WEST POINT

AMERICA'S POWER FRATERNITY

K. Bruce Galloway and
Robert Bowie Johnson, Jr.

SIMON AND SCHUSTER   NEW YORK

SBN 671–21441–1
Library of Congress Catalog Card Number: 72-90391
Designed by Jack Jaget
Manufactured in the United States of America
Printed by Mahony & Roese, Inc., New York, N.Y.
Bound by H. Wolff Book Mfg. Co., Inc., New York, N.Y.

1 2 3 4 5 6 7 8 9 10

*We wish to acknowledge with gratitude the permissions granted by the
following publishers and authors to make somewhat extended quotations
from the works here listed:*

Jerry W. Asher, "Danger in Disarmament," *The World Wars Officer
Review,* January–February 1971. Copyright © 1971 by The Military
Order of the World Wars. Reprinted by permission of The Military
Order of the World Wars.

Donald Barthelme, *Unspeakable Practices, Unnatural Acts.* Copyright
© 1964 by Donald Barthelme. Reprinted by permission of Farrar, Straus,
& Giroux, Inc.

Martin Blumenson, *Bloody River.* Copyright © 1970 by Martin Blumenson. Reprinted by permission of Houghton Mifflin Company.

J. Lawton Collins, *War in Peacetime.* Copyright © 1969 by J. Lawton
Collins. Reprinted by permission of Houghton Mifflin Company.

Fred J. Cook, *The Warfare State.* Copyright © 1962 by Fred J. Cook.
Reprinted by permission of The Macmillan Company.

Donald Duncan, "And Blessed Be the Fruit," *Ramparts,* May 1967.
Copyright © 1967 by *Ramparts.* Reprinted by permission of the editors.

Thomas J. Fleming, *West Point: The Men and Times of the United
States Military Academy.* Copyright © 1969 by Thomas J. Fleming.
Reprinted by permission of William Morrow & Company, Inc.

Roger Hilsman, "Must We Invade the North," *Foreign Affairs,* April
1968. Copyright © 1968 by Council On Foreign Relations, Inc. Reprinted
by permission of Council On Foreign Relations, Inc.

Foreword by Roger Hilsman in Vo Nguyen Giap, *People's War,
People's Army.* Copyright © 1962 by Praeger Publishers, Inc. Reprinted
by permission of Praeger Publishers, Inc.

ACKNOWLEDGMENTS

First acknowledgment must go to the United States Military Academy itself, whose immediate and sometimes stifling presence provided the continuing motivation for this book. Special thanks go to Louis P. Font, a reconstructed Academy graduate, who wrote the Latin American and South American sections and gave invaluable material and guidance to the rest of the work.

Our lasting gratitude to Kathy Cade, Cheryl Fisher, Janet Greenspan, Lisa Hayward, and Tran Vu Zung, all of whom assisted in the crucial tasks of research and organization. Without the persistence and insight of these dedicated persons, the book could not have been completed.

Friends and colleagues who gave generously of their time, experience, and advice include Dr. Gordon Livingston, Greg Hayward, Ron Bartek, Bart Osborn, Craig Blurton, Luther C. West, Josiah Bunting, and a writer who has fought alone against the academies for many years, J. Arthur Heise.

The cadets and officers of West Point who openly or anonymously provided valuable information deserve praise for their concern and courage. We are also indebted to the families that showed us such warm hospitality during our stays at the Point. Other Academy people who were not so directly helpful are thanked for acting in character.

For their timely assistance in the preparation of the manuscript, we thank Sandy Rutter, Linda Probeck, Cheri Clark, Cindy Clair, Otis, Uki, and Paguda.

We are especially grateful to Tran Van Dinh, whose continuous advice, encouragement, and understanding kept us moving and thinking.

ACKNOWLEDGMENTS

And finally, our gratitude to our wives and children is quite inexpressible. Their patience and thoughtfulness over the many months of work were truly amazing and vastly appreciated.

BRUCE GALLOWAY
ROBERT JOHNSON

Annapolis, Maryland
August 1972

For Terry, Tracy, and David.
You will take home with you a good country.

To two men who have cared for Nancy and me.
Gary Battles and Mike McCusker.
We hope to see much more of them.

A special dedication to the memory of
Charles Lynn Hemmingway.
He lived for others.

AUTHORS' NOTE

Because of the delays involved in publishing this book, the rank, military status, and assignment of many of the individuals mentioned have changed since our last check. The personal data that appear are those which were last known to us. Our apologies to anyone who is thereby literarily demoted or kept in the service after his time.

CONTENTS

FOREWORD

Anthony B. Herbert

LT. COL., RET.

THIS book could not be more timely. West Point and its place in our nation's history, in the light of the tragedy called Vietnam, must suddenly be vital to us all. And nowhere else in our literature can one find such a dramatic, penetrating examination of the enigma of the corps of professional officers and its role in this disaster as in these pages.

For the first time in the history of this great nation we have lost a major war—the full aftermath of which is yet to hit us. Somehow, on the field of battle our Army—manned by the very best of raw material, the cream of America's youth, and they were the cream: bigger, better, healthier, better educated, brighter than any who came before them, and at least as brave; backed by the most willing, supportive and patriotic citizenry of the world, the people of the United States; armed with the most horrendous weaponry ever entrusted to the hands of man anywhere—managed to lose. To lose decisively to what can be considered at best a fifth-rate military and even less than fifth-rate economic power.

Whether one considers himself hawk or dove does not make the slightest difference—it is imperative to all that we understand why we lost and then make the necessary corrections before it is too late.

With B-52s, massive artillery, chemical agents, computerized rockets and bombs, we were defeated by an enemy armed, by comparison, with sticks and stones. And accordingly, we must consider what would be the outcome if with that same army we were to have to confront an enemy as well armed as ourselves, such as the Russians or the Chinese. The answer is all too evident, and there are identifiable reasons.

Bob Johnson and Bruce Galloway present a theory backed with impressive, instructive factual data. And if they are correct, then someone somewhere is to blame—and that someone, contrary to what our so-called leaders are expounding today, is not the American people. The people are not to blame! And the stab-in-the-back theory as propounded by the German General Staff in the aftermath of World War I must not be permitted to be accepted here. Neither the climate nor the conditions are the same. To assume this theory is to assume its horrifying consequences.

The responsibility for the tragedy of Vietnam is clearly established. Vietnam was no accident of fate, but rather the goal toward which our Army had been doggedly headed for years. And now the line is drawn; the professional officer corps, the "clique," must accept responsibility for the major role it played.

And we must accept our responsibility for that which we permit to be done without protest, and therefore in effect condone, for as citizens in a democracy we must bear the burden for that which is done in our name. Ignorance of the facts this late in the game is no longer an acceptable excuse. If we are ignorant, then we must educate ourselves at once. We must make decisions and we must act.

Bob Johnson and Bruce Galloway cannot act for us, but they have taken the first big step for all of us in gathering this evidence. They have, in effect, got the ball rolling. It is now our turn —to read, to think, and then to act. The time is short!

INTRODUCTION

When the sphere of their actions, the ends of their lives, and their very existence are confined to the plains of West Point, it is natural that the reverence in which they hold the institution should become a fixed principle, to the detriment of its national character. Under other systems of government than that of the United States, this might not be objectionable, but where the sovereign power is so directly in the hands of the people, to associate any class of public servants too closely with their particular institutions may well be fraught with evil. The aristocratic tendency of which complaint is made may be actually and viciously developed.

—JOHN R. THOMPSON, editor and proprietor
of the *Southern Literary Messenger,*
February 1851

THE overwhelming majority of young men who enter West Point do so out of a desire to serve and defend the American people. But from the day they are sworn in to the day they graduate, these idealistic youths are taught a set of values and attitudes designed to produce an officer who believes he is morally and intellectually superior to those he is charged to protect. His only equal is another West Pointer, one of the illustrious chosen few whose self-imposed mission is to determine our country's destiny. This is the "West Pointer" of whom we write. Should Americans trust an institution that produces men who don't trust them? We think not and feel that the Academy rests at the heart of the separation of the American Army from the American people. A military class dominated by West Point is not needed for the effective defense of this country and its citizens.

There has been no conscious, evil conspiracy on the part of graduates to dominate the military and assume an inordinately powerful role in civilian affairs. West Point has simply taught them to expect and accept these functions as part of the natural scheme—the cream rising to the surface. These men and their institution must be understood by people outside the armed forces if America's military system is to be intelligently controlled. This book seeks to provide some of that understanding.

West Point has for many years been above criticism, a sacred cow never closely examined. We reject that image. Some will accuse us of a lack of objectivity, a dogmatism that approaches that of West Point, but the fact is that since World War II the only view presented has been West Point's insular conception of itself. A U.S. President from the Academy, scores of puff books, an insipid TV series, and Hollywood movies all demand a serious response. We record our interpretation of what graduates have done and are doing, we repeat many of the things they have said and are saying, and where we can we let their own actions and words perform the analysis. We accept the criticism of emotional bias—against the backdrop of a morally repugnant war in Southeast Asia and West Point's eager and crucial contributions to that war it is impossible for us to write without feeling.

West Point belongs to the American people. It is theirs to do with what they will. If they cannot come to West Point, let the Military Academy go to them. There are now four regiments at West Point with approximately 1,000 cadets in each. Let these regiments be placed, one each, along with its uniforms, officers, instructors, books, rifles, and all other baggage necessary for discipline and grooming, in little West Points in San Francisco, Dallas, Minneapolis, and Harlem. If they are truly not elitist, they should feel comfortable among those they serve. Of course, some of the residents of these cities may not admire the pomp and precision of a full dress parade held in a vacant lot, the instructors might have difficulty finding a place to park, and some of the old grads may feel ill at ease returning for a class reunion after dark, but West Point, like all old soldiers, deserves a chance to gracefully fade away.

CHAPTER 1

The Gray Hogs

Nonetheless, style, like sheer silk, too often hides
eczema.

—ALBERT CAMUS,
The Fall

". . . THERE is not on the whole globe an establishment more
monarchial, corrupt, and corrupting than this, the very organization of which is a palpable violation of the constitution and laws
of the country, and its direct tendency to introduce and build
up a privileged order of the very worst class—a military aristocracy—in the United States." [1] The "establishment" is the Military Academy at West Point and the speaker is the third superintendent of the Academy, Alden Partridge, himself a member
of the Class of 1806. Although he spoke these words in 1830,
they were never more true than today.

Taking its cue from Mr. Partridge, what follows is not an
apologetic expansion of the West Point myth. Rather it is an
attempt to cut away the fairy tales and present a critical look
at one of the most powerful and oppressive institutions in the
country, a "school" that professes to train "defenders of freedom" but instead hammers out an elitist group of automatons
who are prisoners of their education and afraid of the very
concept they are supposed to defend.

West Pointers have played a major role in the reduction of this country to a democracy without a people, and they are fearful of any effort to change this condition. The power and influence to prevent any move from the status quo is theirs—the Army and the Air Force are under their control, they boss the foreign and domestic intelligence community, they act as the lubricants in the military-industrial-educational machine, and, above all, they hold top policy positions in government both here and abroad. This is a dangerous situation because these are dangerous men—men whose personal code is identical to the one that appears again and again in the ideology of totalitarianism: "Duty, Honor, Country." This code leaves little room in the life of a West Pointer for a more familiar one, the one that says "Liberty and justice for all."

The dictator of Nicaragua and 1946 graduate of West Point, Anastasio Somoza, euphemistically known as the "President of the Republic," was performing just like one of the boys—his collar was open, his short-sleeved shirt was beginning to dampen in the armpits, and he good-naturedly paid for the drinks when his turn came. The scene was the bar of the Thayer Hotel, a government-subsidized institution on the grounds of West Point that frequently caters to defense-industry conventioneers. On June 4, 1971, however, the bar was filled with members of the West Point Class of 1946, all wearing dark berets and dubbed the Black Class because of their uniformly poor performance in Army service schools after graduation. They were attending their twenty-fifth class reunion during June Week.

"Tachito" Somoza was among friends, the same friends whom he had flown to Nicaragua in May 1967 to attend his inauguration. At that event he had provided them all with transistor radios so they could hear the simultaneous translation of these words: "As a graduate of the Military Academy of the United States of America, I warmly welcome my classmates who, in demonstration of their friendship to the people of Nicaragua, are present today at the inauguration of the third graduate of West Point to be elected to the presidency of his nation.* They, as myself, have been inspired by, and live by the motto of our Alma Mater:

* He forgot one! Jefferson Davis (W.P. 1828), President of the Confederate States of America.

Duty, Honor and Country." [2] Tachito's private plane, a new BAC-111, had picked up his classmates in Miami and, amid wine and food, had flown them directly to Managua, the capital. During their three-day stay Tachito "escaped" a number of times to be alone with his friends. One of these bull sessions in the presidential palace went a little overtime and the commandant of the Nicaraguan military academy, along with his entire corps of cadets, cooled their heels for an hour waiting for their President's friends to come to a review in their honor. His classmates left convinced that Tachito had "outlined a bold program leading toward true democracy" and wished him "success and Divine protection." [3] Tachito's brother, father, great-uncle, and great-grandfather have all been "Presidents" of Nicaragua.

The bar at the Thayer that day was overrun with the Secret Service personnel of two countries—ours and Tachito's. One, a particularly beautiful U.S. agent, was continually forced to rebuff the advances of young bachelor officers in the bar by flashing her identification. Somoza's protection had been provided by Richard M. Nixon. Two days before, Nixon had given a White House dinner in Tachito's honor. Of the thirty-four American guests, fourteen were Academy graduates and ten of them were from the Class of 1946. One of these, Brig. Gen. George S. Patton, son of the well-known World War II general and Somoza's roommate at West Point, commented, "He played the discipline game as a cadet better than the average—a team player, interested in the Academy and, above all, interested in the things for which it stood. I believe retention of those principles have guided his entire life." [4] In other words, Somoza started playing dictator early. Nixon, in a toast reporters were not allowed to hear, fondly recalled a trip he had made to Nicaragua as Vice-President.

The official deference shown at the White House was not greatly in evidence at the Thayer Hotel bar—the bartender even looked exasperated when Tachito blocked his path behind the bar by stretching a telephone line across it. But Tachito was undismayed, laughing it up and talking over old times with his buddies. A member of his entourage was also enjoying himself: Frank "Pancho" Kelly (W.P. 1963) was busy slapping backs and renewing old friendships. When Pancho graduated, he did not become a second lieutenant like the rest of his classmates; rather he became personal secretary to Somoza and the third most powerful man in Nicaragua. He is now the Chief of Staff of the Nicaraguan Army, a rank somewhat higher than that attained by his classmates in the bar. Among those gathered was Maj. Robert Foley (W.P. 1963), whose Congressional Medal of Honor paled the scores of Vietnam service ribbons and decorations displayed on the other uniforms. Tachito and Pancho continued to drink, talk, and have group pictures taken. They whispered quite often.

On another part of the reservation, General of the Army Omar N. Bradley (W.P. 1915) was far more serious as he solemnly laid flowered wreaths on the graves of his classmate Herman Beukema and Beukema's son, Henry (W.P. 1944). There was no fanfare, no Army photographers. Buried nearby is Col. David Marcus (W.P. 1924), who died fighting with the Israelis and was, as his epitaph reads, "a soldier for all humanity." Fifty yards away lies astronaut Edward H. White II (W.P. 1952), the first man to walk in space, who died when his space capsule burned during a ground test in January 1967. In an older part of the West Point Cemetery, George Armstrong Custer (W.P. 1861) and his wife, Elizabeth, rest under a monument covered with reliefs of buffaloes, Indians, and a saber-waving, long-haired cavalryman. In 1868 Custer led the massacre of hundreds of Cheyenne men, women, and children on the Washita River in what is now Texas. One hundred years later, in 1968, George S. Patton sent out Christmas cards featuring a photograph of a pile of dismembered Vietnamese bodies and the inscription "Peace on Earth, Col. and Mrs. George S. Patton III." [5] Custer was a product of frontier America, Patton was a product of a dehumanizing war, but both were products of West Point.

Walking past tombstones inscribed with parachutist's wings and combat-infantryman badges, Gen. Bradley and his wife returned to the limousine provided for the man President Truman described as the "ablest general the U.S. ever had." [6] It is impossible to imagine Gen. Bradley ordering the destruction of villages or inflating body counts for his personal glory. Gen. Bradley was an honorable soldier and rendered great service to his country, but he is now a civilian and chairman of the board of Bulova

Watch Company. His classmate Dwight D. Eisenhower once warned in an oft-quoted speech about the dangers of the growing military-industrial complex. Bradley, as a manufacturer of precision armament parts, may not see such danger: "For many years I have been aware of the continuing need for close co-ordination between our laboratories and the armed forces." [7] Others have also clearly seen the need.

On the eve of the American Civil War, Henry Du Pont (W.P. 1833) accounted for half of all gunpowder production in the United States. The fact that his friend and classmate William Wallace Smith Bliss was for two years the personal secretary of President Zachary Taylor did not harm his progress. Henry's request that Du Pont workmen be exempt from the Civil War draft was granted by the government, but his son, Henry A. Du Pont, who graduated first in the West Point Class of May 1861, was itching for action. While his father was busy building and consolidating his gunpowder empire, Henry A. earned the Congressional Medal of Honor as an artillery commander under Gen. David Hunter (W.P. 1822). It was under orders from Hunter while campaigning in the Shenandoah Valley against Confederate Gen. Jubal Early (W.P. 1837) that Du Pont's artillery fired mercilessly on the Virginia Military Institute. He left it a gutted ruin.

Henry Algernon Du Pont served a decade in the peacetime army, then devoted full time to the powder company and the management of his Wilmington and Northern Railroad before becoming involved in politics. He served two terms in the U.S. Senate after a long and bitter political struggle with the robber baron John Edward O'Sullivan Addicks, a struggle which left a Delaware Senate seat vacant for years and led ultimately to the adoption of the Seventeenth Amendment to the Constitution in 1913 providing for the direct election of Senators. According to the Delaware state chairman of the Democratic Party, the ruthless Addicks was defeated by Henry Algernon because Addicks didn't know how to buy votes like a gentleman. [8]

After the war Henry Du Pont consolidated his empire through the establishment of the great powder trust operating under the name of the Gun Powder Trade Association. By 1889 Du Pont controlled 95 percent of the rifle powder and 90 percent of the blasting powder produced in the United States, powder that was used by scores of West Pointers, including that last man in his son's class, George A. Custer, to drive the American Indians onto reservations. "Better things for better living through chemistry."

But gunpowder needs guns, and West Pointers did not neglect that end of the war business. In 1816 a group of New York State industrialists established the Cold Spring Foundry, commonly called the "West Point Foundry," for the production of armaments and engines. One of the founders was Joseph G. Swift (W.P. 1802). Robert P. Parrott (W.P. 1824) was its superintendent for forty-one years and Thomas J. Rodman (W.P. 1841) revolutionized ordnance construction in the plant with his inventions. The West Point Foundry "dominated the armament industry in the United States, making almost all the heavy cannon for the United States Government from its early days to the end of the Civil War." [9] Swift, Parrott, and Rodman supplied the North and Joseph R. Anderson (W.P. 1836) took care of the South. He was superintendent of the Tredegar Iron Works in Richmond, Virginia, for twenty years and the "foundry continued to grind out guns, shells and small arms for the South until gutted by fire when Richmond fell." [10]

West Pointers provided the gunpowder and guns for the Civil War and West Pointers provide a similar service for the Vietnam war. From May 16, 1962, until February 29, 1964, Maj. Gen. Nelson M. Lynde, Jr. (W.P. 1929), was commanding general of the Army Weapons Command. As such, he played the major role in negotiating and awarding the production contract for the prime weapon of the Vietnam war, the M-16 rifle. This multi-million-dollar gold mine went to Colt Industries, Inc. Lynde retired from active duty on March 1, 1964 and five months later, on August 3, he accepted a $20,000-a-year job as "executive consultant" to the president of Colt Industries.* His duties include "evaluating current products or projects, particularly in the area of military weapons." [11] He is not alone at Colt,

---

* The acceptance of such a position may not violate any federal law, but its ethics and whether the best interests of the U.S. are served thereby are certainly questionable.

however; E. J. Roxbury, Jr. (W.P. 1946), is in overall charge of the international marketing of Colt's military arms, and J. B. Hall (W.P. 1948) is vice-president of the Pyrodynamics Division. In 1967 Hall handled Colt's government sales in Southeast Asia.

Among the hundreds of other graduates in key positions in the defense industry is Rodney C. Gott (W.P. 1933), president of American Machine and Foundry Co. Gott did over $100 million in business with the Pentagon in 1969. Other graduates have been equally successful. Brig. Gen. William T. Seawell (W.P. 1941) was president of the ill-fated Rolls-Royce Aero Engines Inc. venture. Rolls-Royce went bankrupt because of these engines, but Seawell emerged unscathed and was recently appointed to the presidency of Pan American World Airways. The leading capitalist of the Class of 1946, however, has an undiminished record of success and naturally attended the June Week reunion. He is Saul Horowitz, Jr., president of HRH Construction Company (skyscrapers in New York City) and mayor of Scarsdale, New York. One of his classmates, Warren E. Hearnes, dabbles in government also as the current governor of Missouri. Another 1946 graduate, J. Fred Buzhardt, works at the federal level as general counsel for the Department of Defense. At still another level works Rocco Petrone, the Director of the Apollo Program for NASA. Some old grads didn't have to come very far for the reunion: Col. Amos Jordan is the head of the Department of Social Sciences at West Point and Col. Roger Nye is a professor in the History Department. Another classmate, also an educator, who returned was Wesley W. Posvar, chancellor of the University of Pittsburgh. Five months later in Pittsburgh, Posvar's wife would entertain a national television audience with her rendition of "The Star-Spangled Banner" on the occasion of the first night baseball game in World Series history. Fittingly, the game of baseball was invented by yet another graduate, Abner Doubleday (W.P. 1842).

Circulating among all of these dignitaries at June Week were two young members of the Class of 1968, Louis P. Font and Robert Firehock. Although recent graduates, both were very well known to the assembled high-ranking civilian and military

West Pointers. Firehock, the son of an Academy man, had been discharged, while a captain, as a conscientious objector. Font, some four months earlier while a first lieutenant stationed at Fort Meade, Maryland, had preferred formal war-crimes charges against Lt. Gen. Jonathan O. Seaman (W.P. 1934) and Maj. Gen. Samuel Koster (W.P. 1942) for their activities in Vietnam. Font based his charges on the statements of forty Vietnam veterans who testified at a war-crimes inquiry in Washington, D.C.—where Font, while still a lieutenant, had made one of the summary speeches.* Even more embarrassing for the Army and the Academy, the young lieutenant had preferred the charges against these generals with the help of Congressmen—and in full view of the press. "I learned at West Point," Font had said, "that the truth should not make exception for military rank, that what applies to privates and sergeants can also apply to colonels and generals." The Academy lashed back. In May 1971 Maj. Gen. William Knowlton (W.P. 1943), superintendent of USMA, singled out the name of Louis Font for vilification and innuendo in a speech before the Congressional overseers for the Academy, the Board of Visitors. "During war," the general said, "not all young men who come to West Point do so from a desire to serve. Louis Font's file contained clear indications from his peers that they thought he would ride the education gravy train and then try not to repay in service." [12] Another general knew him. Army Chief of Staff William C. Westmoreland (W.P. 1936) had been asked about Font at a Congressional committee meeting and said, "He was assisted considerably by the ACLU. The ACLU advised him and used him, and he made an absolute nuisance of himself to the point where he is affecting the morale of the station—at least his contemporaries on the station where he is now posted—and we feel the best thing for the Army is to get rid of Font." [13] And now Font and Firehock, ex-lieutenant and ex-captain, were back at the Academy for June Week. "I was in the area," said Font, "so I thought I would drop in and see what's happening on campus."

Font, unshaven, and Firehock, with a beard and wearing a

* General Ralph E. Haines, Jr. (W.P. 1935), Continental Army Commander, later dismissed the charges, citing lack of evidence.

medal identifying him as a grad, strolled down Thayer Road past a group of officers. Two of them, both lieutenant colonels, snapped off crisp salutes to Firehock, mistaking his beard and slightly shabby clothes as a sign of old age and, therefore, an old grad. Others stopped the pair and read the class year off the identifying medal, then stood wondering how members of the Class of 1968 could be back at the Academy—and in civilian clothes! West Point officialdom didn't wonder too long, however; it immediately swung into action. A rumor developed that the two were camping out near the reservation accompanied by scores of disgruntled veterans on the scene to protest the war. Police were immediately dispatched to ascertain the location and intentions of the camper-demonstrators. Cautiously approaching Campsite H-1, the police found Firehock, two blankets, a tent, and some New York suburbanites out for a weekend in the country. Slightly abashed, the police left to file their report. That afternoon another rumor surfaced: Font and Firehock were going to attend the alumni luncheon and give speeches attacking Vietnam policy. They were going to beard the lion in its den! Soon after the luncheon, reports began to filter down. "They chickened out and didn't come," said a major. "They both stood on a table and harangued everyone for half an hour," commented a lieutenant colonel. "We had the place surrounded with Military Police so they couldn't get in!" said another major. At the time of the luncheon Font and Firehock were both at the West Point Chapel talking with friends. "Look," Font was saying, "West Pointers can move into a home in my neighborhood, but I'll be damned if I'm going to let my daughter marry one. In other words," he laughed, "they can be on the same military reservation with me, but I refuse to intentionally sit down at a table and eat with one next to me." They had never been near the luncheon.

Font and Firehock weren't the only off-key notes at West Point during June Week. Occasionally a group of shaggy-haired, bearded young men dressed in soiled T-shirts could be seen lolling in the grass; they were in stark contrast to the sharp, starched, athletic cadets. Has that LSD-soaked former cadet Timothy Leary (ex-Class of June 1943) returned? Hippies at the Military Academy? Capt. Buddy Bucha (W.P. 1965) explained, "They're former drug addicts we've hired to help maintain the grounds. It keeps them off the streets and gives them a chance for a new start." Nothing is done at West Point without a reason, and this one appears very altruistic on the surface. Looking again, we must ask how this particular program helps shape our future officers. In a normal day the cadet sees three types of people: enlisted men assigned to the Academy (clean, straight, and military), officers assigned to the Academy (clean, straight, and military), and other cadets (clean, straight, and military). But wait, there is one more type—the hippie, the only non-member of the tight little fraternity called West Point. Our hippie is the only civilian a cadet sees on a daily basis, and he is unclean, unstraight, unmilitary, and, above all, unhealthy —a former drug addict! The Military Academy is there to help this poor creature and also to make him a living exhibit of the moral degeneracy rampant in the outside world. West Point always has a reason for what it does—sometimes more than one.

Most of the old grads didn't notice the freaks, however—they were too busy marching around, saluting, shaking hands, eating, drinking, and, in general, behaving like alumni at any gala reunion. There were a few differences, though. Few alumni groups have a 4,000-man parade in their honor. First, the grads formed up and marched to the parade ground (The Plain), each class moving as a unit. The entire corps of cadets then poured through three "sally ports," maneuvering in ponderous groups and looking more than anything else like thousands of white-and-gray ants attacking in column. The waiting grads stood their ground, however, and accepted the salutes of the cadets as the corps passed in review. Only one alumnus had a hard time. The major in charge of alumni "care and feeding" described it this way: "All of a sudden, this guy from the Class of 1931 lets out a tremendous shout, falls down, and knocks over four or five other old boys like tenpins." Maybe the nostalgia had been too much for him. Other events were calmer. William F. Buckley, the conservative columnist, was on hand to address the grads, as was Secretary of Defense Melvin Laird, and, of course, Superintendent Knowlton had a few words to say at various times throughout the week about how the Academy really hadn't

[30]

changed and how the cadets weren't really having an easier time of it. Between the parades, the picnics, and the Thayer Hotel bar a good time was had by all. At the end of the festivities, the spirit of fellowship extended beyond simple back-slapping for some: "Having lined up a flight to Denver from Andrews, I accepted the kind offer of George Brown (W.P. 1941) to hop back to D.C. At exactly 2100 hours the staff car whisked us over to Stewart where a shiny T-39 awaited the CO AF Sys Cmd (Commanding Officer Air Force Systems Command—Brown) and his fair lady. Bob Johnson (W.P. 1941) and I (Burton Andrus, W.P. 1941) piled in after Skip and George and we were soon scooting down the runway. As we lifted off into a beautiful starfilled summer night, we had one more chance to feel the spell as the lights of W.P. slowly faded into the distance." [14] As one major put it, "The fairy gradfathers really eat this stuff up"—especially when the taxpayers foot the bill.

Some grads had to miss all the fun. Gen. Westmoreland couldn't get away from his Chief of Staff job at the Pentagon until later in the week, Gen. Creighton W. Abrams (W.P. 1936), in Vietnam as commander of MACV,* was too busy, and Lt. Gen. Alfred Starbird (W.P. 1933) dared not waste a minute away from his job of overseeing the development of America's ABM defense system. In fact, none of the West Point generals who occupied key Joint Staff positions at the Department of the Army could get away. Some other military men were too far away. General Chih Wang (W.P. 1932), personal secretary to Chiang Kai-shek on Taiwan, couldn't have been expected to come. Neither could General Manob Suriya (W.P. 1937), the former Air Marshal of Thailand. Others were as close as Washington, D.C., but didn't show. Brig. Gen. Alexander M. Haig (W.P. 1947) was evidently occupied in the White House with his duties as Deputy Assistant to the President for National Security Affairs, as were Lt. Col. Bernard Loeffke (W.P. 1957) and John Holdridge (W.P. 1945), two other Kissinger assistants. Haig, in fact, is busy enough to make the newspaper gossip columns: "The good-looking young general who heads Henry Kissinger's office when Henry is away, Alexander Haig, said he

---

* Military Assistance Command—Vietnam.

was the go-between in the Danielle Hunebelle–Henry Kissinger situation which produced the extraordinary *Dear Henry* book by the French newswoman who claimed to be in love with Kissinger." [15] Presidential advisor John Ehrlichman must have kept his aide, Lt. Col. Dana Mead (W.P. 1957), very busy also. Nearby in Washington but unable to attend were Lawrence K. White (W.P. 1933), comptroller of the Central Intelligence Agency; George Olmsted (W.P. 1922), financier and president of the International Bank of Washington; John Shaffer (W.P. 1943), administrator of the Federal Aviation Administration; and Lt. Gen. Donald Bennett (W.P. 1940), director of the Defense Intelligence Agency. At Columbia University in New York City, Professor Roger Hilsman (W.P. 1943), about to be embarrassed by public disclosure of secret documents containing contingency plans for the overthrow of South Vietnam's President Diem he composed while Assistant Secretary of State, Far East, under President Kennedy, taught classes and waited for the whistle to be blown. This book seeks to blow that whistle, not only on Mr. Hilsman, but on one of the most powerful and corrupt institutions in America—the Military Academy at West Point.

Other schools, notably those in the Ivy League, have produced powerful and sometimes immoral men, so why single out West Point? The answer lies in the fact that the Military Academy offers an ideology, not an education, and because of this and the uniform, the graduates find themselves anointed with access to America's ruling elite. The process can best be described by imagining that all television news broadcasters were alumni of Bob Jones University—only the ideologically correct need apply at NBC. Most schools are as proud of an artist as they are of a corporation president, as proud of a poet as an engineer; they seek to produce diversity, and a large part of their intellectual richness derives from this. West Point, however, seeks to produce sameness, not variety: military officers, not musicians. The graduate who has learned his lessons well applies this educational narrowness to his own children who for some reason can't water at the West Point trough: "My own son, Wolfgang, is a sophomore at Trinity U. . . . and No. 1 in ROTC. . . . He couldn't make the Point. . . . But he is doing all right and, thank God, has no time or patience for the 'Flower Children' or the hippies. And neither do his friends, which gives one a renewed belief in our offspring." [16]

At a time when introspective, thoughtful soldiers are needed, West Point imposes a system of Prussian-type discipline, of rigorously enforced externalized morality, and of bite-sized, spoon-fed doses of knowledge on the young and defenseless minds of all who enter its gates. The rigidity of the system is designed to enable cadets "to overcome their character defects," or, in other words, to force the development of the "appropriate" attitudes and values. The extreme to which these values are taken is illustrated by the following exchange. Col. Alexander G. Stone (W.P. 1930): "Do you think that today's West Point graduate, faced with open insubordination, would risk his life rather than compromise his standards of military discipline?" Maj. Gen. William Knowlton (W.P. 1943 and superintendent of the Military Academy) provided the answer: "That's a tough question. But the answer is 'Yes.' " [17] This four-year trauma of indoctrination is the most crucial experience of a professional soldier, for it entails the formation of a way of life. The graduate will always be associated with a particular graduating class and he must of necessity find means of accommodating to these lifetime colleagues. It is not too difficult, for the common identifications produced by the years of shared experience forge a strong like-mindedness, a sense of group solidarity, and a network of intimate personal contacts.—"There was some discussion of keying the uniform to hard hats, and to take advantage of our togetherness to take some stands on certain issues regarding our profession and the Country. But the cooler and wiser heads pointed out rightly that this was a unique opportunity these days to replenish the spirit and urged that we not encumber that great occasion (June Week) with the dreary problems we must face the other 362 days of the year. The uniform accordingly consisted of the usual arm band and medal, but the hat was a white golf hat surmounted with a chenille patch bearing a black '41 on gold. On each lapel was a small but conspicuous American Flag. We may be off active duty as officers, but we remain on active duty as citizens." [18] All large organizations develop factions, but the Army is unique in that it guarantees only one basic division—

West Pointers and non-West Pointers—and it is the West Pointers, a small group of ideologically secure men, who set the standards of behavior for the rest of the Army. The graduating group disperses very gradually and is bound together in a clique that is constantly telling itself how important and well educated it is. These orgies of self-congratulation occur officially when, at frequent intervals all over the world, the local chapters of the West Point Society meet, and unofficially whenever and wherever graduates are found. "We looked with interest at one another, some *in,* some *out,* some bald, some almost, all pretty well settled into lifetime patterns, but all holding on to the spark of West Point, so hard to describe to anyone else." [19] The grads frequently have occasion to run into each other. As officers they find that their careers are constantly crossing and recrossing; as civilians they tend to concentrate in their specialty, the defense industry; and as retirees they live in communities that understand them, retirement villages catering to the military or a town like Washington, D.C. Graduates have basically the same interests, seek the same ends, and exist within the same tight world. To non-grads the influence and cohesiveness of this group, bitterly known as the West Point Protective Association (WPPA), represent a threat to the military profession. To graduates the WPPA does not seem to produce undue favoritism; rather it is believed essential to the effectiveness of the Army. After all, is not West Point the wellspring of "Duty, Honor, Country" and does not devotion to these ideals reside in every Academy man by virtue of his graduation? Of course. Whereas the loyalties of a Harvard graduate might be tied to a broad social or economic class, the loyalties of a West Pointer are tied to an institution—the Academy. It exists as the source of his political, social, and economic thought and contacts and, therefore, his strength. "All of us here—and all 20,000 of us everywhere—are motivated basically by the love and pride that we have for and in West Point." [20] His loyalties are institutional, not human, and the purpose of his education is to transform him into a member of this callous fraternity. Each member of this closed order is dependent on the group both for his ideas and for his emotional support. In the face of the My Lai crisis, one 1941 grad noted: "It would appear that we could properly take a Class stand.

With the massive and treacherously inspired pressures being exerted on our profession it seems we could *encourage* those still standing muster, *decry* those who have sullied our uniform, *stand firm* behind those who are being falsely accused, and *consider* the things we can do to insure that our Alma Mater will continue to be the impeccable and inexhaustible mold from which our nation's military leaders are drawn." [21] Reality is beginning to be structured for the Class of 1941. When group support fails (rarely) and reality crashes through (even more rarely), the West Pointer turns to a not-so-unique solution: the Kuniholms (W.P. 1924) have decided to settle down in the vineyards above Lake Geneva where there are "no hippies, no smoking of pot, no student protests, no labor strikes, no Black Power, and the lowest incidence of crime in this turbulent world." [22] Sounds like a rather opulent way of "dropping out." But "Duty, Honor, Country" forms a reality of its own and grads believe that the attitude of others must be based on the same "reality." While they believe they understand differing opinions, they are in fact distorting others' motives to fit their world: "Some joker of a reporter, whose name didn't appear, was taking Walt Woolwine (W.P. 1941) to task over testimony he made on the Hill regarding the M-16. Obviously full of distortion, the article was another example of the carefully planned efforts to discredit our profession. We all know exactly where the inspiration for this kind of journalism comes from." [23] This illusion of understanding is preserved by a solid lack of contact with "distasteful" worlds and by an iron discipline. After all, effective communication often requires changing one's own view of reality. This is a little too much to expect from "America's best."

The construction of a West Pointer's group dependence and the accompanying non-compromising view of the world begins at the Academy. The tremendous physical and mental pressures used to destroy each cadet's individuality and replace it with mental mimickry and blind obedience are discussed in detail in the next chapter, but a few general observations of the results can be made now. The rigid discipline that governs every minute of the cadet's time teaches him to regard himself as a single cell in a massive, coordinated organism, an organism filled with corporate strength but at the same time compliant, without its own will, no more than a tool. Each man is taught to abandon his own will for the sake of the efficient functioning of the group. This crushing of spirit involves much personal suffering, but each cadet who "makes it" has habituated himself to his lot and, by extension, to the suffering lot of all humans. By devaluing himself, he has devalued all life. With this crucial step accomplished, the cadet is ready to replace his stripped personality with something else, and only one psychological compensation presents itself at West Point: he must pattern himself after those who have authority over him. The threats and prohibitions of his four-year training are built into a new consciousness, and the rigors and commands can now be defended because they have become his own. He has adopted the attitudes of his superiors and, like a child endowing his father with great powers, expects them to know everything and therefore to think for him.

Within this framework of seemingly benevolent thought control our young man learns the stuff of soldiering. He discovers that West Point's base reference is routine. Life at the Academy is filled with thousands of standardized, conservative rituals which penetrate every aspect of daily living and exercise a continuous, stifling influence. The banality of hundreds of cadets buying Corvettes immediately upon graduation and getting married in the Cadet Chapel to fill the plush empty car seat next to the driver's is but one of many examples of the effects of this suppression. Everyone knows what is going to happen next. In fact, everyone must know. Surprises are not tolerated in a secure environment. Preparation for the untroubled career progression and the tranquil artificiality of garrison living begins with the routine of the Academy. Manifestations of this security are often ludicrous, as evidenced by the following description of Gen. Matthew B. Ridgway's (W.P. 1917) move into the official residence of the Army Chief of Staff at Fort Myer:

> Here, as in Panama, Tokyo, and Paris, Mrs. Ridgway carried out one of her superlative jobs of renovation and redecorating. It was her idea that since the house was to be the residence of the Chief of Staff, it should in its decoration reflect the mood and spirit of West Point, which is the repository of the ideals and the

ethics, the creed of conduct that guides the members of the Officer Corps whatever their school.

She chose the gold and gray of the Academy colors as her color scheme, therefore, and, with the help of Eastman Kodak laboratories, she covered the walls of the dining room with huge murals—blown-up photographs of scenes at West Point which all graduates treasure in their memory, and which we hope, in years to come, will give pleasure to all those who come to share its hospitality.[24]

Admittedly there is little likelihood, but what if a Virginia Military Institute graduate becomes Chief of Staff?

Deviation from the standard course and expression of what little individuality remains are allowed, but are defined within very narrow and acceptable limits. Our man learns to judge himself by the standards of the military community and allows himself to be molded by rules of etiquette and ceremony that reach far beyond the way he performs his duties. The isolation, cohesion, and dominance of this community reinforce the development of our young man's inherited values and characteristics. Steps outside this closed world bring shocks.

Reporting on a classmate's adventure beyond the gates, one graduate commented that "the thing that intrigued them most were the dirty, smelly, disheveled, American hippies spreading 'culture' especially in Italy and Spain." [25] When a grad is suspected of deviant tendencies, he is quick to defend himself to his peers: "[He attended the Reunion] beardless, and denied vigorously that he had ever worn a beard, not wishing to be classed with the bearded and bath-less beatnik students roaming the streets of Chapel Hill." [26] On one level this behavioral code instructs the West Pointer in the appropriate conduct for every phase of his life cycle, but, more importantly, it binds its members together and acts as a filter through which the outer world is perceived. The affairs of the world are not routine, they are unstable and unpredictable, so the West Pointer through his filter perceives that his "qualities" of plodding steadfastness and stubborn toughness are indeed great moral virtues. After all, didn't his leaders at the Academy tell him he was the "cream of the crop"? And doesn't his community continue to tell him so?

The illusion is maintained at all costs: "To us, it seems that the handout is becoming a way of life and we wonder what will happen when we all decide to live on welfare. In many respects, maybe we ought to throw out the whole bunch in Washington and start from scratch again. Let's get rid of the politician and go back to practical commonsense." [27] This "tough pragmatist" from West Point doesn't seem to realize that an end to "handouts" would wipe out many of the advantages of being in the Army—the children of a career officer are delivered without charge, he himself is buried without charge, and in between he enjoys free medical care, free dental care, subsidized housing, cut-rate food prices, cheap luxury goods at the PX, etc. Without these, our hardened graduates (free education with pay, of course) would find the Army a very austere place indeed.

The filters work overtime where integrity is concerned. "Honor" is supposedly the graduate's most prized possession, and an elaborate system based on the phrase "A cadet does not lie, cheat, or steal" has been designed to ensure its inculcation. This system is fully discussed in a later chapter; suffice it now to say that it fails because in application it protects the integrity of the institution and ignores the integrity of the individual. A hint at its orientation is given by Maj. Gen. A. S. Newman (W.P. 1925): "I believe the 'communication gap' that produces misconceptions about the nature and purpose of our Honor System at the Military Academy can be narrowed if we adapt and publicize an *Officers Creed* as a direct extension of the West Point Motto. By adding in our active duty principle, 'for the good of the military service,' this officers creed (or motto) could be: Duty-Honor-Country-Army." [28] Newman is not saying anything new, he is simply acknowledging the current situation. It poses no contradiction for a West Pointer to report false body counts or falsify medals and at the same time praise and preach the honor system, because it has always been the image of the Army, not some abstract morality, that determines what is good or bad. Integrity, in other words, resides not in the individual but rather in the institution. This principle is everywhere in evidence at West Point. For example, it is an honor violation to discuss individual themes or papers with fellow cadets after "pen has touched paper," but in the case of Rhodes

Scholarship qualifying essays faculty members have been assigned to aid applicants in their efforts.[29] "Honor" drops by the
wayside when the image of the Academy is involved, yet graduates persist in their illusion—Newman again: "Guarding against
possible injustice is part of it, too, but as with a woman's virtue,
there are no degrees of honor in spite of heartaches and tragedies
involved."[30] The ritual and ceremony surrounding a West
Pointer's integrity breed vast amounts of self-esteem and group
solidarity, but invariably substitute for solutions to the very real
contradictions they confront. Gen. Westmoreland demonstrates
the process when he offers this advice for a West Pointer facing
a problem: "Don't be a meathead. . . . It's a man with an
inflexible mentality. Try to see all sides of the question. Don't
fall into the trap by thinking you know all the answers. . . .
Now, realize, gentlemen, that many problems defy full solution
and must be lived with. Despite the fact that you might strive to
solve these problems, some of them defy solution. We just
don't deal nowadays, or at any time, I think, in the history of
civilization, with blacks and whites, with complete rights and
complete wrongs. . . . In my view, the positive approach is
the key to success. . . . And it's the one that has a strong
influence over people. Men welcome leadership."[31]

The West Point technocrat is sometimes hard pressed to
recognize that a problem or contradiction even exists, and when
he finally does, he has not been taught that there is an emotional
and intuitive side to issues that demands compassion and understanding, not discipline and obedience. I. F. Stone, writing in
In a Time of Torment, accurately describes this moral blindness
with these words: "In reading the military literature on guerrilla
warfare now so fashionable at the Pentagon, one feels that these
writers are like men watching a dance from outside through
heavy plate glass windows. They see the motions but they can't
hear the music. They put the mechanical gestures down on
paper with pedantic fidelity. But what rarely comes through
to them are the injured racial feelings, the misery, the rankling
slights, the hatred, the devotion, the inspiration and the desperation. So they do not really understand what leads men to
abandon wife, children, home, career, friends; to take to the
bush and live gun in hand like a hunted animal; to challenge

overwhelming military odds rather than acquiesce any longer in humiliation, injustice or poverty. . . ." [32]

Observations such as "The Class of '30 should draw up a resolution supporting Rhodesia and South Africa. They have better solutions than we to some of our problems. Both countries are rich and beautiful" [33] or "Remember, when young men seek means to avoid military service, and young women condone and encourage them, and parents question the need for it, national objectives may be seriously impaired" [34] are typical examples of the abstract and objective, not human, parameters that West Pointers assign to problems. This is an absolutely essential definition, for the complexity and ambiguity introduced into an equation by human concerns would spoil the West Pointer's functional, straight-line approach: "I find it most difficult in the face of massive virulent attack on our profession, coupled with signs of national decay, to compose normal chatty phrases that help escape into soothing nostalgia. . . . Individually we can and should discharge our duties as citizens with the same vigor we did our military duties in the past" [35] or—and this is a serious quote—"[Harold K.] Johnson [W.P. 1933, Army Chief of Staff 1964–68] sides with those who feel that the key to national security and moral rearmament may lie in having more barber shops. Johnny told of one beatnik who looked most frustrated when his long locks were shorn but then became much more mature and cooperative." [36] It is doubtful that close-order drill, parades, and haircuts can solve America's problems, but when a man's focus is on action, competition, and individual achievement to the total neglect of contemplation and cooperation, no other solution can be expected. His spirit is tied to team loyalty and mimickry rather than individual integrity and imagination. To him, truth is obedience and obedience is truth. It is not difficult, then, to understand why the few men who have broken out of this mold look back on their West Point careers with considerable distaste. The famous Robert E. Lee (W.P. 1829) said, "The greatest mistake of my life was taking a military education." [37] A more recent graduate, Gen. Joseph Stilwell (W.P. 1904), well known for his exploits in China, added, "It is common knowledge that an Army officer has a one track mind, that he is personally interested in stirring up wars so that he can get promoted and be decorated, and that he has an extremely limited education, with no appreciation of the finer things of life." [38] Confirming Stilwell's opinion but viewing it as a virtue is William C. Westmoreland (W.P. 1936): "I bet the Russian Army is jealous as hell. Our troops are here [Vietnam] getting all this experience, we're learning about guerrilla warfare, helicopters, vertical envelopment, close artillery support. . . . Those Russian generals would love to be here. . . . Any true professional wants to march to the sound of gunfire." [39] Another graduate explains the gap between Stilwell and Westmoreland: "There are, of course, intelligent generals, highly intelligent ones; but intelligence is not the same as intellectuality. . . . Military men are not thinkers." [40] The truth of these statements is best illustrated by the depth of understanding reflected in the statement of another grad: "We have sit-ins and sleep-ins galore, so why not drink-ins?" [41]

In reality, it is not necessary for a West Pointer to think, for because of his authoritarian, freedom-fearing attitudes most of his actions are based on ideas that have been funneled into him from above. Our man sees nothing wrong with this narrow funneling and, indeed, seeks to make it the norm for transmitting knowledge. Maxwell Taylor (W.P. 1922) speaking of the Pentagon Papers: "What is a citizen going to do after reading these documents that he wouldn't have done otherwise? *A citizen should know those things he needs to know to be a good citizen and discharge his functions . . .*" [42] (emphasis added).

The grad has suppressed any uncertainties and believes uncritically in the superior traits he is told he possesses. Because he produces nothing of economic value in a commercial society, his self-image transcends capitalistic concerns and he is taught to regard himself as a standard-bearer, a self-sacrificing leader whose mission is to protect the weaker members of society whose social and moral ideals are inferior. Westmoreland again in a speech to cadets: ". . . you're going to be dealing with just ordinary people. . . . All people aren't honest. Many have a low, if any, sense of duty. . . . Many citizens go to extremes to avoid any type of military service or any type of service to their country. I feel that the West Pointer must be different, and that is why as a group they have been universally and uniquely successful throughout history." [43] To Westmoreland, the graduate is not a soldier, he is a priest: "[West Pointers] have a sacred trust to provide the dedicated leadership and service to our nation which is so essential to our national security. I certainly view this, and I'm sure you [the cadets] view it, as a very high calling and a noble cause." [44]

His role, then, is that of national guardian and his special virtue is a profound sense of "Duty, Honor, Country." In reality, his sense of Duty springs from the interests of the Army and not from any deeply felt character trait; his sense of Honor means that his product is always the better and the other's is always the worst; and his sense of Country is a kind of artificial self-confidence gained by identification with the "greatness" of his West Point forebears. This code prepares the graduate to defend vigorously the Army's point of view to the public, to reinforce interservice rivalries, and to avoid paying attention to the political consequences of his actions. Despite all the hypocrisy, the ecstasy derived from these notions is genuine and highly demonstrative. West Pointers are constantly dwelling on their sense of duty and honor, their bravery and self-control, they are forever citing attributes, which are strongly at odds with the reality of their personal behavior.

Whereas there have been men who were truly honorable and responsible, brave and controlled, without making a stir about it, the graduate constantly broadcasts and preaches these supposed virtues and has even institutionalized them in the form of famous West Pointers. The helpless cadet feels a highly pronounced identification with these figures, and his need for protection from what is initially a hostile environment is disguised by feeling at one with them. In one graduate's words, "I was MacArthur, Patton, Eisenhower, Grant." The grad perceives himself in these figures and on this basis feels himself to be a defender of the national heritage and the nation, but this does not prevent him from, at the same time, despising non-graduates as lesser creatures who do not belong to his exalted group. The absurdity of his situation is so overshadowed by these identifications that he ceases to realize how completely he has sunk to a position of insignificant blind obedience. He is so dependent on tradition and government authority for his position that his social consciousness is defined by his attitude toward the government and the "nation." This means total identification with and submission to the state power. In 1970 one graduate put his privileged moral position as a representative of authority this way: "We've made it! The in group has become us! And it's only the beginning! The splendid old soldiers of '41 and their even more splendid brides clearly represent middle, and not so silent, America. And, in uniform or out, we remain committed to continue to serve God, Country, and Fellow Man. The pendulum is swinging, and the 'losers' are in deep trouble!" [45] The authoritarian social system of West Pointers is reproduced in the emphasis given the genealogical succession and the "Long Gray Line." The inheritors of the West Point tradition develop a strong identification with their "fathers" and thus form the personal basis of subservient identification with every kind of authority. The Long Gray Line is the factory where West Point's reactionary ideology is produced, and the protection of this "family" is what is meant by "Duty, Honor, Country." The "greatness of the nation" personified by the traditions and heritage of West Point becomes the authoritarian father of our seventeen-year-old cadet—"I know now what makes this place what it is. West Point is like the rock; it is built on ever-lasting. I have only been here two months. I am not yet a member of the Corps, but the feeling of Duty, Honor, and Country has already begun to build in me. I know now why Patton, MacArthur, and other men like them have given so much to their Country. It is because West Point has instilled in them a faith in God and in our Country that overrules all other feelings. . . . What I have written may be hard for you to understand. It is just a feeling that comes from being a part of this place. . . . This sums up what I am trying to say: '. . . With eyes up, thanking our God that we of the Corps are treading where they of the Corps have trod. . . .' " [46] The fear of dissolving these old institutions makes the graduate unequal to freedom. The words of a veteran West Point teacher sum up the problem: "In my system of values, West Point comes first, the Army comes second, and the country comes third." [47]

CHAPTER 2

The Cream of the Crop

I want to tell you so you won't be surprised. They'll first strip off your clothes, but they'll go deeper than that. They'll shuck off any little dignity you have—you'll lose what you think of as your decent right to live and to be let alone to live. They'll make you live and eat and sleep and shit close to other men. And when they dress you up again you'll not be able to tell yourself from the others. You can't even wear a scrap or pin a note on your breast to say, "This is me—separate from the rest." [1]

—JOHN STEINBECK,
East of Eden

AT 1:30 a.m. the Phantom was just beginning his nightly sneaking and creeping. Dressed in tennis shoes, a raincoat with a flapping cape, black gloves, and a hood over his face topped with a full-dress hat, he crept through the halls of East Barracks. Selecting a room, he silently opened the door and turned on the lights. Throwing the cape over his arm and holding it just under his eyes, he fixed the sleeping cadet with a maniacal glare and began a gentle tapping to wake him up. Rising with a start and seeing the black apparition, the cadet clambered to the head of his bed and pressed himself against the wall, nervously facing his assailant. The Phantom merely uttered a low, cackling laugh, flicked off the lights, and slipped off down the hall.

[44]

THE CREAM OF THE CROP

The nervous cadet was "pinging"; he had lost control when faced with a situation that fell outside his normal routine. An uncontrolled event is a rare occurrence at West Point; the Phantom had created one only by breaking regulations—being out of his room at an unauthorized time, being in another cadet's room at an unauthorized time, and wearing the uniform in an unauthorized manner. Hundreds of such regulations bind and constrain the behavior of every cadet, preventing the unusual through fear of recrimination. Everything is regulated: eating, sleeping, smoking, drinking, driving, dating, dressing, and so on, ad infinitum. Every movement and decision takes place with an awareness of this all-encompassing framework of codified "proper behavior."

These regulations are alive. For the administrators of West Point they are the embodiment of years of cherished tradition; for the cadet they form four years of stupefying routine that must be borne without criticism. The Academy says, "Charges of harassment, degradation, and humiliation usually emanate from those cadets who, somehow, were not really meant to be West Point Officers." [2] Gen. Maxwell Taylor (W.P. 1922) says it a little differently: "I should not have to say (although in every class there are a few who would need to be told) that you cannot 'beat the system.' Don't undertake to change the Military Academy on your own. It has been there a long time. It has a justified reason, as I said, for the things it does. Yet, some young men do try to change the Military Academy. Usually they spend most of their time [walking punishment tours] on the Area to the detriment of the enjoyment of cadet life, or, at least, until they conclude that crime doesn't pay." [3] The cardinal virtue, then, is obedience, unquestioning obedience. Cadets who adopt this "virtue" (and only those who can and do adopt it remain at West Point) soon find every minute of their day programmed and overseen. The underlying assumption is that if a cadet's time is not programmed he will not use it wisely. This programming is an obsession: cadets are even monitored through "time studies" of their activities to discover new ways of improving "efficiency." Everyone becomes a guinea pig in the service of statistically justifying four years of living like a computer punch card.

If a cadet deviates from the programmed path, his superiors immediately decry a "poor attitude." Incompetence in conforming to routine never has a physical or intellectual cause; it is inevitably a result of "poor attitude." Indeed, the worst that can be said to a cadet is "Mister, I don't like your attitude!" This translates into "You must not want to 'make it' because you obviously can't 'take it.' " "Making it" and "taking it" comprise "attitude," and the "right attitude" consists of conformance, and conformance means graduation.

This is not to say there are no breaks in the routine; in an environment as structured as West Point is, the cadets hunger for, and sometimes create, small bits of diversion. The Phantom was one of these: he performed for a month in 1965 and retired before being caught. Graduates remember pleasant events like the visitations of the Phantom, and, like everyone else, they tend to gloss over the unpleasantries in their education. In the case of a West Pointer, however, these unpleasantries overwhelm and shape him to such a degree that they must be examined in detail to gain even a cursory understanding of the kind of man he is.

The cadet routine consists of a hectic yet monotonous rhythm of bells, formations, commands, classes, bells, formations, commands, and so on, repeated in never faltering cadence and pattern. A typical weekday goes like this. . . . At 5:50 a.m. the signal to begin is given by the firing of a cannon pointing out over the Hudson from Trophy Point. Soon after, a drum-and-bugle band called the Hellcats starts pounding out Reveille over and over again. At 6:05 a long bell sounds and plebes (freshmen), standing in every hallway of every barracks, are shouting, "Sir, there are ten minutes until assembly for reveille-breakfast formation. The uniform is as for class under short overcoat. For breakfast we are having fried eggs, toast, cereal, and sausage. TEN MINUTES, SIR!" This must be done perfectly, the right words with the right inflection, or the plebe is likely to see a head pop out of a room and hear, "Squeeze your head in, SMACKHEAD, and drive around to my room after breakfast and we'll go through the drill by the numbers. Do you understand that, SMACKHEAD!" "YES, SIR!" shouts the plebe. At 6:10 there are five short bursts from the bell and the plebes repeat their performance. Eleven minutes after six brings four bells and a recitation that excludes the menu, three bells includes the menu, two bells does not, and then the plebe screams, "This is the last minute to be called before this formation, SIR!" and runs outside to take his place. The rest of the plebes are already "standing tall." They have been there for the last five minutes locked at rigid attention and looking a little foolish because each is standing alone on a memorized spot (a crack in the concrete or a patch of tar) in a huge imaginary formation. Policing the scattered cadets are the "head plebe-chaser," a junior, and the regular plebe-chasers, sophomores. They are there to make sure that the plebes have performed efficiently that morning. The name of the game for the rest of the cadets—the upperclassmen—is to stay in bed as long as possible. They have become super-efficient in performing the morning minutiae; they waste no motion as they dress, make their beds, clean up their rooms, and place their "buckets" (wastebaskets) outside in the hall. The uniform they put on is determined by regulation. It varies by activity, season, humidity, temperature, rainfall, and time of day. The class uniform alone has five variations: standard; with gray jacket; with short overcoat, scarf, and gloves; with raincoat and rain cap cover; or with long overcoat. A uniform flag (there are twelve of them) in each regimental area announces the proper variations throughout the day. These uniforms, along with fatigues, khakis, gym clothes, a blazer, and the full-dress costume, are paid for by the cadets out of their approximately $2,500 annual salary and, of course, hang on authorized hooks in authorized locations in each room. Other standard room equipment includes a desk, a metal bed, a chair, a bureau, a wastebasket, a locker or closet, and one cadet per complete set. Roommates are assigned under the "theory of interchangeable parts"; every cadet should be able to live with any other cadet. Contrary to practice in most other colleges, cadets are rarely allowed to choose those with whom they will live. There is very little extraneous matter in the room; plebes are not even allowed to have radios until the second semester. Each desk contains the same books (they are normally taking the same courses) and each drawer contains the same material arranged in the same order. All unauthorized possessions—e.g., food, shoeshine spray, popcorn poppers, etc.—are kept in a duffel bag and hidden during inspections. Excerpts from the "Standard Operating Procedure for Room Arrangements" give a good impression of the sterility of a cadet room: "Rooms will be presentable at all times and *articles will be in their prescribed places* when not in use. . . . Rooms will be subject to inspection *at all times.* . . . Cadets may keep in their possession *only such articles that are issued or specifically authorized.* . . . ASH TRAYS: Optional one per cadet; at least one per room mandatory. Displayed on upper right corner of desk; must be washed frequently and empty for inspection. . . . BLUE BOOK [Regulations, USCC]: Figure 10E [referring to a photograph], tangent to right front edge of top shelf of wardrobe. . . . BOX STATIONERY: Figures 5E and 6E, maximum of two, purchased from Cadet Store or Pointer, containing only writing supplies, plain end forward. . . . BROOM: Under left side bed, bristles down and away from door. . . . PHOTOGRAPHS: Figure 4E, one frame or studio mount per man. . . . WINDOW SHADE: To position one half the height of windows, pulled taut by rope . . ."[4] (emphasis added). All that is needed to complete the impression is bars on the windows.

At the final bell, all cadets are in the "area," at attention, and in formation. The "area," a concrete courtyard surrounded by granite barracks buildings, resembles, more than anything else, a prison exercise yard. Each of the four cadet regiments (approximately 1,000 men apiece) forms in a separate "area." After reports are taken, announcements are made, and sometimes inspections are performed; then the entire corps of cadets is marched off to breakfast.

They stride through a setting that resembles a too perfect movie set. The buildings are solid and imposing, the grass is brilliantly green, the panorama of richly forested hills and the broad Hudson River is incredibly beautiful, and the entire affair is overlooked and sanctified by a monumental church. If there is a God, and if he is Christian and American, he surely resides high on a hill at West Point surrounded by the Gothic splendor of the Cadet Chapel.

The mess hall is shaped like a gigantic asterisk. Its cavernous interior looks like the sound stage for the dining scenes in a multimillion-dollar production of *Good-bye, Mr. Chips*. Approximately 400 identically set ten-man tables, surrounded by oil paintings of distinguished alumni, scores of flags, and massive wooden beams, all wait for hundreds of young men to enter and begin knocking over chairs, throwing mashed potatoes, and, in general, behaving like any large group of adolescents in close proximity to each other and food. The sound stage waits in vain, for what files in is cadets, and cadets, above all, don't misbehave. The Academy itself provides the best description of what *does* occur in the mess hall in a document called *The New Cadet: Information for the Parents of the Class of 1975:*

The first point of instruction about dining hall decorum describes the exact place outside of the building at which the cadet should remove his headgear. (Of course the rule takes into account the possibility of inclement weather.) Once inside the hall, New Cadets are taught that only certain aisles are reserved for their use, and "doubletime" is the accepted mode of movement.

Once the cadets have taken their seats, New Cadets learn that they will "sit erect on all of the chair at a normal position of attention with their back not resting against the chair." New Cadets, no longer civilians but not yet a part of the Corps, will gaze only at their plates in the dining hall unless otherwise directed by an upperclassman. While eating, New Cadets will "not begin to chew their food until their utensils have been properly placed on their plate, and will not pick up another portion of food until they have completely chewed and swallowed their previous bite; a similar policy applies to liquids."

All New Cadets at a given table are responsible for knowing the beverage preferences of the one or two upperclassmen at their table and the first name of the waiter. Beyond that, there are four cadets who perform specific duties at the table. The "Hot Beverage Corporal" and the "Cold Beverage Corporal" sit at predesignated positions and keep the table supplied with the respective liquids. The "Gunner" is responsible for replenishing foods that have been depleted and the "Dessert Cutter" cuts and serves desserts. Both Gunner and Dessert Cutter may speak only prescribed phrases when performing their duties.

Allotted time in the mess hall is 25 to 30 minutes. Usually, the entire Corps requires only 12 minutes to enter the mess hall and get to their seats. After a short benediction, cadets take their seats and begin the meal; the time left in which to eat is 15 to 18 minutes. It may have already become obvious to you that dining hall procedures can easily interfere with the ability of a Plebe to leisurely consume a full meal. Occasions may arise when your son's appetite may indeed be unsatisfied as he leaves the dining hall, but several precautions guard against the possibility of insufficient food intake.[5]

In addition to these inane eating rules, the plebe is obliged, at the whim of an upperclassman, to recite certain vitally important facts from a body of information known as "Plebe Knowledge." The conversation goes like this:

"Well, Mr. Jones, you've tied up again. Let's have the definition of leather, beanhead."

"If the fresh skin of an animal, cleaned and divested of all hair, fat, and other extraneous matter, be immersed in a dilute solution of tannic acid, a chemical combination ensues; the gelatinous tissue of the skin is converted into a non-putresible [sic] substance impervious to and insoluble in water; this, sir, is leather!" [6]

"I don't like your tone, meathead. You sound like a little girl. Now pop off in a military manner. Who do you rank, anyway? . . . Don't just sit there, dullard, who do you rank?"

"SIR, the Superintendent's dog, the Commandant's cat, the waiters in the mess hall, the Hellcats, the Generals in the Air Force, and all the Admirals in the whole damn Navy, SIR!" [7]

"Well, you tied up again. How many 'sirs' in a statement, smack?"

"One sir, SIR!"

"Are you trying to be wise, beanbrain?"

"No, SIR!"

"EAT!"

The plebe instantly reaches for a tiny piece of bread he has placed on his plate specifically for the smooth execution of this command and shoves it into his mouth.

"Not fast enough, meathead, SIT UP! Let's try it again. Are you listening up?"

"Yes, SIR!"

"EAT!"

The plebe quickly discovers the "snowball effect"—the more mistakes he makes, the wider his reputation as a foul-up becomes and the more harassment he receives. Soon he is in too deep to get out—better to just play the game, know your stuff, and don't complain. The Academy explains: "The Fourth Class (Plebe) System is an artificially generated stressful situation which facilitates the socialization and equalization of cadets, assists in the identification of the maladjusted cadet and provides an opportunity for leadership experience by the upperclasses." [8] This is the stuff of West Point.

Near the end of the meal a light goes on and the First Classmen (seniors) are allowed to leave; then another light for the Second Classmen (juniors), and so on. The plebes, of course, are the last to leave. The precious commodity, extra time, is parceled out sparingly: the rich get richer, while the poor get poorer. Eventually, all the cadets are back in their rooms with roughly thirty minutes to finish cleaning them up and, maybe, read a newspaper. At 7:30 another bell sounds, reminding them that there are fifteen minutes until the first class. The cadet lives by his watch and these bells.

Classes normally last until 11:50. At 12:00 one long bell sounds, the minute-caller begins his monotonous shouting, the plebes and plebe-chasers perform again in the area, and by 12:10 everyone is back in formation ready to march to lunch. At 1:00 the corps is on its way to class again, all wearing the right uniform and all carrying the right books. A 1968 graduate recalls a time when he was the only member of his English class who brought the proper book: "The instructor was incensed at the rest of the class, and when the next composition rolled around, their papers were raped. My grade, of course, was very high." Classes end at 3:15, and at 3:30 another bell sounds, sending cadets off to the first possible variation in their day. Depending on the weather, the season, the day of the week, and the overall training schedule, the next activity could be intramural sports or a parade, "Corps Squad" athletics, walking punishment tours, or even some time off.

Intramural sports are normally held twice each week. Each cadet has fifteen to twenty-five minutes to change out of his class uniform into his gym uniform and be in a formation arranged by intramural team. The available sports cover a wide variety, and by the time a cadet graduates he has fired a pistol, played handball and lacrosse, boxed, raced around a compass course, and so on. Corps Squad training is held at the same time for those on the football team, the tennis team, etc. West Point competes in most college sports, and athletes receive some important privileges, among them the opportunity to travel and to eat at Corps Squad tables free from harassment. For the less athletically inclined, performing well on a company intramural team at least helps with their "military aptitude" rating.

Parades are normally held three times a week—twice on weekdays and once on Saturday. The weekday parades are practice for the Saturday performance before the public. During his four years the cadet will participate in literally hundreds of these affairs, spending countless hours preparing, standing at attention, and marching. He wears starched white pants, a spotless full-dress coat, a polished full-dress hat, clean shoulder belts with a shined breastplate, a clean and polished waist belt, a cartridge box containing a piece of wood, and, of course, glistening shoes. Add to this a rifle with bayonet and the resulting caricature does not need further description.

"SIR, there are fifteen minutes until assembly for parade formation. The uniform is full-dress gray under arms. Fifteen minutes, SIR!" Our minute-calling plebe does his piece and the cadets are off and running, the plebes often going straight to an upperclassman's room for a "special inspection." One of their functions while there is to help their superior don his uniform.

The parade itself is stirring: thousands of ramrod-straight, grim young men marching in never deviating patterns to the sounds of martial music. The scene is so perfect that the spectator hungers for a flaw—a company of cadets abruptly halting before the reviewing stand, executing a perfect right-face, and, on command, raising their fingers in an obscene gesture to the superintendent; then a perfect about-face and a mad dash back to the barracks, the entire company never to be seen again. If the form and the execution of the maneuver were good enough, it would surely be overlooked—no one ever examines the substance of a parade.

On those rare days when nothing is scheduled after classes, the cadet has few ways to use his free time. Sleep normally has the first priority. The less passive cadets may work out in the gym, walk around the Academy, visit the library, or study. As limited as these options may seem, the cadet savors the opportunity to freely choose one of them. For some, this time off is used up in another way: walking punishment tours. One punishment tour consists of shouldering a rifle and walking back and forth across the "area" for one hour. Demerits and confinement also are used as disciplinary measures. For upperclassmen, nine demerits in one month means loss of weekend privileges. Each demerit above the monthly limit of thirteen means one hour walking the area. "Ordinary confinement" is served by members of in-season intercollegiate athletic teams in lieu of walking the area. Cadets in ordinary confinement are restricted to their rooms during hours when privileges are normally given. "Special confinement" is reserved for cadets caught committing what Academy officials consider particularly gross offenses, and it includes heavy doses of punishment tours. Possible offenses and punishments are many and varied. The following are a few that were meted out in the 1970–71 academic year, as listed in official Academy special orders: [9]

Offense: Engaging in money-making activity, i.e. selling pizza pies for a profit in area of barracks during CQ [Charge of Quarters], 2 Feb. 71. Punishment: Twenty (20) demerits, forty-four (44) punishments, and confinement to restricted limits for two (2) months.

Offense: Extremely poor judgment, i.e. making an obscene gesture during "Howitzer" picture taking formation, 7 Jan. 71. Punishment: Fifteen (15) demerits and twenty (20) punishments.

Offense: Public display of affection, i.e. allowing young lady to kiss him in Grant Hall, 1745 hours, 20 Jan. 71. Punishment: Ten (10) demerits and fourteen (14) punishments.

Offense: Surly or disrespectful attitude, i.e. displaying belligerent [sic] when asked by guard to move from officers' seat in Chapel, 1055 hours, 17 Jan. 71. Punishment: Fifteen (15) demerits and twenty (20) punishments.

Offense: Gross lack of judgment, i.e. leaving Chapel formation without authority and disrespectful behavior at Chapel by creating a disturbance, talking in relatively loud tone, and having collar unhooked, 7 Feb. 71. Punishment: Twenty-five (25) demerits, sixty-six (66) punishments, and confinement to restricted limits for three (3) months.

Offense: Withholding Form 2-1s, intentional, 30 Nov. 70. Punishment: Twenty (20) demerits, forty-four (44) punishments, and confinement to restricted limits for four (4) months.

Offense: Failure to comply with general instructions, intentional i.e. wearing love beads on wrist while in uniform, 12 Mar. 71. Punishment: Ten (10) demerits and fourteen (14) punishments.

Offense: Gross lack of judgment, reflecting discredit upon the Corps of Cadets, i.e. hitch-hiking in cadet uniform on New Jersey Turnpike, aggravated by unkempt uniform, disreputable shoes, long sideburns, in need of haircut, and wearing a mustache, 29 Dec. 70. Punishment: Twenty (20) demerits, forty-four (44) punishments, confinement to restricted limits for two (2) months, and reduction to the grade of Cadet Private.

Offense: Public display of affection, i.e. walking on Merritt Road with arm around young lady approximately 1730, 18 Mar. 71, in class uniform with gray jacket. Punishment: Ten (10) demerits and fourteen (14) punishments.

Offense: Gross lack of judgment, i.e. returning to post while on weekend leave without authorization and attending cadet hop in improper uniform while intoxicated, 24 Apr. 71. Punishment: Twenty (20) demerits, forty-four (44) punishments, confinement to restricted limits for two (2) months, and reduction to the grade of Cadet Private.

Offense: Gross lack of judgment, i.e. misuse of privileges by driving an automobile on post, leaving post without authority (with young lady rather than parents, guardians, etc.), speeding on Palisades Interstate Parkway, 11 Apr. 71. Punishment: Thirty (30) demerits, eighty-eight (88) punishments, and confinement to restricted limits for four (4) months.

Offense: AWOL, off post, intentional, i.e. visiting Lady Cliff College, 1600 hours, 20 Jan. 71. Punishment: Thirty (30) demerits, eighty-eight (88) punishments, and confinement to restricted limits for four (4) months.

Offense: Escorting at unauthorized time and unauthorized place, i.e. in stairwell between 4th floor and 4th floor mezzanine, USMA Library, at 1355 hours, 16 Feb. 71. Punishment: Fifteen (15) demerits, twenty-two (22) punishments, and confinement to restricted limits for one (1) month.

Offense: Displaying gross lack of judgment, after sleeping in and missing class on 29 Mar. 71, asking instructor to not report his absence. [Reworded] Punishment: Thirty (30) demerits, eighty-eight (88) punishments, and confinement to restricted limits for four (4) months.

Offense: Extremely poor judgment, i.e. bending silverware in the Mess Hall, 21 Feb. 71. Punishment: Ten (10) demerits and fourteen (14) punishments.

Offense: Bellig Att/Abus Lang to Individual in performance of his duty, 1500 hours, 14 Dec. 70, i.e. using extremely abusive lang. when corrected by cadet superior. Punishment: Fifteen (15) demerits, twenty-two (22) punishments and confinement to restricted limits for one (1) month.

Offense: Laxness, inattention to detail in preparation of written requirement, 23 Mar. 71. Punishment: Fifteen (15) demerits and twenty (20) punishments.

Offense: Leaving ceremony or formation without authority, i.e. leaving breakfast formation, 13 Feb. 71, aggravated by a belligerent attitude to a cadet superior in the performance of his duty. Punishment: Twenty-five (25) demerits, sixty-six (66) punishments, and confinement to restricted limits for three (3) months.

Offense: Horseplay in barracks resulting in damage to government property, intentional, i.e. breaking window while wrestling in barracks, 6 Apr. 71. Punishment: Fifteen (15) demerits and twenty (20) punishments.

The Special Orders awarding these punishments go on almost endlessly, as do the regulations the wary cadets must obey. Some challenge the system, however, and by doing so soon learn its crushing weight. The experiences of a recent Academy graduate are instructive.

His problems began in 1968 when he sought answers to the question of compulsory chapel at the Academy. Although his methods were entirely legal, he and three other cadets were threatened with arbitrary court-martial and doubts were expressed as to whether or not they would graduate. After illegal searches of their rooms, during which personal papers and letters were read and confiscated, the lieutenant complained to the Inspector General. The complaint brought an end to the harassment, but the four involved were given large punishments for an offense and sentenced to walk the area until graduation. The lieutenant marched eighty hours in a three-week period, including six straight days of walking back and forth with his rifle for six hours at a stretch. He now suffers from chronic bursitis in his right hip brought on by his punishment, and doctors say there may be other organic damage. Others marching with the lieutenant suffered severe foot blisters, hemorrhoids, and reactions to drugs prescribed by Academy doctors to lessen the harmful effects of the walking tours. A direct threat was also made to those marching to the effect that anyone going on sick call would be held after graduation and into his leave time to complete his punishment. The final blow was delivered by Maj. Gen. Samuel Koster, then the West Point superintendent, when he called upon the 1969 graduating class to look at those who were "troublemakers" in the class and see what happened to them in the Army. In the lieutenant's case this meant continued harassment after graduation. He was denied an office on the Junior Officers Council of a southern Army base after being duly elected, and the normally automatic promotion to first lieutenant was, in his case, delayed. In 1971, the lieutenant resigned in disgust and West Point continues undaunted in its mission of producing "acceptable" officers.[10]

The lieutenant is now out of the Army, and West Point continues undaunted in its mission of producing "acceptable" officers.

At 6:05 the ten-minute bell rings and the minute-caller goes at it again. At 6:15 the formation is standing tall and ready to march off for supper after, of course, the reports, the announcements, etc. One 1923 graduate writing to the alumni magazine reports that all this marching and "standing tall" had its effects on later life: He "says his USMA training to walk with his chest, head and eyes up has done him wrong. Early in March, while conforming to his training, he stepped on a manhole cover that was improperly placed. The result was that he had to be fished out and taken to the hospital with abrasions and lacerations on both legs." [11] The dinner drill is a replay of breakfast and lunch, and by 7:00 most cadets are back in their rooms and studying. (The chapter on the academic system covers this phase of the day in detail.) For those not studying, there are extracurricular activities, such as the Spanish Club; official duties, such as the "subdivision inspector"; and additional duties, such as the Squad Book.

The Squad Book is worth a closer look, for it reveals where cadets are forced to place their emphasis. The squad leader, a

Second Classman, prepares a weekly evaluation and rating of the members of his squad for submission to his company commander and the company tactical officer (an Army captain or major). A page from a Squad Book so well done that it was shown to the superintendent is reproduced here:

> Mr. X is earnest in his accomplishment of duties and is determined to do a good job when he finally decides that it is best to begin his thorough task. For example, Mr. X was given the assignment last Monday evening of acquiring a biographical sketch of the squad members. By Wednesday morning he had not begun though he had ample time to do so. However, once he was reminded of what had to be done, he did an efficient, laudable job by Wednesday taps. Mr. X can accomplish a mission strikingly well, but only when he decides that it is time. Response to Mr. X is not thought of as automatic.
>
> Mr. X is not as fidgety and impatient as he once was. For example, I once observed Mr. X being corrected approximately a month ago and his eyes blinked persistently. Also his arms shook; now Mr. X has substantially improved his voice and command of his mannerisms when he is placed under pressure.
>
> Mr. X does lack force in his expression. He speaks in phrases of four words' duration. This is also true of his ability to memorize knowledge. Mr. X is trying to do well in his memorization, but he can do better. Mr. X was enthusiastic about having the best squad in the platoon, but he found it difficult to project his feelings. Also, he said, without being prompted, that he wished to have the best room in the division.
>
> I rate this cadet 1 of 4.[12]

This cadet description adequately summarizes what is meant by "military aptitude"—an all-important quality at West Point.

The guardian of military aptitude is the TAC—the company tactical officer. He is in charge of anything and everything, but has only one function—to watch, to lurk in the background and keep cadets in line. In recent years almost always a decorated Vietnam veteran, the TAC is well equipped to strike fear in the hearts of the recalcitrant. It is better not to be known at all than to be known by the TAC. Some of them become legend: one will always be remembered for his sneak tactics to surprise cadets in their rooms. He put on one tennis shoe and one regular shoe and ran into the barracks. The cadets, hearing only the regular shoe, thought he was walking and reacted accordingly. This famous TAC confiscated many a sun lamp, popcorn popper, and coffee pot. Part of the TAC's job is counseling needy cadets on their lack of "aptitude." He discovers those in need of this service through the use of rating lists and "poop sheets." Once a semester each cadet is required to rank those members of his company who are classmates or are in classes below him in terms of their military aptitude. In each of the four classes in each company two people must be ranked first, and two last. The bottom two cadets in each class get "poop-sheeted"—in other words, specific reasons are given for their ranking. Under this system, each company must always have eight oddballs, and, needless to say, the TAC is watching. If this somewhat strange indicator of aptitude is not enough, the TAC can use grades, number of demerits, general appearance, reports from instructors, and the quality of the company intramural teams to determine his success in keeping the cadets "in line." Because his personal efficiency rating is determined by the "success" of his company, very few report problems and "failure."

At 12:00 the cadet's day is nearly over and now all he must do is find time to go to the bathroom and crawl into bed. But even this last act is fraught with potential trouble, for, according to the regulations, cadets are required "to turn down their bed each night and sleep in the bed, rather than sleep on top of their blankets and use a blanket for a cover. Tactical officers and the officer in charge will report cadets who do not turn down their bed for 'Failure to sleep on sheets' "! [13]

Saturdays bring a slight variation to the routine—a barracks inspection after breakfast and classes beginning at 7:30 instead of 7:45. In the afternoon, after classes, there is the inevitable parade and perhaps a major athletic event. Attendance at sporting events is not officially mandatory, but just as a cadet is required to "prove himself" through intramurals, he must also show his military aptitude by cheering with the corps at a football game. No cadet may sit down at most of these games; he must stand and shout for the duration. The athletic program is intimately tied to the entire effort of indoctrination through a complex network of rewards and punishments (shades of an ex-West Point assistant football coach, Vince Lombardi). Good athletes receive small favors in the form of extra free time, less harassment, trips off post, and the opportunity to form close mutual-protection societies on their respective athletic teams. Poor athletes are punished in the form of low military-aptitude ratings and, most importantly, by the lack of breaks in their routine—there is no escape for them into the camaraderie of a major athletic team. The system as a whole has three functions: to develop physically fit cadets, to foster the proper competitive attitudes, and to control the cadet's time.

The Army-Navy competition is the culmination of all three. This intense rivalry makes the whole athletic program function because it brings rewards to the entire corps of cadets—interruptions in the routine. There are pep rallies, chances for pranks, trips to other cities, and a general orientation away from things military and toward things collegiate. A victory over Navy brings even greater rewards.

This whole approach to athletic competition fosters on the part of the cadets an unquestioning, obedient attitude toward activities that for every other college student require a value judgment. But this is West Point, and value judgments have, for the most part, been eliminated from training. Perhaps the best commentary on athletics and the Academy was given by an officer who is now a coach at West Point. When asked about recruiting, he said, "Our techniques are the same as any other school, but do you know what the Naval Academy does? They bring potential recruits to Annapolis and let them spend a night in the barracks with the Midshipmen! Do you realize what would happen if we did that? We would scare them all away and not have a football team! So I guess we're a little different." [14]

Saturday afternoon also brings the first opportunity of the week for cadets to "escort"—to see their girl friends. Dating is truly one of the strange rites at West Point, for it too is surrounded by regulations. A cadet's behavior is governed by the "Public Display of Affection" rule, which states: "Overfamiliarity with a lady in public is unacceptable and is avoided by every gentleman. Manifestations of affection are reserved for the privacy of each other's company. When escorting a lady in public, a cadet may properly offer his arm to the lady as a courtesy. It is particularly appropriate to assist her in this manner through crowds, through traffic, over rough or icy obstacles, when she is wearing high heels, and when other circumstances indicate that this courtesy is necessary. Customarily, a cadet will walk to the outside (roadside) of sidewalks, but when this places him to the left of the lady, he must be prepared to exchange salutes when appropriate. Under no circumstances is it proper to hold hands with a young lady in public." [15] This rule is enforced with demerits and punishment tours. One can imagine what would happen to the poor cadet whose date made the mistake of wearing a "see-through" blouse—countless punishment tours! West Point, therefore, becomes the only "campus" in America where the highly unusual sight of young men and women walking together and twiddling their thumbs can be universally seen. The Academy in its infinite wisdom, however, has provided a "non-public" place for cadets and their dates to rendezvous. It is a long, forested trail winding along the Hudson bluffs known as Flirtation Walk. Its use is restricted to upperclassmen and their dates; no one else, even an officer, is allowed. The Chapel, which dominates and bulwarks every activity at West Point, cannot be seen from the hidden recesses of "Flirty" and behavior there is conducted accordingly. On any warm and dry weekend and on others not so warm and dry, the bushes and trees along the trail are hung with uniform hats or shirts or, sometimes, a pair of "Beat Navy" panties to mark the location of two not-to-be-disturbed lovers. This rule of etiquette is scrupulously observed by all—cadets are desperate men when it comes to privacy. All this groping and leaf-scattering takes place no more than 100 yards from where a cadet can be punished for merely touching his girl. Such is the "cover-up" mentality of a West Pointer.

If he wishes to take the risk, there are other places a cadet can try to be alone with his date: the hospital parking lot, Fort Putnam (the ruins of a Revolutionary War fort), the Thayer Hall parking lot, the gym, and the small wooded areas scattered on the periphery of the main reservation. If he is truly adventurous, he can try to sneak off post and make it to a motel. All this need for stealth and planning prevents the development of any normal sexual relationship and instead creates strained, artificial, and often sexist attitudes on the part of cadets. Any woman in-

volved in these games is soon required to make a choice. Is the
man worth the foolish evasions necessary to be with him? If the
answer is yes, she accepts the games and will in all likelihood
make a good Army wife.

Fact is difficult to separate from legend when talking about sex
at a school where deprivation is the rule. This is not to say that
the cadets suffer from lack of available and interested girls, for
just as the well-endowed hero of a pornographic novel presents
an irresistible attraction, so does the cadet: his uniform and the
monastic, innocent image that goes with it. Tales abound concerning cadet-worshiping girls who dispensed their favors freely
while hiding in the barracks for days at a time, of nympho-
maniacs in New York hotel rooms on football weekends, and of
sexual conquests in the drained gymnasium swimming pool. One
cadet relates that he conquered a high-ranking Academy official's daughter in the bushes behind the Catholic Chapel, another
says that his entire company once masturbated together in the
showers, and of course all former cadets interviewed spoke of
adventures along Flirtation Walk. The grain of truth in all these
stories is the socially undeveloped cadet. He has difficulty handling social situations where the parameters are not strictly
defined—situations that require understanding and intuition.
Consequently, he avoids all but the most transient new relationships and concentrates on making the old ones, the ones he
understands, more stable. This leads to a large number of marriages between cadets and their high-school sweethearts—immediate marriages, the day of graduation or soon after. The
Chapel is booked months in advance for these weddings. Thus
the West Pointer maintains the security of his environment, surrounding himself with routine and a carefully cultivated and
tested woman. Surprises are not welcome.

Sunday brings the completion of the cadet's ritual—Chapel.
There are three churches on the reservation: Protestant, Catholic,
and Jewish. The Protestant and Catholic chapels are imposing
granite structures, while the Jewish is a nondescript building
located in the cemetery. There is really only one "real" chapel
at West Point, though—the Protestant. It is lovingly described
by the Academy itself:

Approaching the Chapel on foot from the vicinity of Cadet

Barracks, the visitor walks up a steeply winding path which follows the slope of the hill in a northeasterly direction. At different points along the path, glimpses of the Chapel may be seen through the trees until the observer passes along the northern slope. Here, the building may be seen more clearly. It seems almost as if the Chapel had grown from the ground itself.

The appearance of the Chapel seems to vary with the season. In spring, its austere gray walls seem to soften and blend into the newly greened foliage. In the heat of summer, its huge mass seems to offer coolness. In the fall, the neutral gray of its stone stands forth in startling contrast to the vivid coloring of the trees about it, while in winter its granite walls seem to reflect the cold and dreary grayness of the surrounding hills.

It is at Christmas time, however, that the Chapel is at its best. Floodlighted, it seems to rest in space, projected as a picture against the jet black backdrop of the night sky. Visible for many miles, the Chapel, gleaming as though made of translucent alabaster, has come to be a symbol of the Christmas season to the residents of the Hudson valley.[16]

Much has been written on the question of mandatory attendance at chapel for the corps of cadets. The Academy explains: "because the Military Academy accepts responsibility for the total development of the cadet—mental, physical, moral, and spiritual—and because biblical faith is one of the foundation stones of honor and integrity, every cadet is required to attend the chapel of his faith each Sunday." [17] Most cadets tolerate it or sleep through it, but some, like the previously quoted lieutenant, fight. One of these, a cadet who went so far as to file a suit in 1969 challenging the constitutionality of mandatory chapel before he lost, later found he had had some unusual opposition. A letter, written on White House stationery and dated September 2, 1970, from Nixon's military assistant, Brig. Gen. James D. Hughes (W.P. 1946), to Maj. Gen. William A. Knowlton (W.P. 1943), the superintendent of West Point, contained the following observation: "I just want you to know that I feel, perhaps erroneously, that the success we had with the chapel law suit was due to strong, behind-the-scene support from the President." [18] Nixon also, it seems, feels that God resides at West Point.

The single most revealing fact about religion at the Academy, however, is that Jewish cadets go to services on Sunday. The

West Point religion supersedes all other faiths, and, Jewish or not, conformance is demanded.

Our cadet's week is finished. He has gone through the drill and survived—or has he? If he is a plebe, he has three more years of this mind-numbing routine to go through, a routine that repeats in detail daily, endlessly asserting itself until it is second nature—a set of conditioned responses, producing a group of cadets who begin to salivate when the dinner bell rings.

These circumstances demand a particular kind of man—one who will make a virtue of unquestioning obedience. Superintendent Knowlton describes him in this manner: "He wants a system where virtue is rewarded and error is punished. He likes a structured environment. He's a man who believes in absolute values and would tend to reject the situational morality of today. He believes there are unchanging things in this changing world." [19] (This is the same absolutist Knowlton who maintained in a recent television interview that the commandment "Thou shall not kill" really means "Thou shall not murder.") The Academy somehow finds such men and molds them in its own image. The raw material is usually white, Protestant, middle-class, and, most of all, capable of being motivated by the challenge "Are you good enough? Can you take it?" The good cadet will jump through any number of hoops, no matter how high or foolishly placed, simply to show that he can "make it." The pressure to negotiate the hoops derives in substantial part from the cadet's community and parents. The cadet's hometown newspaper is kept constantly informed by the Academy officials of the local hero's progress, and the mother probably carries a photograph of her uniformed son in her pocketbook. Above all, then, the cadet knows that if he were to leave West Point, the rumor would be that he wasn't "good enough," that he couldn't "take it." The Academy itself creates this impression. Addressing the parents in the *New Cadet* manual, West Point describes their sons thus:

> By electing to attend the United States Military Academy, your son has chosen to make sacrifices the nature of which may be unknown to him. On other campuses across our country the life-style of students is undergoing rapid change. Selecting West Point precludes participation in that phenomenon. Civilian stu-

dents have often reacted against institutional controls of any kind in favor of a life-style associated with freedom of choice in housing, curriculum, and extracurricular activities. West Point is not an institution where cadets participate as directly and frequently in institutional decisions. Further, West Point is not tolerant of extreme modes of dress, language, or protest.

Cadets must forgo many of these prerogatives for a highly controlled and disciplined existence in which they can make few important decisions until they have attained an appropriate upperclass status. If your son is an exponent of the former philosophy, or is halting in his desire to make a career of military service, then you and he can expect to find your introduction to West Point more difficult as a result.

The Academy is sometimes charged with harassment, mental cruelty and childish interests by a few malcontented parents and cadets. In the case of unprepared, poorly motivated and undedicated cadets, these are not so much charges as apparent facts of life. What cannot be stressed enough is the fact that West Point and the U.S. Army are not for everyone. Those individuals who can understand the need for strict discipline, authority, control and order should experience few difficulties adjusting to the basic conditions of life at the Military Academy.[20]

Nowhere does West Point ask the parents: "Are we good enough for your sons?" Should a parent become concerned over the callousness of the above material, the cadet son always falls back on "making it" and "taking it." A character in Erich Maria Remarque's *All Quiet on the Western Front* explains: "Suddenly my mother seizes hold of my hand and asks falteringly: 'Was it very bad out there, Paul?' Mother, what should I answer to that! You would not understand, and never realize it. And you never should realize it. Was it bad, you ask.—You, Mother.—I shake my head and say: 'No, Mother, not so very. There are always a lot of us together so it isn't so bad.' "[21]

There are other reasons why a cadet tolerates the suffocating routine. He soon finds he is powerless to change it; the cost in demerits and punishment tours is too great. He is constantly told he is the best, the cream of the crop, a member of the elite Long Gray Line. This is reinforced by incessant references to graduates who have reached high positions and by constant image-polishing of his role in defending America. He begins to

THE CREAM OF THE CROP

equate his improved efficiency with the growth of his character; never before has he accomplished so much in so short a time—classes, a parade, an inspection, a sport, etc., all in one day! Substance is excluded in favor of form. And finally he makes the goals of the Academy his own and "Why" is no longer the question—there is no other way.

A John Steinbeck character puts it in these words: "Once in a while there is a man who won't do what is demanded of him, and do you know what happens? The whole machine devotes itself coldly to the destruction of his difference. They'll beat your spirit and your nerves, your body and your mind, with iron rods until the dangerous difference goes out of you. And if you can't finally give in, they'll vomit you up and leave you stinking outside—neither part of themselves nor yet free. It's better to fall in with them. . . . A thing so triumphantly illogical, so beautifully senseless as an army can't allow a question to weaken it. Within itself, if you do not hold it up to other things for comparison and derision, you'll find slowly, surely, a reason and a logic and a kind of dreadful beauty." [22]

With this realization, the cadet is ready for one of his last official acts at the Academy. According to Paragraph 318 c.(4) of the Regulations, United States Corps of Cadets, "First Classmen will, prior to or during June Week, write to their Congressmen expressing their appreciation for the opportunity to attend West Point. . . ." [23]

CHAPTER 3

Take Seats!

ARMS AND THE BOY

Let the boy try along this bayonet-blade
How cold steel is, and keen with hunger of blood;
Blue with all malice, like a madman's flash;
And thinly drawn with famishing for flesh.

Lend him to stroke these blind, blunt bullet-heads
Which long to nuzzle in the hearts of lads,
Or give him cartridges of fine zinc teeth,
Sharp with the sharpness of grief and death.

For his teeth seem for laughing round an apple.
There lurk no claws behind his fingers supple;
And God will grow no talons at his heels,
Nor antlers through the thickness of his curls.

—WILFRED OWEN

FROM the Hudson River, Thayer Hall looks like a mistake—
the incomplete work of a demented medieval castle-builder. The
dirty brown stones climbing endlessly up the bluff give the
correct sense of strength and bulk, the turrets with their archers'
slits and parapets lend the necessary sense of malevolence, the
acres of tennis courts hugging the base of the wall substitute
adequately for fields of happy serfs, but something is wrong. On
the landward side, where the defense should be the strongest,
there is no wall, no parapet, no archer's slit. The whole affair

simply slides into the top of the bluff, easily accessible to hordes of loudly screaming invaders or, as it turns out, hordes of silently screaming cadets. The masculine image of medieval strength dissolves with the fourth wall and is replaced with the faint repulsion of a massive, angular mausoleum jutting out of a lush riverbank. The finest crypts along the Hudson!

This discordant structure is the Military Academy's main academic building. Named after Sylvanus Thayer, the man who, from 1817 to 1833, instituted most of the academic procedures that are in effect today, it is, after the graduates, the Plain, the Chapel, the monuments, and the football team, the pride of the Academy. Called variously "the finest academic building in the world" (the superintendent), "the cleanest building in the world" (the janitors), and "the armpit of the world" (the cadets), Thayer Hall is nonetheless stage center for the daily drama called education at West Point.

To graduate, each cadet must complete academic courses, a physical-education course, and a military-science course each semester for eight semesters. Six electives are allowed each cadet—one each in the sophomore and junior years and four in the senior. All other courses are required. (A list of required courses by semester is provided in Appendix A.) A cadet will spend approximately 59 percent of his time on academic subjects and 41 percent on military ones.[1] In the words of Col. C. H. Schilling (W.P. 1941), head of the Department of Engineering, he will definitely learn one thing in his four years at the Academy: "As far as I know, we are the only school in the country that trains every student who goes through here how to talk to a computer—the most important modern language of our time." [2] And West Point means it, even to the extent of having cadets plan their academic futures by talking to a computer. The conversation goes like this:

Computer	Cadet
USERID?	e2
PASSWORD?	usma
CADET, STAFF, OR FACULTY?	cadet
YOUR LAST NAME PLEASE?	jones

Computer	Cadet
YOUR ALPHA NUMBER?	07450
JONES & 07450	
IS YOUR NAME & PASS-	
WORD CORRECT?	yes
SYSTEM?	run cadetrec/tss/corps r
FUNCTION DESIRED? [3]	

and so on . . .

The depersonalization process has begun and the cadet will soon realize that attending West Point is much like living inside the computer to which he is forced to speak. At the heart of the computer are mathematics and engineering—the "real" West Point in its traditional role. Existing outside the "real" Academy are the liberal arts—namely, the social sciences and English. These two departments have been selected for emphasis in this chapter, not because they are unusual but because they are struggling to be accepted into the "real" Academy. They have always existed on the periphery, and in their fight for recognition they have left the inherent contradictions of West Point's academic system exposed and near the surface. In fact, they have left them in writing. Most of the quotations on academic procedures and pitfalls in this chapter come directly from the Social Science or English Department teaching manuals.

Shortly before 7:40 a.m. every weekday (7:30 on Saturdays) the approaches to Thayer begin to fill with cadets. They're walking, not marching—that went out in the late Fifties. The building itself is difficult to see, resting on a level much lower than the rest of the grounds and looking buried up to the top floor. Instructors, in fact, drive directly from the street onto the lot on top of the building. If the teacher is the professor of English, his black-and-gold parking sign will read "Reserved—Professer of English [sic]." No one has corrected this sign. It seems to be an academic "in" joke. Cadets enter on the fourth floor after crossing a moat not filled with water but containing the only litter observed at the Academy—a Coke bottle or two, some crumpled cigarette packages, and a few paper bags. The main entrances lead into circular chambers containing glass-enclosed display cases reserved for the various academic departments. A History Department display during June Week, 1971, caught

[68]

the cadet's eye with color transparencies of Fidel Castro in yellow, a Vietnamese peasant in blue, and Mao Tse-tung in, of course, red. The display was entitled "Understanding Revolution." Hallways radiating from these chambers lead the cadets to their classrooms. The hallways themselves, like everything else at West Point, are totally functional. They are a uniform beige, easily washable, and covered with evenly spaced pegs for the cadets' dress hats. The whole effect is that of a long entrance to a bathroom in a large but mediocre hotel.

The instructor, if he is dutiful, has been waiting in the classroom for the cadets' arrival. The Social Science Department says it this way: "The instructor's presence in his section room a few minutes before and after each lesson will encourage informal cadet comments and questions, often invaluable in estimating instructional problems. . . . Department policy requires that instructors make themselves available to cadets by habitually arriving at their section rooms a few minutes early and remaining for a few minutes after each lesson. (However, sections will be dismissed promptly at the prescribed time.)" [4] The instructor-cadet communication problem hinted at in this innocent passage is stated more clearly on signs found in every staircase: "No unauthorized personnel are allowed on the 1st and 2nd floors without authorization of the Building Commandant." The instructors' offices are on the first and second floors of Thayer Hall, and generally cadets are unauthorized personnel.

A typical classroom is as clean and neat as the rest of the building, painted in combinations of subdued red, blue, or yellow, with blackboards on all four walls. The room is, above all, like every other room. The womblike closeness of each classroom is intensified by its lack of windows. The view over the Hudson from Thayer Hall is truly beautiful, but it does not exist for the classroom cadet. The builders obviously took the attention span of our future officers into account. All potential diversions have been eliminated. The room contains twelve to sixteen streamlined metal-and-plastic desks (it's impossible to carve anything in them), an equal number of red or yellow plastic chairs, a gray metal instructor's desk, and, near the door, a bookcase. One desk is set aside for visitors and displays an "appropriate notebook marked for [the] lesson," a "seating chart properly filled

out," and "readings marked for [the] lesson (if appropriate)." [5]
The blackboard contains a brief outline of the main points of the
day's lesson. Department policy states that this outline may be
placed on either the front or the rear board, depending upon
whether the cadets need it for guidance or the instructor needs
it to jog his memory. The room is ready.

At 7:40 all cadets are standing at attention. The Section
Marcher (a name carried over from the march-to-class days)
salutes the instructor and gives the attendance report. The instructor responds, "Take Seats," and at that moment the vast
bulk of the corps of cadets is sitting in proper, hierarchically
ordered positions in Thayer Hall.

If a cadet happens not to be in his seat, he is "displaying gross
lack of judgment." One cadet in March 1971 made the mistake
of sleeping in, missing class, and asking the instructor not to
report his absence. For this transgression he received thirty
demerits, eighty-eight punishment tours, and confinement for
four months!

The tables are arranged in a U shape opening on the instructor's desk. The table to the right of the instructor is occupied by
the Section Marcher—usually the cadet with the highest academic rank in the section. The rest of the cadets are arrayed in
descending academic order around the room. If this is the "first
section," the Section Marcher is the highest-ranking cadet among
all cadets in his regiment taking the course. If this is the "last
section," the last man in the U is the lowest-ranking cadet among
all taking the course. Every man is in his place and knows his
place.

The general ranking of cadets from first to last (or best to
worst) was developed in the days of Sylvanus Thayer, when a
graduating cadet's class rank played an important role in his
future promotions. The only officially cited utility it has today is
to give those high in "General Order of Merit" first choice in
selecting their branch and initial duty assignment. Specific academic ranking by course occurs every week when each cadet's
grade averages are posted. These grades determine his future
section assignment. At resectioning, approximately once a month,
the students doing well are placed in more rigorous sections and

those performing poorly are dropped into a less difficult class. The standards of the school thus adjust to the quality of the cadets. Indeed, West Point itself says, "Very few cadets are required to leave the Military Academy as a result of academic failure." [6] This is easily understandable when, with resectioning, a cadet is offered the opportunity to underperform with the only punishment being an easier class!

The Social Science Department * describes the situation this way: "In general, cadets are resectioned periodically in the standard courses. This provides variety, enables the cadet to be observed by different instructors, and groups cadets according to their demonstrated ability in the course. It is also used as the occasion to rotate instructors among sections. There is a serious drawback in resectioning, however, in that it takes the instructor away from students he knows and with whom he has established rapport. Too frequent resectioning means treating the cadet less and less as an individual, while infrequent resectioning tends to boredom and a 'locked-in' feeling." [7]

The problem of rapport is seriously understated. The gap between instructor and cadet caused by military rank and authority is vast, usually far too vast to be overcome in the short time allowed to both parties under resectioning. By the time the instructor begins to get a sense of his cadets as people, he is whisked away. The students have learned more quickly—they don't attempt any relationship. They do not work through problems with a human instructor, they simply work at problems to arrive at the solution approved by the department. The instructor is there only to convey what the department has decided should be taught. To whom makes little difference to him; whoever they are, they won't be there much longer. A favorite selling point of West Point is its small classes. What difference does class size make when communication is absent?

Our instructor, firm in his knowledge of the cadets' intellectual abilities, if not their identities, begins. His behavior can best be described by the guidance he has received from his department on the "Conduct of the Class."

---

* The quotations from *Teaching in the Department of Social Science* are excerpts that characterize teaching at the Academy in general.

Instructor Should Keep Moving. There is probably a close correlation between the mobility of the instructor and the activity of the cadet mind. . . .

Teaching Aids Should Be Employed Wherever Possible. In general, the higher the sensory appeal of instruction, the better. . . .

Cadets Should Be Kept Occupied. Interest lags when activity— both physical and mental—lags. With this in mind Classroom exercises should be prepared in advance whenever possible. The instructor should always have a plan—such as a surprise "Take boards"—to cope with the challenge of a listless class. . . . Cadets assisting with teaching aids have an extra leverage placed upon their attention, and their activity heightens the sense of cadet participation, thereby stimulating the remainder of the section.

The Instructor Should Know His Cadets. . . . Whenever practicable, cadets should be addressed by name. The seating chart forms provided by the Department are designed to aid the instructor in associating names with individuals and also to place at the instructor's fingertips pertinent information about the background of each cadet. The source of such information is personal contact, conversation with the company tactical officer and other instructors, and the Biographical Data Cards which each cadet completes. These cards are made available to the instructor for the cadets in his section shortly after each re-sectioning. At the end of each re-sectioning period the instructor will be called upon to rate each of his students on the basis of military aptitude and instructor potential. . . .

The Instructor Should Take an Interest in His Cadets. Discussing the outside interests of cadets before and after class is one way of showing that the instructor is human and sincerely interested in his students as individuals. . . .

The Instructor Should Never Allow Cadets to Forget He Is an Officer. The relationship between the cadet and his academic instructors is among the most realistic and useful training in official relations a cadet receives at the Academy. While an air of informality in the section room is a hallmark of successful instruction, this informality must never be achieved at the expense of military courtesy. The instructor will require . . . the correction of nervous habits and mannerisms on the part of all cadets under his instruction. The academic officer must demand of his cadets the same high standard of bearing, dress, and manner as is exacted by the Department of Tactics. . . .[8] [A 1968 Academy graduate remembers standing at the blackboard during an exercise in his junior year and hearing a scuffling at his feet; he looked down and discovered the instructor on his hands and knees trying to roll a pencil under the heel of his shoe. It seems that if the heel of a cadet's shoe is tapered enough from wear to allow a pencil underneath, those shoes are "disreputable" and below the standards "exacted by the Department of Tactics." This is what is meant by not allowing the cadets to forget that the instructor is an officer. His time could better be spent by trying to convince the cadets he is not a spy.]

The anxiety masked by these guidelines was evident when Ralph Ellison, author of *Invisible Man,* was invited to speak to the collected English classes studying his book. He presented himself in a groping, sensitive, inquiring way. In other words, as a fallible human being. The cadets were embarrassed for him. He lacked command presence! He didn't give the appearance of knowing what he was talking about. Students at the University of Wisconsin, hearing the same basic lecture, loved the man for his "real vibrations."

With his command presence assured, the instructor turns to his possible methods of presentation and selects the appropriate technique. He may choose the "Any questions on the lesson?" approach: "By initiating a class period with an appeal for cadet questions, an instructor can often, providing the questions open into the area of his planned discussion, strike an extemporaneous note which stimulates cadet comment and arouses interest. However, questions will sometimes touch on unpertinent, peripheral, or abstruse matter, in which case the reply and discussion hinged thereon should be limited. . . ." [9] Or he may select the "role-playing" approach: he must remember, however, that "to be effective, cadets must be able to play the roles assigned with a reasonable degree of realism." [10] Then there's always the "Devil's Advocate": "The instructor presents a plausible argument in support of a particular viewpoint, with the object of drawing cadets into taking issue with him. Usually an extreme position is adopted for the case and is deliberately overstated to provoke the student, but it is also possible to develop a provocative conclusion from premises and argument which the students have been led to accept. . . . Usually [this] method is enhanced by a degree of subtlety and indirection in setting forth the ploy. However, *the instructor must beware of being taken seriously:* irony escapes some cadets. . . . Emotion may run high and cadets, scenting the chase, may miss the point of discussion in their efforts to sharpshoot or trip up the instructor. Besides, this type of discussion may degenerate into useless cadet-instructor debate [!] rather than exchange of thought among cadets." [11]

He can also try the "playing the expert" technique: "In long or complicated lessons individual cadets can be designated beforehand to pay special attention to some question, issue, or other aspect of the lesson as they study it. This requires that they prepare the study assignment from a particular viewpoint and come to class prepared to enlighten the section or defend a position according to their expertise. Cadets like this technique because it requires little additional work, and because they enjoy 'playing the expert.' " [12] The instructor's trump card is the "written exercise": "Written work done individually in the section room requires all cadets to put on their thinking caps and therefore ensures student participation in class. . . . The written exercise affords the opportunity of instilling the element of shock action in teaching the social sciences. The command 'Take boards' will often arouse a lethargic class, and for this reason experienced instructors will hold in reserve an exercise designed to call forth the desired student participation if other methods fail. Another method of employing 'shock action' is to require cadets to outline at the boards the argument of the authors in the assigned reading. Those who have not read the lesson will be exposed and usually it is only necessary for the instructor to suggest that this fact is apparent in order to produce a favorable impact on future lesson preparations. The great advantage of the written exercise is that it puts the student to work and therefore enhances participation in the learning process. The main disadvantage is that it is time-consuming." [13]

The list continues—the "open discussion," the "topics raised for discussion," the "reference to personal experience," the "reference to current events," the "reference to history," the "short lecture," the "fabricated outline," and on and on.

So go the attempts to break the ice. These techniques so effectively conceal the fundamental lack of communication that few instructors even realize it is missing. The denial of human relationships is so complete that few vestiges remain to be found even by those at the Academy who could become upset about it. The process is made complete by the fact that most instructors aren't even allowed to choose the trick they like the best for their particular class. This is done by means of an "instructor conference." Each teacher must prepare a lesson plan and "instructor notes" for his class, covering the plan of approach, the teaching aids, source materials, etc. He accomplishes this by studying past lesson plans and course diaries, and by talking with other teachers. At the conference these plans and notes are discussed among all the course instructors and the proper approach and lesson content are agreed upon. If a teaching technique is presented that happens to differ from the one used in years past, it is designated as a mandatory technique for one of the new instructors teaching the lesson for the first time. If a response is gained from the subjects, its use is contemplated the next time around—one year later.

Some cadets, however, manage to insinuate themselves into the system as human problems requiring special solutions. Accordingly, instructors must always be wary of the "silent hive" and the "verbose goat." The former is handled thus: "Cadets with considerable ability are often reluctant to express themselves in class or, what is worse, to fully use their talents. Sometimes confidence is lacking; at other times, interest. The instructor can draw these people out in class by reserving more difficult questions for them, and allowing them plenty of time to think. They may be gently prodded to give a special topic or book report. The instructor should show that he is aware of their ability and confident that they can make a real contribution in class." [14] The "verbose goat" requires more sensitive care and direction: "Some cadets like to talk, but are inarticulate; express themselves but do not say anything. Needless to say, such cadets are found primarily in the lower sections. Fuzzy thinking and general lack of comprehension is the main source of this difficulty, though inability to articulate what *is* understood also contributes. In no case should sarcasm be used to silence a verbose cadet. The remedy lies in sharpening ideas and fixing their impression in the cadet mind. Some specific techniques

WEST POINT

include the use of homework exercises, requiring that the note-book be completed prior to class, and requiring the taking of notes during class. In addition, on every essay writ [test] it is good practice to not allow any writing for the first five minutes, which is reserved for thought and organization. In discussion, the instructor must become practiced in the critical art of re-phrasing cadet questions, so that by example he can assist the student to say what he means. One effective method of correct-ing the flow of erroneous information from verbose goats is to ask some other cadet to comment on the goat's presentation. If, as frequently happens, the second cadet agrees with the first, volunteers from the class can be called upon to provide the correct information. If this fails, the instructor has to step in himself. A good way to avoid such situations is to shoot so many questions at the class that there is little opportunity for the verbose goat to get into the act." [15]

Underlying all this collected wisdom on the conduct of the class, the method of presentation, and the handling of certain cadet minds is the chief admonition of all instructors: "Main-tain perspective!" The problem of maintaining logical continuity in the development of perceptions is a universal problem in education. But West Point's solution is truly unique. In the following directive we will again see tricks and games obscuring to the point of invisibility a problem that must be dealt with in any honest learning environment.

"Over and over again veteran instructors emphasize that a major teaching difficulty is the need to provide a unifying per-spective on the course as a whole. This problem arises from the fragmentation of the subject incident to its presentation through a sequence of individual lessons. The method of im-parting instruction in single lesson increments is partly a matter of volition, but is mostly an adaptation to the necessities of cadet scheduling. Whatever the source of the problem, the need to overcome it by finding ways to provide continuity and per-spective is recognized as one of the uppermost tasks of the instructor; in the lower sections it is probably *the* main task of the instructor. . . . The importance of forward planning in the instructor's lesson preparation, to keep the course from being fragmented in his own mind, resulting in each lesson's taking

[76]

on a life of its own, has already been commented upon. [Note: One method discussed was requiring retention by cadets of all social-science textbooks through the senior year!] The remainder of the task is largely a matter of technique. One of the most valuable is to allow a few minutes for *summation* at the end of each hour, the purpose of which is the integration of several lessons by means of a short lecture or discussion which synthesizes the key ideas developed thus far. At the same time, a brief discussion of the high points of the *next* lesson may be undertaken; this will serve as an introduction and as an aid to cadet study. The day's lesson can also be set in perspective by requiring cadets to automatically open their notebooks to the *course outline* at the beginning of each hour; discussion of the lesson may then follow by relating it to the past lesson or lessons. Again, in the *board outline* which instructors are required to employ for each lesson, a sense of continuity may be achieved by including the lesson title and a few points from the *last* lesson and from the *next* lesson in separate blocs above and below the outline of the day. Some instructors also make a practice of maintaining on the blackboard the outline of the *current lesson bloc*. In addition various specific teaching techniques, such as the *front board,* can be employed at the beginning of the hour to provide a transition from the preceding lesson." [16]

This artificial method of providing continuity so effectively directs the cadets away from introspection about what they are being taught that they soon become mere manipulators of each day's lesson and the information it contains. If a graduate ever begins to think, the results are usually embarrassing. One graduate, sent to Oxford on a Rhodes Scholarship, decided that he would not serve in a combat role in Vietnam—and he didn't. Another, sent to Harvard in 1969 for graduate study, decided he was a selective conscientious objector to the Vietnam war—he was let out of the Army. There are very few examples of this type —the kind of graduate who thinks about what he was taught to do at West Point and rejects it. The indoctrination is very effective.

All of the above Alice-in-Wonderland teaching advice is given to a grown man in uniform (even the civilian instructors wear them) who is, in most cases, a graduate of the Academy himself. In the 1971 academic year roughly 60 percent of the faculty members were graduates. The percentage of non-grads to grads was at one time slightly higher in the Social Science Department, thus giving it the reputation of harboring the "liberals" at West Point. The instructors range in rank from captain to colonel, with the vast majority being majors. The normal tour is three years by invitation, not assignment—potential teachers are asked if they would like to return, hence the "instructor potential" rating of each cadet in each course. The short tour requires a large pool of potential instructors limited primarily, of course, by whether or not they are graduates. A problem arises, therefore, in locating "suitable" and academically qualified instructors for particular standard courses. The Social Science Department discusses this difficulty in this way: "The Department does not teach all of the social sciences which are formally presented at USMA, nor are all of the social sciences taught at the Academy. The Department's curriculum includes courses in three main areas of the social sciences: History (now a separate department), Economics, and Political Science. Usually it is necessary for an instructor to teach in at least two of these fields. Ideally, every instructor, regardless of his area of concentration in his graduate schooling, should have pursued at least one course in each field during his preparation for assignment to USMA, but it is recognized that this is not always possible. Occasionally, instructors are asked to teach in three fields during their service in the Department in order to further the integration of the Department curriculum, a policy which also serves to broaden their professional experience." [17] One illustrious former instructor, Gen. Matthew B. Ridgway (W.P. 1917), has recorded his experience with this unique policy:

I went up the Hudson with a heavy heart, too glum to brood overmuch as to what my duties were to be. I expected to teach English, or law, since I'd done fairly well in both these subjects. Or Spanish, since that had been one of my good subjects too, and I had had opportunity to practice it during my service on the Mexican border. When I got to West Point and reported in to Colonel Willcox, the head of the department of modern languages, his instructions filled me with dismay. Spanish had been discontinued during the war [World War I], he told me. I was to teach French to a class that was already well along in its second year in that language. I bluntly told Professor Willcox I didn't know enough French to order a scrambled egg in a French restaurant. I hadn't spoken or read a word of French since my yearling year, and I hadn't been particularly good in it then. I couldn't possibly see how I could do a good job as a French instructor. Professor Willcox listened, saying nothing.

"Your classes start tomorrow," he said dryly, turning back to some papers on his desk.

I hadn't studied so hard since I prepped for my entrance exams in math. Finally, after about three weeks of sitting up half of each night, filling my head with French grammar, and bluffing and blundering my way through classroom lectures, I began to feel a little more at ease. I was catching up with, and passing, that class of bright youngsters who from the start had known more about the language than I did. [18]

At West Point, in the winter of 1971, 24 instructors had Bachelor's degrees, 434 had Master's, and 67 had Doctorates.[19] Col. George A. Lincoln (W.P. 1929), former head of the Social Science Department, says, "In fact, a few of our best teachers have, upon reporting to USMA, been considerably less than completely competent historians, political scientists, or economists. Perhaps, like leaders, a few teachers are born with the aptitude. Most of us can acquire it if not so endowed by birth." [20] Our instructor, then, academically qualified or not, good teacher or not, is left with one indelible impression of his intellectual role at West Point: "more of [his] time [can] be profitably spent on the mechanics of teaching what [he] already [knows] rather than in trying to acquire more knowledge of the lesson." [21]

The tailoring of the instructor to fit the West Point environment and therefore to have the proper impact on the cadets is of crucial importance. One former instructor recalls that he spent weeks practicing his mathematics lectures before TV cameras before he mastered the presentation technique required by his superiors. His chief shortcoming (discovered by instant replay) was his habit of frequently pushing his glasses up on the bridge of his nose. Another teacher, Col. Lincoln, had a more serious fault: "I have a tendency to lower my voice at the end of some sentences. It was too many years before someone was kind enough to point this tendency out to me." [22] Evidently, even TV taping couldn't help Lincoln, for he was known to his students as "Ether Lips." Students in his lectures were allowed the unusual option of standing up in the back of the hall to keep from falling asleep in their seats. Ether Lips' famous sessions always had a large quota of standing, nodding cadets.

The instructor's prime lesson, however, is that his teaching mission *"must be accomplished within the setting of other activities which contribute to the attainment of that mission."* [23] This means that any spirit of free inquiry and criticism that he has developed must be dealt with first: "Cadets are apt to bring up everything from the vagaries of the Tactical Department and the First Class System to an inconsistency or contradiction between our Department and some other. Obviously an instructor generally lacks the facts needed to discuss such matters, and cadet recitation of the facts is often hearsay, inaccurate, and incomplete. The best rule therefore is to scrupulously refrain from making any statement that can be construed as a criticism of another Academy activity. It is our function to know as much as we can about and sympathize with the objectives of other activities of West Point. . . . The best thesis is that everything we are doing is equally important until a positive decision is made to change." [24] If our man balks at this idea, he is told that "the Department's approach to teaching is largely determined by the context in which it is set—the realities of the West Point environment. The experience of many veteran instructors is that an understanding of the realities is not itself disillusioning, although a rapid realization of realities sometimes brings a temporary disillusionment. The realities should be treated as a challenge, and the earlier the individual here at West Point comes to understand this the happier he will be and the more effective both he and our Department effort will be." [25] In other words, "Get with the program, soldier." Finally, he is warned that "everything an instructor says and does during classes, as well as the manner in which he says and does things, reflects his attitude toward his students, his subject, and the training program. His attitudes have a tremendous influence upon student attitudes and morale, because students tend to adopt both the attitude of the instructor and his point of view toward the subject and the training." [26] This admonition recently led to large changes of personnel in the English Department. It seems that because of the reputation of English as a "sissy" subject at the Military Academy, its faculty was being characterized as having distinctly non-masculine traits. This particularly vicious rumor was dealt with by bringing in English instructors with impeccable credentials—Vietnam service, the Combat Infantryman's Badge, and assorted decorations for valor. The quality of teaching in the English Department fell correspondingly.

Who is the man on the receiving end of these excruciatingly detailed attitudinal and teaching formulae? Above all, he is a man who *"can be led. . . .* This is the fundamental premise upon which teaching in the [Social Science] Department is based." [27] If he is a member of the Class of 1972, his score on the Verbal Scholastic Aptitude Test was 579 out of 800 and on the English Composition Test, 559. His scores on the Mathematics Scholastic Test and the Mathematics Achievement Test were 645 and 630, respectively. Seventeen percent of his classmates were in their high school's band, 12 percent were members of the glee club, 13 percent were in a debating or forensic society, 18 percent were on the staff of their high-school paper, 58 percent were Boy Scouts, 12 percent were presidents of their student body or student council, and 75 percent graduated in the top fifth of their class. All but 10 percent of this class participated in high-school varsity sports. Forty-six percent of the Class of 1972 were members of the National Honor Society, 7 percent received the American Legion Award, 14 percent received letters of commendation for their scores on the National Merit Scholarship exam, and 11 percent received some other national award. Sixty-two cadets were valedictorians of their class and thirty-five were salutatorians. Our cadet began to think about attending West Point at an early age. Fifteen percent of the 1972 class said that they "always" wanted to attend USMA. Nearly 25 percent stated that they began to consider West Point prior to the ninth grade, and another 25 percent indicated they began to think about it in ninth or tenth grade. The most often stated reason for finally selecting the Academy was the "academic reputation of the college" (77 percent). The next most important reason (55 percent) was the influence of a parent or relative. (Only 15 percent of the fathers of the Class of 1972 had no military service. Twelve percent of the fathers were on full-time active duty when the class entered in 1968; the class of 1971 boasts nearly 17 percent. Thirteen percent had served twenty years or more and retired. Sixty-seven fathers are graduates of USMA, ten of the Naval Academy, and one of the Merchant Marine Academy.) Twenty-seven percent reported low cost as a major influence, 26 percent spoke of the athletic program, and, finally, 16 percent stated that they felt the perception that "most students are like me" played a major role in their decision. Over half of his classmates want to become community leaders, another half want to become outstanding athletes, three fourths want to become an authority on a special subject in their field, and over one fifth want to make a theoretical contribution to science.[28] In short, our cadet is a good man—young, intelligent, athletic, and serious in his commitment to his chosen profession.

He is, after all, a recipient of the "best undergraduate scholarship in the world"—a scholarship worth approximately $50,000 over his four-year education.

On paper, then, the typical cadet seems eminently prepared to handle a high-quality education. But is he treated accordingly? We've already seen the approaches suggested for use by the instructor in the daily classroom and they are not exactly reminiscent of teaching techniques at Harvard, Yale, or Princeton (all schools to which West Point is fond of comparing itself). A more appropriate comparison, it would seem, would be with an advanced high school. The faculty's unofficial views on cadets are useful in revealing this apparent contradiction. Col. Lincoln says, "West Point is an undergraduate scholarship school without many scholars or any great motivation for learning as far as a material proportion of each class is concerned." [29] The instructor's manual for the Social Science Department contains these observations: "In general, cadet attitudes are oriented more toward the use of imparted knowledge than to the gaining of understanding for its own sake. . . ." [30] "Integration of material which is presumed to be part of their store of knowledge is frequently poor. . . ." [31] "Care should also be taken in assigning subjects which involve considerable evaluation and interpretation (unless this is the subject), as cadets are weakest in this area. . . ." [32] "Our problem is a special kind of military undergraduate with, as a group, a bit more intellectual capability and probably a bit less motivation than the general run of undergraduates in good civilian colleges. . . ." [33] "We have to bear in mind that by the time a cadet is a Second Classman he is thoroughly indoctrinated with the climate of the military aptitude system and also with the military instructor training courses." [34] One instructor (a non-graduate) commented, "The cadets at West Point are fifth rate." Another, a graduate, said in a pleading tone, "The cadets are really very bright, you know." The most illuminating view of cadets and the methods used to teach them, however, is the official one—the mission of USMA.

[The mission] is to instruct and train the Corps of Cadets so that each graduate shall have the qualities and attributes essential to his progressive and continuing development as an officer of the Regular Army. (AR 350-5) Inherent in this mission are the objectives:
  1. To instill discipline.
  2. To instill a high sense of honor.
  3. To provide the knowledge and general education equivalent to that given by our leading universities, and particularly to develop the cadet's powers of analysis so that his mind may reason to a logical conclusion. [35]

The order in which these objectives are listed is an accurate reflection of emphasis.

These sometimes disparaging views of the cadet's abilities and the role of his West Point education are implemented not only by the instructors' teaching methods but also by the manner in which the student is expected to study. Just as the teaching is circumscribed and technique-oriented, so is the homework.

All cadets must be in their rooms by 1950 (7:50 p.m.), at which time the final Call to Quarters is given. At 2300 (11:00 p.m.) Taps is sounded and lights go out for the Third and Fourth Classes (freshmen and sophomores). At midnight, "late" lights are extinguished for the Second Class. A recent change allows First Classmen to leave their lights on all night. With each cadet spending approximately six hours a day in class, this programmed study time allows the Third and Fourth Classmen roughly one half-hour of preparation for each hour of class. The Second Classmen are able to get forty minutes per hour. As we have seen in the chapter on the cadet routine, additional study time is hard to find. Since most colleges recommend at least two hours of preparation per hour in class, how can West Point allow less than forty-five minutes per hour for three fourths of its students and expect them to function knowledgeably in class? The answer lies in enabling the cadet to make "effective" use of his limited time by standardizing the homework. The key is the pre-printed course notebook. Most standard courses taught at the Academy are accompanied by a notebook which neatly capsulizes the knowledge required to pass the subject. For example, a notebook on a second-year history course will contain the title of each lesson and the day it will be taught, the required reading, the recommended additional reading ("you can pass without reading this material"), the learning objectives (e.g., "the major elements of feudal society"), a list of definitions and identification (e.g., "St. Augustine, oligarchy"), and a group of discussion questions ("Whenever you read a Key Reading or Historical Interpretation in the . . . text, look for at least one discussion question in this section").[36] The cadet is completely aware of what he has to know and studies accordingly.

This programmed homework is absolutely necessary to make the programmed instruction work. If the instructor isn't aware of what the cadets are supposed to know for each day's class, his lesson plan is useless and class discussion non-existent.

Requiring students to have a general awareness of the subject matter prior to class is not, of course, in itself unusual or wrong. But "general awareness" is not what is sought at West Point. Uniformity of preparation and the acquisition of specified bits of knowledge is sought and must be obtained to make the teaching system valid. Cadets must not be allowed more time for study, particularly independent, inquisitive study. If this were allowed, seemingly extraneous contradictory questions might arise in class and disrupt the logical, sequenced flow of the lesson plan. If the interruptions were serious enough, they could even prevent the completion of the day's assigned lesson bloc, thereby invalidating the next lesson plan and placing the entire class out of phase with the schedule. Disasters of this type cannot be absorbed.

Another problem could arise. If cadets were allowed time to develop probing questions, they would require instructors capable of answering them—an instructor who could step outside of his lesson plan and use his general knowledge of the subject. This would mean a teacher who was truly qualified academically rather than a technician capable of reading a lesson plan. The experience of a 1965 graduate of the Academy illustrates what can happen when someone gets "out of step" with the instructor. The course was differential equations, taught in the sophomore year, and the cadet was in confinement with little to do but concentrate on academics. Math happened to be a favorite subject, so he began to read ahead in his course book. The problems were of a Step 1, Step 2, Step 3, etc., variety, and in his advanced reading he discovered that an entire series of steps could be eliminated automatically through the use of a simple rule. The next morning in class he was required to take the board (along with the rest of the cadets) and solve the day's problem. He got to Step 3, applied the newly discovered rule, and skipped to Step 7. The instructor was dumfounded and asked for an explanation. The cadet patiently explained and soon realized that the instructor had no idea what he was talking about. A cardinal error had been made: a cadet had embarrassed an instructor in front of his class. Although the solution was perfect, the grade received was somewhat less than perfect and he had learned his lesson: don't read ahead of the instructor. He learned it well and stated that never again did he get out of phase by studying the "wrong" things.[37]

The motivation to study earnestly is provided by frequent grading and privileges that are granted to those with high marks. A cadet in the top 5 percent of his class is deemed a "Star Man" and allowed such luxuries as an additional weekend of leave each semester and an authorized absence from certain inspections. He is also in the top sections where the system of standardization and resectioning begins to break down. He may be able to spend an entire course with the same teacher, be taught in seminar fashion, and be allowed independent study. His instructor is usually the best in the subject and the cadet is the recipient of some very high-quality instruction. Graduates who spent most of their time in the top sections and honors courses have very few complaints about their education. The system, then, can work for a few selected cadets and without the artificial barriers to learning of standardization and resectioning. But, sadly, only a small number can be Star Men, and the rest of the cadets must suffer with the game. An important part of the game is grading—frequent grading. The system used is based on a maximum mark of 3.0 or 30 tenths; a grade of 2.0 is passing. If a cadet receives a score of 2.1 on an English quiz, he will say that he went "one tenth pro"; in other words, he is one tenth better than he has to be. Should he receive a 1.8, he will refer to that as "two tenths deficient." The game is won when a cadet becomes so many tenths proficient that he cannot possibly lose enough in subsequent gradings to fail the course. For example, if a cadet is 90 tenths proficient and facing an exam worth 9.0 or 90 tenths, he knows that he can totally fail the test and still maintain his minimum mark of 2.0. The Social Science Department admits this phenomenon when it says that "motivation is in considerable part up to [the instructor] insofar as it rises above the 2.0 line." [38] The reports are mixed as to whether or not pressure is applied on instructors to give passing grades. Arthur Heise, in his book *The Brass Factories,* reports that "one member of the department of Social Sciences almost exploded in an interview: 'I would revolt anytime they tried such pressure.' A colleague of his agrees: 'Nobody would dare' to tell him what grade to give." [39] Other graduates, however, have told of experiences where pressure was applied on instructors to give passing grades to athletes in particular.

Grading and the opportunity to gather tenths occurs daily in nearly every course during plebe year, putting constant pressure on the first-year student to conform to the acceptable and necessary study procedure—cramming, memorizing, and dealing only with what is known to be required. Grading slows down as the cadet moves toward his First Class year, but in most standard courses he can still expect to be graded a minimum of three times a week. After all, some kind of rank and grade has to be posted at the end of the week. In mathematics most of the grades are based on "recitations"—problems solved at the board on a daily basis. In engineering courses the pattern is similar. The English Department relies on the CRX (Classroom Exercise) for its daily grades. The Class of 1972, studying Plebe English in April 1969, was given the following objective test to ascertain its understanding of Act II of Arthur Miller's *Death of a Salesman*. (This is taken from the Department Lesson Plan.)

1. How old was Ben when he went into the jungle? (seventeen)
2. What is Willy going out to buy when he leaves the restaurant? (seeds)
3. What new "toy" is Howard Wagner experimenting with when Willy visits him? (wire recorder)
4. What does Biff burn up in the furnace after flunking math? (shoes, University of Virginia)
5. What did Willy's father do for a living? (made and sold flutes)
6. What kind of car does Willy now own? (Studebaker) [40]

and so on.

Instructors are forced into this kind of inane lowest-common-denominator quiz because the pressure of frequent grading requires a "fair and objective" means of determining whether or not a cadet has studied. For the cadet, this means that the purpose of reading and studying becomes the memorization of trivial facts for regurgitation the next day in return for "tenths." Longer tests are called Written Partial Reviews (WPR) or Written General Reviews (WGR). No written exam is ever returned to the cadet for his retention. The WPR is given roughly once a month and is worth 6.0. The WGR is the equivalent of a final exam and is given in three parts over a three-lesson period. Each part is weighted at 9.0. This pattern varies, of course, with the subject, and additional grades may be received for research papers, special topics, etc. The English 102 course for the Class of 1972, for example, required a research paper (30.0), two themes (18.0), a WPR lasting two lessons (12.0), and a WGR (27.0). It is possible to receive a failing grade on a theme or research paper if the proper format is not followed—i.e., proper-size paper, one-inch margin, double spacing, personal identification, page numbering, writing (pen or typewriter—a felt-tip pen is not to be used at any time), italicizing, footnoting, and bibliography. General substantive guidance on themes consists of the following information found in the Department of English Handbook: "While objective criticism of national issues is encouraged, he will not make any derogatory remarks about the President, Congress, or his superior officers" and "He will not submit a theme or deliver a speech containing material that is in bad taste. If he is in doubt, he should consult the instructor beforehand." [41] The cadet is required to sign his name at the designated place on each paper he submits. Under the honor system, his signature is his pledge that the paper is "fairly and honorably" his own product. Under penalty of dismissal from the Academy, the rule is that "no discussion is permitted after the actual writing or a computation begins on any outline, preliminary draft, or final paper which the cadet will submit as his own product." [42] Sloppy presentation leads not only to a failing grade but to demerits and punishment. For example, failure to document a written home assignment is termed "laxness and inattention to detail" and typically rates fifteen demerits and twenty punishment tours. Turning in a paper late is called "gross negligence in the preparation and submission of homework" and calls for another "15 & 20." One graduate recalls that "it was the custom to consider a misspelling as a breach of discipline instead of an academic failure." [43] Rigid adherence to form, to the exclusion of substance, is critical in the functioning of the system as a whole. If the forms are followed, the substance is automatically assumed to have been assimilated. Programmed study, standardized instruction, and the frequent evaluation by grade all reinforce this illusion of intellectual progress.

All of these elements are present in the typical standard course—the culmination and embodiment of the learning process at West Point. Our example will be the English 102 course mentioned previously.

Lesson 1 thru 14	Public speaking and the preparation of a research paper.
	Merit Resectioning
Lesson 15	Introduction to Imaginative Literature—the short story

Lesson 16	Boyle's "The White Horses of Vienna"
Lesson 17	Thurber's "The Catbird Seat"
Lesson 18	Faulkner's "A Rose for Emily"
Lesson 19	Clemens' "The Man That Corrupted Hadleyburg"
Lesson 20 thru 24	The novel—Ellison's *Invisible Man*
Lesson 25	Classroom theme
Lesson 26 thru 29	Drama—Miller's *Death of a Salesman*
Lesson 30 thru 32	Introduction to Poetry

Merit Resectioning

| Lesson 33 thru 34 | WPR |
| Lesson 35 thru 41 | analysis of Benét's *John Brown's Body* |

Random Resectioning

Lesson 42	Course Review
Lesson 43–44	WGR
Lesson 45	Course Critique [44]

The ritual is complete, the blocs have been absorbed, and now the cadets can leave the subject alone.

This particular course contains a good example of how West Point tends to view entire academic subjects as blocs of "things to do," with the emphasis on accomplishing the mission and not on questioning its utility or continuity. To acquaint cadets with the problems of blacks, five lessons in English 102 are given over to *Invisible Man,* possibly the most sensitive and searching analysis ever written on what it means to be black in America. These lessons become known as the "race bloc." A few weeks later, in the "poetry bloc," Benét's epic poem on America during the Civil War, *John Brown's Body,* is studied for seven straight lessons. This work contains some of the most racist descriptions of blacks found in popular poetry, constantly depicting them as buffoons and less-than-human creatures. The lesson plan contains nothing on how the cadets are to be helped in absorbing the contradiction posed by *Invisible Man* and *John Brown's Body* in juxtaposition. The reason is clear—they need no help because they have already had their "race bloc"! They've studied it, therefore they must understand it.

All papers and exams for this course and every other course at the Academy are graded and commented upon in great detail, frequently by more than one instructor. These documents are filed and used to counter criticism of the quality of education at West Point—"See how carefully we check!" "Look at how much attention we give!" One point is always overlooked: each paper, each quiz, each test invariably relates to an isolated bloc of instruction and rarely to a thematic perception running throughout the course. The thought that even though a cadet has studied the "race bloc" he yet may not be an emancipated man never occurs in the fragmented course of instruction at West Point. The concept of progressive, questioning, educational development is so lacking that it's not even missed. Thus, any new tolerance gained by the study of race in *Invisible Man* is never tested, never baptized with fire—the intolerance found in Benét is just a new subject, a new "bloc"!

Who controls this system? Who makes it work? *Who decides?* Answers to these questions are difficult to find because their human elements are wrapped in the obscurity of such catch phrases as "tradition," "Thayer-instituted reform," "our mission," and, of course, "Duty, Honor, Country." These words alone somehow contain an explanation adequate for the Academy's prime constituency—its graduates and cadets—but for the outsider they offer little but psychological insight into the system and its manipulators. People, and not slogans, can be found on the Academic Board—the highest level of power and policy at West Point. Its members, almost always West Pointers, are the superintendent, the commandant of cadets, the academic dean, and the heads of the twelve academic departments. The dean and the department heads are, for all intents and purposes, permanently assigned to the school, whereas the superintendent and the commandant serve three-year tours. All questions brought before the board are decided by a majority vote, which gives the real power to the permanent residents of the Academy. The board sets standards and establishes procedures for all matters affecting the academic program and related areas. Its influence has been starkly conservative. One officer says, "A reactionary or a visionary superintendent would be moderated by the Academic Board." [45] The board's prime concern is stability (the guarding of traditions) and this it achieves by reserving all major decisions for itself, by denying faculty members a clear voice in policy—i.e., a faculty senate has never existed at USMA—and by standardizing courses and instruction to negate the influence of "oddball" or critical faculty members. Lt. Gen. Garrison H. Davidson (W.P. 1927), USMA superintendent from 1956 to 1960, and thus the top man on the Academic Board, found that the techniques used by the board to control the faculty and the corps of cadets at West Point do not necessarily transfer to civilian colleges. Upon his resignation after less than a year's service (1965–66) as a vice-president of the University of California at Berkeley, he said, "Some months ago I came to the conclusion that the politics of the administration of the University of California are so contrary to those principles we in the military service honor and believe in, that I could no longer remain a part of the administration, and still retain my self-respect. Therefore, I resigned. It is a shame to see the reputation of a truly great institution needlessly besmirched by an organized and vociferous but relatively minuscule portion of the student body and faculty. Unfortunately, discipline was not among my responsibilities. A good lieutenant could have handled the situation in the first hour." [46] The present superintendent, Maj. Gen. William A. Knowlton, defers to and relies on the Academic Board in this way:

In this era, which is viewed by many as a time of unprecedented change and declining standards in American society, it is appropriate to reaffirm the unique role of West Point. Some observers argue that moral judgments are best left to individual instincts and that specific moral codes are outdated and repressive; others contend that the past is irrelevant—that the study of our history has no purpose. Yet we military men, wrestling with the realities of history, understand that man struggles upward more successfully within society than under moral anarchy.

The special contribution of West Point is a strong system of values, which produces men who have made the transition to maturity—men who willingly accept the discipline and standards of the institution and transform them into self-discipline and self-imposed standards of achievement. I remain inspired by the ideals and philosophy of the Military Academy and wish to reaffirm my commitment to the Academy's objectives and values.[47]

In other words, the "moral anarchy" of an open society should be (and has been) replaced at West Point by the moral tyranny of the system and its protectors, the Academic Board.

The present academic dean and board kingpin is John R. Jannarone (W.P. 1938). A member of his staff says, "In terms of statutory authority, the dean has virtually none; in terms of earned respect, earned authority he has a lot." [48] Jannarone was appointed dean in June 1965. His prior assignments include Special Assistant to Gen. Leslie R. Groves (the commanding general of the Manhattan Project), two District Engineer jobs, chief of the Army Programs Analysis Branch, assistant professor of physics at West Point, and professor of physics and chemistry at West Point. Including cadet time, he has spent twenty-one years of his thirty-seven-year Army career at the Academy. His attitude toward West Point reflects this long commitment: "[Serving at the Academy] is knowing and feeling that you are contributing continually to the greatest institution on earth. You cannot measure that in words." [49] Jannarone avows a deep concern with and faith in the ability of the academic program to evolve ever higher in quality under West Point's system of "continuous review." When asked about any significant changes in the last years, he said, "The principal accomplishment was the change from a completely prescribed program to one which takes into account the differences in cadet interests and aptitudes. In other words, we have curtailed the core curriculum and expanded electives correspondingly. Initially a cadet could select two electives; now the number of electives has increased to eight . . ."! [50] Even with this wrenching change in the educational program, Jannarone retained enough faith in the overall stability of the system to send two of his sons to the Academy in the Sixties—the period of "continuous review" and "evolution."

Assisting on the Academic Board are such men as Col. E. V. Sutherland (W.P. 1936), head of the English Department. A bald, spectacularly mustachioed man, he has been described as having "relaxed on the job. . . . His deputy runs the Department. . . ." It is not at all unusual for English instructors to be in their second year before they have more than a casual greeting from Sutherland. He has one painting in his office at the Academy: a portrait of Field Marshal Douglas Haig, a British commander in World War I.

Another member of the Board is Col. Russ Broshous (W.P. 1933), head of the Earth, Space, and Graphic Sciences Department. He has spent twenty-six of his thirty-six years of commissioned service at West Point, and sums up the curriculum with one comment: "As an instructor in the Department of Engineering in 1937, I taught vector analysis to First Classmen. In [my department] we now teach it to Plebes. We are pushing forward in knowledge." [51]

The members of the Academic Board have additional responsibilities as the senior professors in and heads of their respective departments. These are best described by the following: "The breadth and complexity of the Department's functions are such that detailed supervision by the Professors is not feasible. Hence, the Department is so organized as to render day-to-day supervision unnecessary, to make each instructor, Assistant Professor, and Associate Professor feel that they have both full trust and full responsibility in the discharge of their respective duties, and to provide a body of precedent, policy, and established procedure which are such that, even for matters normally referred to a Professor, there need be added nothing save his additional experience and individual judgment." [52]

This statement emphasizes one important point: "precedent, policy, and Standard Operating Procedure" run the department, not human beings who could hear the cries for change. These department heads were described by a major instructing at West Point as "victims of paper; they have become truly professional in the daily shifting of stacks of documents from their 'in' to their 'out' box." The associate and assistant professors oversee the details of department policy: the preparation of major exams, the conduct of lesson conferences, the submission of course records to the Machine Records unit, the maintenance of course files, and so on. Their substantive role is difficult to assess, for, other than acting out policy, they seem to be invisible men.

The final tools in the control system are the instructors—the transmitters of the approved information to the cadets. In this activity above all, the boat must not be rocked. The following non sequitur describes the instructor's rule: "In all our activities an atmosphere of academic freedom prevails. Cadets are encouraged to exercise full freedom of opinion both in the classroom and in discussions with fellow cadets outside class. This policy presumes a responsible and logical approach to the matters being discussed, and is not intended to license any deviation from habitual high standards of loyalty, military courtesy, and bearing. The instructor is expected to exercise sound judgment and discretion in determining the bounds of propriety and in correcting cadets who transcend those bounds." [53] The misuse of the instructor as a mere extension and conveyor of policy is the saddest note in the mechanics of stability at West Point. The instructors, as a group, are ambitious and highly motivated until they are placed amid the so-called "realities"—until they become a part of the ranking, frequent grading, sectioning, standardization, and "absentee landlord" policy control that are all inextricably wound together, all causing one another and being caused by one another. They form a true Gordian knot; no ends are showing and there is no place to begin untying. The knot has a name, "The Academic Program," and its final arbiters are the instructors. However, they are woven so deeply into the knot's center that they are unaware of their surroundings. They are so completely simple purveyors of policy that it becomes unimportant whether or not any students are around to hear them.

But the students are there and they do hear. What do they learn in four years at West Point? The Ewell Board, a group formed in 1956 to study what qualities and attributes the regular Army officer should possess during 1968–78, decided what they should have learned: they directed that an officer should have the "ability to think." [54] Can our cadets think? Gen. William C. Westmoreland says no. He told the Ewell Board, "Officers can't write because they can't think." [55] Why? As we have seen, cadets are not taught the complexity and ambiguity of reasoning; rather they practice a "no frustration" approach to learning. Lesson plans, cadet notebooks, and "bloc" instruction translate into memorization, repetition, and absolute assumptions—x + y = z in all circumstances. If the cadet has studied the "ethics bloc" and the "race bloc," he is quite obviously a free and tolerant thinker! The contradictions between absolute assumptions never arise—there is no "bloc" on resolving contradictions. Did the underlying moral problem of our presence in Vietnam ever occur to Westmoreland or did he simply view the war as a series of "blocs," of separate campaigns either won or lost? Lt. Col. D. R. Palmer (W.P. 1956), writing a history of the war in Vietnam for the former Department of Military Art and Engineering in 1969, answers this question: "It is possible to speak of the war in Vietnam in the past tense. To be sure, be it peace or an entirely different war, whatever happens in the future will undoubtedly affect how we view Vietnam, will perhaps alter our analyses. Nevertheless, there is a clear starting point, 1954, and an equally clear stopping point, 1968, to the fighting there. . . . The war in Vietnam ended in August of 1968 when sorely battered Communist troops were unable to engage the allied war machine." [56] Lt. Col. Palmer was obviously aware that fighting was continuing in Vietnam. But from his point of view the American Army's war was over in 1968, the "bloc" was complete, and an approved, if not ideal, solution had been found. The body counts, the pacification figures, and the "kill ratios" all add up to a series of successful campaigns which themselves add up to a victory, not final, but still victory. That people are still fighting and dying there does not appear to be of much importance in his version of history.

This ability to appear to be able to think and reason without really being able to do so flows from West Point's emphasis on "getting the job done," on "solving the problem." This process disregards the emotional and intuitive sides of man. Instead of moving the cadets by appealing to their emotions and instincts of compassion and generosity, these faculties are ignored in favor of abstractly and objectively solving the "problem." Dying people are treated like math problems; it is never a suffering human who needs help, but rather that insurgent "problem" or a Communist "problem." Better to solve a problem than save a man. The forms and rituals are followed to the exclusion of the substance. This is substantiated in the language of Vietnam, where "neutralize" means "kill," "external ordnance" means "bombs and napalm," and so on.

This emphasis on action is carried to ludicrous degrees. A major (W.P. 1963) now teaching at West Point said it this way: "The Academy graduate is able to make decisions without data. This is one thing we teach them." In other words, "Don't just sit there, do something!" Another instructor, also Class of 1963, said, "The value of a West Point education is the development of an ability to focus, a single-mindedness of purpose. Cadets don't have much time for anything, but when they do, they focus and concentrate and excel." Yes, they focus on action, competition, and individual achievement to the neglect of contemplation, cooperation, and learning.

Perhaps the summation of the entire educational experience at West Point has been provided by Col. C. P. Nicholas (W.P. 1925), the recently retired head of the Mathematics Department. Writing in *Assembly* Magazine on "Mathematics and the Making of Leaders," he says,

A teacher who expects to influence the mind of a student should begin by knowing something about how the mind operates, and this is the position we take in the training of the mathematics instructors at West Point. Their training program includes a review of the basic facts that recent scientific advances have disclosed with regard to the brain. . . . It is a reasonable thesis that memory corresponds to some form of permanent physical change in the brain, produced by perception and thinking [this is totally hypothetical]. . . . Whatever the physical nature of the change may be, the permanent new imprint in the brain is called an engram. By analogy with the computer, an engram may be compared to stored information, ready to be retrieved when needed.

All learning involves both memory and the readjustment of context, and from the educator's standpoint it is imperative to know that the changes corresponding to engram formation do not take place instantaneously. They require a period of consolidation ranging up to 24 or 48 hours. During the first hour or two, the process is precarious, and in the early stages a violent interruption may erase the traces. Conversely, a period of rest enhances the consolidation. Accordingly, the student should have opportunity for peaceful reflection and tranquil sleep immediately after an evening's study. By next morning, the consolidation process will be well advanced, placing the mind in a state of readiness. Classroom exercises should then be aimed at the final stages, *employing all devices that may combine to hammer the engrams into permanent form while the iron is hot.*

This cyclic process of preparation, readiness, and classroom exercises is a dominant characteristic of instruction in mathematics at the Military Academy. Creative activity in the classroom is the climax of each cycle.

For the preparation phase, the cadet is given a carefully designed text assignment that includes a presentation of new ideas, several illustrations of their relation to previous mathematical context, and exercises designed to let the cadet explore the implications. He is expected to study diligently, in order to probe the new ideas and begin adapting them to previously learned context. The lessons are designed so that from one and a half to two hours of study will be adequate for initial progress in the cycle. The instructor is expected to counsel the cadet as to methods of study, and to assure himself that conditions of study are favorable to the preparation and readiness phases.

The cadet does not know in advance the specific exercise that will be assigned to him in the classroom, but the text makes clear the general nature of what he is to expect. His objective during study is to assimilate the new ideas in the lesson in order to be facile with them during creative work in the classroom.

The class begins with a period of questions from the cadets, aimed at clarification of points that seemed difficult during study. The instructor's answers are expected to be both informative and stimulating, so as to arouse every mind in the room to a high state of readiness. After ten minutes of this the cadets are sent to the blackboards where each is assigned an exercise. In general the exercises involve two phases, each about 30 minutes long. The first is the stage-setting, in which each cadet writes on the blackboard the necessary displays of symbols, equations, and diagrams to support his oral presentation of concepts to the entire class. At the conclusion of this essentially preparatory phase all cadets take seats, and the scene is now set for the culmination in which the teaching process reaches the peak of its effectiveness. This is the second and final phase, and its educational impact is crucial. Each cadet in turn goes to the blackboard, where he presents orally to the class a significant mathematical development, such as proof of a theorem, and application to physical science, the technique and rationale of solving a problem, or an explanation of the logic underlying a methodology.

Ordinarily each exercise is a paired one, involving two cadets at blackboards on opposite sides of the room. The instructor may interrupt the presentation by one of the cadets and require a continuation or a challenge from the other. He may also raise questions to be answered by the cadets who are seated, so that an exercise beginning with a presentation by a cadet at a blackboard may end with a debate involving the entire section. For this reason we refer to these proceedings as "forum exercises."

Ordinarily the forum exercises develop the entire mathematical structure of the day's lesson, and it is this activity that exerts the climactic influence in the day's development of the cadet's mind. His final oral presentation to the class is a critical experience, leading to either triumph or disappointment. The ideas consolidating from the previous evening's study are now brought back into vigorous play. The concepts organized symbolically on the blackboard during the 30 minutes preceding the cadet's presentation are now chiseled into precision by speech. *All the resources of his central nervous system are focused on the adjustment of prior context to new perceptions. The driving force is his own will, and he creates order by means of decision and communication.*

The effect of these methods is cumulative. No miracle of change occurs in the cadet's mind as a result of a single 24-hour learning cycle, *but when his mind undergoes this experience during every day of mathematical education for two years, it is bound to develop along the lines induced by that experience. Each day's preparation by study is a military responsibility,* and it is a challenge of respectable proportions. Each day the cadet finds that he must learn by his own efforts; that no one else can develop his powers for him; that no one can lead him by the hand in ultimate responsibility. Each day in class he faces a new situation requiring him to understand an assigned mission; to prepare a plan of action; and to formulate his mission and his plan in clear language. *He finds that in every crisis of uncertainty, salvation lies only in energy of will, swiftness of decision, and precision of expression.*[57] [Emphasis added]

EPILOGUE

THE PLACE: Long Binh Depot, Vietnam
THE TIME: Late 1969
THE SCENE: A rocket-and-mortar attack on Long Binh being carried out by VC or North Vietnamese hidden behind a nearby mountain.

In the midst of the attack, a West Point general clambers to the top of his air-conditioned headquarters building to survey the assault.

Binoculars to his eyes, he says, "They're coming from behind that hill. Get me my engineer!"

A member of his retinue scurries off and returns with a USARV engineer.

"Case," says the general to his engineer, *move that hill!*"

"What?" replies Case.

"You heard me. In seventy-two hours I want that hill gone."

And it was.

CHAPTER 4

Conquering the Truth

Make us to choose the harder right instead of the easier wrong, and never to be content with a half truth when the whole can be won.

—From the "Cadet Prayer"

LT. GEN. JULIAN J. EWELL (W.P. 1939) assumes command of the field forces in the southern part of South Vietnam. He has made himself quite a reputation as commander of the Ninth Infantry Division in the Mekong Delta and it is said that his unit killed over 100 people a day. Ex-Capt. Greg Hayward (W.P. 1964), a highly decorated Vietnam veteran, explains that "General Ewell amassed an unsurpassed record of body count and it was based on lies. And everybody in the unit knew it. He would claim kills at night with his sniper team firing with infrared scopes at 600 meters—an impossible feat. General Ewell was promoted above several officers to the job of II Field Force commander, and put great emphasis on his body count. He loved the term 'killing fish in a barrel' and used it to describe several operations. I personally heard him brag about killing fish in a barrel." [1]

This newly promoted great captain of history had performed admirably as a division commander. And now, so could the additional forces under his command. Ex-Capt. Ron Bartek (W.P. 1966) describes Lt. Gen. Ewell's first commanders' conference: "He had the division commanders, the brigade commanders, and all the battalion commanders there. I was representing my battalion commander. He spent about thirty minutes giving his formula for success. He began by saying that his unit was only killing, and these are his words, only killing 2,000 of these little bastards a month, and that they were infiltrating 4,000. Consequently, by the end of that month, which I believe was February of 1969, he wanted to begin killing 4,000 of these little bastards a month and then by the end of the following month wanted to kill 6,000. This led to great pressure on the subordinate commanders. As I said, all the subordinate commanders were there. The production of that massive figure for body count lent legitimacy to the falsification of reports. General Ewell gave to the division commanders a quota for that month and for the following month. When it filtered down through the brigades and to the battalion level I had to tell my battalion commander when I went back and briefed him that we had to kill 50 by the end of that month. . . . We did not have a single major fire-fight that month, and we had a legitimate body count of three, but I was told to report 50, and I did." [2]

As a brigadier general, William A. Knowlton had been Gen. Ewell's assistant division commander in Vietnam for four months. Two years later, as a major general, he replaced Maj. Gen. Samuel W. Koster as the superintendent of the United States Military Academy. On April 30, 1971, in a speech before the Board of Visitors, he explained the cadet honor code: "The other night I talked to the Second Class for an hour and a half. The last half hour I leaned heavily on the subjects of honor, integrity and morality. They are going to be next year's First Class, and the response was terrific. In the course of that talk I put on a slide with a quote from Newton D. Baker that is half a century old: 'Men may be inexact or even untruthful in ordinary matters and suffer as a consequence only the disesteem of their associates or the inconvenience of unfavorable litigation; but the inexact or untruthful soldier trifles with the lives of fellow men and with the honor of his government. It is therefore no matter of pride but rather a stern disciplinary necessity that makes West Point require of her students a character of trustworthiness that knows no evasions.' The quote may be fifty years old, but I do not think we can improve upon it." [3]

The *West Point Bugle Notes,* a text for Fourth Classmen on this subject, puts it this way: "Today, the Honor Code is a most cherished possession of the Corps of Cadets and the 'Long Gray Line' of graduates. The Honor Code has never outgrown its original and simple meaning—'A cadet does not lie, cheat, or steal.' " [4]

How is it, then, that there exists such a gap between the ideals of honor as stated officially and the actuality of deceit and deception that has for so long characterized our involvement in Indochina? There are many reasons, but the main one goes back to West Point itself, where cadets learn by example that deceit and deception are often "standard operating procedure" when the image of West Point or the Army is at stake.

The 1966 West Point honor scandal—which never "officially" occurred—provides a clear indication of this kind of honorable deceit. In May 1966 more than twenty members of the Class of 1968, who were part of a large cheating ring centered primarily on the subject of physics, were dismissed. The actual extent of the ring and its gradual development will be discussed later, but the point now is that no one outside the environs of West Point has ever heard about it.

While those to be dismissed were living in the boarders' ward awaiting discharge, Academy officials heard a terrifying rumor that one of them was going to sell the scandal story to *The New York Times.* At 3:00 a.m. the startled and bleary-eyed suspect was awakened by the commandant of cadets, Brig. Gen. Richard P. Scott (W.P. 1941), and two of his aides. He was threatened with court-martial if he did not come clean with his sinister scheme, but two hours of questioning convinced the commandant that the rumor was just that. It may have been more, but at this point the suspect ex-cadet was too frightened to carry out the possible transgression.

Later the corps of cadets was assembled and told the essential facts in order to minimize other unhealthy rumors. The cadets were ordered to decline to answer the questions of reporters. They were told not to discuss the facts in the future with any members of the incoming cadet classes so that the incident would die. The central message of their briefing was this: If the cadets exercised strict discipline, no one outside West Point would ever know, and the image of the Academy would be protected. The authorities purposely dismissed the culpable cadets one or two at a time so that the press would not get wind of the scandal. Those dismissed were told that if people in the outside world found out about their dereliction at West Point, they would be disgraced, unable to get into another school or get a good job. One of those dismissed reports: "Myself and two others were placed in a car and driven to a New York City airport. Before leaving, however, I listed my destination as Washington, D.C. Col. Breakiron seemed quite concerned with this and asked me for what purpose I was going to D.C. when I was from ———. I told him I had friends there and once again he cautioned me to be cautious." [5] Col. Richard C. Breakiron, the action officer for this particular scandal, remembered all too well the effects of negative publicity, as he was a member of the infamous Class of 1951. But there were two other reasons he feared a foundling's trip to Washington. One of the cadets dismissed was the son of a prominent West Point lieutenant general and the latest in a five person lineage running back to 1826. Another, Robert Johnson, was the son of none other than the Chief of Staff of the Army, Gen. Harold K. Johnson (W.P. 1933). One can imagine the trauma caused in the psyches of these generals had the matter become public. The shame of it all —the genealogical succession terminated "without honor"!

In 1967 J. Arthur Heise, while researching for his book *The Brass Factories,* noted the unusual statistical rise in honor violations in 1966 among members of the Class of 1968. He asked the superintendent, Maj. Gen. Donald V. Bennett (W.P. 1940), for an explanation. The commandant, Brig. Gen. Bernard W. Rogers (W.P. 1943), answered instead with a cautiously worded letter saying in part, "I feel certain these variations are related to the environment and background of these individuals during pre-cadet days. As you know, we receive cadet candidates from all walks of life representing a cross-section of American youth subject to the forces and trends of modern-day society. Some of them are faced with a rather abrupt initial change to their concept of honor when they begin to live under the Cadet Honor Code and system." [6] Mr. Heise wrote back to Gen. Rogers and asked specifically (1) how many of the Class of 1968 honor dismissals had been for lying, for cheating, for stealing, for toleration, and (2) the largest number of cadets involved in a particular honor incident and the general date of its occurrence. Gen. Rogers replied:

> With regard to your first question, I do not intend to provide information additional to that contained in my letter of Dec. 22, 1967.
>
> With respect to your second question, our most recent large scale incident occurred in the summer of 1951 when approximately 90 cadets were dismissed for academic cheating.[7]

On February 4, 1968, Gen. Bennett, superintendent of West Point (1966–68), was called before the Special House Armed Services Subcommittee on the Academies formed after the big Air Force Academy scandal in 1965. He was asked about the sensitive 1966 cheating incident at West Point, and, given the evasive and confusing nature of the following testimony, one can understand why Congress has yet to gain a clear picture of the shortcomings in the West Point honor system.

> MR. CHARLES WILSON. There were two major scandals at the Air Force Academy in recent years, and I seem to recall that during one of those years there was quite a large number of honor code violations at the Military Academy, but which were not publicized. Now, is this because the Air Force Academy, as you may have heard or read in the newspapers, was a large group that all participated in an event and yours was spread out over several— I think you had some 40 or 42 one year.
>
> GENERAL BENNETT. Forty-two, I think is the number you are referring to.
>
> MR. CHARLES WILSON. The press never wrote this up, as I recall.
>
> GENERAL BENNETT. No, sir; because they were spread out in the main, sir.
>
> MR. CHARLES WILSON. I wondered if you had better relations with the public press than the Air Force Academy at that time. This was not a planned violation of the whole group?
>
> GENERAL BENNETT. That is correct. We had a major problem in this area, as you just commented on, in 1951 I think it was. This had a traumatic impact, because it was centered in several small subcenters within the corps of cadets. Since then, we have not had such an event in such a small group. It was newsworthy because it was in such a small group.

MR. CHARLES WILSON. It involved quite a few football players at that time?

GENERAL BENNETT. Football players and others. One year the number will go up slightly, the next year it will go down. It is a reflection of many things. It is a reflection of the type of system, the type of control, the type of discipline that the first class will place upon the underclasses. This particular year that we are talking about, I think it was 42 in that year. This is when the class of 1967 were first classmen, and the class of 1967 to me were measurably different than the class of 1966 in their total acceptance of honor and their total acceptance of duty. They were more hardnosed. This is one of the reasons for this. [It should be pointed out that Bennett had known the Class of 1966 for only a few months.] But it does go up, it goes down, and we have not had a major situation the like of which we had in 1951, sir.[8]

Intentionally or not, Gen. Bennett's testimony was misleading on at least three counts. First, at the time of the incident, May 1966, members of the Class of 1966 were First Classmen, not members of the Class of 1967 as he says. Second, he pretends, like Gen. Rogers and the rest, that the 1966 scandal never happened. Third, Gen. Bennett raises an interesting defense of breakdowns in the honor system: that the cadets themselves administer it. . . . In essence, he is saying, "Don't blame me, it is the First Classmen's fault!" He can point to the fact that cadet companies elect their own honor representatives to the cadet honor committee, which then meets behind closed doors to cleanse the Academy of its honor violations. The fact, of course, is that the system is tightly controlled from top to bottom by majors, colonels, and generals tempered with the conservative guidance of the Alumni Association. The cover-up of the 1966 scandal is some indication of this control. It is surprising that Gen. Bennett did not raise another defense common to West Point graduates regarding any breakdown in the honor system, a defense well articulated by Brig. Gen. Rogers: that cadets come from an America plagued by moral degeneracy—an attempt to blame the American people for the bad qualities of the honor system. One wonders at what point in the selection of applicants for the Academy the "cross-section of American youth" becomes "the cream of the crop."

Where the image of West Point is concerned, the practice of

deceit is acceptable, and it is all the more acceptable where the image of the Army and distinguished graduates is concerned as well. West Point sets the example: if an incident reflects unfavorably upon the institution, cover it up.

The cadet honor code is far more complex than its simple words, "A cadet will not lie, cheat, or steal." But whenever their system is under attack, Academy officials point to this simple slogan in defense, and their critics are left helpless. For who can argue with the proposition that not lying, cheating, or stealing is honorable? Over the decades, however, the honor code has outgrown its original and simple meaning and has become encumbered by a system whose rules and regulations serve to control cadets and to inculcate in them a sense of team loyalty and servility rather than individual integrity and imagination. The system crushes the individual's moral development by denying to him the indispensable ingredient of that development— freedom.

One main purpose of the honor code is to enforce difficult-to-enforce regulations. It is used to harness 4,000 aggressive, virile young men living within the narrow gray confines of the reservation, 4,000 young men whose natural propensities must be controlled or an image may be shattered. It is particularly concerned with what can happen at night when cadets might wander off post into the wickedness and perversity of the outside world to indulge in what they see fit, and possibly make fools of themselves in front of the great American public. Regulations require that cadets be present only in specified wholesome places after dark. The honor system ensures that these regulations are followed.

An intricate mix of regulations and honor, enforced by cadets doing their duty, is used to keep cadets in their rooms at night. Any cadet found outside his room on an academic evening is subject to being asked the question "All Right?" The affirmative "All Right" rendered in response has far-reaching meaning. The Regulations, USCC, state that an "All Right" rendered by a cadet outside his room means that "He is going or has been on an authorized visit and nowhere else; that he has observed or will observe other regulations relative to limits." [9] The cadet is honor bound to tell the truth. If he is going to a classmate's room, or has just returned from Highland Falls (a town just outside the Academy gates), he cannot, without lying, state "All Right." He is caught. The hard-to-enforce limit regulations are enforced, and the cadet is punished by a confinement, hours spent walking the area, or, if his transgression is serious enough, by dismissal.

The concept of "All Right" is also applied to cadets inside their rooms—as many as four times each evening, on any academic night. The return answer of "All Right" signifies that "all absentees and all visitors are authorized." If all occupants of the room have gone, for example, to the library, the inspecting cadet then checks the "absence cards." "The absence card is used to account for the authorized absence of a cadet from his room," [10] states the Regulations, but what the authorities mean to account for, of course, are the unauthorized absences. The card has several possible markings: "Unmarked, Authorized Absence, Hospital, and Trip." The cadets who live in the room are honor bound to mark their individual cards truthfully; the marking of the "Authorized Absence" slot of the card is tantamount to a cadet standing in the room and saying "All Right." Once the Inspector (Division Inspector, Subdivision Inspector, Assistant Subdivision Inspector, or Barracks Sentinel) has checked all absence cards and asked any cadets who may be in the hallways the "All Right?" then he, like a jailer, renders a report to higher authority. He also renders a verbal "All Right," which means, according to paragraph 502c (2)(a), Regulations, USCC: "That he has inspected all rooms in his division or subdivision at the times and in the manner described; that during his inspection all cadets were present or accounted for and none were visiting without authority; or that all violations of the foregoing have been or will be duly reported." [11] Cadets are forced to check on each other. The rules are more important than any one cadet.

There are numerous other ways the honor system is used to enforce hard-to-enforce regulations. For instance, paragraphs 505b and d of Regulations, USCC, provide a glimpse of the multitudinous meanings of a cadet's signature: "When a cadet signs out in a Company Departure Book to take advantage of privileges authorized in these Regulations, his signature indicates that he is authorized privileges and will observe the Regulations concerning Limits. It also certifies the correctness of all entries. A cadet's signature on an application for football tickets certifies that he will use the 'Personal Use' tickets he has ordered as prescribed in current regulations." [12]

Indeed, a cadet of integrity will not even get married! Each cadet is required to sign a statement, "I am not married," every time he returns from weekend leave or any extended absence. Thus, the "simple" and "uncluttered" cadet honor code can be better stated in its modern meaning as: "A cadet will not lie, cheat, or steal, or go to a bar in Highland Falls at night, or get married, or violate any other regulations the authorities have difficulty enforcing and expect the cadet to obey."

Aside from regulations, the honor system is closely entwined with and forms an integral part of the academic system. Standardization of academic procedures demands that cadets learning the same lesson at different times be given similar daily tests. An English instructor teaching Chaucer to his four sections over a two-day period will give the same "writ" [test] to his first two classes on Monday and a similar writ to his two classes on Tuesday. The cadets are honor bound not to discuss the test they have taken with those who have not as yet attended that particular class. A cadet may only ask another "Was there a written recitation?" and get a reply of "Yes" or "No." Exchange of information beyond that point is an honor violation. These and other aspects of the academic honor code are likely to be found at most civilian colleges; a cadet is not allowed, when working at the blackboard for a grade, to view another cadet's blackboard; a cadet is not allowed to look over the shoulder of another cadet while taking an examination; in short, the cadet must not cheat. At West Point, though, the cadet who may slip for an instant is honor bound to report himself and he usually suffers immediate dismissal.

There are other facets of the academic honor code which are unheard of in civilian colleges. In writing an essay, no cadet is allowed to converse with another cadet once he has touched pen to paper. Paragraph 512c of Regulations, USCC, is quite specific on this point: "Unless the department specifies otherwise, the rule will be that no discussion is permitted after the actual writing or computation begins on any outline, preliminary draft, or final paper which the cadet will submit as his own product." [13] The code goes even further. When a cadet submits his homework, he is stating that "The manual composition, to include handwriting, typing, sketching, and mark-sensing or key-punching, is the cadet's own." The cadet is isolated from his fellow cadets; he may not, *must not,* ask his roommate how to spell a word; nor can he exchange his ideas, thoughts, or reactions with his friends—the sort of intellectually stimulating process that is encouraged at most educational institutions.

As the cadets move about within the intricately woven web of honor, regulations, and academic rules, they begin subtly to associate their individual standards of integrity with obedience to the rules the authorities have set for them. And it is not an accident. Academy directives remind the student, "Every cadet taking an action involving Regulations, USCC, must ask himself if his actions are in consonance with the principles of the cadet honor code." [14] Here are sown the seeds of the team concept of honor which will carry over into the active Army. Col. Samuel Hays (W.P. 1942), head of Military Psychology and Leadership from 1965 to 1969, explains it this way: "More and more in this country the emphasis tends to be placed on individual achievement, individual growth, individual self-realization. We have to change the focus of a man's loyalty from himself to the group." [15] When this aspect of the system is working, between 7:50 p.m. and Reveille the next morning, six school nights a week, cadets will be doing what they are supposed to be doing, or at least they will be where they are supposed to be: in their rooms, at an evening lecture, at the library, or on an authorized visit to the latrine. When "Saturday Evening Privileges" are in effect, the cadets may be found in more places, but these places will be authorized ones. Yet there are no iron bars on the windows or doors of barracks; there are no armed guards in the hallways. Honor regulations are the bars and guards; the prison is inside the head of each cadet.

The absolute nature of the system makes it difficult for graduates to differentiate between insignificant moral problems and those of great moment, for within their frame of reference it is the form of the situation which matters. Ethical acumen is discouraged where honor and integrity are defined in clear-cut, black-and-white terms. As the new cadets are told at their orientation talks, "Honor is like virginity—you've either got it or you don't." As cadets learn that situational ethics is unrealistic, they suffer the concomitant psychological turmoil.

Consider, for example, the cadet who returns one minute late from Saturday-evening privileges. He must sign in at 1:01 a.m. and thus in effect give himself seven demerits. His disciplinary record may be excellent and those demerits mean nothing to him, or those may be the seven demerits which prevent him from enjoying an otherwise well-deserved weekend away from West Point. In the extreme case they may be the demerits which make him exceed his allotted number for the year and lead to his dismissal. In all cases the sixty-second indiscretion is judged by the same inflexible standards.

This system has its most intense effect on the plebes. They not only must follow the same exacting forms as the upperclassmen, but they must also suffer the humiliation of pointed and inane questions to which they must reply truthfully—such questions as: "When was the last time you took a shower, smackhead?" and "When was the last time you shined those shoes, mister?" It was a wise upperclassman who first ordered the plebe standing in front of him at rigid attention to keep his eyes straight to the front. Otherwise the adroit freshman might be tempted to direct his eyes to the shoes of his intimidator and ask a counterquestion of his own. But the plebe answers the questions faithfully and begins slowly marching to the conclusion that obedience is truth. One unfortunate plebe in the Class of 1966 became the unique victim of a bizarre set of circumstances brought on by the twisted system. Mentally distraught and emotionally upset by the rigors of plebe life, he sought a few hours of solace at an evening meeting of the Cardinal Newman Club, a cadet religious group. He did not think that he was authorized by regulations to attend this meeting, but he went anyway and marked his card "Authorized Absence." Later that evening he returned to his room and had second thoughts about what he had done. He felt guilty, and, as his previous dialogues with upperclassmen had taught him, he confessed to his cadet honor representative. He discovered he had been authorized to attend that meeting. But that did not matter. He was found guilty by the cadet honor committee and was gone the next day, although what he had done did not violate regulations or the honor system in any way. He was guilty merely of thinking he had. Dismissed for a "thought crime."

Or consider a more common case where, in answer to a pop question, a plebe says he has shined his shoes that day when in fact he has not. Unsure in his own mind whether he has simply erred or intentionally deceived his squad leader, he fears making an immediate correction. He becomes less and less likely to correct his statement as time continues to separate him from the verbal transaction. But a roommate who has overheard later turns him in. Such a case involving a member of the Class of 1974 received some notoriety when Congressman Anderson of Tennessee intervened on behalf of the dismissed cadet. The Congressman objected vehemently to what he called the "archaic" cadet honor system and stated that he intended to ask the Board of Visitors to reexamine it. Congressman Anderson claimed that his constituent—the cadet—had been "expelled." The superintendent, Gen. Knowlton, considered the Congressman's choice of words somewhat arbitrary and explained to the Board of Visitors: "He was offered legal counsel and the option of a Board of Officers once the Honor Committee had unanimously found him guilty. He refused the lawyer and the Board of Officers, stating that he wished to resign. His resignation was accepted. The two key points are that the offense was not inadvertent, but deliberate; the young man was not expelled but resigned." [16] Gen. Knowlton obscured the reasons for such a resignation; in actuality, being found guilty by the cadet honor committee is the virtual equivalent of expulsion. The board of officers the cadet would have to face would be appointed and controlled by graduates. If they were to find him guilty, his dismissal for "moral turpitude" would become a matter of public record, and in most communities a mark of disgrace. But if the board of officers, because of some legal technicality, were to find the cadet not guilty, his fate would be even worse. He would return to the corps only to face a very cruel and unusual punishment. He would be "silenced." West Point officers and cadets would not speak to him except in the line of duty for the rest of his cadet days and even thereafter. He would have to live by the same routine as always, but would have to do it in psychological isolation as a spiritually unclean outcast. He would be, in the literal sense, excommunicated.

Such an ordeal was faced by two cadets in the Class of 1962 in their senior year because of transgressions committed during their summer leave. Although they were put in different regiments, they were able to talk with each other during "privileges," which eased the individual burden during their nine muted months until graduation. Silencing was also faced by a plebe in 1966. He was accused of fudging a golf score during a practice match and found guilty. His Congressman intervened, however, and a subsequent officers' board found him innocent. Nevertheless, he was silenced and resigned in June 1966. Had the young cadet defended by Congressman Anderson not elected to resign, his reward would have been more than three years of bitter isolation—an impossible sacrifice. But, as the superintendent said, "the young man was not expelled but resigned."

The honor system tolerates no mistakes, no matter how small. In the realm of West Point ethics, one is not allowed to learn from error. An error is a mortal sin. Since very few cadets can go through the four years without violating the code in some small, private way, there exists a great reservoir of guilty conscience which the system can exploit to support the concept of absolute honor. Such a standard is not only impossible to sustain, but the implied equating of all transgressions means that the sometimes subtle distinction between lies and mistakes (i.e., intent) becomes blurred, requiring that everything must give the appearance of perfection—Cover your ass! Big mistakes require big lies. Thus Maj. Gen. Samuel W. Koster (W.P. 1942) suppressed the evidence of the My Lai massacre. And Col. Robert B. Rheault (W.P. 1946), commander of the Fifth Special Forces Group in Vietnam, rendered a false report to General Abrams (W.P. 1936) regarding the Green Beret assassination of an alleged Vietnamese triple agent.

Thus, the honor system polices a cadet's every movement, indoctrinates in him the principle of blind obedience to arbitrary military authority, and provides a framework within which the graduate need not exercise painful moral judgments, substituting instead a set of rules for the development of that critical faculty. After a few years of career military service, rule worship sometimes entirely supplants moral integrity. If a military superior should give an order to "blow away" a village, search and destroy, inflate a body count, or cover up a massacre of unarmed women and children, the loyal Academy-trained or Academy-influenced officer of whatever rank is well prepared to obey. Lt. Col. Luther C. West (Ret.), whose seventeen years of experience in the Judge Advocate General Corps and continual challenges to the West Point mentality have given him an insight into the nature of the system that few others possess, has written: "Thus at a tender age, the West Point Cadet learns that military rules are sacred and in time readily accepts them as a substitute for integrity. As he progresses through his military career, the rules remain uppermost in his code of honor. In fact, his 'honor' is entwined with the rules, and so long as he obeys the rules, whatever their content, or whatever manner of man or fool may have written them, his honor is sound. The nice thing about a set of principles of this nature is that as soon as the officer himself takes command he can write a good many of his own rules, and the higher he is promoted, the more rules he can write, and the more people will be subjected to his rule-making authority." [17]

The very roots of their system are infected. At West Point itself the system backfires; inevitably, the code breaks down. The cadets are not total automatons and some perceive the essential negativeness of the honor system. They know that it prevents them from doing things and discussing ideas which are in themselves not dishonorable. The absolute nature of the system imposed on their frail human psyches activates their latent cynicism, and even West Point cannot prevent close collusion among men who have struggled through plebe year together.

In formation a plebe is asked: "Did you shine that breast-plate today, Ducrot?"

"Yessir," he replies.

After the parade his roommate, who overheard and knows the truth, comments, "You know you didn't shine your breastplate today."

"What are you going to do? Turn me in?"

They both smile and they know that they can trust each other. . . . they have entered the "gray" area of honor.

The roommates may cautiously remain in that gray area for four years, each tolerating the violations of the other and infrequently committing a minor infraction himself. But as yearlings one or both may be on a varsity athletic team and overhear a classmate in another regiment talk about a test he took that day that they will take the next. They feel that their classmate knows they are listening and they make a decision. Sometime later they meet and begin to exchange test information on a regular basis. These men have entered the black area. Some cadets, of course, remain forever "lily white," but blacks and grays know who they are and avoid them like the plague. The unpublicized ring partially exposed in 1966 developed along much these lines. The exchanging of test information blossomed where friendships and trust were the strongest, on athletic teams. One cadet would ask another who had taken English that day if he had had a test. Yes, the other would reply. Fifteen minutes later during the meal the cadet who had taken the test would discuss how much he enjoyed "Ode on a Grecian Urn" and what in particular about it excited him. Those cadets yet to take the test would get the message. The scope and intensity of information exchange would grow. According to a cadet who was in the center of the ring, there were over 100 cadets that he personally knew were involved. "The football team," he says, "would have lost most of their games because of a lack of players." Academy officials first became aware of something awry when some strange multiple-choice answers were recorded on a physics test by members of the Fourth Regiment. The first cadets to take the test were misled when the approved solution erroneously showed that the answer to question 9 was (c) when in fact it was (a). Those to whom the test answers were passed were not concerned with conceptual understanding. They wanted the letter answers, and that is what they got. Subsequently an unusual number of cadets in the Fourth Regiment answered (c) to question 9. It should be noted that suspicions of the academic department were based not on variation in cadet knowledge and cadet performance on tests ("The instructor should get to know each cadet") but on a formal discrepancy. Scores of cadets came under suspicion but the evidence was only circumstantial until an athlete, about to compete away from West Point, was permitted to take a physics exam early. He related the contents of the exam to, among others, two roommates, each of whom the athlete had cheated with individually but neither of whom knew the other had cheated. In the general atmosphere of suspicion, each roommate was afraid of the reaction of the other and individually they reported the athlete's indiscretion to their honor representative. In a perverse way, the system was working. The roommates had placed more faith in it than in each other. The athlete, found guilty by the honor committee, was kept at the Academy and threatened with a court-martial unless he revealed the names of the others involved.

Stephen Phelan, one of those on the periphery of the ring (taking advanced physics, he had on one occasion provided his roommates taking the standard courses with relevant information), describes the subsequent events. "At this point things really started to heat up. Several of the Ring members had been investigated by the honor board before for assorted other real or imagined offenses. I was called and asked if I knew of anything my roommates or anyone else had done. I said no. For a while everything cooled down. I know that the Ring had a number of meetings during this time to coordinate stories; they were very careful not to match them precisely, but to allow minor differences as would normally happen. I was present during at least one in my room. The Blackhawks [Academy officials] were evidently unable to pierce the shield. Then [my roommate] decided that it was only a matter of time before they caught him, and wishing to beat them to the punch, turned himself in for lying to his girl friend, of all things. He reasoned that it was considerably better to get thrown out for that than for cheating. So he was found. Then came the kicker. The honor board told him he would remain in the boarders' ward until he did as they asked. And so the Hawks called my other roommate up to their HQ and left him in a room alone with [the first roommate], who told him that the Hawks had a sworn witness who had spilled the whole thing. The only course was to confess. And so he did. I was called next, and brought to a room where the two of them were sitting. They filled me in on what had happened. I was pretty sure that the Hawks had set the thing up, but [my roommate] had already confessed, so I followed suit." [18]

After this initial crack, other men were either called in by the committee or turned in by other cadets. During this period, the remaining hard core of the ring met in a New York hotel room while the Corps was in the city for Memorial Day. They decided that two of their number would turn themselves in, take full responsibility, and thus end the witch hunt. (They were as well organized as the honor committee, for one of them had clandestinely reviewed the committee's current files on its suspects and intentions.) The two men did turn themselves in, but in the meantime the athlete who had been reported by the two roommates succumbed to the pressure and implicated a wide group of cadets. One of those called was Robert Johnson, the son of the then Chief-of-Staff. Under questioning, he acknowledged that he knew of the existence of a ring and was found guilty of tolerating the violations of his friends.

Fifteen years before, at West Point, news of the Korean war was temporarily pushed to the inside pages of newspapers as the headlines in August 1951 read: WEST POINT OUSTS 90 CADETS FOR CHEATING IN CLASSROOM, FOOTBALL PLAYERS INVOLVED . . . "CODE" IS VIOLATED. Even with this great purge, the cheating was far more extensive than reported. One of those dismissed estimates that hundreds of cadets were involved at the time, and that the cheating had gone on for years. The involvement of many stemmed from the knowledge that once they were aware that others were taking or giving aid and failed to report it, they were just as guilty of violating the honor code as the rest. The Army team's highly touted football coach at the time, Earl Blaik (W.P. 1920), in a chapter of his book *You Have to Pay the Price* aptly entitled "The Ninety Scapegoats," writes that members of the football team when called before the investigation board would tell the board anything it wanted to know about them personally, but under no circumstances would they involve other cadets. Blaik knew how widespread the cheating had become: "It was up to the other cadets to involve themselves. . . . I now had a list of those involved from all three upper classes and would soon have a list of the plebes involved. I knew now how terrible and deep was the defection." [19] He continued:

> As to their ideals of honor, most of the ninety boys condemned themselves by telling the truth. Since their acts had not involved cheating in the classroom, there was no evidence against most of them. To remain, all they had to do was to refuse to answer or to plead innocence. To them, this would have been dishonorable. Square this alongside their exploitation of the repetitive writ system and you have, in attitudes, a stranger paradox.
>
> Some of the cadets involved were advised by officers not stationed at the Academy to admit nothing. Others involved chose on their own to admit nothing. These stayed on at the Academy.
>
> Dramatic scenes that included the pressure of parents and tearful entreaties not to tell on others were, in the end, revolting to those who had chosen honestly to implicate themselves.[20]

Academy officials knew that cheating was rife. The investigation had been triggered on April 2, 1951, when two cadets reported irregularities. Although there was ample evidence showing widespread participation by First Classmen, they were allowed to graduate, and the scandal was not announced until two months after their departure. The ninety dismissed belonged only to the classes of 1952 and 1953. And those dismissed were those who told the truth, those who admitted they had made what the institution defined as a mistake. Speaking of the thirty-seven members of his football team and the fifty-three others dismissed, Coach Blaik wrote: "Certainly, ninety fine young Americans of good families and records do not suddenly become 'men without Honor' unless something basic in a system is wrong and extraordinary conditions and circumstances are affecting them." [21]

The percentage of black, gray, and lily-white cadets can vary from year to year, but the system Blaik speaks of will not change. In fact, virtually the same system was imposed upon West Point–West, the U.S. Air Force Academy, when it was established in 1955. It is no small wonder, since the superintendents, commandants, and academic deans were all West Point graduates, that no new, highly imaginative approaches were used. But it would take the Air Force Academy officials time and hard experience to learn how, like their classmate counterparts on the Hudson, to become masters of the cover-up.

Robert F. McDermott (W.P. 1943) had been dean at the Air Force Academy for eight years when in 1965 there occurred, according to *Look* Magazine, the "worst cheating episode in college history." [22] One hundred and five cadets, including most of the varsity football team, were dismissed. The fact that exams were stolen and sold by a highly organized ring indicates that hundreds of cadets, perhaps a majority, had entered the gray and black areas of honor, and, as in the West Point episodes, it was not an instructor who first had indications of the ring, but a lily-white air cadet. McDermott treated the press with contempt. His instant analysis of the situation when he first secretly briefed the faculty on the events was that "These young men come to us from a society where moral fibers are weakening and where respect for law and honor and morality is decaying." [23] (Now there were two academies charged with preserving the precious bodily fluids.) He told the faculty members not to talk to the press, and the superintendent, Maj. Gen. Robert H. Warren (W.P. 1940), later threatened cadets and enlisted men with court-martial if they discussed the incident because, echoing Gen. McDermott's words, "We do not want members of Congress to interfere with this thing." [24]

The modus operandi of the ring or "Clan" is discussed on five buried pages within the 114-page annual report of the superintendent. Much of those five pages is reproduced below. The reader can judge for himself how extensive was the cheating, how long it had gone on, and how corroded the system had become in ten short years. (All emphasis and parenthetical material added.)

> On January 7 1965, a cadet told an officer that there was cheating in the academic examinations throughout the Cadet Wing. He said that most of the cheating was done during examination week by certain cadets who gained prior knowledge in one of two ways. When the same test was given to different groups on different days, a cadet taking the examination on the first day remembered or recorded the answers and exchanged them with an-

other cadet for similar information on another test he would take later. Also a small group somehow obtained copies of examinations and then offered them for sale to certain "customers."

This cadet subsequently stated that several cadets had openly admitted to him that they had cheated through the use of examinations obtained through theft, trading or buying. He also identified 27 other cadets that he believed [were] involved in the cheating ring. The cadet making those allegations stated that he refused to join the ring when invited and as a result he was advised *under veiled threats* not to expose the ring. . . .

[Another air cadet turned informer] stated that he *also received veiled threats* not to expose the ring. . . .

A search for evidence to back up the allegations of the two cadets was begun. An analysis was made of progress reports, graded reviews and final examination grades to determine whether it was apparent that some of the named suspects and others had obtained advance information on examinations.

The account of the 1965 scandal continues, noting that the school's superintendent returned from a trip on January 10 and that on the following day he "called in the Office of Special Investigations (OSI) USAF to advise and assist in the investigation."

Preliminary examination of evidence relating to certain examinations indicated that the cheating allegations were probably correct. The following actions were taken:

—An analysis of grades versus examination grades was made in courses with large enrollment. In this way the Academy hoped to obtain some idea of the size of the ring *without endangering informants,* or tipping off the ring.

—The OSI was asked to furnish advice and assistance in obtaining evidence against and identifying the guilty parties.

—Plans were made to trap the guilty cadets during the graded reviews (tests which usually take a class period to complete) in early February.

During the following week, studies revealed that approximately 115 cadets had probably been involved in cheating during the fall semester; that the majority of these were second classmen [juniors], and that there appeared to be a connection of cheaters in four specific squadrons out of a total of 24 squadrons [in the cadet wing].

The action picked up:

At midnight on 17 January, an Air Officer Commanding [officers who supervise each squadron of cadets] received a call at his home from the cadet chairman of the honor representatives [of the Academy's honor committee]. The chairman stated that two fourth classmen [freshmen] . . . had gone to their respective honor representatives earlier that evening and reported the cheating ring. Both had been approached during finals [final examination] week in December and [had been] offered examinations for a price. After ferreting out more information about the operation of the ring, they decided to report it. *One or both had been threatened with bodily harm if they disclosed anything.* Both cadets named the thief of the examinations and identified 15 cadets as being members of the ring.

When these same fourth classmen were questioned on the following day, they revealed 16 additional names of probable cheaters. They also stated that the price being charged for examinations depended on the demand, and each class had its own distributors. Cost of examinations to distributors ran from $50 to $200 each. Distributors would resell copies of them for $5 to $16 to individual cadets. Payments were always made by checks, with a maximum of $10 per check. . . .

Later this same day a third classman who wanted to resign revealed what he knew of the cheating ring. . . . First classmen in one squadron did a lot of television watching during evening study time yet received high grades. [In this case a cadet was apparently able to see what the faculty could not.]

Many cadets met in certain cadets' rooms [on] evenings before finals. Doors were locked.

The cadet's new roommates told him that it was easy to get advance information, and later tried to get him some. Later, another cadet came in and, when he learned the first cadet was "in," he talked freely about answers for an upcoming quiz. He was also told of another cadet who had been hounded until he joined and how the "clan" could hardly keep him away. It was like a drug—once you got some of it you couldn't stop.

It was rumored that an honor representative had been offered $500 to $1,000 by a cadet up for an honor violation to bribe another honor representative to vote "not guilty" on hearing. [Only one "not guilty" vote is required to acquit a cadet brought before the honor committee.] Furthermore, it was rumored that a first classman of the squadron had offered a bribe under the same circumstances. The honor representative later admitted to the first bribe but denied the second.

Some "clan" members were taking extra privileges, particularly when other members of the "clan" were cadets in charge of quarters.

Even the honor committee itself was not above suspicion:

On 18 January the cadet chairman of the honor representatives reported that he had advised the chairman of the honor committee of developments and may have inadvertently tipped off the ring because *the vice chairman was a suspect.*

An unregistered pistol was found that morning in the room of the suspected cadet burglar. *Since the ring was possibly alerted and the gun discovered, informers might be in serious jeopardy. The OSI, therefore, was formally requested to assume full responsibility for an immediate investigation:* Academy staff members would assist in every way possible. The superintendent advised the Inspector General of the Air Force by phone of the possible existence of a cheating ring of 100–200 cadets and stated that he had asked the OSI to investigate.

By 1800 hours (6 p.m.) that day—18 January—18 OSI agents were present, all AOCs (Air Officers Commanding) were assembled, and the superintendent gave the OSI a search and seizure warrant. At assembly for supper—1825 hours—11 AOCs accompanied by 11 OSI agents removed the 11 "hard core" members of the ring from the ranks and proceeded to the cadets' rooms. A thorough and formal search was conducted for unauthorized examination materials, keys and other incriminating evidence. At the same time, AOCs searched the rooms of about 50 cadets. A considerable amount of evidence, including a card file of names and partial rosters of names of "clan" was found.

After the search, most of the eleven cadets pulled out of the ranks were interviewed by the OSI. Around midnight

all 11 cadets were transported to Lowry Air Force Base [in Denver, about 60 miles north of the Academy] and confined to individual cells overnight *because of violence indicated by earlier threats. . . .*

It became apparent that cadet burglars had entered the academic building and stolen examinations. Access to the building had been gained in two different ways. After the guard left his post at 0100 (1 a.m.) the thieves entered the building by operating the emergency switch on an elevator to permit entry on the second floor under the library. (The elevator had an override device which, when activated, made it possible to stop the elevator anywhere. As a result, they would get on the elevator on the first floor, push the button, and when the elevator was in the area where they thought the second floor was, they would push the emergency switch. Then, by prying the doors open, they could get out. They would leave the building the same way, because the override device controlled only the buttons inside the elevator, but not the controls on the second-floor landing.) This gave them access to all floors of the academic portion of the building. The second method was employed after 0530 (5:30 a.m.). . . . At that time, the academic building was opened to allow cadets to attend chapel services. The thieves entered through open doors on the third floor and then went to the sixth floor where examination materials were stored. A stolen key was used to open storage rooms where the examinations were kept.[25]

Among those discharged were three honor representatives. Of the 105 discharged, 101 were dismissed for cheating, only *four* for toleration.

Presidential study commissions were appointed after the great 1951 West Point scandal and after the 1965 Air Force fiasco. The Hand Commission examined West Point; the White Commission, West Point–West. Both commissions concluded that the honor systems were basically sound and that academy authorities had taken the correct action. How this could happen seems puzzling at first, but a look at who made up these investigative boards and their approaches to the problem sheds some light on the seeming contradiction. The 1951 scandal review board consisted of Learned Hand, retired judge of the Second United States Court of Appeals, Lt. Gen. Troy H. Middleton, President of Louisiana State University, and West Point graduate Maj. Gen. Robert M. Danford (W.P. 1904). This board interviewed none of those dismissed. They spoke only to cadets chosen for them by West Point authorities. (Earl Blaik was not called before the review board nor was he allowed to place his own substantiated record of the affair in the Military Academy Library.[26])

The White Commission consisted of (1) the late Gen. Thomas D. White (W.P. 1920), chairman of the panel and former Air

Force Chief of Staff; (2) Gen. Joseph J. Nazzaro (W.P. 1936), then Vice Commander of the Strategic Air Command; (3) Charles B. Thornton, head of Litton Industries, a giant defense contractor; (4) Dr. Robert L. Stearns, former chairman of the Sterns-Eisenhower Board which recommended the Air Force Academy be established; and (5) Hardy C. Dillard (W.P. 1924), dean of the University of Virginia Law School.

Had these men concluded that the duplicate honor systems were not basically sound, they would have been finding fault with the men who control the systems, the superintendents, the commandants, the academic deans, the chiefs of staff of the Army and Air Force. Had the West Point members concluded the system was not sound, they would have been finding fault with themselves. For it is the same system that educated them, a system which had not been changed from their own cadet days, a system which they revere—a system which had made them "honorable men." It is better and easier to find fault with individual cadets, to talk about "moral decay" outside the fortified walls of West Point and about small men incapable of living up to high standards.

If West Point can dismiss thirty-seven members of a nationally ranked football team and the Air Force Academy can virtually wipe out its intercollegiate athletic program, the system must "know no fear when truth and right are in jeopardy." Never mind that the cheating had been going on for years, that a deeply implicated West Point Class of 1951 had been allowed to graduate unscathed, and that academic instructors with a maximum of sixteen men in each class could not detect constant cheating; never mind the truth. If the system can dismiss the son of the Chief of Staff of the Army for toleration, then the old grads can feel they are worthy of the naïve trust the public places in them. And this points out the most important function of the honor system: it provides a mechanism which allows graduates and the public to believe that our military chieftains are men of integrity.

Above all, the graduate protects the "honor of the corps," a collective integrity into which he blends, and to that extent he is relieved of his individual moral responsibility. It is an experience which leaves the realm of the rational and is "held sacred by every West Pointer." ²⁷ It is a kind of ritualistic participation mystique difficult for those who have not worshiped at the Thayer monument to understand. Gen. Knowlton explains: "The Honor System is the wellspring of all that we strive for at the Academy and our cadets fully understand the importance of holding firmly to a system that will never be compromised or diluted in order to appease the whims of those who do not—and perhaps will never fully comprehend its meaning or purpose." ²⁸

If one of their own attempts to struggle with a personal truth and that individual truth tends to tarnish and sully Alma Mater and Father Thayer, the heresy is dealt with firmly. Cadet Cary Donham, a member of the Class of 1971, found such a truth in his junior year. He became a pacifist, a conscientious objector to war. A duly constituted West Point board of officers ruled that he could not be afforded official conscientious-objector status because he was "insincere." Cadets are not supposed to lie, and Donham was not lying, but the officers refused to believe him—his truth was not acceptable. He was separated from the Academy.²⁹

At West Point, ethical laziness becomes a virtue as the "true believers" with their monopoly on "honor" cleave together, receiving effortless confirmation of their own convictions. The disciples talk loudly and zealously about their moral code, and at times it sounds neat and clear enough, but in the world of real people the actuality of that code is a sorry tatter. Cadet Donham filed as a conscientious objector at about the time Maj. Gen. Koster resigned his post as superintendent to face charges that he covered up the massacre at My Lai. Gen. Koster's "sincerity" was never in doubt. His cover-up of the massacre of men, women, children, and babies provoked no critical analysis of the honor system at West Point. Koster was a general and a member of the Long Gray Line. He was, by definition, an honorable man. His situation did not require understanding but rather an act of faith. The cadets gave Koster a standing ovation in the mess hall and a "spontaneous" march past his quarters. "Don't let the bastards grind you down," Koster told the corps, and the corps parroted that back to him. Class scribe Kenneth F. Hanst, Jr. (W.P. 1942), expressed the general feeling of

Koster's classmates: "The distressing news about Sam Koster has just been released, and I know and speak for every last one of the class when I say that we are 100% behind him and Cherie at this time, and that the entire family is in our thoughts and prayers." [30]

Lt. Gen. Jack Seaman (W.P. 1934) can eliminate countless peasant villages from the face of the earth in the Iron Triangle area of Vietnam and two years later drop the charges against Maj. Gen. Koster for covering up the My Lai massacre ("in the interest of justice"); Maj. Gen. Thomas H. Lipscomb (W.P. 1934) can use his command influence in ninety-three court-martials at Fort Leonard Wood, Missouri [31]; Gen. Julian Ewell can base his military reputation in part on what some of his aides charged were fictitious body counts—but a cadet will not lie, cheat, or steal.

Graduates, like the rest of us in America, sense that something is wrong. Their solution, however, does not involve an examination of their own system and attitudes. Their solution is to project their own inflexible standards with ever increasing zeal upon the rest of us. Gen. Westmoreland, never one to be overcome by pessimism, reveals his plan to revitalize the moral fiber of the Army: "I have made it a personal goal of mine to press home to every leader in the Army—from senior general down to the newest corporal—the need for *absolute* honesty and morality in *everything* they do" [32] [emphasis added].

CHAPTER 5

The Warlord

Well, they've given us a job to do. A tough job, a mansize job. We can go down on our bended knees, every one of us, and thank God the chance has been given to us to serve our country. I can't tell you where we're going, but it will be where we can do the most good. And where we can do the most good is where we can fight those damn Germans or those yellow-bellied Eyetalians. And when we do, by God, we're going to go right in and kill the dirty bastards. We won't just shoot the sonabitches. We're going to cut out their living guts and use them to grease the treads of our tanks. We're going to murder those lousy Hun Bastards by the bushel.[1]

—GEORGE S. PATTON, JR. (W.P. 1909)

IN THE summer of 1832, President Andrew Jackson called upon Maj. Gen. Winfield Scott to command an expedition of 1,000 regulars to help the Illinois and Michigan militias defeat the Indian warriors of Black Sparrow Hawk in the so-called Black Hawk War. Scott sent his family from New York to live at West Point with the commandant of cadets, Capt. Ethan Allen Hitchcock (W.P. 1817), and ordered nine companies of regulars from Fort Monroe to Chicago. On the way up the Hudson he was joined by a detachment of newly graduated West

Pointers, most of the Class of 1832, who came "in joyous anticipation of immediate war service." The graduates included Lt. George B. Crittenden, son of Scott's lifelong friend Senator John J. Crittenden of Kentucky. Among the others were the sons of Generals Jacob Brown, Alexander Macomb, Robert Startwout, and Col. George Bomford. But the expedition met an enemy more terrifying than Indian warriors while still aboard its steamer transports—Asiatic cholera. Hundreds of terror-stricken soldiers grew sick and died. The unshaken Gen. Scott continued forward with 220 of the regulars, but the Military Academy contingent he sent hastily back to West Point—"too many of them were the sons of intimate friends or distinguished public characters to warrant risking their lives for the experience they would gain." [2]

In the early years of the Military Academy, graduates were fortunate to have guardians like Gen. Scott. Today they need no such protectors, for they have learned to care for themselves. And it is no longer simply disease from which graduates need protection. The threat to their survival has changed its character, as one man's story of what happened to him illustrates:

Anthony B. Herbert tried to join the Marines and fight in World War II when he was fourteen years old. He didn't make it until the Korean war, but soon became the Army's most decorated enlisted man. Gen. Matthew Ridgway selected him as the best American soldier in that war, sent him on a tour of United Nations countries, and in 1952, after he received the highest score ever attained at the Army Ranger School, Senator Lyndon Johnson awarded him his Ranger tab on national television. After adding a college degree to these laurels, Herbert was made a commissioned officer and quickly received advance promotions all the way to lieutenant colonel. In 1969 he was sent to Vietnam and eventually offered command of an infantry battalion in the elite 173rd Airborne Brigade. Brig. Gen. John W. Barnes (W.P. 1942) was the commanding general of the brigade, but the man who "kicked ass" was the executive officer, Col. J. Ross Franklin (W.P. 1950). Franklin welcomed Herbert by asking if he realized that he was starting out with two strikes against him—he had not attended West Point or the Command and General Staff College. Lt. Col. Herbert replied that he would try his best. Herbert did try his best and, in doing so, charged that on several occasions he witnessed, stopped, and reported to Col. Franklin what have now become known as routine events in Vietnam—systematic electrical torture, water torture applied by South Vietnamese Field Police under the direction of American officers, and the beating of detainees with bamboo flails. In the midst of a combat operation on Valentine's Day, 1969, Lt. Col. Herbert relates that he witnessed a massacre carried out by the Tan Quan District Provincial Reconnaissance Unit (PRU) led by an American advisor. Herbert happened on the scene of the incident and found about twenty Vietnamese soldiers in the process of killing fifteen detained citizens. One of the soldiers was slitting the throat of a Vietnamese woman as her five-year-old child clung to her leg. Four of the detainees were already dead. Herbert stopped the executions and reported them by radio to Col. Franklin. He demanded that the remaining ten prisoners be taken from the PRU and protected. Franklin declined and ordered Herbert to turn them back to the PRU. Herbert refused. A short time later Herbert's unit was assigned to another mission and "extracted" from the area. The sergeant left behind to safeguard the detainees was immediately overpowered and the remaining ten Vietnamese were murdered. On March 28, 1969, Herbert reports that he spoke to Brig. Gen. Barnes and asked that he and Col. Franklin investigate the total of eight separate war-crimes incidents he had witnessed and reported. The next morning Herbert was called into Barnes' office, summarily relieved, and sent to Saigon. He immediately demanded a formal investigation of his relief. The subsequent hearing was presided over by Maj. Gen. Joseph R. Russ (W.P. 1935) and Herbert's war-crimes allegations were not allowed into the record. So much for "trying your best."

Upon his return to the U.S. Lt. Col. Herbert was to attend the Command and General Staff College at Fort Leavenworth. While working in the intelligence section waiting for his school cycle to begin he continued to press for an investigation of the incidents he had witnessed. Col. George E. Newman (W.P. 1943) bluntly told him that if he wished to get through the college he would have to forget about his charges because he would not have time for both. Lt. Col. Herbert made it clear that he would not forget the war crimes and was quickly reassigned to Fort McPherson, Georgia. During this interval Col. Franklin had been appointed to the Peers Commission which was charged with investigating the My Lai massacre and its cover-up. Three of Herbert's war-crimes reports had been submitted to Barnes and Franklin while their immediate supervisor was none other than Lt. Gen. Peers.

The Third Army commander at Fort McPherson was Lt. Gen. Albert O. Connor (W.P. 1937). Connor had been Gen. William Westmoreland's loyal Deputy Chief of Staff for Personnel at the Pentagon before assuming command of the Third Army. Whether or not Connor was in contact with the Department of the Army is unknown to the authors, but he did take what appears to us to be an unusual step with a soldier of Herbert's stature by assigning him as Third Army Reenlistment Officer, traditionally a dead-end street for a career officer (when he was assigned, the position called for a captain). But Herbert did not surrender as expected and on March 12, 1971, formally charged Col. Franklin and the newly promoted Maj. Gen. Barnes with covering up the occurrence of war crimes. Brig. Gen. John H. Cushman (W.P. 1944), the commanding general of the Military Assistance Command in the Mekong Delta of Vietnam, was given the investigation of Franklin. Such procedure is commonly referred to in the Army as exercising the "trickle theory"—decision responsibility is passed to the lowest possible level in order to give the Chief of Staff an opportunity to plead ignorance of what is going on in case the issue springs back to life after being killed by the lesser officer. Seven thousand miles from everyone but Franklin, Brig. Gen. Cushman dropped the charges for "insufficient evidence." And, true to the "trickle theory," Maj. Gen. Roland M. Gleszer (W.P. 1940) in Washington dropped charges against Barnes, for if Franklin was innocent, how could his superior, Barnes, be guilty? [3]

Lt. Col. Herbert ended his once promising Army career in 1972 by resigning his commission, a victim of an institution afraid to admit its mistakes and of an organization called the West Point Protective Association. From Franklin at the bottom to Westmoreland at the top, Herbert dealt with no one but members of the Association. In a press release in 1971, speaking of the fact that war-crimes charges against Samuel Koster (W.P. 1942) had been dropped, Congressman Samuel S. Stratton characterized the WPPA as a group of men who put the welfare of their classmates "over the welfare of the nation and the fundamental right of the American people to know the facts: never mind what happens to the Army or the country, just make sure we keep our paid-up members out of embarrassment and hot water."

The WPPA does not limit its energies to simply covering up the crimes of its members. Its activities extend as far and wide as the influence of the graduates, and sometimes its operations have lasting ramifications in the civilian community. One example of an artful way in which graduates protected each other is the case of the building of the Kinzua Dam by the West-Point-ruled Army Corps of Engineers. In 1966 a Corps dam inundated the Seneca Reservation, displacing the Indians from their homes on the Upper Allegheny in violation of the oldest existing treaty signed by the United States of America. In 1794 the Senecas had signed the Pickering Treaty whereby they surrendered most of their long-held domain, and in return had received an unqualified promise from the Washington administration that the small remaining reservation would be theirs "so long as the sun rises and the river runs."

An alternative dam site which would have left the Seneca reservation intact and would have provided greater flood control at less cost was proposed in 1958 by one of America's most honored and sensitive engineers, the first chairman of the Tennessee Valley Authority, Dr. Arthur E. Morgan. He advanced a unique and imaginative plan recommending the use of the vastly larger storage capacity of the Conewango glacial depression. As Dr. Morgan wrote, "It seems almost incomprehensible that for more than thirty years this great glacial depression of Conewango was less than ten miles away from the Allegheny River, and that yet the members of the Corps were completely unaware of its major alternative possibilities. But reservoir sites are usually in river valleys. What significance could there be in a depression dug by a glacier? Where is a glacier mentioned in the textbooks or in West Point Classes?" [4]

Because of Congressional pressure exerted by Morgan, the

Division Engineer of the Ohio River Division, Col. Rudolph Ethelbert Smyser (W.P. 1928), agreed to submit Dr. Morgan's plan for analysis by an "independent, civilian engineering firm," even though it had already been strongly condemned by the Chief of Engineers, Lt. Gen. Emerson C. Itschner (W.P. 1924). What Col. Smyser did not tell Dr. Morgan was that three of the four partners of the contracted "independent, civilian engineering firm" were ex-corps members and that one of them, James H. Stratton (W.P. 1920), was a retired Corps of Engineers brigadier general whose last active-duty assignment had been with the office of the Chief of Engineers in Washington. Strangely enough, for over twenty years the Corps had been by far the most important client of the firm.

This consulting firm did not make any general survey of the possibilities suggested by Dr. Morgan although "the Conewango basin offered half a dozen alternative solutions, which required definitive study to determine which would be best. In limiting the consultants' time and funds the Corps compelled them to miss entirely two or three of the best solutions, and to be entirely unaware of the existence of the two best." [5] In Dr. Morgan's opinion, there was not in evidence on the part of the consulting firm or the corps officers any spirit of inquiry: "The aim seemed not to explore the [Conewango] prospect, but to discredit it." [6]

The Corps of Engineers proceeded with its own insensitive plan and the Kinzua Dam was built. The Seneca Indians lost their homes and sacred burial grounds, but West Point's honor remained "untarnished and unsullied," which, after all, seemed to be the main issue from the beginning.

Sometimes as graduates act to protect themselves and each other, the spirit of West-Point-style international interventionism prevails. In the Spring 1965 issue of the West Point alumni magazine, Manuel Q. Salientes (W.P. 1937), then a Filipino businessman, is pictured with two "friends of the class" in Saigon, Gen. William C. Westmoreland (W.P. 1936) and Maj. Gen. Richard G. Stilwell (W.P. 1938). The class scribe reported, "In December, Sal Salientes wrote to Pop Metz about his family which now numbers 9 and also of *his efforts to volunteer Philippine support in Vietnam*" [7] (emphasis added).

The WPPA is not an informal, haphazard organization; it has a real structure. At a yearly spring ritual held in scores of locations throughout the world, graduates gather at exclusive dinners to celebrate Founders Day and renew their loyalties to Alma Mater, Father Thayer, and each other. The occasion is generally sponsored by local West Point societies under the overall auspices of the Association of Graduates, USMA. Over sixty West Point societies have been established from Harrisburg, Pennsylvania, to Seattle, Washington; from Caracas, Venezuela, to Manila, Philippine Republic; from Athens, Greece, to Bangkok, Thailand. On that day, graduates from the armed forces, retired life, and civil life gather to hear the youngest and oldest graduates present formally praise the institution which encased their characters. Usually the youngest graduate tries to allay the great fears of Academy change in the psyches of the older grads. Capt. John S. McGuire (W.P. 1966) spoke at the Denver, Colorado, Founders Day gathering in 1971:

> As I understand it, the purpose of having the youngest graduate present at a Founders Day Dinner to give a short talk is to bring the older graduates up to date on our Alma Mater, with an alternative purpose of assuring them the "Corps has not gone to h---." Normally I wouldn't feel very qualified in this respect as it has been five years since I graduated. I do feel, however, that I might be more qualified than quite a few of my classmates, as I have a younger brother who is finishing up at the Academy this year. We're pretty proud of him—he's a Regimental Commander. Perhaps from the contacts that I have had from him and his friends I can glean an opinion as to how the recent changes at the Academy might or might not have changed the basic fiber of today's Cadet.
>
> Changes have taken place in the physical plant; changes have taken place in the academic curricula; changes have taken place in the Tactical Department's approach to the development of personal character; changes have taken place in the material that is used to fabricate the old "Keydet Gray." In my opinion all of the changes made at the Military Academy have been for the betterment of the institution. These changes represent to me the fact that the Academy is a viable and vital institution of education and not an inflexible organization completely indoctrinated in its own traditions, isolated from the realities of the present,

drifting without the foresight that any institution of its type direly needs. The Academy has kept pace with the realities of the present; but, then, it has not overdone itself on this point, either. I think this can be attributed to the inherent tradition of West Point —that characteristic that makes it so dear to all of us.

. . . For a cadet to survive some of the moods and ideologies to which he is exposed today, he has to be a more responsible individual. I don't think the cadet today has changed so much that you wouldn't recognize him at first glance—your first impression might be that of a sleek, modernistic version, perhaps— but you couldn't fail to detect the presence of that unmistakable fiber—that characteristic that has been termed the Long Gray Line.[8]

The oldest grads often detect some change, but generally view it as a manifestation of the progressive moral degeneracy of the American people. At the Founders Day dinner at West Point in 1969, the oldest grad present, Abbott Boone (W.P. 1907), said that Thayer's prophetic vision "has culminated in the greatest military institution on earth," and many other things before closing with these words: "Well, I guess that this is about the end of this short talk. But I do wish to bring one other point to your attention in passing. It is this: The United States is today drifting slowly but unmistakably into a subtle form of anarchy. The military virtues of governmental authority and self-discipline in its people are gradually being eroded. The time has come when subtle influences are invading the military forces of the country, and only the military virtues hold the key to national and governmental authority and obedience to law. We do not know when the great fountain of honor, duty, and love of country as stored in the hearts and minds of the some twenty-five thousand graduates of West Point and similar numbers of graduates of Annapolis and in the future at the Air Force Academy will be the granite strength which will preserve this country from the evil forces now seeking to undermine it. Again I repeat, authority in the government and self-discipline in the citizenry are the urgent needs of the day." [9]

At Founders Day, 1971, in Nicaragua there was no need for a plea for more "authority in government" since "Tachito" Somoza (W.P. 1946) and sundry lesser West Pointers *are* the government. Among the grads present at the Managua dinner with Tachito were his aide, Frank "Pancho" Kelly (W.P. 1963); his younger brother, Max Kelly (W.P. 1970); several other members of the class of 1963; and Trevor W. Swett, Jr. (W.P. 1949), commander of the U.S. Military Group, Nicaragua.

The kind of attitude which judges that West Point indoctrination gives to its graduates moral insight and character unobtainable elsewhere is the essence of West Point elitism. At the Founders Day gathering in Louisville in 1971 sponsored by the West Point Society of Kentucky, artist Ray Harm presented to the superintendent of West Point a painting which seems to symbolize the way graduates see themselves in relation to the rest of the country. Against the background of the blue sky an American eagle with wings majestically spread grips a limb of dead wood in its talons. In the righthand corner there is a tiny gold West Point crest signifiying an official Academy edition of art. Authorized copies now hang in scores of officers' homes and offices at the Academy. Could the eagle and what it represents—Army, West Point—be the strength of our society, and the dead wood the decaying social structure which finds redemption and meaning only as it supports the weight of the great bird of prey? This interpretation of West Point art may not be too far from the truth. Listen to what Matthew Ridgway (W.P. 1915) said to one of the more than 100 Founders Day gatherings in 1971: "From Thayer's time to today, West Point has been the inexhaustible reservoir of high-principled integrity inculcated through its graduates in our officer corps, and by it transmitted to our NCO's. I know of no substitute for that high moral force. It must not be diluted by any concession to any lesser codes of society." [10]

Here is part of what the president of the Association of Graduates, Paul W. Thompson (W.P. 1929), said in 1971 to the Founders Day gathering at West Point:

A layman, reflecting on the responsibilities for which military leaders must be prepared, can perceive that the crux of the matter —the name of the game—is not education and technology and training (all of which, relatively speaking, may be taken for granted)—the name of the game is Character. He whose shoulders "hold the skies suspended" bears his burden through strength deriving from the attributes of Character which are his, and which have been his throughout the ups and downs of his career.

Reflecting on these attributes of Character, one returns to the precepts of West Point—those precepts which have to do predominantly with Character, and only incidentally with book learning. Truly, and here I paraphrase both the poet and Great Captain: on other fields and other days these precepts will bring Victory—perhaps in situations where the sum of things is at stake.[11]

Class scribe Lt. Col. P. S. Gage, Jr. (W.P. 1936), rounds out our brief study of the meaning of West Point art with this somewhat immodest remark: "The timing for the writing of these notes is governed by the end of all the Founders Day celebrations around the world. This year many important emissaries from the Point spread out to carry the gospel and reaffirm the spirit and development of the *finest group of young men that* HAS EVER BEEN CONCEIVED UPON THIS EARTH"[12] (emphasis added).

Non-graduates do not necessarily have the same appreciation of the moral fiber of the West Point elite. Lt. Col. Edward L. King (Ret.) in his excellent book *The Death of the Army* put it this way:

The Army's top managers are as discriminatory toward the officer corps as toward the enlisted men. But they must be a good deal more circumspect in controlling the officers. Favoritism excludes all but a small preordained group of officers from entry into the controlling of the Army high command. This favoritism must be exercised in such a way that the majority of the officer corps will accept it and yet still work their hearts out to serve the purpose of the high command. This has been accomplished by indoctrinating all members of the officer corps from the time of their commissioning to accept the myth of superiority of an elitist group from West Point. This conditioning has been combined with a program of career incentives that keep all officers busy struggling to achieve various competitive levels of success. Few stop to realize that the program favors the elitist group that controls the Army. At each level the West Point managers weed out increasing numbers of those officers who are no longer useful. Only the most cooperative and best indoctrinated non-West Pointers are permitted to progress to the general officer ranks. Few of them are allowed to go beyond the grade of major general.[13]

Later, Lt. Col. King added these interesting thoughts:

> While the West Point officer almost automatically gets his ticket punched with good assignments, the rest of the officer corps must scurry around desperately trying to avoid the dead-end jobs that so often fall to their lot. This growing feeling of inferiority and resignation to a limited career opportunity is exactly the result that the system is designed to produce in the mind of the non-West Point officer. Events like the Founders Day Dinner serve to reinforce the non-West Point officer's feeling of being isolated. Each year on Army posts about the world, West Point alumni new and old gather to relive the memories of their days at the institution on the Hudson (referred to by non-West Pointers as South Hudson Institute of Technology or SHIT). An alumni meeting of officers from a civilian college, such as the University of California, would not have the use of Army aircraft, buses, and sedans that are provided to transport "old grads" to the annual Founders Day celebration. They would be lucky if they could obtain permission to use the officers' club, since some of their alumni would be enlisted men.[14]

West Pointers are aware that there are thousands of truly dedicated non-graduate officers in the army like Lt. Col. King who resent being ruled by such an elitist clique. They try to control their loyalty by offering those who come closest to acting like West Pointers a crumb or two, and by rewarding West-Point-type attitudes and actions with official and unofficial praise. The graduate-dominated Freedoms Foundation at Valley Forge, Pennsylvania, is designed to dole out the "unofficial" praise. The president of the foundation is Army Chief of Staff General Harold K. Johnson (Ret.) (W.P. 1933). The just-resigned Dick Hoebeke (W.P. 1933) was the vice-president for many years. Gen. Bruce Clarke (W.P. 1925), Governor Warren Hearnes (W.P. 1946), Gen. Omar Bradley (W.P. 1915), and Gen. Nathan Twining (W.P. 1919) all serve as trustees. The two current chairmen of its award jury are Dr. M. Norvel Young, the president of Pepperdine College, and the omnipresent Lt. Gen. William A. Knowlton (W.P. 1942). In 1970 Lt. Gen. Jonathan O. Seaman (W.P. 1934) presented non-graduate Maj. Gen. Roland F. Kirks with the "coveted" Freedoms Foundation George Washington Honor Medal for his speech before the reserve officer graduates of the Command and General Staff College. Here are some of the things Maj. Gen. Kirks said:

There is a cult of violence in the land, in the cities and on the campuses. Today we find scholars, writers, poets, artists and students glorying in the apocalyptic spectacle of burned and looted cities, in the anarchic turmoil on campuses, and in the general disruption of law and order. Yet no society can tolerate a breakdown of its laws and expect to survive. This is so regardless of how misguided idealists or spineless educational and governmental leaders rant about freedom and democracy, crying aloud the myth that violence is an inevitable result of correcting just grievances and civil rights issues.

It is true that a just society must strive with all its might to right every wrong even if righting wrongs is a highly perilous undertaking. We need mayors of cities and presidents of universities who will delight in battle. They have to be encouraged and supported by an informed and aroused citizenry. You have the talent and training and you have taken an oath to act. I am sure you have been awaiting the clarion call. It has been sounded. . . .

Do you demand respect and obedience in your home and in your office as you do in your military unit?

Do you exercise the same forthrightness in stamping out permissiveness and incompetence in your civilian environment as you do in your military command? . . .

In asking you these questions, I seek to stimulate in each of you a dedication in your civilian approach to life equal to the dedication inherent in your military outlook, and to urge you to take positive, constructive action to counteract those forces that would destroy our society. You must stimulate to action and lead the silent majority of our nation.[15]

Perhaps if Lt. Col. King had felt comfortable saying these kinds of things he would be a general in today's Army.

Hundreds of other Freedoms Foundation awards are annually presented to members of the armed forces and reserve components whose understanding of liberty meets the criteria set by Dr. Young and Gen. Knowlton. Seeing American freedom in business or corporate terms can earn $100 and a George Washington Honor Medal. "Our forefathers made the down payment on our freedom and passed the responsibility of paying off the mortgage on to each generation." [16] Some other examples: "Nearly 200 years ago an unknown company of design engineers —Constitutional Convention Inc.—drew up a blueprint for a new type of machine. They called this type of machine a Republic, and named this particular machine the United States of America." [17] "My God gave me life but I must live it. My employer gave me work but I must perform it! . . . My forefathers gave me freedom but I must keep it." [18]

The Freedoms Foundation tends to reward those who view liberty not as an inalienable right but as a privilege—"If the privilege of freedom is to survive, then every American has the obligation to prove the value of this way of life to all of humanity." [19] "Freedom is a privilege willed to us by our forefathers who yearned for something better than the perilous gratification of animal existence." [20] And a George Washington Honor Medal went to a young West Point graduate who said this: "The weakness in America's armor is the inability to unite its home forces to support its fighting Army abroad." [21]

West Point is beginning to pay more attention to the "home forces." Certainly the American people are beginning to pay more attention to West Point. And the Americans who are beginning to catch on to the Military Academy's game may ultimately prove to be the weakness in West Point's armor. But it has been around for a long time and it has survived some bitter attacks. To understand West Point better, we must look closely at its origins and growth. Let us begin with a disastrous war for America and her people but a good war for the consolidation of West Point power.

At a late evening meeting with his Cabinet on March 28, 1861, President Lincoln disclosed the plans of his general-in-chief, Gen. Winfield Scott, for dealing with seceded Southern states: abandon Forts Sumter and Pickens in a conciliatory move to the eight slave states that still had not abandoned the Union. Gen. Scott, then seventy-five, foresaw a long and bloody fratricidal war, and understood that risks for peaceful reconciliation were well worth taking. Secretary of State Seward agreed. But the other Cabinet members were opposed, particularly Postmaster General Montgomery Blair (W.P. 1835). Stoutly against concession or compromise in any form, Blair delivered an impassioned denunciation of Gen. Scott's plan.

Secretary Seward, faced with overwhelming Cabinet opposition to Scott's and his strategy, saw the necessity for drafting plans for the military relief of Forts Sumter and Pickens. For this task he called upon Montgomery C. Meigs (W.P. 1836), an engineer captain then on duty in Washington superintending the construction of the two wings being added to the Capitol. This engineer officer with no previous combat experience was taken by Seward to the White House, where he assured Lincoln that Fort Pickens could easily be reinforced if "the Navy would do its duty." [22] Capt. Meigs and Gen. Scott's military secretary, Col. Erasmus Darwin Keyes (W.P. 1832), drew up the detailed plans for the relief of the forts. But on April 12, before the designs of these enthusiastic West Pointers could be put to the test, Jefferson Davis (W.P. 1828), President of the Confederate States of America, ordered Maj. P. G. T. Beauregard (W.P. 1838) to fire on Fort Sumter. The firing continued for thirty-six hours until Maj. Robert Anderson (W.P. 1825) surrendered his surrounded and outgunned Union garrison to his fellow alumnus from the South.

Four years later on Palm Sunday, 1865, Robert E. Lee (W.P. 1829), his army divided and beaten, accepted the unconditional surrender terms of Gen. U. S. Grant (W.P. 1843) at Appomattox Court House.

West Pointers began the fighting, West Pointers put an end to it. And the sanguine middle of the conflict was dominated by their courage and brilliance, their timidity and stupidity. West Point provided 294 general officers to the Union, 151 to the Confederacy. In 55 of the 60 major battles, both sides were commanded by graduates. Later tales of their feats reached heroic proportions, but, as a cynic might point out, West Pointers lost as many battles as they won.

The turning point of the war had been reached in July 1863. Near the first of the month Confederate Gen. John Clifford Pemberton (W.P. 1837) had surrendered Vicksburg to Grant, and Robert E. Lee, without his "right arm," T. J. "Stonewall" Jackson (W.P. 1846), and after ignoring the advice of his "brain," Gen. James Longstreet (W.P. 1842), led his Army of Northern Virginia in retreat from Gettysburg and Gen. George

G. Meade (W.P. 1835). Gen. William S. Rosecrans' (W.P. 1842) army in Tennessee hesitated. He awaited the move of Grant's army to protect his right flank and the advance of Gen. Ambrose Burnside's (W.P. 1847) from Cincinnati to Knoxville to protect his left. Lincoln's Chief of the Army, Gen. Henry W. Halleck (W.P. 1839), irked by Rosecrans' caution, peremptorily ordered him to advance against the cadet-gray-clad army of Gen. Braxton Bragg (W.P. 1837) and seize Chattanooga. At Chickamauga Creek the two great armies would clash and West Pointers would oversee the slaughter on both sides. Among Rosecrans' subordinate commanding generals would be Gordon Granger (W.P. 1845), George H. Thomas (W.P. 1840), Alexander McCook (W.P. 1852), H. P. Van Cleve (W.P. 1831), Philip Sheridan (W.P. 1853), Thomas Wood (W.P. 1845), R. W. Johnson (W.P. 1849), and Absalom Baird (W.P. 1849). Bragg's subordinate generals would include John B. Hood (W.P. 1853), William H. T. Walker (W.P. 1837), and Simon Bolivar Buckner (W.P. 1844).[23] Bragg would divide his forces into two commands, one commanded by Longstreet, who was sent by Lee to the scene of the most critical action, and the other by Leonidas Polk (W.P. 1827). Before the initiation of hostilities, Polk, the first West Pointer elevated to the episcopate, had been Bishop of Alabama, Missouri, Arkansas Territory, and the Republic of Texas. Jefferson Davis, a close friend of the holy man at West Point, had asked Polk to bring the word of God to the battlefield and Leonidas hesitated not. Another West Point minister of the Gospel had died the year before in Shanghai after translating the Bible into Chinese. Had Michael Simpson Culbertson (W.P. 1839), a classmate of Halleck's, lived to see Bishop Gen. Polk's human-wave attacks against the lines of Union Gen. Thomas, his Chinese converts on the sidelines might have been prompted to observe that "Confederates don't seem to value life the way we Orientals do." The Chickamauga campaign cost the two sides 34,633 casualties.[24]

During the early stages of the war, West Pointers were not immune to severe criticism. Political intrigues by graduates during the volatile 1850s and the dismal failures of Union generals in the beginning of the war aroused the suspicion and ire of Congress. William L. Crittenden (W.P. 1845) gave a hint of what was to come when he attempted to "liberate" Cuba in America's nineteenth-century version of the Bay of Pigs fiasco. Backed by his powerful uncle, Senator John Crittenden of Kentucky, and other Southern fire-eaters, he planned to convert Cuba into the sixteenth and seventeenth slave states. Crittenden was killed by a Spanish firing squad in Havana in 1851. The unnatural caution and political arrogance of Gen. George B. McClellan (W.P. 1846) prompted Lincoln to relieve him and replace him with Burnside. During the Antietam campaign McClellan went so far as to entertain a pro-Southern Democrat, Fernando Wood, and outline his plans for less war, more conciliation. This political general would run against Lincoln in the Presidential race of 1864.

In 1862 Congress fumed. The defection of hundreds of West Pointers to the insurgent South (Lee had been superintendent of the Military Academy under Secretary of War Jefferson Davis) provoked one Congressman to rail that West Point had produced more traitors "within the last fifty years than all the institutions of learning and education that have existed since Judas Iscariot's time." [25] During the debate on a bill to increase the number of cadets at West Point in January 1862, Senator James H. Lane of Kansas stated that "there was no possible method of telling which men at West Point had brains and which men lacked them." [26] Lane also maintained "that the greatest evil we have in our present Army grows out of the stupidity of the graduates from West Point who have been placed in high command." [27] The expansion bill was defeated 25–12. But in January 1863 a bill to abolish the Academy altogether was also defeated 29–10. Senator Sherman, brother of Gen. William T. Sherman (W.P. 1840), had doubts whether "a military education at West Point has infused into the army the right spirit to carry on this war." [28] Senator Benjamin F. Wade of Ohio, a leading radical Republican, commented, "I do not believe there can be found, on the whole face of the earth, or in the history of the world, any institution that has turned out so many false, ungrateful men as have emanated from this institution." [29] Senator Wade called West Point "a closed corporation," "exclusive" and "aristocratical."

Charges of a West Point "aristocracy" were not new and they

had much substance. Henry Du Pont (W.P. 1833) was the grandson, and Henry A. Du Pont (W.P. 1861) the great-grandson, of Pierre Samuel Du Pont de Nemours, landowner, private advisor to the court of Louis XIV, friend of Jefferson, Franklin, and Hamilton, and refugee from the French Revolution. Robert E. Lee was the son of "Light Horse" Harry Lee of Revolutionary War fame; Rufus King (W.P. 1833) was the son of the president of Columbia University and descendant of a wealthy family; Henry C. Wayne (W.P. 1838) was the son of James M. Wayne, Associate Justice of the Supreme Court, 1835–67; Alfred Sully (W.P. 1841) was the son of the eminent artist Thomas Sully; a son and a grandson of Ethan Allen graduated from the Academy; and Schuyler Hamilton (W.P. 1841) was the grandson of Alexander Hamilton.

Although some members of Congress attacked the privileged order of West Point, others did not hesitate to appoint their favorites. John B. Hood was admitted in 1849 through the agency of an uncle in Congress; the son of Senator William M. Gwin of California resigned in 1861 to join the Confederacy; the guardian of William T. Sherman, Senator Ewing of Ohio, gave him his appointment; George B. Crittenden (W.P. 1832) was the son of Senator John Crittenden of Kentucky; and Fitzhugh Lee (W.P. 1856) was the nephew of Senator Mason of Virginia and Robert E. Lee.[30]

The attacks on West Point had their roots in the Revolutionary War. The Revolution had been a battle fought by the American people against a British aristocracy and its foreign mercenaries. Washington's rout of the mercenary Hessians represented more than a tactical military success, it was meant to be a victory for the idea of a people's army and a people's revolution. The irregular, harassing tactics used by guerrilla fighters Thomas Sumter, Andrew Pickens, Francis Marion, and Ethan Allen's Green Mountain Boys became legend and the norm for warfare, so it was only logical that the American Constitution was constructed in fear of a large, powerful military establishment—only the Congress could declare war, appropriations for the military would be made for two years only, and an elected civilian official, the President, would be commander-in-chief. America was a wide, open land surrounded by vast oceans and weak neighbors; it did not need a large standing army, for citizens themselves were the riflemen, the protectors of families and towns. Men stamped by the Revolutionary War did not look with favor upon an autocratic military elite.

The introduction of House Resolution No. 7 of the 21st Congress on February 25, 1830, inaugurated the federal legislative aspect of the fight against the growing dominance of West Point. The bill was introduced by a Tennessee Congressman, hunter, pioneer, and populist who would lose his life defending the Alamo—Davy Crockett. Congressman Crockett submitted the following resolution:

1. RESOLVED, That if the bounty of the Government is to be at all bestowed, the destitute poor, and not the rich and influential, are the objects who most claim it, and to whom the voice of humanity most loudly calls the attention of Congress.

2. RESOLVED, That no one class of the citizens of these United States has an exclusive right to demand or receive, for purposes of education, or for other purposes, more than an equal and ratable proportion of the funds of the national treasury, which is replenished by a common contribution, and, in some instances, more at the cost of the poor man, who has but little to defend, than that of the rich man, who seldom fights to defend himself or his property.

3. RESOLVED, That each and every institution, calculated, at public expense, and under the patronage and sanction of the Government, to grant exclusive privileges except in consideration of public services, is not only aristocratic, but a downright invasion of the rights of the citizen, and a violation of the civil compact called "the constitution."

4. RESOLVED, FURTHER, That the Military Academy at West Point is subject to the foregoing objections, in as much as those who are educated there receive their instruction at the public expense, and are generally the sons of the rich and influential, who are able to educate their own children. While the sons of the poor, for want of active friends, are often neglected, or if educated, even at the expense of their parents, or by the liberality of their parents, or by the liberality of their friends, are superseded in the service by cadets educated at the West Point Academy.

5. RESOLVED, THEREFORE, and for the foregoing reasons, That said institution should be abolished, and the appropriations annually made for its support be discontinued.[31]

Between 1833 and 1843 four state legislatures (Tennessee, Ohio, Connecticut, New Hampshire) passed resolutions calling for the abolition of the Military Academy. The attacks culminated in a Congressional debate over the appropriation bill for West Point in 1844. Congressman Dana of New York was one who wanted no more money spent on a "military nobility": "out of a population of 18 to 20 million about 100 individuals are annually selected as the exclusive recipients of the national bounty. . . . No man, whatever may be his talents or qualifications or his thirst for military fame, can get into the army unless he enters through the gates of the West Point Academy, the only portal open to ambition." [32] Congressman Dana urged his fellow Congressmen to join him in ending the monopoly at West Point that made cadets "proud and vain" and allowed them to look with "scorn and contempt" upon the American people. The appropriation bill carried by a single vote.

Did this narrow victory for the defenders of West Point mean that they, unlike Davy Crockett and other Academy opponents, had renounced their revolutionary heritage in favor of a powerful military elite? It did not. Those who defended the Academy, in general, defended it not as a military school but as an engineering college which supplied our young nation with much-needed scientific knowledge and engineering skill. West Point greatly changed in character during the first thirty years of its existence. Its legitimate roots are at times distracting but well worth reviewing in some detail.

The first official recommendation under the federal government for adopting a system of military instruction in the Army of the United States is to be found in a report dated January 18, 1790, made by Gen. Knox, then Secretary of War under President George Washington. This military education was to be of a practical nature. The "advanced corps," says the report, "are designed not only as a school in which the youth of the U.S. are to be instructed in the art of war, but they are in all cases of exigence to serve as an actual defense to the community." [33] Congress did not act on the proposal.

But on May 9, 1794, "an act providing for raising and organizing a corps of artillerists and engineers" was passed by Congress giving the President authority to purchase "books, instruments and apparatus" for the use of the corps. In his annual message to Congress of December 7, 1796, President Washington recommended the establishment of a Military Academy in direct terms, but he did not disclose the details. President Washington also recommended the establishment of a national university for the study of the science of government.

Acting on a recommendation of the Secretary of War, Congress on July 16, 1798, passed an act providing "that the President of the United States be . . . authorized to appoint a number, not exceeding four, of teachers of the arts and sciences necessary for the instruction of the artillerists and engineers."

President John Adams in January 1800 submitted the plan of his Secretary of War, Mr. McHenry, to Congress. It provided for the establishment of a "Fundamental School" where theoretical knowledge of all the sciences involved in the art of war were to be taught, and three practical army schools, one for the engineers and artillerists, one for cavalry and infantry, and one for the navy. Those who through their own education had mastered the principles taught in the fundamental school could move directly to one of the practical schools. But this plan, like the other plans for military education, was designed only for those who constituted a portion of the actual military or naval force. Congress considered but did not act upon President Adams' proposal.

On December 30, 1801, the House of Representatives adopted the following resolution: "Resolved, that it is expedient to reduce the military establishment of the United States." An outgrowth of the resolution was "an act fixing the military establishment of the United States," passed into law on March 16, 1802. By this act the Corps of Artillerists and Engineers created by the acts of 1794 and 1798 was dissolved and a new corps of artillerists and a new corps of engineers, as distinct bodies, were created; the engineer corps was to consist of seven engineer officers, one major, two captains, two first lieutenants, two second lieutenants, and ten cadets. The same act provided "that the said corps, when so organized shall be established at West Point in the state of New York, and shall constitute a Military

Academy." The use of the words "military academy" did not mean a substantial change in the character of the institution since the cadets were still part of the actual military forces of the nation, subject at all times to service as the President might direct.

The Act of April 29, 1812, did alter the character of the Academy in significant ways. With war with Great Britain brewing, the Congress increased the maximum number of cadets to 250. Entering cadets for the first time had to meet age requirements. They had to be older than seventeen but not yet twenty-two to qualify for entrance. When the War of 1812 was terminated, the occasion for the operation of the army and militia on its expanded scale was at an end, and, supposedly, so was that of the Academy. The army and militia were accordingly reduced, but no corresponding reduction was made at the Military Academy. "The extension of the Academy, under the operation of the Act of 1812, may, therefore, be said to have survived both the original occasion and original design of it." For the first time men were being educated at the public expense who did not belong and were not essential to the active and actual military force of the government. After 1815, West Point began to take on the character of both a military academy and a national engineering institution.

Some maintain that this was President Jefferson's actual intention when he signed the 1802 act. One author says, "President Jefferson, who was 'no great lover of military affairs but a warm friend of science' . . . when he signed the act establishing the military academy, contemplated an institution which would supply the country with engineers for civil as well as military purposes, an institution which would serve as a model for training in the practical sciences." [34] Another author maintains that Jefferson "wanted a national university, and as the foremost apostle of progress in America he wanted that university to teach science, not the musty classics that prevailed at other American schools. But the tug of sectionalism was too strong for Congress to agree even on where such a school should be situated, much less what it should teach. Jefferson, therefore, decided that he would smuggle his national scientific school into the nation under the guise of a Military Academy." [35] Jefferson's actual intent will probably never be known. He may well have favored educating civil engineers but certainly not excess professional soldiers.

In 1837 a select House of Representatives Committee on Military Affairs studied the origin of the Military Academy and its changes by legislation and practice in great detail. It concluded in part that: "From the minute historical view which has been taken in the preceding pages, it must be apparent to all that the institution at West Point is not in principle, nor in practice, what it was under Washington, under the elder Adams, and under Jefferson, nor what it was only designed to be under Mr. Madison. What it now is it has attained to independent of the authority of their illustrious names, if not against their authority." [36]

But the character of West Point was just beginning to deviate from the visions of its founders. In 1815 Secretary of War Monroe sent Maj. Sylvanus Thayer (W.P. 1808), on Thayer's request, to France to gain a knowledge of European military establishments and to collect rare books, maps, plans, and instruments for the Military Academy. Thayer was ordered home by President Monroe in 1817 to take the reins of the school. Few men had precise ideas about what West Point ought to be and how it ought to function. Unfortunately, Thayer was one of those who did have ideas and they were gleaned largely from the operations of foreign, authoritarian armies and institutions.

Thayer brought back much more than an academic philosophy for engineering education. When he accepted the West Point superintendency in 1817 he imposed upon the fledgling Military Academy a total system which had as its aim the molding of the entire personality. Academy historian R. Ernest Dupuy described the Thayer system this way: "the discipline was—and is— embraced in the four year enmeshing of the student within a rigid military framework governing his entire existence while at the Academy. It constitutes a novitiate, in which every man suffers equally, and every man is rewarded according to his performance, moving toward a common goal, under an impartial impersonal command." [37]

Thayer himself graduated from Dartmouth College before spending one year at the Military Academy and graduating with the Class of 1808. Although many of his admirers have attributed to Thayer "meritorious and valorous" service during the War of 1812, he actually "performed Quartermaster duties well removed from the sound of cannon." [38] His initial success can probably be attributed to his apple polishing, particularly with Army Chief of Engineers Joseph G. Swift and Army Inspector General Daniel Parker. Parker wrote to Gen. Porter in 1815, "This war has not afforded [Thayer] a chance to distinguish himself in the field still it is the opinion of all who know him that he is a most meritorious officer. I want to get a brevet [promotion] for him and pray you to send a recommendation to the Secretary of War enclosed to me that I may bring up that subject at a proper time." [39]

And it was his "affectionate friend" Swift who persuaded acting Secretary of War Monroe to send Thayer and Col. William McRee (W.P. 1805) on their junket tour of Europe. Thayer had a way of ingratiating himself with superiors while holding himself haughtily aloof from subordinates.

A great devotee of Napoleon, Thayer brought back from France with him Gen. Simon Bernard, one of Bonaparte's engineer officers and for a time the Corsican's aide-de-camp. For seventeen years Thayer ruled West Point in what Dupuy called "Sylvanian majesty," adding that his was "an inflexible, Spartan rule." [40] Thayer thoroughly organized the cadet schedule so that hardly a minute of the cadets' fifteen-hour day was not devoted to drill, study, policing their rooms, or some other controlled activity.[41] Evidently it was Thayer's dim view that if cadets had more free time they would not use it wisely. He began the practice of requiring every cadet to attend Sunday chapel services, and it was his idea to use cadet officers to enforce his rules against other cadets and report them for violations. The overall intent of his system is best described in his own stern dictum, "Gentlemen must learn it is only their province to listen and obey." [42]

A great number of the cadets exhibited an independent spirit and simply refused to comply with Thayer's Prussian discipline. During the heart of the Thayer era fewer than two out of five cadets continued to graduation. The detailed Congressional study of the Academy in 1837 examined the disciplinary records of

West Point and concluded that they exhibited "the most con-
clusive evidence of the moral inefficiency of the institution" and
"its inherent weakness against the spirit of insubordination to
which young men are ever inclined to give indulgence." [43] This
select committee added that no other American educational
institution could equal the annual delinquencies and malconduct
in the Academy at West Point. Thayer's rigid rule and regulations were not considered part of the solution. The report continued, "The error of these [regulations], if any there be, will, it
is believed, be found upon the side of too much rigor than
otherwise, for both the freedom of speech and of the press are
subjected to a censorship, so far as the rights of cadets are concerned, unlike everything elsewhere to be found in our land. It
is, therefore, in the nature of the institution itself, as has been
already remarked, that its moral weakness and inefficiency
are to be found." [44]

Thayer's rigor was greatly appreciated by those who graduated. According to one writer, "Thayer obviously understood the
value of shared hardship in creating a spirit that would animate
West Pointers for the rest of their lives. How well it worked
can be seen from the speeches of graduates in later years, in
which they invariably recalled with pride the freezing rooms, the
mediocre food, drilling on the plain when it was covered with
ice." [45]

But those who did not share the four years of hardship, discipline, and common study under the Thayer system saw the
West Point camaraderie for what it was, and is—elitism. The
1837 Congressional study committee recognized that "the officer
educated at West Point will cherish, and, at times, carry into his
intercourse with coadjutors, a sense of personal superiority
over another of his own grade, or even of a higher grade than
his own, who has entered the army through some other avenue
and with less imposing pretensions." [46] The Congressional report
continued:

> In a nation like ours, based, as has been justly remarked by the
> Committee on Military Affairs of a late session of Congress, upon
> the great principle of amalgamating all orders of society, the feel-
> ings and prejudices of the soldier are to be in a measure consulted.
> A nation thus constituted cannot be forced into submissive obedi-

ence to a class of military or other officers, towards whom all previous observation has excited in the citizen feelings of aversion
and disrespect. Make it the known condition of filling up the army
of the United States at any juncture of danger that the citizen
soldier's wishes are not to be consulted in the selection of your
officers, and that, so far from it, all his wishes and feelings are
to be violated by placing over him men whose education, habits,
temperament, and feelings, he has been accustomed to regard with
a feverish dislike, and what will be the consequences? Either a
failure in filling up the desired ranks, or the earliest discharges
of their musketry will be to rid themselves of their obnoxious commandants, and to devolve the duty of command upon some more
congenial comrade.

Ask the old soldiers and officers from among the people who
have served in the battles of our nation, if they have not seen these
very results effected beyond all reasonable doubts, in cases where
such disaffection has been general between privates and their officers; and the answer will be in the affirmative. Can it be doubted
that when the "bone and muscle" of our countrymen shall come
into the field they will demand for their captains and their generals men who have feelings in common with themselves—men
who, like themselves, know well the temperament of mankind
from having mixed with them in all the various pursuits of life? [47]

The committee recommendation on this matter applies as well
nearly a century and a half later:

The army of the United States, in all its grades, should be kept
open to the fair, manly, and impartial competition of all citizens,
like every other department of government; and no discourage-
ment, much less actual exclusion, of any one denomination, who
are able of body, from seeking its honors, ought to be counte-
nanced, and certainly not to be reduced to system. Such a policy
is adverse to the genius of our free institutions and is suited only
to those governments under which distinctions and privileges are
hereditary, and men are made the creatures of government, and
not government the creature of men. It is alike the interest and
the duty of Americans to repudiate it, and to guard their institutions against every similitude of it. [48]

Naturally Thayer and his alien system were repudiated by
many Americans. President Jackson is reported to have said,
"Sylvanus Thayer is a tyrant. The autocrat of all the Russias

couldn't exercise more power." America did not need Thayer and his oppressive, un-American regime, but America did need engineers. West Point survived because it was the first American educational institution capable of providing the critical engineering skills needed by a growing nation during the long peace following 1815. Coastal harbors had to be improved, inland harbors built. Transportation to link domestic and foreign markets with the vast resources of the interior of the continent had to be constructed. Uncharted land required survey for the location of canals, overland roads, and railways. The relationship between internal commercial improvements and military defense was then accepted almost without question. Capital expansion and regional competition for markets and resources were America's business, and West Point would explore, recommend, and build the transportation network for it. West Point's association with the powerful men in government and business who made money and materials move would ensure the survival of the institution and ease its graduates into the power elite. Unfortunately, Sylvanus Thayer and his system of developing "character" came as part of the bargain.

The Army Topographical Engineers, 85 percent of whom were graduates, would survey most of the yet uncharted regions of the central continent under the direction of their chief, John James Abert (W.P. 1811). In 1824 Chief of Engineers Alexander Macomb would send William G. McNeill (W.P. 1817) and his brother Albert to plan and survey the best routes to connect the Ohio, the Potomac, and Lake Erie; Captain W. G. Williams (W.P. 1824) would survey the route from Charleston to Cincinnati for Senator Calhoun; Gen. Bernard and Col. Joseph G. Totten (W.P. 1805) would survey the Ohio and Mississippi rivers from Louisville to New Orleans and determine the most practical means of improving navigation; and West Pointers would build the 750-mile stretch of road between Cumberland and St. Louis (U.S. Route 40).

In 1827 avaricious Baltimore businessmen, motivated by intense commercial rivalry with the seaports of New York and Philadelphia for more western trade, and desiring to prevent Georgetown, Washington, and Alexandria from gaining profit advantage through the Chesapeake and Ohio Canal, would request and receive engineering aid from the federal government to construct the Baltimore and Ohio Railroad. William G. McNeill (W.P. 1817) would serve on the board of the B&O, and George Washington Whistler (W.P. 1819) would be the superintending engineer. Whistler and McNeill became the most noted engineers of their day. Whistler served as superintending engineer on numerous railroads and went to Russia (1842–49) at the request of the Czar to build the Moscow-St. Petersburg railroad connection. McNeill attained eminence as the chief engineer of many railroads and by 1835 had achieved such prominence that he personally selected the men who built the first railroad in Cuba. They were, of course, all West Pointers.[49]

The early government proponents of West Point engineering aid to state and private enterprises developed strong personal ties to the institution. One of them, President Monroe, saw his nephew and namesake, James, graduated from West Point in 1815. By the time Calhoun became Monroe's Secretary of War, the Federal Engineering Department included the Corps of Engineers, the Topographical Engineers, and the Military Academy, all controlled by the Chief of Engineers, Gen. Alexander Macomb, who reported directly to Calhoun. Macomb sent a son to West Point, and Calhoun's son, Patrick, graduated from the Academy in 1841. Calhoun's plans for federal engineering aid were supported by advocates of Speaker of the House Henry Clay's "American System"—Clay sent two sons to West Point. The first graduate of the Academy, Joseph G. Swift, later became the Chief Engineer of the Army and as such worked closely with the Congress, the Secretary of War, the President, and prominent capitalists. He naturally favored the appointment of relatives of his political friends. In his own words, "From an early day I had advocated sending the sons of the most talented men in the country to that institution as a better plan than selection by Congressional district that was beginning to have sway at Washington."[50] Swift thought enough of his own talents to send a son and a grandson to West Point (Alexander J. Swift, Class of 1830, and Joseph G. Swift, Class of 1866).

During the administrations of Andrew Jackson and Martin Van Buren, West Pointers would become firmly entrenched within the ruling circles. These administrations coincided with the decade of the greatest expansion of railroad construction in American history, and graduates working as engineers on private and state projects made their greatest gains during this period. President Jackson's Cabinet was rife with West Point political nepotism: the son of his Postmaster General, William T. Barry, graduated in 1830; the son of his Secretary of State, Robert M. McLane, graduated in 1837 (he would later serve five terms in Congress and four years as Ambassador to France); and his Secretary of War, Lewis Cass, sent two nephews to West Point. One of these, George Washington Cass (W.P. 1832), became president of the Adams Express Co. and several railroads with the help of his uncle. The other nephew, Irvin McDowell (W.P. 1838), was to become in 1861 the first commander of the Army of the Potomac. Jackson's rich and powerful supporter Francis P. Blair sent his son to West Point in 1831. Montgomery Blair (W.P. 1835) became a lawyer, judge, and ultimately Postmaster General under President Lincoln. The son of Jackson's appointee to the collectorship of the Port of New York graduated in 1832. President Jackson himself had two nephews graduated. Andrew Jackson Donelson (W.P. 1820) served his uncle as personal secretary for two terms. The connections of Jackson's first Vice-President, Calhoun, with the Engineers and West Point have been mentioned. Martin Van Buren was Jackson's second Vice-President, and his son, Abraham Van Buren (W.P. 1827), would serve him as personal secretary during his Presidential administration from 1837 to 1841. When Davy Crockett introduced his bill to abolish West Point in 1830, he did not, we imagine, know quite what he was up against.

Soon after Crockett's resolution, West Pointers intensified their infiltration of the civilian power structure. In 1831 Secretary of War Eaton praised the engineering work of Academy graduates and encouraged them to join the civilian calling of their choice if not needed by the Army. The Florida Indian wars hurried the choice of many patriotic graduates. Although many West Pointers fought against the elusive Seminoles, hundreds more decided that the Everglades, the disease, the boredom, and the Army did not need them and resigned. Most followed Eaton's advice and moved directly into positions of power in engineering, railroading, education, and business.

An analysis made in 1868 showed that of the 2,218 graduates between 1802 and 1867, some 139 had entered the field of education and 334 had taken up pursuits of a technical nature. Those in education included 26 presidents of universities and colleges, 23 principals of academies and schools, 5 regents and chancellors of educational institutions, and 85 professors and teachers. In specialized callings were 1 superintendent of the Coast Survey, 6 surveyors-general of states and territories, 14 chief engineers of states, 35 presidents of railroads and other corporations, 48 chief engineers and 41 superintendents of railroads and other public works, 155 civil engineers, 30 manufacturers, and 4 architects.[51]

The Prussian elitism at West Point, the political nepotism, and the mass resignations during the Seminole campaigns gave West Point's critics nearly enough ammunition to do away with it in the early 1840s, but the peculiar collective psychology of a victorious foreign war against Mexico muted public and Congressional criticism.

On May 11, 1846, President Polk demanded from Congress a declaration of war against our southern "neighbor" already provoked and engaged by American forces under Gen. Zachary Taylor. (That year Polk sent his son to West Point.) The Southwest Territory was largely unknown. Land had to be surveyed, rivers had to be forded, mountain ranges negotiated—all tasks for West Point engineers. Participating in the war with Mexico were 523 graduates, and Regular Army graduates and resigned cadets leading volunteer militias rekindled many old friendships. Almost all of the key generals in the Civil War fought side by side in Mexico. U. S. Grant served in the war with Simon Bolivar Buckner (W.P. 1844) and John Pemberton (W.P. 1837). Later Buckner would surrender Fort Donelson to Grant, and Pemberton would give up the entire town of Vicksburg to the Union general.

The Mexican war would be the last fought with non-graduates in the key command positions, but even though the West Pointers didn't lead, the war made its impressions on them. "Old Rough and Ready" Taylor would teach U. S. Grant that the glitter and polish of garrison life meant nothing on the battlefield. In Grant at Appomattox, stooped and disheveled, wearing a dusty borrowed uniform with gold stars sewn on his shoulders, one could see the image of the general whose troops in Mexico often could not tell him from a farmer—until the fighting started. Robert E. Lee served as an engineer under Winfield Scott and would learn a different lesson. "Old Fuss and Feathers" was a commanding and majestic figure, acting and looking the part of a bold and demanding soldier. He would control his subordinates just enough to allow their own leadership abilities to bloom, and Lee never forgot. On the other hand, George G. Meade (W.P. 1835), classing the volunteer soldiers in that war with the Biblical plagues of locusts, would learn next to nothing.

Scott and Taylor, great generals with no formal military education, led their armies to quick and successive victories, and both men found their ties to West Point tightened. Col. Joseph G. Totten (W.P. 1805) was Scott's Chief Engineer, and two of his most trusted staff officers, besides Lee, were George B. McClellan (W.P. 1846) and P. G. T. Beauregard (W.P. 1838). After the war Taylor's aide-de-camp, William Wallace Smith Bliss (W.P. 1833), found himself in the White House as President Taylor's personal secretary (1849–51). Bliss married one of Taylor's daughters, and Jefferson Davis (W.P. 1828) eloped with the other.

By this time the work of the Army engineers was moving westward. Through the efforts of men like William H. Emory (W.P. 1831) the great Southwest would lose its status as an unknown. Lt. Joseph Ives (W.P. 1852) would become the first American to reach the floor of the Grand Canyon. G. K. Warren (W.P. 1850) would compile one of the first detailed maps of the trans-Mississippi West. Alexander Center (W.P. 1827) would construct the Panama Railroad. Davis himself directed the survey of four routes from the Mississippi to the Pacific. This railroad work has been called the most notable effort of the Army Engineers, and many of these Pacific railroad explorers working under the direction of Davis and Gen. Totten would eventually earn wartime fame. Among them were Henry L. Abbot (W.P. 1854), John B. Hood (W.P. 1853), Andrew A. Humphreys (W.P. 1831), George B. McClellan (W.P. 1846), John G. Parke (W.P. 1849), John Pope (W.P. 1842), and Philip H. Sheridan (W.P. 1853).

In little more than half a century the graduates of an institution that had begun in 1802 with seven officers and ten cadets grew to dominate the policy level of the Army and greatly influence politics and business. Among many others, George Sears Greene (W.P. 1823) became the founder and first president of the American Society of Civil Engineers; Henry Du Pont's (W.P. 1833) gunpowder-manufacturing profits had put his family well on the way to becoming the richest in the country; and William B. Franklin (W.P. 1843) had made his fortune as a twenty-year vice-president of Colt's firearms-manufacturing company. After the war Americans looked to familiar military names to stabilize the chaotic political situation. Grant would serve two terms as President (1869–77). Gen. Winfield S. Hancock (W.P. 1844) would barely lose to Garfield in 1880, and McClellan, after having been defeated by Lincoln for President in 1864, would become governor of New Jersey. Gen. Burnside would govern Rhode Island for three terms; George Stoneman (W.P. 1846) would be governor of California; Francis R. T. Nicholls (W.P. 1855) led Louisiana; John S. Marmaduke (W.P. 1857), Missouri; and Adelbert Ames (W.P. 1861), Mississippi.

Up to the Civil War, businessmen and the civilian elite had required West Point's grasp of technology to move ahead quickly, and graduates naturally took advantage of the situation. If West Point was not entirely a school for the sons of the rich and successful, it was at a minimum almost a guaranteed ticket for upward mobility to the highest level. A century later the process would reverse. After World War II, the civilian world-view would disappear and the new-found military view would require businessmen and political leaders to follow the lead of the military elite.

In the meantime, after the Civil War, the standing army dwindled to 25,000 men, and with the war behind them, graduates who may at one time have been uncertain about the military role of their alma mater became professional soldiers.

The two most influential military thinkers of this period were prolific naval historian Capt. Alfred Thayer Mahan, son of Thayer's academic protégé at West Point, Dennis Hart Mahan (W.P. 1824), and Maj. Gen. Emory Upton (W.P. 1861), a protégé of Gen. William T. Sherman (W.P. 1840). Although Upton's manuscript *The Military Policy of the United States* was not published until 1904, more than twenty years after his death, his views were well known especially among government leaders and the professional officer corps. Elihu Root, who became President McKinley's Secretary of War in 1899, looked to Upton's writings for guidance because of his own unfamiliarity with military affairs. By 1903 Root had done much to advance the army to European-style professionalism. He followed a great number of Upton's recommendations, including one to establish a general staff system based on the German model.

Upton believed that the military suffered from too much civilian control. According to Upton and his followers: "in 1861 as before and since, the United States paid a heavy price for ignorance and complacence. The regular army was grossly neglected. In every war since 1775, the small band of regulars had borne the brunt and saved the day. Yet politicians pandered to popular sentiment and to foolish state pride by insisting upon the imaginary excellence of the amateur soldier. The Confederacy could have been crushed at the outset, on that heartbreaking day at Bull Run, if only the regular army had been maintained at a reasonable strength, and if only the militia had been organized federally as a genuine force instead of being a temporary rabble." [52]

Upton himself had been a general's aide at the first Battle of Bull Run and wrote with laconic contempt about the ninety-day militia, although two of the most disgraceful acts of the battle were committed by Army regulars. Union division commander Dixon S. Miles (W.P. 1824) became more and more drunk and incapable as the battle wore on, and Ambrose Burnside (W.P. 1847) "pulled his brigade back without permission, and later in the day was seen by a newspaper correspondent galloping away from his men with the unlikely excuse that he must arrange for their rations." [53]

Like Sylvanus Thayer, Upton was a great admirer of Napoleon and trusted alien structures as models for America's army. In 1876, after five years as commandant of cadets at West Point, he departed on a round-the-world tour to study foreign

[157]

armies. "He returned with an unabashed affection for the German war machine with which Bismarck had recently humiliated France and Austria and forged the modern German state. In his report, entitled *The Armies of Asia and Europe,* Upton recommended that America abandon its dual military system and adopt a unitary professional army patterned after Germany's. In peace, the regular officers would prepare for war by attending a system of military schools; in war, the expanded army would consist entirely of forces led by these thoroughly trained professionals." [54]

West Pointers immediately practiced their professionalism against the American Indian, but those heathens were eliminated all too soon, and, in a move with ominous overtones for the future, the more zealous among the grads began to look abroad for enemies. One man ready to accommodate them was Ismail Pasha, the ruler of Egypt. He had watched the Civil War closely and felt that experienced soldiers would have much to offer in the way of modernizing Egypt and expanding his personal empire. To this end, Ismail hired a total of forty-four war veterans during the 1870s—sixteen of them were graduates of West Point. Most of the men were recommended for Egyptian service by Gen. William T. Sherman (W.P. 1840), head of the U.S. Army, who even released a few of his younger officers so they might "round out their Civil War experiences in the land of the Pharaohs." [55]

The man in charge of this early military-assistance group was Brig. Gen. Charles P. Stone (W.P. 1845). He reported directly to Ismail and held his position as Chief of Staff of the Egyptian Army for thirteen years (1870–83). Henry H. Sibley (W.P. 1838), formerly a brigadier general in the Confederate Army, devised plans for the coastal defense of Ismail's land; and Eugene O. Fechét (W.P. 1868) became Chief of Survey and charted the royal domain from Aswan to Khartoum and Cairo to Suez. Soon after he arrived in Egypt in 1875 Samuel H. Lockett (W.P. 1859) visited the Egyptian Military academy in Cairo. Lockett, a colonel in the Confederate Army and a West Point instructor, was astonished at the complete lack of the discipline for which his alma mater is famous: "the professors sit cross-legged on their divans to hear recitations, smoke all the time, and frequently have a cup of coffee brought to them during a class. When one cadet recited, the others wandered around, lounged, talked and paid no attention." [56] Lockett later admitted rather uncomprehendingly that "in spite of all this they seem to learn something." [57] Although the West Pointers failed in their attempts to import Prussian discipline to Egypt, they were very successful with their mapping, and soon Ismail began to dream of expanding his empire to the Red Sea and the Indian Ocean. All trade from central Africa would pass through Egyptian territory and pay fees into the ruler's coffers in Cairo. His American crew was to supply the technical knowledge and leadership for these endeavors.

Abyssinia was to be the first to fall. At Stone's insistence, the "native" commanders were replaced by his fellow graduates and they marched at the head of the invading army. The West Pointers had trained an excellent staff of mapmakers, bookkeepers, and logisticians, but they had failed to train the troops in the aiming and firing of weapons. The result was predictable, and Stone's men were soon marching at the head of a rapidly retreating army. Ismail's power began to decline after this debacle, and our soldiers of fortune, like small, furry animals deserting a sinking ship, began to leave Egypt. Fechét later became the U.S. Consul in Mexico; James A. Dennison (W.P. 1870) became Deputy Attorney General of New York; Charles W. Field (W.P. 1849), a leader in the Abyssinian campaign as the commander of the totally ineffective Egyptian artillery, eventually found a home as military advisor to the King of Korea. But the most successful of all was the leader, Charles P. Stone, who was asked by the federal government to design and construct the base for the Statue of Liberty. In October 1886 the work was completed and a cold, rainy day saw Stone riding bareheaded and leading the dedication procession. On January 25, 1887, Stone passed away, having never recovered from the chill he had taken at the ceremony. Gen. William T. Sherman (W.P. 1840), John M. Schofield (W.P. 1853), and Col. Fitz-John Porter (W.P. 1845) escorted the body to its resting place in the cemetery at West Point. In some cases even irony finds its way to graduates of the Military Academy.

In 1916 the eager West Point warriors found themselves

chasing Pancho Villa around Mexico. The almost comical Punitive Expedition was, of course, commanded by graduates from top to bottom and provided some soon-to-be famous names with their first combat experience: Second Lt. George S. Patton (W.P. 1909) bagged two Mexicans from his touring car, lashed them to the fenders like deer, and won a promotion to first lieutenant for his daring; First Lt. James L. Collins (W.P. 1907) investigated a shooting incident involving Americans and friendly Mexicans, found the Americans innocent despite the protests of the Mexican government, and almost had the expedition thrown out of the country; and Brig. Gen. John J. Pershing (W.P. 1886), who practiced "Mexicanization" long before the delusion was popular—"these forces can be maintained here indefinitely as an incentive to Carranza [government] forces to kill or capture Villa." [58] But perhaps the most revealing story of this whole adventure is that of Lt. E. M. Zell (W.P. 1903). Ordered to report to a barren, inhospitable base camp on the Mexican border, Lt. Zell alighted from his train, took one look around, and cried out, "Great God! Is this Columbus, New Mexico?" A few minutes later Zell shot himself in the head, inflicting a fatal wound. [59]

During World War I, 74 percent of the 480 army generals were West Pointers—they comprised the Supreme Commander, 90 percent of the corps commanders and nearly 80 percent of the division commanders. Their performance is best summarized by the disproportionately high American casualty figure of 320,710 and the following remark of Gen. Pershing: "The fact is that our officers and men are far and away superior to the tired Europeans. High officers of the Allies have often dropped derogatory remarks about our poorly trained staff and high commanders, which our men have stood as long as they can. . . . [I now have told the Allies] in rather forcible language that we had now been patronized as long as we would stand for it, and I wished to hear no more of that sort of nonsense." [60] But he did hear more, and this time from home, with Dr. Charles W. Eliot, president emeritus of Harvard, stating, "West Point is an example of just what an educational institution should not be. . . . This was shown by the inefficiency and failure of its graduates in the World War." [61] Eliot later added, "In my opinion, no American school or college intended for youth of between 18 and 22 years of age should accept such ill-prepared material as West Point accepts. Secondly, no school or college should have a completely prescribed curriculum. Thirdly, no school or college should have its teaching done almost exclusively by recent graduates of the same school or college who are not teachers and who serve short terms. West Point, so far as its teachers are concerned, breeds in and in, a very bad practice for any educational institution." [62] This blast was answered by Col. James G. Steese (W.P. 1907) with a full-page reply in *The New York Times* in which he pointed out how many graduates had found a place among the elite, "including seventeen mayors of cities, eight bank presidents, seven presidents of railroads and no less than forty-six presidents of universities and colleges." [63] Near the end of his rebuttal Steese held up the blind spot of West Pointers for all to see: "We admit that West Point is hard and we admit that it is narrow. We consider that it is well that at least one institution should continue in the United States which holds that the duties of its students are more important than their rights." [64]

During the defense of the Philippines at the beginning of World War II, when Gen. Douglas MacArthur (W.P. 1903) asked Gen. Jonathan Wainwright (W.P. 1906) which command he wanted, Wainwright answered without hesitation or reference to the tactical situation, "The place where some distinction can be gained." [65] He gathered his distinction as the commander on Bataan in 1942 and, subsequently, as a Japanese prisoner of war until 1945. Although his method wasn't the most comfortable, Wainwright had the right notion of how to get ahead in the Army: move in the right circles and get into the limelight. This attitude is the key to the involvement of West Pointers in World War II.

At the start of the war, graduates comprised less than 7 percent of the officer corps and near the end they formed roughly only 1 percent of a total of some 890,000 officers.[66] Their influence, however, acted in inverse proportion to their small numbers. A tabulation of World War II ground-force commanders alone reveals the dominance of West Point at the high command level: [67]

	No.	West Point Graduates	Percentage
Supreme Commanders	3	3	100.0
Army Group Commanders	9	7	77.8
Army Commanders	20	11	55.0
Corps Commanders	31	20	64.5
Division Commanders	92	48	52.2
TOTAL	155	89	57.4

That West Pointers reached the top is not in itself surprising; after all, they were designated the most "professional" of the "professionals" and it was assumed that great accomplishments and responsibilities were a natural part of their daily life. This image was the result of years of careful cultivation that raised the Academy to the level of a sainted institution capable of spewing out nation-savers on demand. In 1965 Maj. Gen. Robert M. Danford (Ret.) (W.P. 1904), USMA commandant of cadets after World War I and one of its chief image-builders, described the "priceless value of West Point to our country" in these words: "It makes no difference when our nation faces the tragedy of war, there will always be a number of West Pointers to rise to high rank and positions of great responsibility and thereby give us names that will embellish the pages of our country's history throughout all time." [68] This, then, is what West Pointers tell each other and what the nation seems to have accepted without any real reluctance—but is it true? Did graduates rise to the top in World War II because of demonstrated competence, thorough training, and dedication—in other words, natural selection—or was there some less glorious process in operation? An experience of Gen. Danford while a lieutenant provides a clue: "So you see, I became Commandant of Cadets because Lady Luck, for over two years (1908–09), led me around the golf course at Fort Riley with [Maj.] Peyton C. March (W.P. 1888, Army Chief of Staff during World War I) as my partner. Of course he would have selected someone else if he had not known me. And had the selection been left to MacArthur, he, of course, would have chosen a combat officer, probably one associated with him

[162]

in the 42nd Division. Truly, 100 percent unadulterated luck! The result: my most cherished assignment." [69] Lieutenants playing golf with majors for over two years can be called luck, but it seems more likely that Danford learned quickly the importance of "moving in the right circles" as an aid to natural selection.

Gen. Danford's tour as commandant of cadets provided the makings of another interesting phenomenon. Speaking of the Tactical Officers who served under him during his three years at the Academy, Danford gushes, "I thought them wonderful at that time, but after World War II I knew that they were great! Permit me to call the roll: There was Courtney Hodges (ex-cadet W.P. 1908) who became a 4-star general in command of an army. . . . Then there was Willis Crittenberger (W.P. 1913), a 3-star general in command of a corps in Mark Clark's (W.P. 1917) army. . . . Then there was Oliver [Oscar] Griswold (W.P. 1910), a 3-star general in command of a corps. . . . The following were major generals and almost all of them division commanders: Arch Arnold (W.P. 1912), Charles Bonesteel (W.P. 1908), Ernest Dawley (W.P. 1910), Douglass Greene (W.P. 1913), Charles Gross (W.P. 1914), Leland Hobbs (W.P. 1915), John Homer (W.P. 1911), Paul Newgarden (W.P. 1913), Vernon Prichard (W.P. 1915), Stanley Reinhart (W.P. 1916), Charles Ryder (W.P. 1915), Charles Thompson (W.P. 1904)—and a number of others who were brigadier generals. In short, that group of TACs at West Point was almost 100 percent on the first team in World War II. . . . I do not mean to convey the impression that these officers became great because they served in the Tactical Department, but rather that they were potentially great when they were selected and assigned to it. At that time there were a number of potential 'greats' in the academic departments, men like Omar Bradley (W.P. 1915 and commander of American Ground Forces in Europe), Matt Ridgway (W.P. 1917 and deputy commander of the 82nd Airborne Division), J. Lawton Collins (W.P. 1917 and deputy commander of American Ground Forces in Europe), Wade Haislip (W.P. 1912 and commander of the Seventh Army), and others." [70] The personal alliances formed among West Pointers while sharing duty assignments go a long way in explaining the dominance of graduates in high command positions. Non-graduates call the phenomenon the West Point Protective Association (WPPA); graduates call it luck—Gen. Danford: ". . . in my service I am certain that luck did far more for me than skill." [71]

For many West Point commanders in World War II, luck came in the form of an assignment to the Infantry School at Fort Benning, Georgia, in the years 1927–32. The deputy commandant at Benning during this period was George C. Marshall, a 1901 graduate of the Virginia Military Institute (he followed his brother there), who would become Army Chief of Staff during the war and, as such, would make nearly all of the personnel selections for key military posts in Washington and Europe. Marshall received his high appointment through the considerable efforts of Gen. Frank McCoy (W.P. 1897) and Gen. John J. Pershing (W.P. 1886), and his selection represented a significant departure from form: he was the first non-West Pointer to become Chief of Staff in over twenty-five years and would be the last until 1960. If McCoy and Pershing left the club to boost Marshall, the new Chief of Staff stayed right within it in choosing his new commanders. Reaching back to his Fort Benning days, Marshall elevated many of his former associates—Omar Bradley (W.P. 1915), J. Lawton Collins (W.P. 1917), Joseph Stilwell (W.P. 1904), Jacob Devers (W.P. 1909), Courtney Hodges (former cadet), Harold Bull (W.P. 1914), Thomas Hearn (W.P. 1915), Norman Cota (W.P. 1917), William Eagles (W.P. 1917), Edwin Harding (W.P. 1909), and so on. In all, a total of 160 members of the Infantry School during Marshall's tenure became general officers in World War II. Collins' experience is illustrative of how Marshall worked. He had been impressed by Collins' work as an instructor at the school, and when in 1936 Collins became disillusioned with the progress of his career (he had been a lieutenant for seventeen years), Marshall personally dispelled any doubts that one of his favorites may have had with these words: "[The Army would be] showing signs of real modernization when they reach down and pick you and several others of your stripe, which I imagine will be done, and shortly." [72] Collins stuck it out and Marshall made good his words by making Collins a corps commander in the army under Gen. Hodges. Collins seemed to have forgotten the fatherly benevolence of

Marshall when he recently said, "Only a limited number of people combine the necessary qualities of character, integrity, intelligence and a willingness to work, which leads to a knowledge of their profession, to become successful leaders. These are God-given talents we inherit from our forebears." [73] God's name, in this instance, begins with an M.

Not all the top officers in World War II had a chance to meet Marshall at Benning; some met him on his assignment as an infantry brigade commander in Washington State, 1936–38. One of these was Mark W. Clark (W.P. 1917), who wrote, "I would say my association with George Marshall [in Washington] . . . probably was one of the greatest breaks I ever had." [74] Soon after Marshall became Chief of Staff, Clark was called to Washington, D.C., for work on the staff of the commander of Army ground forces, Maj. Gen. Lesley J. McNair (W.P. 1904). He soon jumped from lieutenant colonel to brigadier general and by the end of the war had his fourth star and the command of the Fifteenth Army Group. Speaking of his call to Washington, D.C., Clark says, "They could have picked one of fifty fellows that I know for the job I got, who would have done it at least as good, maybe better; but I happened to be there at the time, in the proper grade and age, and Marshall was looking." [75] Marshall of course wasn't alone in carrying officers to the top. Clark did some boosting of his own on behalf of an old friend. In 1941 Marshall asked Clark for a list of ten men suitable to head the very important War Plans Division, and Clark responded by giving him only one name—Dwight Eisenhower (W.P. 1915). Clark said of Eisenhower, "He was two years my senior at West Point, but we had been in the same company and had lived in the same division of barracks. We saw a lot of each other. . . . I had long admired his sterling qualities." [76] The influence of his friends was not lost on Eisenhower, for when asked why he was selected for his new job, he replied, "I think Gerow [then head of War Plans] and Mark Clark and possibly Wade Haislip (W.P. 1912) suggested me. . . ." [77] Ike's connections, however, went much deeper than these three men. He had been tutored by Maj. Gen. Fox Conner (W.P. 1898) in Panama, had become close friends with George S. Patton (W.P. 1909) because of a common interest in the tank corps, and, most important, had served as Douglas MacArthur's (W.P. 1903) senior assistant both in the 1932 operation against the Bonus Marchers and in MacArthur's later assignment as Field Marshal of the Philippine Army. But Eisenhower could rise only so far without the direct assistance of Marshall and he soon received it. In 1942 a conversation occurred wherein Ike told Marshall, "I don't give a damn about your promotion and your power to promote me. You brought me in here for a job. I didn't ask you whether I liked it or didn't like it. I'm trying to do my duty." [78] Speaking about this supposed blunder some years later, Eisenhower said, "You know, from that day on he started promoting me. Well, not that day, within ten days. He had written the request for the promotion to major general to the Senate himself. He said the operations division as he had set it up in the United States Army was not truly a staff position. He said I was a commander since I was making deployments, etc. This was his rationalization. It wasn't too long after that that he decided to send me to England, and when he sent me there he gave me another star and then another, etc." [79] Again Eisenhower was not loath to acknowledge the role of luck and friendship in his meteoric rise: "I probably would have finished the war as the Operations Officer of the War Department if it hadn't been for that conversation with General Marshall." [80] One of Eisenhower's classmates, James A. Van Fleet (W.P. 1915), was not so fortunate in his initial relations with Marshall. The Chief of Staff personally turned down repeated requests for Van Fleet's promotion to brigadier general because (it was widely believed) he confused him with an officer named Van Vliet (pronounced Van Fleet) who had gotten on Marshall's black list during the Infantry School days. It wasn't until Omar Bradley (W.P. 1915) and J. Lawton Collins (W.P. 1917) took a personal interest in the case that Marshall realized his error and began to promote Van Fleet with suitable rapidity.[81]

Another notable West Pointer, Gen. George S. Patton (W.P. 1909), also needed the personal intervention of his friends to ensure his high position in the face of his well-known indiscretions. For this purpose Patton's career had provided him with many well-placed comrades. Chief among them were Gen. John J. Pershing (W.P. 1886), with whom Patton served in Mexico and World War I; Secretary of War Henry L. Stimson, whom Patton served as an aide; Gen. Douglas MacArthur (W.P. 1903), whom he accompanied against the Bonus Marchers; * Gen. Fox Conner (W.P. 1898), who shared his interest in tanks; and Gen. Dwight Eisenhower, whom he had known since 1919. Against the advice of his staff, Eisenhower gave his old friend his first chance in World War II by selecting him as a division commander in North Africa. Although the planned operation never occurred, the selection marked the beginning of Ike's fatherly guidance of Patton. His patience was tried many times: "I'm just about fed up. If I have to apologize for George once more, I'm going to have to let him go, valuable as he is. I'm getting sick and tired of having to protect him. Life's much too short to put up with any more of it." [83] Eisenhower did, however, and Patton ended the war with four stars and the command of an army. This was the same Patton who commented after his success in the eventual North African invasion, "I guess I must be God's most favorite person." [84] God must have appeared to Patton in strange ways—i.e., Eisenhower, Stimson, et al.

Scores of other West Pointers reached high command in World War II and their stories read much like the ones above—the Academy caste system is thoroughly efficient in its operation and only rarely is an old friend overlooked. The danger posed to men's lives when an institution like the West Point Protective Association rears its head is best illustrated by a battle that occurred in Italy at the Rapido River in 1944. The cast of characters includes Mark Clark (W.P. 1917), friend of Eisenhower and commander of the Fifth Army; Geoffrey Keyes (W.P. 1913), commander of II Corps in Clark's army; and Fred L. Walker, commander of the 36th Division (a Texas National Guard unit) and a part of Keyes' II Corps.

Walker, a Regular officer though not a West Pointer, had been given command of the 36th Division in 1941 and had spent two years training it for the combat it finally saw on the Salerno beaches in 1943. The unit performed well in the landings and

---

* *The New York Times* ran a story on Patton's role in this adventure, highlighting the fact that he "was compelled by duty last night to evict from the main camp . . . a man who saved his life on the field of battle fourteen years ago." [82]

continued the fight with few breaks until the offensive reached the Germans' Gustav Line south of Rome in late 1943. In January 1944 Walker was ordered to crack the Gustav Line at the Rapido River as an adjunct to the landings at Anzio which were designed to outflank the German defenses and open the way to Rome. Walker felt that the crossing had little chance of success, but did not protest, probably out of fear of losing command of the men he had been with for so long. Nonetheless, Walker was bitter. He had been senior to Clark and Keyes for his entire career and now found himself serving under both of them. In addition, he was disgusted by some of their tactical policies. "I doubt very much," he wrote, "if this bombardment of a village [Altavilla] full of helpless civilian families, many of whom were killed or injured, contributed any real help in capturing the dominating ground in that vicinity." [85] After visiting the town of Battipaglia, he noted, "Not a single building was intact. The town will have to be rebuilt—it cannot be repaired. One could smell the odor of dead bodies, not yet recovered from the rubble. Such destruction of towns and civilians is brutal and quite unnecessary and does not assist in furthering the tactical program . . . " [86] With such a strong aversion to unnecessary death and perceiving that some of his men might meet this very fate, Walker nevertheless did not protest—he must indeed have felt that his men would suffer more heavily if he were replaced. A few hours before the attack Clark's other corps commander, British Gen. McCreery, advised that the 36th Division's assault be canceled because it had "little chance of success on account of the heavy defensive position of the enemy west of the Rapido." [87] Clark disagreed and said, "I maintain that it is essential that I make that attack fully expecting heavy losses in order to hold all the [German] troops on my front and draw more to it, thereby clearing the way for [Anzio]." [88] The two-day battle that followed cost the 36th Division 1,681 casualties and comprised one of the most shocking American defeats in World War II. Walker wrote that "Yesterday two regiments of this Division were wrecked on the west bank of the Rapido." [89]

The executive officer of one of the devastated regiments later said that it was common knowledge that the attack would fail because the defenses along the river were too strong for an infantryman to attack and remain alive. Indeed, the attack had been so weak that the German commander turned it back without even calling on the local reserves for assistance. One of the regimental commanders explained the weak attempt in these words: "Losses from attacks of this kind are tremendous in manpower and materiel; and in addition have a devastating demoralizing effect upon those few troops who survive them. . . . As long as leaders . . . have the guts to plunge into hopeless odds such as this operation, [and men] are sacrificed like cannon fodder, our success in battle will suffer in proportion and disaster will eventually come." [90] What he was trying to say was that the attack was ill-fated from the beginning and should not have been undertaken.

Clark, however, had no regrets and wrote: "In deciding upon the attack some time ago, I knew it would be costly but was impelled to go ahead with the attack in order that I could draw to this front all possible German reserves in order to clear the way for [Anzio]. . . . Some blood had to be spilled on either the land or [the Anzio] front, and I greatly preferred that it be on the Rapido, where we were secure, rather than at Anzio with the sea at our back." [91] Clark never again during the course of the war referred to the battle in writing. He obviously regretted the casualties, but made no apology for ordering the attack that ended so disastrously.

Walker, on the other hand, felt that his division had been badly hurt for no justifiable reason and noted the following in his diary: "I fully expected Clark and Keyes to 'can' me to cover their own stupidity. They came to my headquarters today but were not in a bad mood. Clark admitted the failure of the 36th Division to cross the Rapido was as much his fault as anyone's because he knew how difficult the operation would be. He has now decided to attack over the high ground to the north of Cassino. . . . This is what he should have done in the first place." [92] A few days later he added: "The great losses of fine young men during the attempts to cross the Rapido to no purpose and in violation of good infantry tactics are very depressing. All chargeable to the stupidity of the higher command." [93] Walker was unaware of other larger military operations which in Clark's view dictated haste along the Rapido, and thus came to suspect that the failure was due to the incompetence of his superiors brought on by their exaggerated personal ambition.

Shortly after the end of the war the 36th Division Association met for a convention in Texas to exchange war stories and meet old friends, but all they seemed to be able to discuss was the Rapido River. Giving vent to their feelings, they passed a resolution calling for a Congressional investigation of the battle and branding it "as one of the colossal blunders of the Second World War." [94] The resolution read in part as follows: "Every man connected with this undertaking knew it was doomed to failure because it was an impossible situation. . . . Notwithstanding this information . . . contrary to the repeated recommendations of the subordinate commanders, General Mark W. Clark ordered the crossings of the Rapido. . . . The results of the blunder are well known. The crossings were made under the most adverse conditions . . . [resulting in] a methodical destruction of our troops. . . . [An investigation is necessary] to correct a military system that will permit an inefficient and inexperienced officer, such as Gen Mark W. Clark, in a high command to destroy the young manhood of this country and to prevent future soldiers being sacrificed wastefully and uselessly." [95]

A clamor quickly arose in Texas that resulted in the State Senate endorsing the Association's stand. The War Department responded to the charges by maintaining that "General Clark exercised sound judgment" in planning and ordering the operation. This decision met with added uproar in Texas and soon the Military Affairs Committees of both houses of Congress became interested and asked that witnesses from the 36th Division appear before them. The president of the Association spoke before the House committee and said that he hoped to correct "a military system that permits elevation of officers to high command regardless of their known ability and [to help eliminate] a gross discrimination of National Guard and Reserve components in favor of the Regular Establishment and I am including the West Point Protective Association"—meaning, of course, Clark and Keyes.[96] A former regimental commander in the 36th Division added, "We could not help feeling that a fine National Guard Division was being destroyed by faulty orders from a West Point commander, with a ruthless determination to eliminate for all time National Guard officers, and Regular Army officers [Walker] in sympathy with the National Guard. . . . It was very obvious to even an inexperienced soldier that an attack such as the one ordered had practically no chance for success. All the teaching of sound military tactics would be violated by such an attack." [97] In spite of such testimony, no strong case emerged against Clark, and the War Department's findings stood: the attack had been necessary.

Whether or not the Rapido assault was a faulty tactic or, further, whether or not it was dreamed up by West Pointers with the intent of harming non-West Pointers is not the point of this discussion. The point is that graduates, simply because they were graduates, were blamed. The specter of the selfish interest of West Pointers, real or not, is always present.

In August 1945 Russian troops entered Korea. One month later American forces followed suit and the country was effectively divided at the 38th Parallel. In December, at the Moscow Foreign Ministers Conference, this split was formalized and a five-year joint trusteeship of Korea by the U.S. and Russia was organized. With the belief that after forty years of Japanese occupation the Koreans were incapable of forming their own government, the trustees set up a Joint Commission directed to form a unified Korean government. The chief delegate for the U.S. was Maj. Gen. Albert E. Brown (W.P. 1912). The commission met in 1946 and could not reach agreement on which Korean groups should be consulted, the Russians excluding all "rightist" organizations and the Americans wanting to talk only with groups controlled by the "rightest" leader of the South, Syngman Rhee. One historian has noted that Maj. Gen. Brown "was known to feel that war with Russia was not far away and his conduct was colored by this belief." [98] The commission met futilely once more in 1947 and referred the entire matter to the United Nations. In December 1948 the U.N. adopted a resolution declaring the government under Syngman Rhee in Seoul to be the only lawful government in Korea and recommended that all foreign troops be withdrawn. The U.S. and Russia complied, and in 1949 President Truman outlined a policy of non-intervention in Chinese affairs. Secretary of State Acheson put it more bluntly: he spoke of continuing the construction of a "democratic Korea," but offered no guarantees in the event of a military attack.[99] It seemed that the U.S. had totally given up on the Asian mainland when, in May 1950, Senator Tom Connally, chairman of the Senate Foreign Relations Committee, said that "he was afraid that South Korea would have to be abandoned" to the Communists.[100] But Gen. Douglas MacArthur (W.P. 1903), Commander-in-Chief of the Far East Command, Military Governor of Japan, and Supreme Commander for the Allied Powers in Japan, had different ideas. With his close friends Rhee and Chiang Kai-shek, the leader of Nationalist China, he had long before begun work to ensure U.S. involvement and, if necessary, military aid in Korea. In 1948 MacArthur told the South Koreans that "this barrier [the 38th Parallel] must and will be torn down" and that "nothing shall prevent the ultimate unity of your people as free men of a free nation." [101] In 1949 he said to Rhee: "You can depend upon it that I will defend South Korea as I would defend the shores of my own native land." [102] Later, in 1950, the MacArthur-Rhee-Chiang trio gained a powerful ally in the person of John Foster Dulles, who was acting as the Republican advisor to the State Department. Speaking to a friend, Dulles said, "Our material might was exemplified by the atomic bomb; our moral might is exemplified by General MacArthur." [103] On June 21, 1950, Dulles and Mac-Arthur went to Tokyo for talks with Secretary of Defense Louis Johnson and Omar N. Bradley (W.P. 1915), chairman of the Joint Chiefs of Staff. Soon after the meeting Dulles predicted "positive action by the United States to preserve the peace in the Far East." [104] When asked for an explanation, Dulles said that the conclusions of the group would lead to "some positive action but I cannot forecast what." [105] Four days later, on June 25, the war broke out, with the South Koreans in immediate retreat. Historians are still debating who initially attacked whom and whether or not anyone was really surprised by the "sneak attacks," but a West Pointer there at the time made one point absolutely clear. Two members of the staff of Brig. Gen. William L. Roberts (W.P. 1913), chief of the U.S. Military Advisory Group in Korea, assured the U.N. commission one month before the fighting that "MAG" had "confidence in the ability of the

Army of the Republic to handle the forces of the Northern regime in case of attack." [106] Gen. Roberts retired later in 1950.

As the military situation worsened, MacArthur was quickly given the opportunity to make good his grandiose earlier promises to Rhee. On June 27 Truman ordered U.S. air and sea support for the South Koreans, with the limitation that they be used only south of the 38th Parallel. On June 29 MacArthur ordered Lt. Gen. George E. Stratemeyer (W.P. 1915), his Far East Air Force commander, to bomb north of the parallel. Stratemeyer's message to Maj. Gen. Earle E. Partridge (W.P. 1924), commanding general of the Fifth Air Force, read as follows: "PARTRIDGE FROM STRATEMEYER. TAKE OUT NORTH KOREAN AIRFIELDS IMMEDIATELY. NO PUBLICITY. MACARTHUR APPROVES." [107] This message was sent twenty-four hours before Truman rescinded his bombing restrictions. One must ask if a non-West Pointer inserted in this command chain would have objected to the blatant disregard of Presidential orders. It doesn't seem likely, but later events prove it a valid question. On July 25, 1950, in his first report to the U.N., MacArthur maintained that "the character and disposition of the Republic of Korea Army indicated that it did not expect this sudden attack." Eighteen months later Maj. Gen. Charles A. Willoughby, a non-graduate and MacArthur's intelligence chief, spoke about the "alleged 'surprise' of the North Korean invasion" and said, "The entire South Korean army had been alerted for weeks and was in position along the 38th Parallel." [108] Better late than never, Gen. Willoughby. Something had obviously changed in the man who formalized the honor code at West Point and made it a part of the Academy's basic mission. But then, he was a graduate, and the honor code, after all, is designed for cadets. These events were merely the beginning of a long series of deceptions and indiscretions that would eventually lead to MacArthur's removal from command in Korea.

On June 29 MacArthur requested that U.S. ground troops be committed, and on June 30, after consultation with Truman, the Joints Chiefs of Staff informed the Korean commander of the President's approval. The JCS at this time consisted of Gen. Omar N. Bradley (W.P. 1915), Gen. J. Lawton Collins (W.P. 1917), Gen. Hoyt S. Vandenberg (W.P. 1923), and Adm.

Forest P. Sherman (Naval Academy). Collins has this to say about his partners: "Bradley, Vandenberg, and I had a common background of training at West Point and the additional bond of service together in combat in Europe, where Vandenberg's bombers frequently furnished air support for Bradley's First Army, of which my VII Corps was a part. Brad and I had been tactical instructors together under General Marshall at the Infantry School at Fort Benning and had served on the Secretariat of the War Department General Staff. I had played softball and squash with Vandenberg while he was a student and I an instructor at the Army War College just before World War II." [109] There are no strange bedfellows for a West Pointer on his way to the top.

The first American army troops to fight in Korea were led by Lt. Col. Charles B. Smith (W.P. 1939). He arrived on July 1, 1950, with a force of 406 men to block the main route of advance of the North Koreans. On July 4 he was joined by a detachment of artillery under the command of Lt. Col. Miller O. Perry (W.P. 1931). Brig. Gen. George B. Barth (W.P. 1918) was sent forward the same day to oversee the operation. This task force was soon beaten back with heavy casualties, and by the beginning of August the American and South Korean units found themselves compressed into the Pusan Perimeter and fighting for their lives. In command of the combined forces was Lt. Gen. Walton H. Walker (W.P. 1912), who had been stationed with Gen. Collins at West Point after World War I. His army consisted of the badly depleted 24th Division led by Brig. Gen. J. H. Church from MacArthur's staff; the 25th Division, commanded by Maj. Gen. William B. Kean (W.P. 1919), Bradley's chief of staff in World War II; and the 1st Cavalry Division, led by Maj. Gen. Hobart R. Gay, Patton's chief of staff during World War II. (Gay's son graduated from West Point in 1946 and flew in Korea with the Air Force.) MacArthur immediately demanded additional troops and Gen. Collins dispatched Lt. Gen. Matthew B. Ridgway (W.P. 1917) to assess the situation. Collins describes his choice of Ridgway thusly: "Matt Ridgway and I had been classmates at West Point, and his 82nd Airborne Division had fought brilliantly in my VII Corps in Normandy. I knew that I could depend on his ability to evaluate the situation in Korea and the further needs of the Far East Command. I knew also that he had the confidence of MacArthur, under whom he had served as Director of Athletics at West Point while MacArthur was Superintendent." [110] Collins obviously knew what experiences in a man's past were important, and MacArthur got his troops.

On September 15 the X Corps, under the command of MacArthur's former Chief of Staff, Maj. Gen. Edward M. Almond, landed at Inchon to outflank the North Koreans, and by the end of the month the newly designated "U.N. Forces" were back at the 38th Parallel. This return caused some in the U.S. and in the U.N. to say that the objective of repelling the invasion had been accomplished and the situation could now be stabilized. The U.N. began to work toward this end, but Truman and MacArthur had different ideas. On September 27 Truman authorized MacArthur to send troops north over the parallel. Instead of immediately moving, he issued an unconditional-surrender proclamation to the North Koreans on October 1. It said, in part, "I, as the United Nations Commander in Chief, call upon you [the North Korean commander] and the forces under your command, in whatever part of Korea situated, forthwith to lay down your arms and cease hostilities under such military supervisions as I may direct." [111] Fifteen minutes before this message was broadcast, the South Korean 3rd Division advanced across the 38th Parallel.[112] The U.N. had been presented with a fait accompli: a crossing of the parallel without U.N. instructions and a surrender proclamation without U.N. concurrence as to its terms. On October 7 it could do little but rubber-stamp its approval of U.S. actions. Collins and Vandenberg could not have been surprised by MacArthur's actions, for in mid-July he had told them: "I intend to destroy and not [merely] to drive back the North Korean Forces. . . . I may have to occupy all of North Korea." [113] The old grads were all in agreement, the prospects for peace notwithstanding.

By late October advance elements of the U.N. forces had reached the Yalu River on the border of China, and on November 8 Stratemeyer's planes were bombing along the border itself. He later gave a description of one of these raids, the bombing of Sinuiju, a city on the Yalu. The attack began "when fighter planes swept the area with machine guns, rockets, and jellied gasoline bombs." They were followed by "ten of the superforts" which "dropped 1000-pound high-explosive bombs on railroad and highway bridges across the Yalu River and on the bridge approaches. . . . The remaining planes used incendiaries exclusively on a two-and-one-half-mile built-up area along the southeast bank of the Yalu." Stratemeyer said that all targets were military and that the planes "had kept away from the city's hospital areas." At the same time, the Air Force claimed the destruction of 90 percent of the city.[114] This miniature Dresden on China's border occurred while U.N.-sponsored peace talks were under way. MacArthur seemed determined to keep peace from breaking out.

On November 24 the Chinese arrived at the U.N. for what many hoped would be the beginning of real peace talks, but again MacArthur had a different idea. On the same day he announced the beginning of his "Home by Christmas" offensive, and the Eighth Army under Walker and the X Corps under Almond began to advance. The Chinese counterattacked on the 27th, and on November 29 MacArthur authorized withdrawal. Lt. Gen. Walker was killed in a jeep accident on December 10 and was replaced by Lt. Gen. Ridgway while the Eighth Army steadily retreated toward the south. A *New York Times* correspondent described Korean reaction to the retreat: "When the Koreans saw that the Communists had left their homes and schools standing in retreat while the United Nations troops, fighting with much more destructive tools, left only blackened spots where towns once stood, the Communists even in retreat chalked up moral victories." [115] The Air Force was also doing its share: "Crews on B-26 light bombers of the 452nd Bomb Wing reported scarcity of targets at Hamhung today." One airman reported: "It's hard to find good targets, for we have burned out almost everything." [116] Ridgway was pursuing a scorched-earth policy which left millions of Koreans hungry and homeless. But MacArthur had no intention of leaving this burned-out country to the Communists, for when the JCS notified him that if he was driven back to Pusan an evacuation would be ordered, he immediately offered a series of strategic alternatives, first, "blockade the China coast"; second, "destroy China's war industries through naval and air attacks"; third, "reinforce the troops in Korea with Chinese Nationalist forces"; and, fourth, "allow diversionary operations by Nationalist troops against the China mainland." [117] Maj. Gen. Emmet O'Donnell (W.P. 1928), commander of the Far Eastern Air Force Bomber Command, wanted to go even further and use the atomic bomb on the Chinese. "They'll understand the lash when it is put to them," he said.[118] All this was too much even for the JCS, and Collins and Vandenberg met with MacArthur on January 15 in Tokyo to discuss the situation. After the meeting Collins announced, "As of now, we are going to stay and fight." [119] On his orders, the U.N. command stopped retreating and turned to face the Chinese. Other orders were issued on the 15th which removed Maj. Gen. O'Donnell from command and assigned him to a post in California. He was replaced by his deputy and classmate, Brig. Gen. James E. Briggs (W.P. 1928), of whom O'Donnell said, "[He] also is a disciple of the Air Force's strategic bombing doctrine." [120] Later that year Briggs joined his old boss in California.

On January 25 Ridgway began his new northward offensive and soon afterward a naval task force began the bombardment of Wonsan, a city of 35,000 people. Rear Adm. Allen E. Smith described it as "the longest sustained naval or air bombardment of a city in history." "In Wonsan," said the admiral, "you cannot walk in the streets. You cannot sleep anywhere in the twenty-four hours, unless it is the sleep of death." He said this treatment was also being given to two other ports in the same area, Songjin and Chongjin, and that the population of the cities had been reduced to "suicide groups." [121] The slaughter that accompanied the new advance was not confined to the hands of the Navy— the following story was written by a *New York Times* correspondent who was with an advancing armored column when they "recaptured" a village early in February:

> A napalm raid hit the village three or four days ago when the Chinese were holding up the advance, and nowhere in the village have they buried the dead because there is nobody left to do so. This correspondent came across one old woman, the only one who seemed to be left alive, dazedly hanging up some clothes in a blackened courtyard filled with the bodies of four members of her family.

The inhabitants throughout the village and in the fields were caught and killed and kept the exact postures they had held when the napalm struck—a man about to get on his bicycle, fifty boys and girls playing in an orphanage, a housewife strangely unmarked, holding in her hand a page torn from a Sears-Roebuck catalogue crayoned at Mail Order No. 3,811.294 for $2.98, "bewitching bed jacket—coral." There must be almost two hundred dead in the tiny hamlet.[122]

In light of these events, the name of Ridgway's second advance on February 21 assumes a new meaning—he dubbed it Operation Killer. I. F. Stone in his *Hidden History of the Korean War* describes a press conference held by Ridgway two days before Killer was launched: "[Showing captured bamboo spears to a group of correspondents, Ridgway commented:] 'In the year of our Lord 1951, they attack our troops with these crude spears that were in style five thousand years ago.' In the year of his Lord 1951 this was how a Christian general leading a crusade against 'godless' Communists and Oriental heathen sneered at the inferiority of their weapons of destruction." [123]

Ridgway's weapons were indeed superior, and by late March his troops were back at the 38th Parallel. At this juncture, on March 20, MacArthur received a message from the JCS which said:

> State planning a Presidential announcement shortly that with clearing of bulk of South Korea of aggressors, United Nations now prepared to discuss conditions of settlement in Korea. United Nations feeling exists that further diplomatic efforts toward settlement should be made before any advance with major forces north of the thirty-eighth parallel. Time will be required to determine diplomatic reactions and permit new negotiations that may develop.
>
> Recognizing that the parallel has no military significance, State has asked Joint Chiefs of Staff what authority you should have to permit sufficient freedom of action for next few weeks to provide security for United Nations forces and maintain contact with the enemy. Your recommendation desired.[124]

In other words, a major attempt at negotiation to end the war was to be made and the key was MacArthur—he was not to cross the 38th Parallel in force until diplomatic efforts had begun. But once again MacArthur had a different idea. On March 24 he issued his own cease-fire proposal to the Chinese, offered to accept their surrender, and authorized Ridgway to cross north of the parallel. By April 7 elements of nine divisions were across the line and hopes for peace talks were ruined. On April 11, after showing total disregard for all efforts to curb him, MacArthur was removed from command. An old grad had gotten a little too old.

Lt. Gen. Ridgway took over MacArthur's command and was replaced by Lt. Gen. James A. Van Fleet (W.P. 1915) as Eighth Army commander. Gen. Collins remembers Van Fleet: "Van was two years ahead of me at West Point, a member of the distinguished class of 1915, which included Dwight D. Eisenhower and Omar N. Bradley. As I remember, Van had not played football at the Point until Coach Charlie Daly persuaded the husky cadet to give it a try in his junior year. Van quickly developed into one of the most versatile backs the Army team had in those days of nonspecialists, helping mightily to kick the Navy 20 to 0 in the fall of 1914." [125] Van Fleet later served under Collins in World War II and received his promotion to brigadier general upon Collins' recommendation.

Van Fleet immediately resumed Ridgway's offensive and met with a Chinese counterattack on April 22. The fighting bobbed back and forth through May, but by mid-June a line above the 38th Parallel had been stabilized. Later in the same month Maj. Gen. O'Donnell traveled from his new post in California to Washington, D.C., to testify before Congress on his hopes at the beginning of the conflict and his observations of present conditions:

GENERAL O'DONNELL: It was my intention and hope, not having any instructions, that we would be able to get out there and to cash in on our psychological advantage in having gotten into the theater and into the war so fast, by putting a very severe blow on the North Koreans, with advance warning, perhaps, telling them that they had gone too far in what we all recognized as being a case of aggression, and General MacArthur would go top side to make a statement, and we now have at our command a weapon that can really dish out some severe destruction, and let us go to work on burning five major cities in North Korea to the ground, and to destroy completely every one of about 18 major strategic targets.[126]

Van Fleet exhibited these same "soldierly qualities." When the first round of peace talks began on July 10, Van Fleet was steadily attacking. Between July 10 and the end of September his casualties totaled nearly 10,000 Americans alone. Explaining to critics why he felt it necessary to continue attacking during the talks, the general said it was "imperative that the Eighth Army remain active to forestall the dreaded softening process of stagnation. . . . I could not allow my forces to become soft and dormant. . . . While these attacks served further to cripple the Communist aggressor, United Nations forces were working at their trade . . . absorbing new lessons and gradually learning the profession of fighting." The Eighth Army, he said, "was utilized more and more as a combat school." [127] Unfortunately, these live field maneuvers tended to kill people. Now Americans were not being asked to die to repel aggression; they were being asked to die in a training exercise.

The negotiations ended on August 23 and resumed on October 25 to continue fitfully until the armistice. In May 1952 Ridgway was replaced as U.N. and Far East commander in chief by Gen. Mark W. Clark (W.P. 1917). Clark had been a classmate of both Ridgway and Collins at West Point. In February Lt. Gen. Maxwell D. Taylor (W.P. 1922) replaced Van Fleet as Eighth Army commander. Collins describes him thus: "Max Taylor had jumped into Normandy at the head of the 101st Airborne Division on D Day in World War II and had distinguished himself in the subsequent drive across the base of the Cherbourg peninsula under my command in the VII Corps. After World War II he had served as Superintendent of West Point and as U.S. Commander in Berlin before I brought him to the Department of the Army staff as Assistant Chief of Staff, Operations, G-3, in 1951. In this capacity and later as Deputy for Operations and Administration he had closely followed the Korean war and was thoroughly familiar with its problems. I recommended to the JCS and President Eisenhower that he command the Eighth Army. Max fully maintained the fighting tradition of that army established by Walker, Ridgway, and Van Fleet before him." [128]

The armistice was finally declared on July 27, 1953, and the war can be summed up in true West Point fashion by using the words of Gen. Van Fleet: "Korea has been a blessing. There had to be a Korea either here or some place in the world." [129] To ensure that this kind of thinking would not die, the U.S. left the South Koreans an important legacy—a Korean military academy with a four-year curriculum patterned after West Point. Little did Van Fleet know, but in a few short years Asia was to witness the appearance of another "blessing" and his counterparts from the Korean Long Gray Line would be presented with a wondrous opportunity to practice their lessons.

Buried inside the April 28, 1970, issue of *The New York Times* was the following tiny article: "The President met with Secretary of State Rogers, Defense Secretary Laird and his special advisor on national security affairs, Henry A. Kissinger. The President also saw Arthur K. Watson, the new Ambassador to France. At noon the President met with the American Society of Association Executives. Later in the afternoon, he met with representatives of military, veteran and patriotic groups to discuss foreign policy." [130]

The *Times* did not consider the names of the "later in the afternoon" groups significant enough to mention, but it, like the Foreign Relations Committees of the Congress and the American people, were in the dark about the imminent invasion of Cambodia. The groups were National Guard Association, Navy League of the U.S., Reserve Officers Association, The Retired Officers Association, Air Force Association, American Ordnance Association, the Association of the U.S. Army, Marine Corps League, American Security Council, Military Order of World Wars, and of course those noted foreign-policy experts, the National Rifle Association. Nixon looked for and found support for his "bold" move into Cambodia among his strongest constituency, the paramilitary-industrialists. Their support was certain. He was, after all, their commander-in-chief.

Most of the paramilitary groups whose representatives met

with the President are directly influenced by West Pointers and enjoy an institutionalized form of their mentality. Two of the eleven who met with Nixon were themselves graduates: William K. Ghormley (W.P. 1929), executive director of the American Ordnance Association (AOA), and Lt. Gen. (Ret.) Charles G. Dodge (W.P. 1930), executive vice-president of the Association of the U.S. Army (AUSA). Both these groups could certainly be counted upon to justify whatever war moves Nixon would make and spread the good word through their massive propaganda networks. In the past, AUSA has been more than pleased to help the American people understand Vietnam policy in particular: "A white paper on Vietnam published in 1968 was also a notable landmark. Called 'Vietnam in Perspective,' it described the war, the opposing armed forces, the consequences of disengagement, and then drew some penetrating conclusions. Fourteen thousand copies were distributed to executives in business and industry, professional people, senior military leaders of all Services, educators (including the presidents of all colleges that have Army ROTC), and to other influential Americans. Its purpose was to explain to the recipients, and through them to the American people, our commitment in Vietnam, the reasons for it, and what this country must do to meet its obligation there. We believe it provided fresh insights into this serious problem for many American opinion leaders and made them more aware of the magnificent performance of the men and women of our Armed Forces serving in Vietnam." [131]

These loyal paramilitary organizations would never consider questioning the wisdom of America's President—they "love" their country too much. As an example of their devotion, one California chapter of the Military Order of World Wars (MOWW) has been busy raising $25,000 for the erection of the tallest (125 feet) floodlighted flagpole. At the regional meeting of all MOWW Southern California chapters, a number of interesting resolutions were offered: "to decrease unemployment by refurbishing mothball ships and military hardware . . . strengthen internal security by weeding out subversives in Federal government . . . expose subversive influence in ACLU . . . return military control to General Abrams . . . blockade

North Vietnamese ports . . . loosen Free Chinese. . . ." [132]
In a seeming non sequitur, the Los Angeles chapter demanded
"a resolution condemning South American seizure of fishing
boats and one commending Lawrence Welk's Thanksgiving program." [133]

In the meeting with Nixon, MOWW's 12,000 "male commissioned officers, active and reserve, emergency and retired who
have demonstrated or are demonstrating their love of country by
full time active duty in the Armed Forces during a period of
hostilities" [134] were represented by Vice Adm. George Dyer, but
the man who conducts MOWW's day-to-day business is its chief
of staff, Brig. Gen. (Ret.) Albert R. Brownfield (W.P. 1939).
His current post is far less exacting than his recent assignments.
In 1960 he was posted to Laos as the operations and training
officer for the Military Assistance Advisory Group, where "he
found that most of his time was spent in advising the Royal
Laos Army in combat operations." [135] In 1966, as associate
director of the Joint Public Affairs Office, an adjunct of the
Saigon American Embassy, he developed and directed all psychological operations against the Viet Cong and their supporters,
and in 1967 he became Gen. Westmoreland's operations officer.
He retired in 1969, but was recalled briefly to write some of the
official history of the Vietnam war. Brig. Gen. Paul Holland
(W.P. 1945), the recently elected commander-in-chief of
MOWW, helps Gen. Brownfield in his current task of directing
psychological operations at the American people.

The chairman of MOWW's legislative committee, Brig. Gen.
(Ret.) Lester L. Wheeler (W.P. 1935), feels that patriotism is
related directly to a tranquil "law and order" atmosphere. In his
bi-monthly column for the *World Wars Officer Review* titled
"The Law and the Order," he praises the Nixon-Mitchell-initi-
ated Public Law #91-358, commonly referred to as the D.C.
Crime Control Package, which authorizes no-knock search and
arrest warrants, wiretapping and electronic surveillance, and
pretrial detention for up to sixty days. Brig. Gen. Wheeler encourages the members of MOWW to "work, now, for the
incorporation of [this] precedential Federal legislation into the
whole fabric of American jurisprudence at every level of gov-

ernment." [136] In another issue Wheeler provides his readers with an inside-out military-industrial litany printed in the form of a poem:

> We should insist that
> our elected representatives
>
> in the Ninety-second Congress
> subject the managers of
> public monies for public welfare
> to the same intense scrutiny
>
> and accountability
>
> that has characterized
> Congressional efforts
>
> and attitudes
> in
> the field of
>
> defense expenditures.[137]

The telephone on Gen. Brownfield's desk is his link with the Southern California chapter, the painting of John J. Pershing on the wall of the tiny office in Washington his link with the past. There, with no apparent sign of work to be done, the general edits the *World Wars Officer Review* and wonders why young people don't understand the danger. In Brownfield's magazine P. A. "Dick" Horton, chairman of MOWW's Americanism Committee, describes the purpose of the United Nations Education Scientific and Cultural Organization (UNESCO).

UNESCO is a United Nations protected organization with their own charter, own funds and own headquarters in Paris and are entirely independent in their operations. It was charged that UNESCO was set up:
1. To destroy all religion
2. To destroy all family influence
3. To destroy all patriotism in this country
4. To rewrite our text books.
These charges were proven at the American Legion National Convention in Miami and a Congressional investigation was demanded.
We hear of many demands for a Congressional investigation

of the cause of the riots, disrespect, and law breaking, much of
which is inspired by UNESCOites on the school faculty. Investi-
gators should look to UNESCO. It was planned that way.[138]

Another author, writing in Brownfield's magazine about "Danger
in Disarmament," does more than complain. He offers twenty-
six (A to Z) constructive measures he feels must be taken to
"protect the public and lessen the impact of the recession."
Among them:

(b) Win the War in Southeast Asia thru the use of American air and naval power against North Vietnam, carrying the
fight to the enemy, and discouraging their offensives into Laos and
Cambodia by telling strikes on camps, bases, supply lines, dams,
bridges, railroads and factories, saturating military targets until
all enemy troops and guerrillas are withdrawn, and they recognize
the war to be unprofitable and sue for peace; close Haiphong
harbor by naval and air action;

(c) Impose a tight naval blockade against North Vietnam until
all Prisoners of War are exchanged; . . .

(f) Move rapidly against Communist conspiracies, revolutionary activity, fomented strife, lawlessness and treason; enact the
Internal Security Act of 1970; subject sources of Communist
propaganda to investigation; arrest, try and incarcerate enemy
agents operating illicitly here, persons in the pay of foreign powers
levying war against the United States, and leaders of front-
organizations attempting overthrow of our Constitutional government; support orderly college campuses; . . .

(i) Pacify the Caribbean, regaining the traditional American
position, effecting the collapse of Castro's terrorist state in Cuba
by firm measures, shipping an OAS stabilization contingent to
Cuba to supervise elections and the resettlement of returning
exiles; use all bases in Puerto Rico to advantage American services; construct a second Panama Canal at sea level; retain American control of the Canal Zone; double-track the Panama Railroad
and add a new rolling stock and special military railroad cars;
construct a freeway across the Isthmus in the Zone on the west
side of the Canal; emplace modern military facilities of permanent
character in this protected area; . . .

(r) Incorporate the ROTC into the Reserves of the Armed
Forces, permanently expanding its college programs so that this
country has leaders ready for mobilization; reduce Federal sub-
sidies where pink "academic Senates" debase the Services; . . .

(x) Restrain excesses in Chile by arranging with Brazil and Argentina for special local roles in the region; plan protection for the majority of Chileans who did not vote for a Communist President.[139]

So much for Gen. Brownfield's editorial instincts.

The Retired Officers Association (TROA) shares two important goals with the MOWW: "to defend the honor, integrity, and supremacy of our national government and the constitution of the United States" and "to inculcate and stimulate love of our country and the flag." [140] The 138,000 mature, responsible, and dedicated members of TROA, Nixon realized, could be depended upon to write letters, make calls, and send telegrams to him and the Congress in overwhelming support of the invasion of Cambodia. Consequently, he met with TROA's president, Vice Adm. William R. Smedbert III, a retired Naval Academy graduate. The presidency of the multi-service TROA seems to rotate between Naval Academy graduates and West Pointers. The leader of TROA from 1964 to 1968 was William P. Corderman (W.P. 1926). Currently, the second vice-president is Lt. Gen. (Ret.) Andrew T. McNamara (W.P. 1928), ex-Quartermaster General of the Army and, in retirement, president of the Defense Supply Association. The directors include Lt. Gen. (Ret.) John W. Carpenter III (W.P. 1939), Lt. Gen. (Ret.) Benjamin O. Davis (W.P. 1936 and the first black general in the Air Force), Gen. (Ret.) Barksdale Hamlett (W.P. 1930), and Lt. Gen. (Ret.) John W. Bowen (W.P. 1932).

President Nixon himself is one of the 62,000-plus members of the Reserve Officers Association (ROA), founded in 1922 by General of the Armies John J. Pershing's (W.P. 1886) close friend and confidant Brig. Gen. Henry J. Reilly (W.P. 1904). ROA's executive director, Col. John T. Carlton, is a registered lobbyist, and resolutions adopted in 1971 by his group include support for extension of the draft and recommendations to the House and Senate Armed Services Committees "that the Selective Service System be made permanent with the continuing responsibility of registering, cataloging, and evaluating the Nation's manpower." [141] A meeting with the President is not uncommon for the leadership of the ROA: "In March of 1968 when discussion was prevalent in the country over the nation's policy in

Vietnam, ROA leaders called on the President [Johnson] in the White House to assure him that our Association endorsed the course then being followed to achieve victory and ultimate peace." [142] This group included Col. Carlton. The purpose of these more routine meetings in the White House is obscure, however: "Since World War II, ROA has found an open door and open ears at the White House, where the highest echelon of policy making operates. It is improper to mention in detail what has gone on behind those portals, but ROA's representatives go there and are heard." [143]

Five national staff officers, including Col. (Ret.) Joseph L. Chabot (W.P. 1937), director of Army affairs, work with ROA's $2 million in assets at its new Minute-Man Memorial Building in Washington supporting "a military policy for the United States that will provide adequate National Security and to promote the development and execution thereof," [144] or, in plain language, selling military hardware and policies to the public. Nixon understands propaganda and had Westmoreland congratulate the ROA for its Pentagon salesmanship: "The Reserve Officers Association has made and can continue to make a significant contribution to national security by furthering public understanding and support of our defense team." [145]

Nixon's choice to include Louis F. Lucas, the executive director and treasurer of the National Rifle Association (NRA), in his meeting with the paramilitary-industrialists was a wise one. The members number over one million and are active in writing letters to Congressmen and the White House. Special bulletins keep them informed of bills and Presidential actions of an emergency nature that require letter-writing support. The NRA has a number of West Point patrons (contributions of $500 or more) and one of NRA's many national officers is Lt. Gen. (Ret.) Louis W. Truman (W.P. 1932). For two years Ben Truman commanded the Third U.S. Army at Fort McPherson, Georgia, made a number of pleasant industrial contacts, and, upon retirement in 1967, found himself executive director of the Georgia Department of Industry and Trade in nearby Atlanta. The number-one man in NRA is a retired major general, Maxwell E. Rich. He is not a graduate of West Point, but shares enough of West Pointers' beliefs to be a member of the West

Point-dominated Advisory Board of Directors of the Association of the U.S. Army (AUSA).

Besides Nixon's favorite, Charles Dodge, AUSA's national leadership includes Maj. Gen. (Ret.) Earle F. Cook (W.P. 1931); Gen. (Ret.) Barksdale Hamlett (W.P. 1930); Gen. (Ret.) Hamilton H. Howze (W.P. 1930), a developer of the air mobile concept, now working for Bell Helicopter; and Lt. Gen. (Ret.) William W. Quinn (W.P. 1933), a vice-president of Martin-Marietta. AUSA claims to be a "private, voluntary, non-profit, educational organization made up of Americans, both civilian and military, dedicated to the premise that a strong, modern mobile army is essential to our national defense." *The Membership and Information Guide to the Association of the U.S. Army,* second edition, describes precisely what AUSA has done and seeks to do in its programs. These activities include lobbying for the extension of Selective Service legislation, support for "accelerated procurement of the most modern weapons and equipment for the Army," support of the C5A, "full support of our country's objectives in Southeast Asia," endorsement of "worldwide deployment of U.S. Forces," support for the "development of an ABM system," and support of "efforts to make disrespect for the flag a federal offense." Page six of the pamphlet describes the methods and targets of AUSA's policy programs: "The accomplishments of the Association are many. Its objectives are reflected in resolutions adopted each year at its Annual meeting, which become the AUSA 'platform' and guide for our efforts for the coming year. These resolutions are disseminated to all members of Congress, key personnel at the White House and the Department of Defense, senior military leaders, other influential citizens throughout the country, and to all AUSA Chapters. Special memoranda, pamphlets and articles in *Army* magazine are published from time to time to implement and support these resolutions."

It is not the industrialists and West Point generals who pay for AUSA's lobbying campaign. This burden rests upon the backs of low-ranking officers and non-commissioned officers who are virtually forced to join the organization. Objections to such coercion by a young West Point lieutenant in the South afforded him an opportunity to get out of an Army he had come to view as fat and corrupt. The following account is drawn from a complaint filed November 16, 1970, by the West Point officer. In February 1970, during a massive AUSA membership drive, the lieutenant was ordered to join the organization by his battery commander. The first sergeant considerately filled out the application form for the lieutenant, and, not wishing to "rock the boat" before he had full information and a considered course of action, the lieutenant reluctantly joined. His commander was under pressure himself. He, like all other unit commanders in his airborne division, had received a letter personally signed by the commanding general, a two-star member of the Class of 1942, "encouraging" members of his command to join AUSA. Those with experience in the armed forces can understand the meaning of "personal encouragement" by a general officer. In this instance it meant the following: the airborne division staff prescribed AUSA membership goals for all subordinate units based on their personnel strengths; personnel rosters indicating who had not joined AUSA were required to be forwarded to higher headquarters; government transportation was used to transport enlisted men to a gala AUSA picnic; the post Public Information Office sent AUSA news releases to the local media; Army message-center facilities were used to distribute AUSA printed matter and propaganda posters; and official-business mailing envelopes of the Department of the Army were used.

Unit goals for AUSA membership at this post were met or exceeded. Some officers, however, wanted to know what they would get for their $7.50 yearly dues. One cynic replied, "A worthless magazine the Army loses before you receive it." An NCO asked a captain if they could get a day off for joining. He replied "Yes, next Sunday." But it is not true that the $7.50 is a total waste; there are rewards.

Members are supposed to receive AUSA's monthly magazine, *Army,* in which they can read such provocative articles as: "From Army of the '70s: 'A Flawless Performance' " by Gen. W. C. Westmoreland (W.P. 1936); "New Weapons, Realistic Training Mark NATO Vigil" by Gen. James H. Polk (W.P. 1933); "Innovations Applied at AMC [Army Materiel Command] in Face of Budget Cutbacks" by Gen. Ferdinand J.

Chesarek (W.P. 1938); and "Two-Decade Vigil Forges a Strong South Korea" by Gen. John H. Michaelis (W.P. 1936).[146] In short, for $7.50 a year, young officers and NCOs can have West Point generals tell them what a wonderful job the West Point Army is doing.

The army post's membership drive provided 3,632 new members and $27,756 for AUSA. In the entire Army, men recruited by these campaigns provide AUSA with an operating budget in excess of $300,000. What is done with their money? We don't know, but there is no mistaking that Edward C. Logelin, AUSA's president and the treasurer of U.S. Steel, gets some good fiscal advice from AUSA's Advisory Board of Directors:

W. S. Blakeslee, Vice Pres., Chrysler Corp.
Maxwell E. Rich, Vice Pres., National Rifle Ass'n
Mrs. Olive Anne Beech, Pres., Beech Aircraft
Harvey Gaylord, Pres., A division of Bell Helicopter
Peter MacDonald, Manager, Goodyear
Cruse W. Moss, Vice Pres., Kaiser Jeep
G. Paul McCormick, Vice Pres., North American Aviation

"Traditionally, the U.S. Army had been expressly forbidden to play any political role or exert any political influence; this is a cherished and precious part of our American heritage which we in the Army must jealously guard." [147] Ironically, these are the words of Gen. Bruce Palmer, Jr. (W.P. 1936), published in the October 1970 issue of *Army*. Of course, Gen. Palmer does not find it necessary to "jealously guard" our country from the undue political influence of AUSA. Army Regulations 600-20, paragraph 42, stating: "They are prohibited by 18 USC 602 and 607 from soliciting, receiving from, or giving to, any other officer, employee, or person paid from Federal funds, any contribution, subscription, or assessment for any political purpose, or for the promotion of any political object," is enforced to prevent organization by GI's United Against the War, Vietnam Veterans Against the War, and the anti-war Concerned Officers Movement, but not against AUSA. It was such a double standard to which the lieutenant objected. In a ten-page complaint to the commanding general of the XVIII Airborne Corps, Lt. Gen.

J. J. Tolson III (W.P. 1937), and filed under the provisions of
Article 138 of the UCMJ, he described in detail the nature
of the illegal activities carried out against powerless members
of the Division and himself. The lieutenant called upon Lt.
Gen. Tolson to order the following: "(1) The cessation of
AUSA membership recruiting and fund raising at this post. (2)
Remove AUSA posters and advertisements from government
buildings and the military reservations as a whole. (3) The
cessation of AUSA use of government buildings and facilities
for meetings and dinners unless these facilities are made available to political groups of the opposite view. (4) The cessation
of the granting of administrative leave to members of the military
to attend AUSA conventions which develop and vote on a
political 'platform.' " [148] The lieutenant found he had touched a
sensitive nerve and, in spite of a five-year service commitment,
was allowed to resign. The words of Gen. Palmer, therefore, seem
especially ironic, for he has written (also in *Army* Magazine),
"We must not allow a double standard—one we talk and write
about, but a different one we actually live by in the real world.
Failure to practice what we preach can only lead to professional
'phonies'—people skilled at giving higher authority a 'snow job,'
but lacking in basic qualities. Fortunately, such pseudo-leaders
don't fool the troops; unfortunately, the troops suffer as a result of
such leaders' lack of professionalism." [149] Nobly said, but Palmer
seems to be in the time-honored position of not being able to
see the forest for the trees.

The Air Force Association (AFA) is similar to AUSA
except, of course, that its focus is directed toward "maintaining
adequate *aerospace power* for national security and world peace."
Its three goals do justice to cold war logic: "(1) Support armed
strength to maintain security and peace. (2) To educate themselves and the public in development of adequate aerospace
power for the betterment of all mankind. (3) To help develop
friendly relations among free nations based on respect for principles of freedom and equal rights to all mankind." Like AUSA,
AFA has an industrial-associate program, with more than 200
corporate members ranging from AVCO Corp. to Westinghouse.
The industrial associates are provided with Air Force, Army,
Navy, Department of Defense, and NASA organization charts

listing key positions and contacts, while Industrial Service Marketing Reports keep them abreast of Air Force and Department of Defense activities, special events, military budgets, and Congressional reports. They also make active use of AFA's research department to find the more obscure answers to their corporate questions. The AFA annual convention is the largest aerospace meeting in the nation, and industrial affiliation permits unlimited attendance at the hundreds of seminars and luncheons.

In addition to AFA's corporate members there are 105,000 individual members who pay $10 annually for dues. Membership is open to anyone interested in promoting the Air Force and aerospace. *Air Force* Magazine, AFA's monthly publication, assists in that promotion with its emphasis on exotic research-and-development programs, national strategic deterrence through air power, and national and international military affairs (meaning Soviet aerospace progress). This unbiased and intellectual publication is required reading at the Air University and the National War College. The directors of AFA help sell the Air Force–Aerospace Industry point of view with soothing propaganda, but they are not averse to using their rhetoric to frighten. One director, Milton Caniff, is famous for his virile comic strip "Terry and the Pirates." Another, Gen. Curtis E. LeMay, is known for his prophecies of impending strategic disaster, his run for the White House on the George Wallace ticket, and his low-key fright book, *America Is in Danger,* co-authored, it happens, by Maj. Gen. (Ret.) Dale O. Smith (W.P. 1934). West Point directors of the Air Force Association include Gen. (Ret.) Carl Spaatz (W.P. 1914), and retired Air Force Chief of Staff John P. McConnell (W.P. 1932). Fortunately, the Air Force Association is no more political than, say, the Association of the U.S. Army or MOWW. Its resolutions call upon Congress and the administration to develop and deploy the Minuteman Hard-Point defense system as a key element in the ABM program, support deployment of the B-1 bomber, urge a full-scale SST prototype construction program, and so on. Gen. Bruce K. Holloway (W.P. 1937), commander of the Strategic Air Command, sums up their aims: "The Air Force Association ought to consist of 100,000 emissaries for adequate national defense through airpower—emissaries in the greater sense that national defense is not possible without airpower—and that the Air Force is its essence. Our emissaries should ever keep in mind some words General Arnold (W.P. 1907) spoke before it was born: 'A modern, autonomous, and thoroughly trained Air Force in being at all times will not alone be sufficient, but without it there can be no national security.' " One hundred thousand common voices speaking out to those unfortunates who are "not conversant with the complexities of defense issues"! [150]

But Nixon's Cambodian collaborations did not end with the West Point-dominated paramilitary organizations. In May 1970, as American troops of the 25th Infantry Division, commanded by Maj. Gen. Edward Bautz, Jr., the 11th Armored Cavalry Regiment, commanded by Brig. Gen. D. A. Starry (W.P. 1948), and the 1st Cavalry Division, under the late Maj. Gen. G. W. Casey (W.P. 1945), all under the provisional command of Lt. Gen. Michael S. Davison (W.P. 1939), continued their marauding, the President symbolically reported to the Pentagon warlords to get his usual "overwhelming success" briefing. It was there, in an off-the-cuff speech, that he referred to dissident students as "bums" and called the uniformed brass surrounding him "true Americans." In a sense, it was fitting that he reported to them for his briefing, for he was only fulfilling the long-standing recommendations of the key Vietnam policy advisors during the critical years 1964–68. The West Point triumvirate of Earle G. Wheeler (W.P. 1932), Chairman of the Joint Chiefs, Harold K. Johnson (W.P. 1933), Chief of Staff of the Army, and William Childs Westmoreland (W.P. 1936), COMUSMACV,* had incessantly recommended that enemy "sanctuaries" be "cleaned out," only to be rebuffed by President Johnson and his political considerations.

Whether these men or the Pentagon are the "true Americans" is open to question, but there can be no question about their being the truly powerful Americans. It is the West Point generals and their concomitant ideology that control a military empire that extends to all continents including our own. The commanding general of U.S. Army, Korea, is Westmoreland's classmate Gen. John H. Michaelis (W.P. 1936). Command of IX Corps

---

* Commander, U.S. Military Assistance Command, Vietnam.

and the Ryukyus falls to Okinawa's military governor, West-moreland's classmate, and ex-superintendent of the Military Academy, Lt. Gen. James B. Lampert (W.P. 1936). Others have found their way to the Pacific—"Taiwan was the scene of the 4th Annual . . . [Special Forces Commanders' Conference] . . . on 16 June 71. Woodie Collins (W.P. 1946) and Bill Simpson (W.P. 1946) arrived there then and were flown by the Chinese to their showplace, Kinmen Island, a few miles off the coast of Communist China; a heavily fortified island, receiving incoming arty every other night like clockwork. As they stepped off the plane, they were greeted by the only American on the island, classmate Dan Moriarty (W.P. 1946) who then had served a few weeks of a one-year unaccompanied tour as Sr. Adv., Kinmen Island, JUSMAG, China. Bill wrote to inform us of the little Class meeting on Kinmen. He was stationed on Okinawa till late Aug., when he left for the . . . [Army War College], after 26 months of fine command time with the 1st Special Forces Group. Others on Okinawa include Brick Bentz (W.P. 1946), CO 7th Psychological Opns. Gp.; Jack Sadler (W.P. 1946), Proj. Latern Dir. (human relations); Dick Day (W.P. 1946), W. Pac. Engr.; and Bill Webb (W.P. 1946), a civilian with Gulf." [151] In Vietnam, Westy's classmate Creighton Abrams (W.P. 1936) runs the show. With Vietnamization now in style, three of the four senior "advisors" are graduates. The commander of U.S. Support Command Thailand, Brig. Gen. David E. Ott (W.P. 1944) was recently replaced by non-grad Brig. Gen. John W. Vessey, Jr. His Thai counterpart, Manob Suriya (W.P. 1937), who was chief of the Thai Air Forces, will now have to hold things together on Founders Day.

On the other side of the world, Westmoreland's protégé Gen. Michael S. Davison (W.P. 1939) commands United States Army, Europe. Westy and Davison sealed their friendship at West Point, where Davison served as commandant of cadets under *Time* Magazine's 1965 "Man of the Year." Gen. Davison's classmate Gen. Frank T. Mildren (W.P. 1939) commands Allied Land Forces, Southeast Europe. And the combined NATO forces of the United States, Canada, Iceland, Norway, United Kingdom, Netherlands, Denmark, Belgium, Turkey, Luxembourg, Portugal, France, Italy, Greece, and the Federal Republic of Germany are controlled by the Supreme Allied Commander, Europe, another classmate, Gen. Andrew J. Goodpaster (W.P. 1939). In the torrid Mideast, where the U.S. has no tactical Army units, Westy's classmate Lt. Gen. John A. Heintges takes up the slack as U.S. Representative to the Central Treaty Organization (U.S., United Kingdom, Northern Ireland, Turkey, Iran, West Pakistan, East Pakistan).

In Latin America and other areas of the Third World the United States Army maintains an intricate network of schools, military missions, academies, and advisory groups whose main purpose is to maintain "stability." Father Thomas R. Melville, an American priest who had spent ten years in Guatemala, wrote a letter to Senator William Fulbright dated February 14, 1968, outlining this American policy. Melville worked with the peasants of Guatemala, establishing credit unions, agricultural cooperatives, one industrial cooperative, and helped in the formation of a dozen other cooperatives. "I didn't accomplish much because we forever ran into government indifference at best, and government interference at worst," he wrote Senator Fulbright. "If any program showed signs of success, the Alliance for Progress men were right there to offer money in exchange for the right to hang their publicity signs." [152] He described the social ferment in Latin America in these words: "The masses of Latin America are becoming more and more restless. Their Governments do not want any real progress, because it would have to come at the expense of the landed oligarchy, which in turn control these governments. . . . This insignificant minority maintains itself in power by paying the national armies. The United States sends technical help, money and armaments, to modernize these armies. Last year four new troop-carrying helicopters were donated to Guatemala; 2,000 new policemen were added to the force with their salaries, uniforms, and latest weapons all paid for from the Alliance for Progress. American experts in antiguerrilla warfare, with the help of professional torturers of Cuban, Puerto Rican and Dominican nationalities, keep the country terrorized." [153] Toward the end of this letter Father Melville had words of warning for all Americans: "If the United States government continues with its policy of believing that all national insurrections are manipulated by Moscow or Peking, then it is going to find itself in more than one Vietnam in Latin America." [154]

There are a number of ways in which the U S. armed forces intervened in Latin America. Later we will see how Gen. Frank R. McCoy (W.P. 1897), with the help of some 5,000 U.S. marines, suppressed the revolutionary efforts of Augusto César Sandino and conducted the 1928 Nicaraguan elections— elections in which only U.S.-approved candidates could run, and in which only U.S.-controlled areas could vote. These elections, of course, proved fruitful for the United States, eventually leading to the establishment of the present dictator of Nicaragua, Gen. Anastasio Somoza (W.P. 1946), who, as might be expected, parrots U.S. foreign-policy goals and aims. Some Americans are familiar with the U.S. intervention in Guatemala in 1954, when the CIA-backed Gen. Castillo-Armas overthrew the democratically elected Arbenz regime. Most Americans (and Latin Americans) are familiar with the Bay of Pigs fiasco, in which the United States trained and supported Cuban exiles and encouraged them to overthrow the government of Fidel Castro. Also, many persons are aware of the 82nd Airborne Division operations led by Gen. Bruce Palmer (W.P. 1936) in the Dominican Republic in 1965 for the purpose of "saving American lives."

Few Americans, however, are familiar with the day-to-day and far more subtle programs of U.S. military aid, equally effective, whose end result is the support of the "landed oligarchy" and "significant minority" of which Father Melville speaks.

This more subtle control is accomplished through an extensive network of schools and the crisscrossing careers of American military personnel and Latin American military personnel, training in the United States or American-controlled schools, working together to keep the lid on the Latin American social ferment. This gossamer of control, this spreading of the "military reality," extends from West Point itself, where conferences on Latin American affairs are held bringing together business, military, and academic elites, to the U.S. Army's Command and General Staff College, where scores of foreign lieutenant colonels and colonels are taught "counter-insurgency" and "stability" operations; to the Inter-American Defense College in Washington,

D.C., strongly influenced by West Pointers; to the U.S. Army Ranger School at Fort Benning, Georgia, where young Spanish-speaking cadets are taught in schools patterned after West Point. The Special Forces is an integral part of this network, as is the U.S. academic community. The system encompasses some seventeen military missions in Latin American countries and career officers who serve for two or three years in these missions, then spend a year in Vietnam and return to Latin America, specializing in repression. The control includes foreign graduates of West Point who return to their native land and add an air of legitimacy to the entire affair; and it includes the millions of dollars in military aid and equipment passed from the Pentagon to dictatorial and fascist regimes like those of Brazil, Argentina, Nicaragua, and Venezuela.

The military domination of Latin America begins in the United States itself—with West Pointers in the forefront. In 1961 a Counter-insurgency Committee was appointed to enhance "the nation's capability for unconventional warfare." It was chaired by Gen. Maxwell Taylor (W.P. 1922). With Taylor showing the way, the Pentagon's West Pointers have consistently supported militarist Latin regimes with military aid and equipment. During the period 1952–68 the U.S. military hardware supplied to Latin America amounted to some $687 million, not including some $178 million worth of excess hardware supplied to Latin American armies. In 1968–69, for example, Brazil was the recipient of six Bell Iroquois helicopters specially equipped for counter-insurgency warfare. At the same time Bolivia received twelve Hughes 500-M helicopters, also armed for counter-insurgency. In 1968 Argentina acquired four Bell Iroquois helicopters for use in guerrilla warfare.[155]

More important than equipment, however, is indoctrination. Foreign students attend approximately 150 U.S. military and police schools in the United States. These schools range in location from the Army Language School in Monterey, California, to Laurence G. Hanscom Field in Massachusetts. One of the most important institutions for teaching foreign personnel is the International Police Academy (IPA). This school was originally located in the Panama Canal Zone and called the Inter-American Police Academy. In 1964 the Academy was relocated in the

Georgetown section of Washington, D.C., and its student body expanded to include members from the entire Third World, although Spanish-speaking students still constitute a majority of the student body. By 1969 well over 3,000 police officials had graduated from IPA, with instruction including three days at the John F. Kennedy Special Warfare Center at Fort Bragg, North Carolina, for training in "civil-military relationships in counter-insurgency operations and police support in unconventional warfare." [156] The flavor of IPA was related by one journalist who visited the Academy: "Much of the Academy's instruction takes place in a room called the Police Operations Control Center (POCC). . . . At the front of the POCC is a magnetic game board on which has been constructed the map of a mythical city, Rio Bravos. . . . From the control booth, faculty rifle commanders alert the students to a communist-inspired riot at the city's university, or to a bombing attempt by communist subversives from the neighboring country, Maoland. The students deploy their forces on the board and plan strategies, much as they would from a real police control center." [157] Such instruction is not confined to IPA. The Command and General Staff College at Fort Leavenworth, Kansas, and the Inter-American Defense College at Fort McNair, Virginia, also engage in such playful tactics.

The Inter-American Defense College is controlled by a group known as the Inter-American Defense Board. It prides itself on being a representative board of Latin American nations gathered together in mutual hemispheric defense. In actuality, the U.S. military are firmly in control. According to a U.S. government pamphlet entitled *An Introduction to Mutual Security Planning by the American Republics,* the rationale for U.S. control is as follows: "The Chairman [of the Inter-American Defense Board], the Director of the Staff, and Secretary are officers of the Armed Forces of the American State in which the Board functions. Since the seat of this international organization is in the United States of America, these officers are selected from the Armed Forces of that nation." [158] Of course, the board will never leave the United States. For Latin American officers, requirements for admission to the college include having attained the rank of lieutenant colonel or above, military command experience, and advanced command and staff college. As of June 30, 1972, the college, established in 1962, had graduated 373 students. Most courses are taught in Spanish, and as part of the nine-month program of study students take courses on the social, economic and political aspects of hemispheric security and make a trip to West Point. In turn, West Point cadets (all members of the Spanish Club) make an annual trip to Washington, D.C., usually in April, to tour the Inter-American Defense College and exchange views with the Latin American officers.[159]

Three thousand miles south of Washington, D.C., lies another focal point of U.S. military influence in Latin America. This is the U.S. Southern Command, known as SOUTHCOM, and located in the Canal Zone. It is one of four major commands the U.S. military maintains around the world (the others are the European Command, the Middle East Command, and the Asian Command). The Southern Command, started in the 1940s, controls a general staff of several hundred officers and enlisted men from the Army, Air Force, and Navy; maintains logistics bases, logistics schools, equipment storage, and a number of tactics schools; and is responsible for all U.S. military activities in Central and South America. According to Gen. Matthew B. Ridgway, former commander of SOUTHCOM, "the Commander in Chief of the Caribbean, and his component service commanders, exercise a tremendous influence on the military establishments and, therefore, on the political regimes of the Latin-American republics. Our military establishment is their model, and the U.S. Army, particularly, is the model for the armies of most of the Latin-American republics. And it is their armies which exercise the controlling influence over their governments."[160]

In the Canal Zone alone, SOUTHCOM runs an entire series of schools designed to supplement and complement instruction given in the United States. "Stability," "counter-insurgency," and "military civic action" programs are taught. The U.S. Army School of the Americas, located at Fort Gulick, Canal Zone, teaches courses exclusively in Spanish for Latin American personnel and has trained an estimated 22,000 Latin Americans in counter-insurgency operations. Courses range in length from two to forty weeks. According to *Army Digest,* the Irregular Warfare

Committee of the school "teaches various measures required to defeat an insurgent on the battlefield, as well as military civic action functions in an insurgent environment." The article continues with equal candor, emphasizing that the school's alumni "have risen to such key positions as Minister of Defense and Chief of Staff in Bolivia, Director of Mexico's War College, Minister of War and Chief of Staff in Colombia, Chief of Staff for Intelligence in Argentina, and Undersecretary of War in Chile." This training "paves the way for cooperation and support of U.S. Army Missions, attachés, military assistance groups and commissions operating in Latin America." [161] In the late 1960s the School of the Americas was commanded by Gen. Vincent Elmore, Jr. (W.P. 1938), whose qualifications included four years' service as military attaché in Havana, Cuba, during the Batista regime.

Beginning in 1963, the Inter-American Air Forces Academy (IAAFA), also in the Canal Zone, joined the counter-insurgency club by offering joint courses with the School of the Americas in such activities as aircraft supply operations for counter-guerrilla forces, airborne operations, etc.

SOUTHCOM also maintains a research arm which devises and tests jungle weapons for use against guerrillas. The U.S. Army Tropic Test Center (TTC) serves both Latin American and Southeast Asian U.S. interests, testing such items as counter-guerrilla surveillance systems using infra-red sensors, counter-infiltration devices using acoustic detectors, and tactical communications equipment. This center was established in Panama in 1962 as part of the Army's Test and Evaluation Command.

Another key element in the Southern Command is the Eighth Special Forces Group, located in Panama. This Green Beret unit is a vast training arm of the Southern Command (one of four such training centers the U.S. Army maintains around the world, the others being in Vietnam, Okinawa, and West Germany) and provides an immediate-response capability for the command. The Special Forces personnel are organized into two dozen Mobile Training Teams (MTTs) of up to thirty men each and are available to be dispatched to a South American country at a moment's notice. According to one journalist who visited Fort Gulick, "the principal mission of the Special Forces is to advise, train, and aid the Latin American military and paramilitary forces to conduct counter-insurgency activities, and to do so in support of the objectives of the United States of America within the framework of the Cold War." [162] In 1965 alone, the Green Beret teams made at least fifty-two incursions into Latin America, including parachute drops into guerrilla zones.[163] Although many Special Forces operations are clandestine, it is known that Green Beret teams have entered most Latin American countries, with the exception of Haiti, Cuba, and Mexico. In 1966 and 1967 the Green Berets aided the Guatemalan Army and even suffered some combat casualties. A Mobile Training Team is known to have been operating in Nicaragua in 1967. Under the direction of Col. Joseph P. Rice (W.P. 1951), head of the Army Mission in Bolivia, and Maj. Robert "Pappy" Shelton, a group of sixteen Green Berets trained a battalion of 600 Bolivians during the summer and winter of 1967. In October 1967, with the help of the CIA, this group was instrumental in capturing and murdering Ernesto Che Guevara and his guerrilla band. (See Gott, 409–483 for a descriptive account of American aid in eliminating Che Guevara.)

Col. Rice had been well trained for his job. In 1962–63 he was a student at the Army Language School in Monterey, California. In 1965 he obtained a Master's degree from American University in foreign-area studies. Rice then participated in the U.S. Army Foreign Area Specialist Training Program in Colombia and went on to Bolivia. It should be noted that Julio Sanjines (ex-W.P. 1945) was the Bolivian Ambassador to the U.S. during this period.

For some high-ranking U.S. Army officers, several schools and commands—SOUTHCOM, the Inter-American Defense College and Board, military missions, teaching West Point cadets—form the strands of a single career. Thus, in 1964–66 Maj. Gen. James D. Alger (W.P. 1935) was commander of the U.S. Southern Command, and in 1967, when promoted to Lieutenant General, he was assigned to Washington, D.C., as head of the Inter-American Defense Board. In 1967–70 Maj. Gen. C. L. Johnson (W.P. 1937) was head of SOUTHCOM, while earlier he had been Army attaché in Mexico City. Gen. Robinson Mather (W.P. 1932), the current commander of U.S. forces in the southern hemisphere, was prepared for this duty by working in the Civil Disturbance Office of the Pentagon, 1968–69. Col. Elery M. Zehner (W.P. 1937) has held several Latin American assignments. In 1950–52 he was part of the U.S. Military Mission to Venezuela, where he aided one Dictator Jiménez, who was finally overthrown by the people in 1958. Col. Zehner then worked in the Pentagon at the Office of the Chief of Civil Affairs and Military Government, 1958–61. Next he flew to Buenos Aires as chief of the Army Mission to Argentina, again aiding a repressive and unrepresentative regime. In 1964–67 he served on the staff and faculty of the Inter-American Defense College. It is interesting to note that the participation of West Pointers in the Inter-American Defense Board and College is not necessarily limited to American graduates. Col. Bey Mario Arosemena (W.P. 1934), Army of Panama, represented his country at the Inter-American Defense Board in the late 1940s.

Several West Pointers have made a career of working with the Green Berets in different parts of the Third World. Col. Eleazar Parmly IV (W.P. 1946) trained with and led the 77th Special Forces Group, Airborne, at Fort Bragg, 1959–60. From there he was assigned to Laos in 1960–61, then to the Department of Tactics at West Point for three years. In 1964 he arrived at the U.S. Southern Command as aide to Gen. Andrew P. O'Meara (W.P. 1930). His next tour of duty was with the Fifth Special Forces Group, Republic of Vietnam, 1966–67. Then, about ready to retire, he became professor of military science at Johns Hopkins University in Baltimore. Lt. Col. Bernard Loeffke, a White House Fellow, worked with the Green Berets in Brazil during the early 1960s and then returned to West Point to teach a foreign language. Maj. Daniel Arthur Smith (W.P. 1960) teaches Spanish to West Point cadets and has also been a Green Beret. Maj. Smith trained with the First Airborne Battle Group at Fort Bragg, 1960–62, and then worked with the Eighth Special Forces Group in the Canal Zone for four years. After attending the Army Infantry School at Fort Benning in 1966, he took his Green Beret talents to South Vietnam, where he joined the Fifth Special Forces Group. Following this hardship tour, he brushed up his Spanish at the University of Madrid in Spain and returned to his alma mater to teach cadets the Spanish language.

The career of Gen. Matthew Ridgway is laden with service in Latin America. He accompanied Gen. Frank McCoy on the Nicaraguan electoral commission of 1928, and then on the Bolivian-Paraguayan Conciliation Commission the following year. During the course of his career he commanded both the Inter-American Defense Board and the U.S. Southern Command. It is from Gen. Ridgway that one gains an appreciation of the curious combination of responsibility and luxury that some of these high-ranking jobs—missions, commands, attaché positions—may be. In a chapter of his memoirs entitled "Panama Idyll" Ridgway describes his duties as commander of SOUTHCOM, 1948–49. "The months I spent in Panama as Commander in Chief, Caribbean, were an idyllic interlude which will long linger in my memory. . . . I needed a few months of rest," wrote Ridgway. " 'Panama' in the aboriginal speech means 'place where the fish abound,' and Penny [Ridgway's wife], who shared my love for fishing for salt-water game fish, soon found that this was no misnomer. We fished for marlin and big sail in the Pearl Islands, eighty miles west of Balboa, and for fine tarpon in the Chagres River, which empties out of Gatun Lake." [164] Of course Ridgway also attended to his official duties. "We had flown to Ecuador," he wrote, "to attend the inauguration of President Galo Plaza, a distinguished gentleman who had been a star football player at the University of California. . . . We were there for fifty-two hours. We must have fished for forty-five of them. We fished for tuna, on light tackle. . . . There were great sailfish in these waters, too." [165]

West Pointers seem to have a lock on certain of these work-filled assignments. In 1964 West Point's alumni magazine, *Assembly,* boasted: "Recently, the Panama Canal celebrated its 50th anniversary. Although the event received appropriate attention in the public press, West Pointers might well have noted that all 13 governors of the Canal Zone during the 50-year period have been USMA graduates. Canal Zone Governors are Presidential appointees, and while the law does not require it, traditionally the men chosen have been Army Engineer officers on active duty. The incumbent is R. J. Fleming Jr. '28." [166] The Lieutenant Governor during 1963–65, David S. Parker (W.P. 1940), had served as assistant to the governor ten years earlier and had also served with the Defense Intelligence Agency in the Pentagon. Col. Harold Robert Parfitt (W.P. 1943), Lieutenant Governor of the Canal Zone 1965–68, had earned a Master of Science in civil engineering at MIT and had been the District Engineer in Jacksonville, Florida. Prior to becoming the Lieutenant Governor, Richard Hartline (W.P. 1945) served as the Chief Engineer Advisor in South Vietnam, 1967–68. And, of course, the House Panama Canal Subcommittee is chaired by Rep. John M. Murphy (W.P. 1950).

Aside from teaching facilities, Green Beret operations, and total control over the Canal Zone, the U.S. Southern Command also supervises U.S. military missions in Latin America. As of July 1, 1970, there were seventeen U.S. missions in Latin America with 505 U.S. personnel and 88 native employees. This includes military missions ranging in size from five personnel in Costa Rica to 102 persons in Brazil. In addition, there were seventeen U.S. employees advising the armies and internal security forces of Nicaragua, 41 persons "helping" in the Dominican Republic, and 44 in Ecuador. These missions—distinct from military attachés on embassy staffs—provide information on how civic action programs may win the peasants away from the guerrillas and advise on the optimal use of the weapons supplied by the United States.

West Pointers, it would be safe to say, have served on most, if not all, of the military missions in Latin America and have filled many of the attaché slots. Col. John B. Stanley (W.P. 1934) was a member of the Mission to Venezuela in 1947–50 and went on to the Office of the Chief of Psychological Warfare, 1951–53. Col. Charles Parsons Nicholas (W.P. 1925), who later became head of the Department of Mathematics at West Point, was military attaché to Venezuela in 1948. Col. Ronan Calistus Grady (W.P. 1943) was in the Mission to Venezuela, 1959–61, and later served as Army attaché at Asunción, Paraguay. Lt. Col. John R. Shaffer (W.P. 1950) was in the Mission to Venezuela in 1965. Col. LeRoy Bartlett (W.P. 1930) served in the Mission to Bolivia before becoming the director of the Nicaraguan military academy in 1944–46. Col. William P. Francisco (W.P. 1940) earned a law degree at the University of Virginia in 1951, studied Spanish at the Defense Language Institute, and then became chairman of the U.S. Military Group in Nicaragua, 1965–69. Christian H. Clarke (W.P. 1930) spent four years as Army attaché in Argentina, two years as attaché in Mexico, and then for two years was commanding general of Fort Jackson, South Carolina. Burton Oliver Lewis (W.P. 1945) served in the Mission to Argentina, 1963–66; Robert W. Tribolet (W.P. 1946) was in the Armed Forces Mission in Argentina, 1964–67; and Paul A. Coughlin (W.P. 1951) spent two years in Argentina in the FAST program (Foreign Area Specialist Training), learning the language and geography of Latin America, and specializes in that field. Col. Trevor Washington Swett (W.P. 1949) has served in the missions to El Salvador and Nicaragua. Maj. David Wilson Patton (W.P. 1955) was advisor to the army of Guatemala in 1968. Academy graduates have served in Honduras, Peru, Colombia—the list is almost endless.

Like a Johnny Appleseed of militarism, the United States has sprinkled West Point seedlings in Latin America. During the 1920s, the U.S. Marines, with the help of Gen. Frank McCoy, established and ran the Nicaraguan military academy. In 1939 this school sprouted into a full-grown Latin West Point—superintended, in fact, by a graduate, Col. Charles Love Mullins (W.P. 1917). The next four superintendents, until 1956, were also West Pointers. The original executive agreement made between the United States and Nicaragua concerning the academy and dated May 22, 1941, is instructive. It reads in part: "The Government of the United States of America shall place at the disposal of the Government of Nicaragua the technical and professional services of an officer of the United States Army as Director of the Military Academy of the National Guard of the Republic of Nicaragua." Article 8 of the agreement provides for the immediate promotion of the assigned officer: "The President and Commander-in-Chief of the Republic of Nicaragua will grant the officer detailed under this agreement the assimilated rank of Brigadier General for the duration of this agreement and said officer shall have precedence over all Nicaraguan officers of the same rank." The agreement stipulated that Col. Mullins "shall be governed by the disciplinary regulations of the U.S. Army," yet "shall be responsible directly and solely to the President and Commander-in-Chief of the Republic of Nicaragua."

With regard to pay, the U.S. Army rented out its soldier: "this officer shall receive from the Government of Nicaragua such net annual compensation expressed in U.S. currency as may be agreed upon between the Government of the United States and the Government of Nicaragua." [167] In 1947, after his graduation from West Point, Anastasio Somoza, our future dictator although then only a colonel, became the superintendent of the Nicaraguan military academy.

Similar executive agreements have been executed between the United States and other Latin American countries. An agreement entitled "Detail of Military Officer to Serve as Director of Polytechnic School of Guatemala" was signed between the United States and Guatemala on May 27, 1941. As with the Nicaraguan agreement, the officer assigned, in this case Lt. Col. Edward L. N. Glass (W.P. 1914), was assigned the rank of brigadier general and was made responsible "solely and directly to the Minister of War of Guatemala." [168] He was paid by the Guatemalan government, yet was a member of the American military and subject to U.S. Army rules and regulations. An agreement was also made with El Salvador for the United States to supply a superintendent for the military school and academy of that country, the American lieutenant colonel to receive from the "Salvadoran Government an annual compensation of One Thousand Eight Hundred and Ten Dollars." [169] Agreements were also made with Argentina for the U.S. to provide military aviation instructors,[170] and with Haiti for American military personnel to "cooperate with the President of Haiti, the Chief of Staff of the Garde d'Haiti, and with the personnel of the Garde d'Haiti with a view to enhancing the Garde d'Haiti." [171] Other military academies have been influenced by West Point and some are as patterned as the W.P. model, notably the military academies of Mexico, Chile, Bolivia, and Paraguay. Others have simply been allotted U.S. military advisors. The West Point model is also exported via West Point cadets. For example, during the summer of their junior year four cadets usually participate in a two-week exchange trip with the Mexican military academy in Mexico City. The young West Pointers spend a few days at the academy and tour Mexico City, and then take a short excursion to Acapulco, where they are wined and dined by U.S.

and Mexican officials and put up at Las Brisas Hotel. In turn, the following month four Mexican cadets travel to the United States and receive the red-carpet treatment in Washington, D.C., and at West Point. All excursions are not annual events, however. In September 1967, for instance, four West Point cadets and the superintendent of the Academy, Maj. Gen. Donald V. Bennett, flew to Santiago, Chile, to participate in a parade and ceremonies honoring the 150th anniversary of the founding of the Chilean Republic. The cadets stayed at the Chilean military academy in Santiago, where they commingled with cadets from a dozen Latin American military academies who were also present for the ceremonies.

No study of U.S. influence in Latin America can be complete without at least a quick look at West Point business interests in the area. In much the same manner that, upon retirement, West Point procurement officers find it lucrative to go into defense-related industry, graduates who have been associated with Latin America often partake of Latin-oriented business upon retirement. Just as their Army duties required them to seek "allies" willing to adjust national laws and policies to meet the requirements of the U.S. military establishment, so does big business ask them to find "client states" willing to adjust to their corporate demands. These demands are aimed at gaining monopolistic control over sources of supply and markets to allow the company to do business on its own terms whenever and wherever it desires. "Trading partners" are not a part of this scheme; "client states" are, and the West Pointer, trained in preventing defections from the military "free world," needs little adjustment to begin preventing defections from the corporate "free world."

The Inter-American Development Bank, located in Washington, D.C., is attractive to retired officers. Col. Roderic Dhu O'Connor (W.P. 1941), part of the U.S. Air Mission to Chile in 1946–49 and air attaché to Venezuela in 1963–66, became the representative of the Inter-American Development Bank in Asunción, Paraguay, in 1968. Lt. Col. Walter James Hutchin (W.P. 1943) was a student at the Army Language School in 1960 and then Army attaché in Honduras before working for the Defense Intelligence Agency. Upon retiring in 1965, Hutchin obtained employment with the Inter-American Development

Bank as an analyst. Herbert Davis Vogel (W.P. 1924) was the Lieutenant Governor of the Canal Zone and vice-president of the Panama Canal Company in 1949–52. He later applied his expertise as an engineer advisor for the World Bank in 1964–68. John Abell Cleveland (W.P. 1933) taught Spanish at West Point as an associate professor from 1948 to 1951 and, upon retirement in 1957, became assistant manager of the Valdez Sugar Company, a firm dealing in Ecuadorean sugar. He is now the U.S. agent for Ecuadorean sugar. Walter Hale Frank (W.P. 1910) retired in 1945 and by 1960 was president for South America of Sears, Roebuck and Company. Caesar Frank Fiore (W.P. 1935) was Army attaché in Spain in 1951–54 and when he retired in 1957 became vice-president for Latin America of Western Union International, located in Balboa, Canal Zone.

Besides bringing West Pointers to Latin America, the Academy encourages Latin Americans to come to West Point. Some ninety foreign cadets have graduated from the U.S. Military Academy, partaking of four years of "education" and then returning to their native countries, usually to assume positions of leadership and influence. The rationale for imbuing foreign cadets with the West Point ethic is perhaps best expressed by the following passage alluding to U.S. military and economic expansion from *Assembly:* "In a world in which the U.S. has constantly increasing responsibilities, our military officers and leaders must make many contacts with foreigners. The problems with which they will be confronted, while serving either at home or abroad, are almost certain to involve many foreign nations, their governments and their civilian nationals as well as their military." [172]

Another reason for admitting foreign cadets was pointed out by Col. Jose Joaquin Jimenez (W.P. 1933), Army of Venezuela, in *Assembly:* "Venezuela, like all the other Latin American countries, has a quota of two foreign cadets at West Point but has been unable to fill the spaces for the past five or six years. We feel it is important that a few of the officers of the Venezuelan Army be West Point graduates and thus be instilled with a strong sense of duty, honor, and dedication to democratic and constitutional government." [173] Better wording for "dedication to democratic and constitutional government" might be "dedication to governments supported by the United States, regardless of character." Col. Jimenez himself writes to *Assembly* that he and other members of the Venezuelan West Point Society "will be constantly striving to support West Point and the Association of Graduates, and to bring before the people and the armed forces of Venezuela the ideals, standards, and dedication to duty that so typify the graduates of West Point." [174] It should be pointed out that from 1948 to 1958 Venezuela was ruled by a ruthless dictator, Pérez Jiménez, his regime complete with prisons, torture chambers, and American aid. President Dwight D. Eisenhower (W.P. 1915) was thoughtful enough to present Dictator Jiménez with the Medal of Freedom on behalf of the American people. In 1948 Col Jose Jimenez, the West Pointer, had served as head of the dictator's military household. Other graduates from Venezuela have served in the Venezuelan armed forces during the rule of President Jiménez, among them Miguel A. Bethancourt Jimenez (W.P. 1953) and Vance S. Brown, Jr. (W.P. 1950). Ramon Benigno Aguilar Sanchez (W P. 1954) has spent much of his career as a teacher or student. He attended the Command and General Staff College in Venezuela, 1961–63, and was an instructor at the Army Supply School in Venezuela, 1963–65. He then became chief of the Academic Department of the Army Engineer School and, later, deputy secretary of the Schools Command of the Venezuelan Army. By 1970 Lt. Col. Aguilar Sanchez was dean of the Armed Forces School in Caracas. Barnabe Ramirez Serrano, Venezuelan cadet (W.P. 1954), and Angel Eduardo Olmeta (W.P. 1960) round out the foreign cadets from the oil republic.

Along with these foreign graduates are a handful of ex-cadets. They are usually dismissed because of language difficulties. For the same reason, perhaps, most foreign cadets graduate near the bottom of their class. An exception is Luis Manalong Mirasol (W.P. 1958), a foreign cadet from the Philippines, who graduated fifteenth in a class of 573. Foreign cadets have come from nearly all countries of Latin America as well as China, Thailand, the Philippine Islands, and, more recently, Spain and South Vietnam. Many foreign cadets upon graduation continue their studies at another school, usually in engineering. Gabriel Jose de La Guardia (W.P. 1945), from Panama, pursued a Master's degree in civil engineering at MIT in 1949 that propelled him in his career as a general agent for Pan American Life Insurance Company in 1959, and later president of the Xerox Corporation of Panama in 1965. Arnoldo Cano Arosemena (W.P. 1967), also from Panama, studied industrial engineering at Virginia Polytechnic Institute, earning a Master's degree in 1969. Joaquin Weber Parez, cadet from Chile, graduated from West Point in 1968 and then began study at Louisiana State University. One foreign cadet from Costa Rica, Jose B. Quiros (W.P. 1957), received a Master's degree in business administration at Columbia University and is now influential in Latin American markets for American Airlines.

The Philippine Islands has sent the largest number of foreign cadets to West Point, about two dozen, beginning with Jaime Velasquez (W.P. 1931), who later, as a colonel, was military attaché at the Philippine Embassy in Washington. Lt. Col. Manuel Quiaoit Salientes (W.P. 1937), of the Philippines, was back "home" in the United States as military attaché of the Philippines in Washington in 1950–52. He later became Undersecretary for Defense in the Philippine government. Brig. Gen. Rafael Ileto (W.P. 1943) is currently Deputy Chief of the Philippine Armed Forces. The Philippine military academy, established, of course, by American West Pointers, has been dominated by Philippine West Pointers. Pastor Martelino (W.P. 1920) was president from 1937 to 1941. After the war Pedro FlorCruz (W.P. 1942) helped reestablish the academy and welcomed Rafael L. Garcia (W.P. 1916) as its new leader. In 1946 Tirso G. Fajardo (W.P. 1934) took over and was joined a year later by Antonio P. Chanco (W.P. 1938) as commandant of cadets. Fajardo remained at the academy until a few years ago, when he became chief of staff of the Philippine Army. Chanco retired in 1958 to become vice-president of the Philippine division of the Vinnell Corp.

Several Philippine West Pointers have had the opportunity to rub elbows with their American classmates on the Vietnam battlefield. In 1965, trained, equipped, and paid by the U.S. government, the Philippine Islands "volunteered" a combat division for Vietnam. The ranks of the Philippine battalions hired to put the Vietnamese in their place included Ramon M. Ong (W.P. 1963), who later had the opportunity to explain his experiences to eager cadets during a tour in the Mechanics Department at West Point. Lt. Col. Fidel Valdez Ramos (W.P. 1950) joined Ong in Vietnam and was placed in charge of operations for the Philippine Civic Action Group. Prior to Vietnam duty, Lt. Col. Ramos was chairman of the Committee on Unconventional Warfare, Headquarters, Armed Forces of the Philippines, and had been the commanding officer of the First Special Forces Company in the Islands. After his Vietnam tour, Ramos became military aide to the President of the Philippines and is now Deputy Chief of Staff for Home Defense Activities, supervising, nationwide, the non-combat aspects of counter-insurgency and counter-subversion.

Other foreign graduates have also proven useful to the U.S. in Southeast Asia. At least seven West Pointers, beginning with Camron Sudasna (W.P. 1930), have been Thai citizens. Sudasna rose to be commandant of the Command and General Staff College of the Royal Thai Army and was later advisor to the Thai Ministry of Defense. The Class of 1932 boasts two Thai nationals: Brig. Gen. Bun Mar Praband sought advanced West Point education at the Command and General Staff College in the U.S. and later became Chief of Engineers of the Thai Army; Mom Laung Chuan Chuen Kambhu (W.P. 1932) retired in 1955 as a colonel in the Thai Army and became director general of the Thai Economic Relations Department with a Wall Street address. The most illustrious graduate is Manob Suriya (W.P. 1937), who rose to be Air Marshal of the Thai Air Force.

West Point's earliest imperial emphasis, however, appears to have been with cadets from China. Two graduates from the Class of 1909 returned to their native land of China and rose to positions of considerable influence. One of these, Ying Wen, reached the rank of lieutenant general of the Nationalist Chinese Army and was the commanding officer of the Revenue Guard which fought Mao Tse-tung and the Japanese. These forces later became the new "First Army" of China under the leadership of Chiang Kai-shek. From 1946 to 1951 Ying Wen was a senator in the Nationalist Chinese government. He died in 1968 in Silver Spring, Maryland. The other Chinese member of the Class of 1909, Ting Chia Chen, graduated last in a class of 103, but by 1931 had risen to the rank of major general in the

Chinese Army. In 1918 Linson Edward Dzau, born in China, graduated from West Point. In 1922–26 he was professor of military science and commandant at Tsing Hua University. He later became advisor to Marshal Chang Tso-lin and counselor to the Ministry of War and the General Staff. He resigned as a major general in 1928 and began a career in education by becoming headmaster of Linson College in Formosa. In 1941–45 Tao Hung Chang (W.P. 1924) was Finance Minister of the Chinese government and later worked in the Ministry of Agriculture in Shanghai. Another major general in the Nationalist Chinese Army and West Pointer, Chih Wang (W.P. 1932), is military counselor and secretary to President Chiang Kai-shek. Aside from their extensive military connections, some Chinese West Pointers have been active in business. One of these, Posheng Yen (W.P. 1937), was Chinese consul-general in Rangoon in 1938–40 and in 1946 became Chinese consul in New York City. By 1956 he had become a senior engineer with Western Electric.

Asian business connections have proven quite lucrative for several old grads. D. W. Samuelson (W.P. 1951) was Senior Counsel–Far East for International Telephone and Telegraph in 1967 (he is now a vice-president); the former commanding general of the Army Matériel Command, Ferdinand J. Chesarek (W.P. 1938), has considerable interests in land and apartments in the non-U.S. Pacific area; and Maj. Gen. James E. Landrum (W.P 1936), the former head of Army Information and Data Systems, is now Director of Pacific Requirements for Computer Planning Corp. Individual Asian countries all have their quota of West Point businessmen capitalizing on the war, and a few names from Thailand will illustrate their diversity of interest: John H. Ruth (W.P. 1959) is managing director of Thai Ltd. (John Deere equipment); in 1968 Joseph W. Benson (W.P. 1943) was "Mr. Philco-Ford" in Bangkok and his boss was Peter S. Tanous (W.P. 1941), Manager of International Activities; and Charles Van Way (W.P. 1924) recently returned from a stay in Bangkok as consultant to the Thanaloai Business School, where he might well have been entertained by Mom L. C. C. Kambhu, who has given up his Wall Street office and is now managing director of the Jalapranthan Cement Co. in

Bangkok. As one of his classmates notes, Kambhu is doing quite well: "Johnny Kambhu (M. L. Chuan Chuen Kambhu is his formal name) sent me a copy of the Jalapranthan Cement Co., Ltd, of which concern he is Managing Director. You should see the list of Directors: GENs, LTGs, doctors with names unpronounceable to me. Two of them seem somewhat familiar. They are listed as Mr. J. M. Garoutte and Mr. Nick P. Petroff —likely French and Russian. He also sent a copy of the supplement of the Bangkok *Post* with front page pictures including His Majesty, the King, alighting from a yacht to the pier of the factory, plus his unveiling the cover over the company's sign, plus our Kambhu escorting His Majesty on a tour of the plant and another of Her Majesty Queen Rambhai Phanee of the late King Rama VII escorted by our classmate enroute to perform the anointing ceremony for the new cement carrier, 'M. L. Xujati' christened in honor and commemoration of the late M. L. Xujati Kambhu, one of the prominent promoters and developers of the company. The similarity of names indicates a relationship to our classmate. Very interesting contribution, Johnny, and we thank you and wish you continued success. I wish there were room to fully cover this event which was represented worldwide by advertisements of Japanese, Chinese, Swedish, German, and American concerns—the latter to include Goodyear, Westinghouse, and Otis Elevator. Advice—if you go to Bangkok and get in a jam, just tell them you know Kambhu." [175]

Panama, Costa Rica, and Venezuela boast the most Latin contributors to West Point. Five members of the prestigious Alfaro family of Ecuador and Panama have attended West Point; three graduated and two became ex-cadets. Richard J. Alfaro, born in 1882, did not attend West Point, but rose to be President of Panama, 1931–32. In 1936 he negotiated a treaty with the United States on modifications in the terms of the Panama Canal agreement and later helped rewrite the Panamanian Constitution. He represented Panama at the first United Nations conference in San Francisco and served as Ambassador to the U.N. from Panama. He was also an honorary member of the American Bar Association. It was probably not too difficult, then, to have a son and another relative appointed to West Point: Olmedo Alfaro, ex-cadet, Class of 1904, and Colon Eloy

Alfaro, ex-cadet, Class of 1913. Although he didn't make it to graduation, Colon Eloy Alfaro rose to positions of prestige in his government. In 1928 he accompanied U.S. President Herbert Hoover on his visit to Ecuador and was later involved in a number of other diplomatic missions and assignments. The *Who's Who* of Panama, *Quien es Quien,* lists Colon Eloy Alfaro as special minister to Mexico (twice), Nicaragua, Costa Rica, Cuba, Colombia, the Dominican Republic, and the United States (1933–36). From 1936 to 1944 Colon E. Alfaro was Ecuadorean (not Panamanian) Ambassador to the United States. He was then representative of Ecuador in the Pan American Union, 1947–48, and was on an Inter-American economic consultative committee in Washington, D.C., soon thereafter. At the same time he was director of a major shipping company of Ecuador and was listed as a member of the Bankers Club of New York, the Golf Club of Panama, and the Army-Navy Country Club in Washington. For these services he was awarded a presidential medal from Nicaragua and a Liberty Medal from the United States.

This eminent ex-cadet sent all three of his sons to West Point: Eloy and Jaime Eduardo Alfaro graduated in 1939, and Olmedo Alfaro in 1942. Following in their father's footsteps, these three brothers have been influential in Ecuador, Panama, and other parts of Latin America. Eloy Alfaro became aide to the President of Ecuador in 1942 and accompanied him on a tour of the U.S. and Latin American countries. Eloy, like his father, is a member of the Golf Club of Panama and the Army-Navy Country Club in Washington. The three brothers control and operate the Alfaro Company of Panama, Eloy as president and Jaime Eduardo and Olmedo as vice-presidents. Eloy is also director-general of the Eloy Alfaro International Foundation. The Alfaros are also familiar with William C. Westmoreland: "Among his [Westmoreland's] additional chores during that year [1936] had been escorting visiting dignitaries about the academy, and among them had been the Alfaro family, most conspicuous political lineage in Ecuador. Several Alfaro sons had been West Point cadets. In appreciation for the hospitality, the family invited Westmoreland and a few other outstanding cadets to Ecuador as guests of the government. The Spanish he had studied as a first classman was hardly enough to enable Westy to see the country without a guide, but that mattered little, for the proud young officers were made to feel as if just graduating made them heroes. The Quito newspapers ran long articles about where they came from, what they looked like and what they said." [176] Westy stayed for two months.

Also influential in Panama, though to a far lesser extent than the Alfaros, is the Arosemena family. Bey Mario Arosemena graduated from West Point in 1934 and his son Arnoldo Cano in 1967. The elder Arosemena obtained a Master of Science in sanitary engineering at Harvard and served on the Inter-American Defense Board as a colonel in the Panamanian Army. In 1944 he became general manager of Clay Products, Inc., in Panama. His son studied for a Master's degree in industrial engineering and, as of 1970, was an industrial engineer for the Panama Canal Company in the Canal Zone (governed, remember, by a West Pointer). There are yet other Panamanian graduates. Diego Alonso Jimenez (W.P. 1951) was manager of a large bank in Panama (Cia Nacional de Seguros) in 1965. Julio E. Heurtematte (W.P. 1957), born in Costa Rica but listed as a foreign cadet from Panama, is an assistant to the executive vice-president of the Inter-American Development Bank. In 1970 he became chief of the bank's loan area. One foreign cadet from the class of 1961, Dominador Bazan, obtained a Master's degree in civil engineering from Stanford in 1962 and now works for a construction company in Panama, Ingenieria Caribe. A more recent graduate, Hermogenes Derek de la Rosa Perigault (W.P. 1966), studied at Carnegie Tech and is now a communications engineer with the Tropical Radio Telex Company.

Some seven foreign cadets are citizens of Costa Rica. The first such graduate is Teodoro Picado, Jr. (W.P. 1951), who upon graduation became aide-de-camp to the chief of staff of the Campo de Marta, the Costa Rican police. Costa Rica's police force substitutes for the more typical Latin American army in matters of domestic control. Picado resigned in 1954, having attained the rank of captain, and became general manager of a textile company in Nicaragua, the land of fellow alumnus Somoza. Jose Rafael Gonzalez Lutz (W.P. 1965) earned a Master's degree in electrical engineering at Catholic University, became a mechanical engineer of the Holderbank Technical Center in Switzerland, and finally a project engineer in Costa Rica.

Another dozen West Pointers hail from Central America. Four Guatemalans graduated in the 1950s and 1960s, and one of these, Oscar Morales Duvall (W.P. 1952), taught at the Guatemalan military academy and rose to be vice-chairman of the Guatemalan Army in 1966. In preparation, he was the air attaché to the Embassy of Guatemala in Washington. Another, Luis Arturo Getella (W.P. 1963), was part of the President's Guard of Guatemala. There are two foreign cadets from Honduras, one of whom, Hugo Enrique Elvir (W.P. 1966), worked as an engineer in the Ministry of Communication and Public Works in Tegucigalpa, Honduras, before going into private enterprise. In Ecuador, Raul Alejandro Roca (W.P. 1947) is general manager of Forhans-Zonite of Mexico. During the repressive Batista regime, Cuba sent two foreign cadets to West Point: Arthur Emil Gay (W.P. 1946) and Francisco Roberto Prieto y Castro (W.P. 1953). Gay was in the export business in Latin America until his death in 1958. Prieto y Castro became a project engineer with M. Chinchilla Varona and Associates in Miami Beach, Florida.

There are also Academy graduates from South American countries, though not nearly in such numbers as from Central America. Luis Pinillos Montero of Peru is an ex-cadet from the Class of 1951. He studied agronomy at Cornell, 1949–52, and in 1960 began managing his own plantation in Pisco, Peru, became president of Public Works for the State of Ica, Peru, and, all the while, remained a captain in the Peruvian reserve army. Marcial David Samaniego (W.P. 1962) from Paraguay taught at the Paraguayan military academy in Asunción for four years after graduation from West Point, and later studied at Texas A&M. In 1969 Onofre Torres of Colombia graduated from West Point. Since 1962 four Chilean cadets have graduated from the Academy. One of them, Ricardo Enrique Cesped Doering (W.P. 1962), is a project engineer for Kaiser Engineers in Oakland, California. In 1970 a cadet from Spain graduated, and in 1973 the first cadet from South Vietnam will receive his diploma.

The end result of these schools, advisory groups, military missions, and business connections is a tight network of control that sometimes becomes entangled in itself. Interestingly enough, when insurrection broke out in 1962 in Guatemala, both sides had received military training at the U.S. guerrilla-warfare school at Fort Gulick in the Canal Zone. Interviewed on February 14, 1962, President Ydigoras, dictator of the republic, stated: "One of our great difficulties is that both sides have been trained in the same tactics by the same experts. Our commanders are very smart, but the rebels are very smart too." [177] One of the rebel leaders, Lt. Turcios Lima, had attended the military academy of Guatemala and soon thereafter, as a second lieutenant in the Guatemalan army, was sent to the U.S. Ranger School at Fort Benning, Georgia. Asked about his U.S. training, he replied that "from the military point of view it was very good." Later he explained the "non-military" view: "We had the officers' club, 15-ounce Texas steaks, good clothes, the best equipment, plenty of money, too; every month I sent $150 to my mother. What worries did I have?" [178] Despite his best efforts and the training, Lima's guerrilla operations were short-lived—primarily because he could not avoid the efforts of the men who had trained him. According to Richard Gott, an authority on guerrilla movements in Latin America, "It seemed improbable that the Guatemalan army could have dealt with the guerrillas so speedily had it not been for [Green Beret] outside assistance." [179]

The U.S. has reaped considerable benefits from Nicaragua and, likewise, Nicaragua from the United States. Gen. Tachito Somoza, President of the Republic, can always be counted on to praise U.S. interventionist policy and to help in any other manner possible. Thus, in 1954, while director of the Nicaraguan military academy and head of the armed forces of Nicaragua, he aided Castillo-Armas in the overthrow of the Arbenz regime in Guatemala—American pilots flying in support of Castillo-Armas departed from the Managua International Airport. During a lull in activities of the "Liberation Army" of Castillo-Armas, Gen. Tacho Somoza, Tachito's father, invited Miguel

Ydigoras Fuentes, who later became President of Guatemala, to lunch. Noticing that the Liberation Army was advancing on Arbenz only very slowly, Somoza asked: "What kind of crummy military school did Castillo-Armas go to?" Ydigoras replied, "The same one I did." [180] Both had attended the Guatemalan military academy. Castillo-Armas had also spent two years at the U.S. Army Command and General Staff College at Fort Leavenworth.

In 1961, during the Bay of Pigs fiasco, Tacho Somoza generously offered Puerto Cabezas, Nicaragua, as the disembarking point for the Cuban exile forces, and it was from there that the exiles left for the Cuban shores.[181] Somoza Jr. is consistently counseling other Latin nations on the U.S.-style perils of Communism, helping to spread the military mentality and reality, and all the while holding his millions (dollars and people) close to his bosom. As insurance for the future Somoza has Frank J. Kelly (W.P. 1963) following in his footsteps. After graduation Kelly served as secretary to the President of the Republic, and is now secretary/chairman of the Nicaraguan armed forces. As more insurance, a younger Nicaraguan, Maximiliano Bozco Kelly, recently graduated from—need it be said—West Point.

For some persons, usually West Pointers, contemporary American influence in Latin America is not complete. From a recent issue of *Assembly:* "A recent letter to the secretary asked for assistance in locating a graduate who might be interested in helping to found a privately owned military preparatory school on the outskirts of the capital city of Panama." [182]

All these West Pointers spending all their time keeping America "secure" could very well prompt Nixon to call them "true Americans," but, as such, they have "security" plans so secure that even the Congress isn't aware of them, although some members would like to be. In August 1971 President Nixon invoked executive privilege to prevent the Senate Foreign Relations Committee from obtaining the programmed future funding of the Pentagon's Military Assistance Program (MAP). Maj. Gen. Edward M. Flanagan (W.P. 1943), however, knows how much money is to be used for military "assistance." At that time commander of the JFK Center for Military Assistance, he was in a good position to know how much it costs to enforce a "generation of peace." The Military Assistance Program is an integral part of U.S. collective-security arrangements and a "vital instrument of foreign policy." Military Assistance Advisory Groups (MAAG) see that the MAP money is spent wisely. On Formosa, where runways have been lengthened to accommodate the B-52s soon to be displaced from Okinawa, the MAAG commander is Maj. Gen. Livingston N. Taylor, Jr. (W.P. 1939). In Ethiopia, a key link in the Pentagon's worldwide communications system, Brig. Gen. John W. Collins III (W.P. 1943) oversees America's military aid as well as the activities of the Special Forces. Domestic criticism of another Vietnam occurring in Cambodia effectively prevents the Department of Defense from sending a MAAG mission there, but in its place Brig. Gen. Theodore Metaxis commands a Military Equipment Delivery Team (MEDT) with fifty-nine men in Pnom Penh and sixty-three in Saigon. Periodically, Brig. Gen. Metaxis and his subordinates travel in the countryside to determine that MAP material is being "properly used." In most countries there is one military man assigned for every $1 million provided by the Military Assistance Program. In Cambodia, then, the total should be 185, and it may not be long before there is a PX in Pnom Penh along with a full-fledged Military Assistance Command–Cambodia. Advice for businessmen wishing to sell to this new PX can be obtained from the former head of the Army Air Force Exchange System, Harlan C. Parks (W.P. 1929), who is president of a counseling service for businesses selling to the worldwide PX arrangement. Another possibility is the president of Military Purchase Systems, Inc., William A. Fio Rito (W.P. 1953).

Headquarters Command, United States Air Force, logistically supports the MAAG and MEDT missions throughout the world. HEDCOM's responsibilities extend from its central headquarters at Bolling Air Force Base, Washington, to more than 800 worldwide locations from Saudi Arabia to Taiwan. HEDCOM's commander is Maj. Gen. Nils O. Ohman (W.P. 1937). Other organizations supported by HEDCOM's special-activities units include the North Atlantic Treaty Organization (NATO), the North American Air Defense Command (NORAD), the

U.S. Strike Command (STRICOM), the Pacific Command (PACOM), the Federal Aviation Administration (FAA), the Defense Supply Agency (DSA), the Defense Intelligence Agency (DIA), and the Defense Atomic Support Agency (DASA). Ohman's command is also responsible for the First Composite Wing at Andrews Air Force Base, Maryland, which controls the Airborne Command Post of the Joint Chiefs of Staff and Nixon's *Air Force One*. In 1968 Ohman's HEDCOM assumed command of the Civil Air Patrol–USAF, its fifty-two wings, and its volunteer membership of 73,000. Gen. Ohman has been far-sighted enough to see that CAP offers "a comprehensive aerospace education and youth motivation program for its 36,000 teen-age cadet members." [183]

At home in the United States, West Pointers have the key command positions sewed up. The Continental Army, commanded by Gen. Ralph E. Haines, Jr. (W.P. 1935), is responsible for four separate armies and the Military District of Washington (MDW). Command of MDW was given to Maj. Gen. Roland M. Gleszer (W.P. 1940), who used to work for Westmoreland at the Academy. Three of the four continental armies are commanded by graduates:

First Army	Hq, Fort Meade, Md.	Lieut. Gen. Claire E. Hutchin, Jr. (W.P. 1938)
Third Army	Hq, Fort McPherson, Ga.	Lieut. Gen. Albert O. Connor (W.P. 1937)
Sixth Army	Hq, Presidio, San Francisco, Calif.	Lieut. Gen. Alexander D. Surles, Jr. (W.P. 1937)

In addition to these armies, there are two continentally based strategic forces with worldwide striking capability under the command of Gen. J. L. Throckmorton (W.P. 1935), Commander-in-Chief, U.S. Strike Command. Lt. Gen. George P. Seneff, Jr. (W.P 1941), commands one of them, the III Armored Corps. The other, the XVIII Airborne Corps, settled the Dominican Republic problem under Gen. Bruce Palmer (W.P. 1936) and can now be airlifted by C-5A to almost any trouble spot in the "free" world. Lt. Gen. John H. Hay, a non-grad, recently succeeded Lt. Gen. John J. Tolson III (W.P. 1937) as commander. Maj. Gen. William B. Latta (W.P. 1938) serves both these units with his Strategic Communications Command.

The group within the Army that has been most heavily dominated by West Pointers throughout history is the Corps of Engineers. The corps legitimately traces its beginnings back to the days of exploring, mapping, and conquering Indians in the West, and it takes full credit for the opening of this new empire: "These things were all accomplished by the application of America's greatest power. That is the power of Engineering Character, Engineering Leadership, and Engineering Knowledge. All employed to fulfill our destiny." [184] The direct descendants of the West Pointers who are at the heart of this slightly chauvinistic appraisal control the corps today. Lt. Gen. F. J. Clarke (W.P. 1937) is currently Chief of Engineers, and all but one of the seven generals on his staff are fellow grads. These men and roughly 200 other officers in the civil-works section of the corps control over 40,000 full-time civilian employees and projects totaling $13.5 billion in cost. Their mission is explained by Lt. Gen. Clarke: "With our country growing the way it is, we cannot simply sit back and let nature take its course." [185] To this end, the corps straightens rivers, builds dams, digs canals, and, in general, seeks to introduce military order and stability into the natural environment. The catalogue of their misadventures is enormous and has led Justice William O. Douglas to term the corps "public enemy number one." [186] Senator Gaylord Nelson has added, "The Corps of Engineers is like that marvelous little creature, the beaver, whose instinct tells him every fall to build a dam wherever he finds a trickle of water. But at least he has a purpose—to store up some food underwater and create a livable habitat for the long winter. Like the Corps, this little animal frequently builds dams he doesn't need, but at least he doesn't ask the taxpayer to foot the bill." [187] In the same vein, a writer concerned about corps projects in Alaska wrote, "As any small boy knows, the presence of running water is a compelling reason to build a dam. Most boys when they grow up turn to other things, but a select few go on to join the U.S. Army Corps of Engineers." [188] With such criticism and a publicly stated disdain for the ecological effects of their work—"This business of ecology, we're concerned, but people don't know enough about it to give good advice. You have to stand still and study life cycles, and we don't have time" [189] (Director of Civil Works Maj. Gen. F. P. Koisch '42) —how does the corps continue getting its massive amounts of money? Former Governor Leslie A. Miller of Wyoming provides the simple answer: "The Corps is undoubtedly the most powerful lobbying and pressure group in the Government today." [190]

The corps begins to sound like a conspiracy, but is not. The leaders are quite honest and aboveboard; the real difficulty is that they are West Point engineers. Steeped as they are in technique, they see all questions as "problems" to be solved in a straight-line, machine-like fashion. The anesthetic qualities of the technological approach along with their Academy education totally insulates them from the human and lifelike aspects of the "problem." Brig. Gen. R. H. Groves (W.P. 1945), Deputy Director of Civil Works, explains: ". . . our nation is engaged in a struggle to survive its technology and its habits. It is a fact, too, that we are defiling our waters, polluting our air, littering our land, and infecting our soil and ourselves with the wastes which our civilization produces. These are serious problems, but we cannot permit ourselves to yield to an emotional impulse that would make their cure the central purpose of our society. Nor is there any reason why we should feel guilty about the alterations which we have to make in the natural environment as we meet our water-related needs." [191] This triumph of technique has led to such Corps-sponsored projects as the $50-million Cross-Florida Barge Canal, of which one writer said: "I looked at a flood-control map of central and southern Florida, it showed in garish red and green the existing and proposed networks of canals, levees, dams, pumping stations and control centers with which the Engineers are transforming all the bottom of the state. It [the map] is an uncaring and terrifying symbol of the triumph of the Engineers and the rape of America." [192] After a long struggle by conservationists, this project was canceled, but the corps did not lose the battle for lack of West Pointers in Florida—the Division Engineer for the area is Maj. Gen. Richard H. Free (W.P. 1940); Col. Avery S. Fullerton (W.P. 1949) commands the Engineer District from Jacksonville (12 of the 17 division chiefs and 24 of the

37 district heads around the world are grads—14 of the district heads are from the Class of 1950 alone); William F. Powers (W.P. 1932) is the general manager of the Florida Intra-coastal Waterway, and came to the job after presiding over the cost-plagued construction of the JFK Center for the Performing Arts as Executive Director of Engineering; and Giles L. Evans (W.P. 1937) is the manager of the Florida Canal Authority. The canal was definitely a family project.

One of the major benefits of serving in the Corps is the jobs that present themselves on retirement. If the conscientious officer can't develop lucrative contacts for the future while building his dams, he can always find them within the Society of American Military Engineers (SAME), one of whose aims is to "foster and develop relations of helpful interest between the engineering profession in civil life and that in the military service." Eighty percent of the 25,000 members of SAME are civilians, but the leadership is dominated by active-duty or retired West Pointers: the full-time executive secretary is William C. Hall (W.P. 1931), the president is Maj. Gen. Guy H. Goddard (W.P. 1941), the treasurer is Charles G. Holle (W.P. 1920), and six of the ten members of the executive committee are graduates, as are four of the eleven vice-presidents-at-large and three of the five regional vice-presidents. The sustaining members of SAME include some of the largest engineering firms in the world: Bechtel Corp. (two West Pointers—a vice-president and a past president of Canadian operations); Sver-drup & Parcel & Associates (a vice-president); Peter Kiewit Sons' Co. (a vice-president); Ralph M. Parsons Co. (a vice-president); Vinnell Corp. (a vice-president); Kaiser Engineers (Project Manager, England); Tumpane Co. (Assistant to the President); and Pacific Architects and Engineers (Contract Manager—Vietnam; General Manager—Greece; Chief of Management Review and Audit—U.S.). Scores of additional grads work for these and other firms, among them the former Chairman of the Tennessee Valley Authority and Engineer Advisor to the World Bank Herbert D. Vogel (W.P. 1924); he and his classmate Peyton F. McLamb, former vice-president of the First National City Bank of New York, are both board members of Planning and Development Collaborative International. Washington, D.C., subway construction has also attracted its share, as these quotes from *Assembly* illustrate: "Tom [McManus, W.P. 1927] was a low bidder (utilities) on the D.C. subway system . . . perhaps Tom and son James can really get the District subway project out of its long-time low gear!" [193] "Bud and Helen Buehler [W.P. 1934] may soon be making a visit to D.C. as Bud's division of Bechtel Corp. successfully negotiated a contract to provide Project Management for the D.C. Metropolitan Transit Project (Man, they need it). A real accolade for Bud." [194] "Will [Wilhoyt, W.P. 1937] will hold one of the major positions in the D.C. Metro construction agency and, judging from the many problems the company is having getting the huge task underway, he has a tremendous job ahead of him." [195] The opportunities for economic incest in the tight little world of West Point engineers are many and varied, and it's back to Florida for an example. Herbert C. Gee (W.P. 1935) and his firm of Gee and Jenson were consulting engineers on the new Disneyworld complex in Orlando, along with Robert S. Palmer (W.P. 1937), who handled similar chores for Howard, Needles, Tammen, & Bergendoff. The man who brought these two to Orlando was the president of Disneyworld, William Potter (W.P. 1928).

From the atomic bomb to the fantasies of Walt Disney, West Point engineers have been in on it all, but their secret for "success" remains unrevealed. A hint, however, is contained in the following quote from the SAME magazine, *The Military Engineer*: "The engineer is . . . especially qualified to understand and to help others understand the great fundamental truth which is being ignored in human affairs today: that there are similar fixed and unchanging principles governing human nature and human relations in life on this planet." [196] One must wonder whether this "great fundamental truth" is a differential or a quadratic equation.

The West Point elite understands the importance of controlling the indoctrination system that precedes high positions and ensures that its graduates control the Army's key school networks. The two important schools or "tickets" for senior Army officers are the Army War College, at Carlisle Barracks, Pennsylvania, commanded by Maj. Gen. George S. Eckhardt (W.P. 1935),

and the Command and General Staff College at Fort Leavenworth, Kansas, commanded by Maj. Gen. John J. Hennessey
(W.P. 1944). At these schools, officers from the U.S. Army and
more than thirty foreign countries learn to do it by the book,
the West Point book. It is, of course, easier to indoctrinate a
seventeen- or eighteen-year-old, and West Pointers will never
relinquish control of their alma mater on their own. Since 1812
every superintendent, every commandant, and every dean of
academics has been a graduate. By making no move to change
this policy, West Point can perpetuate itself and its institutional
values forever. Since its founding in 1956 the Air Force Academy
too has been controlled by West Pointers. The current superintendent is Lt. Gen. Albert P. Clark (W.P. 1936), and the
commandant is Brig. Gen. Walter T. Calligan (W.P. 1945).
West Pointers will continue to indoctrinate the young air cadets
until Air Force Academy graduates have an opportunity to
consolidate their own protective association. But even then a
West-Point-type mentality will continue to boss America's air
power.

Gen. John D. Ryan (W.P. 1938) replaced Gen. John P.
McConnell (W.P. 1932) as Chief of Staff of the Air Force in
1969. His service accounts for the expenditure of more funds
than any other single government agency. The comptroller who
ensures that this wealth is properly distributed is none other than
a fellow graduate, Lt. Gen. Duward L. Crow (W.P. 1941).
Much of this money goes to keep the Strategic Air Command on
twenty-four-hour "defensive alert." These front-line troops operate from a three-story underground control room surrounded by
an exterior ramp and walls of concrete and reinforced steel
twenty-four inches thick. If necessary, it could be sealed off for
weeks to ensure survival (of the SAC generals and staff). In
the event of atomic attack, most of SAC's 450 B-52 bombers
and their nuclear bombs could be airborne in minutes. Should
the SAC underground headquarters be a target of sabotage, flying ready is the SAC airborne command post, *Looking Glass,*
named perhaps for the Alice-in-Wonderland nature of SAC's
mission and its commander, Gen. Bruce K. Holloway (W.P.
1937). SAC crews are the most proficient in the Free World:
in fact, four of Holloway's B-52s recently brought home the

little-known but nonetheless coveted Blue Steel Trophy for the best bombing team in RAF Strike Command competition. His SAC team compiled 1,531 points—177 more than the second-place team! [197]

Holloway finds it difficult to understand how America's defense team with its high standards of excellence can come under such bitter attack by the news media. On March 23, 1971, he voiced his criticism to a closed-door session of the House Appropriations Subcommittee: "One of the things that has bugged me," the four-star general said, "is the vast amount of information over television and other instant news media that, one way or another, in my judgment is a disservice to the security of the country." He suggested it was a matter of "outright efforts, perhaps, to give an erroneous picture. . . . One thing that would be as valuable as anything I could think of right now today for the American people and the security of the country," Holloway testified, "is a national information program, such as every week a half-hour program that would treat some critical problem of the country, starting out with the defense issues." To give the program "impact," Holloway suggested that if the "material" could be declassified it "would serve tremendously" to give it "authenticity." Demonstrating his astuteness in public relations, he added that "you would have to have the President starting it off with a thirty-second introduction." The general also said the program should provide "entertainment," but, unfortunately, he did not elaborate.[198]

Coming on top of the Justice Department's efforts to prevent publication of the Pentagon Papers and the government's attempts to cite CBS for contempt in regard to the controversial documentary "The Selling of the Pentagon," Holloway drew fire from both the left and the right. Humbled but undaunted, the general returned to his task of modernizing his 1,000 Minuteman missiles with the addition of 550 Minuteman IIIs capable of carrying Multiple Independently-targeted Reentry Vehicles (MIRV) and overseeing SAC's secondary and conventional missions. Holloway sees to it that all Air Force fighters, bombers, and reconnaissance aircraft are refueled, and it is under his direction that waves of B-52s, each carrying thirty tons of 500- and 750-pound bombs, bomb three Southeast Asian countries daily. His efforts have contributed substantially to the more than five million bomb craters in that area of the world, making parts of it look like that other great American strategic objective, the moon. Holloway should stick to these humanitarian functions and let his fellow graduates, like Paul W. Thompson (W.P. 1929), vice-chairman of the eminently fair *Reader's Digest,* worry about informing the public of the truth. If Thompson needs help with a balky citizenry, Stephen R. Hanmer (W.P. 1931), former administrator of Radio Free Europe, James Patterson (W.P. 1944), vice-president and assistant managing editor of the New York *News,* Charles J. Windsor (ex-cadet, W.P. 1961), promotion manager for *True* Magazine, Ben Schemmer (W.P. 1954), president and publisher of the *Journal of the Armed Forces,* or Peter J. Foss (W.P. 1951), who handled the press relations for the My Lai trials, would all surely be glad to come to his assistance. The way these gentlemen can come together to present the proper image is illustrated by a book called *West Point: The Men and Times of the United States Military Academy,* published in 1969 and written by an academy apologist named Thomas J. Fleming. His Acknowledgments tell the story: "The same generous spirit of cooperation was displayed by Lieutenant General Leslie Groves, head of the Association of Graduates, who first approached me with the possibility of writing a biography of Sylvanus Thayer, an idea that broadened into this full-scale history of the Academy. . . . For editorial counsel I wish to thank Fulton Oursler, Jr., and Hobart Lewis of the *Reader's Digest,* who not only provided the funds that sustained this project but also devoted many thoughtful hours to helping me shape the manuscript. . . ." With these revealing facts behind him, Fleming forges ahead and adds: "I wish to make it clear that in the best West Point tradition I take full responsibility for everything—facts as well as judgments—in this attempt to see West Point in the context of the American experience." [199] Sure, Tom.

Gen. Holloway will receive the new B-1 bomber by the late Seventies. His classmate Gen. George S. Brown (W.P. 1941) is now working on that along with all other Air Force modernization marvels. "Within the Department of Defense today, there is one technology program which truly stands out with the potential to make a profound and lasting impact on military operations. This technology advancement, the high-energy gas laser, is of great national significance." [200]—Gen. Brown. He commands the Air Force Systems Command (AFSC) and is responsible for "developing and producing modern aerospace systems, weapons and equipment ranging from microcircuits to missiles and bombers, . . . from advanced fiber composite materials to air superiority fighters, . . . from computers to command and control networks to space foods and space satellites." [201] Gen. Brown's command directs the expenditure of 28 percent of the Air Force budget and administers contracts having a total face value of about $42 billion.[202] Where does this money go?

I have a few new marvels here I'd like to discuss with you just briefly. A few new marvels that are just about ready to be gaped at by the admiring layman. Consider for instance the area of realtime online computer-controlled wish evaporation. Wish evaporation is going to be crucial in meeting the rising expectations of the world's peoples, which are as you know rising entirely too fast. . . . The development of the pseudo-ruminant stomach for underdeveloped peoples is one of our interesting things you should be interested in. With the pseudo-ruminant stomach they can chew cuds, that is to say eat grass. . . . We could, of course, release thousands upon thousands of self-powered crawling-along-the-ground lengths of titanium wire eighteen inches long with a diameter of .0005 centimeters (that is to say, invisible), which, scenting an enemy, climb up his trouser leg and wrap themselves around his neck. We have developed those. They are within our capabilities. We could, of course, release in the arena of the upper air our new improved pufferfish toxin which precipitates an identity crisis. No special technical problems there. That is almost laughably easy. We could, of course, place up to two million maggots in their rice within twenty-four hours. The maggots are ready, massed in secret staging areas in Alabama. We have hypodermic darts capable of pie-balding the enemy's pigmentation. We have rots, blights, and rusts capable of attacking his alphabet. Those are dandies. We have a hut-shrinking chemical which penetrates the fibers of the bamboo, causing it, the hut, to strangle its occupants. This operates only after 10 p.m., when people are sleeping. Their mathematics are at the mercy of a suppurating surd we have invented. We have a family of fishes trained to attack their fishes. We have the deadly testicle-destroying telegram. The cable companies are cooperating. We have a green substance that, well, I'd rather not talk about. We have a secret word that, if pronounced, produces multiple fractures in all living things in an area the size of four football fields.[203]

These are the words not of Gen. Brown, but of author Donald Barthelme. His language and concepts may seem ludicrous, but they come painfully close to the dreams of those imbued with the West Point functional mentality: "The Air Force Materials Laboratory . . . has developed a paint which, when spread over aircraft parts or other material, then exposed to heat or light, changes color to signal the relative porosity of that part."[204] So much for language. "People sniffers" are currently in use in Vietnam. They detect movement in remote parts of Vietnam by measuring the urine content of a particular area. The Viet Cong have been hanging buckets of urine in strategic spots to confuse this particular technological marvel. "Spooky" gunships, converted C-123s, patrol the skies of Vietnam with their 7.62 miniguns capable of firing 4,000 rounds a minute. The armed-forces training film introducing Spooky to the troops pictures hundreds of evenly spaced balloons on a football field being "popped" by a single long burst from Spooky. Gen. Brown's Systems Command was also responsible for the development of the 17,000-pound blockbuster bomb, the most powerful conventional bomb ever developed. As one might expect, its impact leaves a big hole and causes "multiple fractures in all living things" within a mile radius. Is there any truth to the rumor that the bomb was developed when the Air Force calculated statistically that 8.5 tons of expended ordnance are required to kill one Viet Cong? We do not know.

These wonders are not random developments that have accidentally found their way into America's war arsenal. They are part of Gen. W. C. Westmoreland's dream of the automated battlefield: "I see battlefields or combat areas that are under 24-hour real or near-real time surveillance of all types. I see battlefields on which we can destroy anything we can locate through instant communications and the almost instantaneous application of highly lethal firepower."[205] Westmoreland's dream, a nightmare for its victims, is not far off: "Hundreds of years were required to achieve the mobility of the armored division. A little over two decades later we had the airmobile division. With cooperative efforts, no more than ten years should separate us from the automated battlefield." [206] This concept made its formal debut in October 1969 at the annual meeting of AUSA in Washington, and two new groups were quickly organized to move the battlefield along. One, STANO (Surveillance, Target, Acquisition and Night Observation), was formed to pull together the more than 100 classified electronics and weapons projects already under way. The other, Project MASSTER (Mobile Army Sensor System Test and Review), is a highly secret operation at Fort Hood, Texas. Also a special *tri-cap* (triple capability) army division has been established at Fort Hood for operational testing of certain aspects of the automated battlefield. The totally integrated electronic war game that Westmoreland described will evolve slowly from the most successful of the components now in use in Vietnam. Project Igloo White, which has played a key role in the Laos air war, integrates the three basic components of the new system—a sensing device, a communications link, and an attack mechanism. Acoustic and seismic sensors contained in long spears are flung from high-speed aircraft and stuck into the ground in series. A radio/microphone is dropped near the spears by a parachute designed to snag in a tree. Any or all of these devices can pick up sounds or disturbances caused by troops or trucks moving nearby and transmit them to a surveillance plane flying in the area, which in turn relays the signals to a ground control station. The information is then fed into a computer, and "skilled target analysts" decide whether the electronic "tracks" were made by the enemy or by friendly forces (or by water buffalo). Should the computer print-out conclude it was enemy, an air strike would follow. Additional Igloo White weapons, "Wappum" and "Dragontooth," by-pass the "skilled target analysts" altogether. They are anti-personnel devices dropped from the air, arming themselves as they spin to the ground. These weapons themselves "decide" what or whom to blow up. They can stop people but leave vehicles intact: "The only kill mechanism is blast. GRAVEL will blow a man's foot off but it will not blow a hole in a truck tire." [207]

West Point's Army works hand in hand with West Point's Air Force on the future battlefield that will make personal responsibility for war crimes obsolete—Gen. Brown's pal Lt. Gen. W. C. Gribble, Jr. (W.P. 1941), is the chief of the Army's research-and-development effort. On page 13 of the April 1971 issue of *Air Force* Magazine, two of their respective subordinates are pictured in a revealing pose. Army Maj. Gen. John R. Deane, Jr. (W.P. 1942), and Brig. Gen. William J. Evans (W.P. 1946) are shown beaming like five-year-olds on Christmas Day as their hands and eyes delicately fondle camouflaged, antenna-like models of the electronic sensors used to "report" on enemy supply routes in Southeast Asia.[208] Both generals testified before the Electronic Battlefield Subcommittee of the Senate Armed Services Committee, and Senator Goldwater became intrigued with one of General Deane's Captain Video devices as it sat squawking on a display table:

SENATOR GOLDWATER: Does that beep at regular intervals?
GENERAL DEANE: Just when it detects something, but right now, because there is so much disturbance here, it keeps beeping. It beeps and then stays silent, for, oh, about 10 or 15 seconds and then it will beep again. . . .[209]

Gen. Evans explained to the enthralled Senators how the system worked: "An assessment officer monitors sensor activations in his area of interest. When he recognizes a target signature from a (classified exhibit) particular sensor string, he calls up on his cathode ray tube a sketch of the road net which that string of sensors is monitoring; the computer automatically displays and updates on the CRT the movement of the target along that road (deleted). He then can instruct one or a number of the (deleted) F-4's, which I mentioned earlier, to enter those (deleted) coordinated into the aircraft's computer. This gives the aircraft the course to steer to that point and produces an automatic release of ordnance at the proper time to hit the target. Using area-type ordnance, excellent results have been obtained with this blind-bombing method." (Early in March 1971 the Air Force claimed that Igloo White had made it possible for U.S. aircraft to find and destroy some 80 percent of the traffic coming down the Ho Chi Minh Trail in Laos since October 1970.) [210] Goldwater was ecstatic: "I personally think it has the possibility of being the greatest step forward in warfare since gunpowder." [211]

Gen. Brown's experience as Seventh Air Force commander in Vietnam intensified his own excitement for the continuing perfection of the automated battlefield. As he said in an April 1971 interview with *Air Force* Magazine concerning his Air Force Systems Command, "One of the most productive areas of work undertaken by AFSC in recent years involves technological programs in support of limited war. I should know. I was a user of these technologies for two years in Southeast Asia. A significant achievement, which is fully operational and working extremely well, involves laser-guided bombs and electro-optional systems, both conceived and developed by AFSC. We have also made great improvements on our gunships, the AC-119s and AC-130s, and they have proved of enormous importance to tactical warfare. Further, we have modified the B-57 to incorporate very sophisticated target-acquisition devices. We also have a program in progress that adds low-light-level TV and other sensor gear to the OV-10 FAC aircraft. This will make it possible for us to acquire targets at night and to use laser designators so that strike aircraft can attack the targets." [212]

Gen. Brown, like Westmoreland, squints into the future as he describes what he can of the AFSC's top-secret five-pronged automated destruction program curiously code-named "Have Lemon": "it is of great value to limited war, and for that matter, any kind of warfare. In essence, it seeks to provide defense suppression and stand-off capabilities with regard to various forms of defenses. We have set up a special office at AFSC Headquarters, whose staff pulls together information from various AFSC Centers and Laboratories on the five project areas involved. The headquarters staff works directly, without diffusing layers in between, with the project people in such places as [the Armament Development and Test Center at] Eglin, Rome [Air Development Center], and the Air Force Laboratories at Wright-Patterson. We expect to verify the feasibility of those technologies through field demonstrations in about a year." Gen. Brown further told *Air Force* Magazine that "at this time there are no major areas of known technology relating to limited war that have not been covered by AFSC programs." [213]. . . The hut-shrinking chemical?

Need we worry that all this wondrous technology might be employed without regard to the ethical implications? Will we actually be destroying "anything we can locate"? Gen. Deane answered these questions before the subcommittee: "You say the sensors won't tell you. And the sensors might give you an indication if over an acoustic sensor you heard voices and determined from the conversation that they were enemy, that is the only way I would know you would be able to tell. Now, when you get into that kind of a problem, you have to bring to bear your knowledge of where your friendly forces are and use your best judgment. I think the commanders that I have known, if they had doubts, they would not fire." [214]

Westmoreland too is greatly concerned that these ethical standards remain at their current high level: "I have made it a personal goal of mine to press home to every leader in the Army —from senior general down to the newest corporal—the need for absolute honesty and morality in everything they do." [215]

And so, as Barthelme's fictional chief engineer put it, "The interesting thing is that we have a moral sense. It is on punched cards, perhaps the most advanced and sensitive moral sense the world has ever known. It considers all considerations in endless detail. . . . It even quibbles. With this great new moral tool, how can we go wrong? I confidently predict that, although we could employ all this splendid new weaponry . . . we're not going to do it." [216]

CHAPTER 6

The Apolitical Politicians

I don't want to be a hard hat, I just want to be
me. My strong suit isn't group philosophy, but
somehow I've got to believe that our crowd—who
with their brains, energy, and dedication helped
solve World War II, the Cold War, Korea, Cuba,
and now Vietnam—can solve drugs, Black Pan-
thers, and hippies without too much overtime.[1]

—FRANK LINNELL (W.P. 1941)

FANTASIZING in 1964 about the year 2000, Col. Elvin R.
Heiberg (W.P. 1926) envisaged a U.S. made perfect by West
Point: "Picking up a paper on the Dean's desk, we note that
President Peter M. Dawkins ('59) has decided not to seek reelection. We are sorry to hear this as it will bring to a close the
term of the fourth Academy graduate to serve in the White
House. The third USMA-educated President, we all remember,
was Andrew Goodpaster ('39). He was the dark-horse candidate who won such spontaneous support when the deadlock
developed between Goldwater and Nixon in 1972, after President Johnson's third term. We also note, from the Dean's newspaper, that Secretary of State Lee Olvey ('55) has predicted the
end of the Cold War, and the return of all troops from Vietnam
before Christmas. Secretary of the Treasury Colin Kelly ('63)
has promised a tax cut before the end of the year. On the other

hand Postmaster General Tom Dooley ('64) warns that the high cost of transportation will require 1st class postage to be inched up another penny to 25 cents. On the editorial page we see a snide reference to the many USMA grads on Dawkins' Cabinet which the press refers to as the 'Long Gray Line-up.' It is claimed to be almost as powerful as the Harvard influence of 40 years ago." [2]

Was Heiberg dreaming? We have twenty-eight years to find out, but in 1972 the indications are that Dawkins and company are far more than dark-horse candidates. West Pointers have already laid siege to the White House. Brig. Gen. James D. Hughes (W.P. 1946) is Military Assistant to the President; Brig. Gen. Brent Scowcroft (W.P. 1947) is also a Military Assistant; Frederic V. Malek (W.P. 1959) is Special Assistant and chief "talent scout" for Nixon; Brig. Gen. Alexander M. Haig, Jr. (W.P. 1947), is Deputy Assistant for National Security Affairs and Henry Kissinger's right-hand man; John H. Holdridge (W.P. 1945) is Kissinger's China expert on the National Security Council staff; Lt. Col. Dana Mead (W.P. 1957) is an aide to John Ehrlichman on the President's Domestic Council; and Richard W. Streiff (W.P. 1946) is a Deputy Special Assistant to the President and Peter E. Millspaugh (W.P. 1958) is with the White House Transition Office. On a different level, Lt. Col. Arthur D. Dewey (W.P. 1956) serves on the President's Commission on White House Fellows, overseeing the activities of such current friends and Fellows as Bernard Loeffke (W.P. 1957), Dick Stephenson (W.P. 1957), Warne Meade (W.P. 1957), and Bob Dey (W.P. 1958). Trailing these members of the advance party are such distinguished soldiers as former Brig. Gen. George A. Lincoln (W.P. 1929), Director of the Office of Emergency Preparedness and member of the National Security Council; David M. Abshire (W.P. 1951), Assistant Secretary of State for Congressional Affairs; Michael Collins (W.P. 1952), Assistant Secretary of State for Public Affairs; John H. Shaffer (W.P. 1943), Administrator of the Federal Aviation Administration; Clare F. Farley (W.P. 1943), Executive Officer of NASA; Glenn Schweitzer (W.P. 1953), Secretary of the Marine Resources Council; and Harry J. Shaw (W.P. 1945), an official in the Office of Management and Budget. The battle has been joined and the "Long Gray Line-up" seems far ahead of Heiberg's Year 2000 schedule.

This trend gained the approval and support of President Kennedy: "I am sure that many Americans believe that the days before World War II were the golden age, when the stars were falling on all the graduates of West Point—that that was the golden time of service and that you had moved into a period where military service, while vital, is not as challenging as it was then. . . . The fact of the matter is that the period just ahead in the next decade will offer more opportunities for service to the graduates of this Academy than ever before in the history of the U.S., because all around the world in countries which are heavily engaged in the maintenance of their freedom, graduates of this Academy are heavily involved. . . ." [3]

Soldiers in government have come a long way since the day President Woodrow Wilson threatened to abolish the Joint Board (the Joint Chiefs of Staff) when they disputed a Presidential decision. Wilson's threat reflected the popular sentiment that military men were the instruments of policy and not the formulators. This concept of the apolitical soldier has roots deep in American tradition, and the Constitution itself carefully defines and delimits the role of the military by designating the President as Commander in Chief, by giving Congress alone the power to declare war and appropriate military funds, and by providing no institutionalized channels of communication between the military and their civilian leaders. Early American society embraced the fear of a powerful military establishment implicit in the Constitution and rejected the professional soldier. American populism declared that it was every citizen's duty to defend his country and its ideals, and that a professional army was both redundant and dangerous in this context. Consequently, the role of West Point at its founding was not to produce specialists in military science but rather to train specialists in the engineering skills necessary to build a country. This atmosphere persisted until the Civil War, when a society ravaged by unprecedented violence and slaughter totally rejected anything military and isolated the remnants of the professional army. The Army reacted by withdrawing and turning inward to examine its values and mission. It was during this period that Gen. Emory Upton (W.P. 1861) and Gen.

William T. Sherman (W.P. 1840), influenced by the work of H. Wager Halleck (W.P. 1839), led the movement that resulted in the creation of the modern professional soldier—an apolitical man who is an expert in the management of violence. The new soldier gained an identity that distinguished him as a professional and defined his role as such in society. His identity was that of a specialist in military art; his role was that of the self-sacrificing defender of the nation. He was to operate as a tool of the government in a totally apolitical fashion. The military had only slightly deviated from this pattern when they were slapped down by President Wilson in the early 1900s. This apolitical definition of military professionalism persisted until World War II. The military leaders had even extended it to cover voting. Gen. Patton remarked, "I am in the pay of the United States government. If I vote against the administration I am voting against my commander-in-chief. I am being bought." [4] Gen. Spaatz said, "I have always felt that career officers of any of the services should not be concerned with politics. If they vote, that means they are siding with one party or the other. I think there should be the same separation of the military from the political part of the government as they say there should be of separation of church and state." [5] Gen. William Simpson added, ". . . it didn't make any difference to me who the constituted government was. I was dedicated to the service of my country." [6] These statements represent the dying gasps of the military's apolitical and "professional" tradition. Since World War II this tradition has become a myth.

Prior to World War II, America did not live in a military neighborhood. War was a distant phenomenon, only briefly interrupting the growth of a peaceful economic and technical giant. America's borders were defined by her businessmen, not by her political or military leaders. This world view was shattered by World War II. No longer could the U.S. remain aloof and untouched by war while there existed the technical means to devastate the country. Americans had joined the world. The professional managers of violence were standing in the wings awaiting the call—they had been preparing for this new world reality for almost 100 years; they had made it their own. Roosevelt naturally gave the management of this new wartime

America to the soldiers. Adam Yarmolinski in *The Military Establishment* describes the situation: "He turned for advice to generals and admirals as well as to diplomats. He decreed that Chiefs of Staff have direct access to him without going through civilian secretaries. During difficult periods after 1940 . . . he frequently sought military advice and, after Pearl Harbor, he leaned even more heavily on the military. . . . In terms of entree to the White House and influence on a broad range of presidential decisions, members of the Joint Chiefs outranked Cabinet Secretaries. Roosevelt sought advice from the Joint Chiefs on a range of issues that he and his predecessors would have regarded before 1938 as primarily State Department business." [7]

Samuel Huntington, the reigning apologist for militarism, offers this description: ". . . the Joint Chiefs extended their activities and interests far beyond the normal military confines and into the areas of diplomacy, politics, and economics. From the initial great decision to defeat Germany first to the last complex series of decisions on the end of the war with Japan, the major strategic and policy issues of the war were resolved by the President, the Chiefs, and Harry Hopkins. The absence of a formal charter for the JCS facilitated the expansion of its functions since it was impossible for any rival agency to argue that it was exceeding its authority. Tied in close to the President, the interests and powers of the Chiefs tended to expand and become coextensive with his. The formulation of the American position preparatory to the great interallied war conferences was normally done by the military and the President. The Chiefs themselves attended virtually all these conferences while the civilian secretaries were left at home. The military carried out diplomatic negotiations for the government, as well as being in constant communication with the British service chiefs. In the fields, theater commanders such as MacArthur and Eisenhower functioned in political and 'diplomatic roles.' " [8]

A West Pointer, of course, was one of the four members of this JCS—Gen. H. H. Arnold (W.P. 1907).

After the war, the Joint Chiefs found themselves with no experience of functioning solely as a military body; they had assumed a political role and had developed a political tradition that has been maintained to the present day. Following the lead of the JCS, other military men quickly moved to entrench themselves in the fertile ground of civilian bureaucracy. Among others in the immediate postwar period, Maj. Gen. Philip B. Fleming (W.P. 1911) became Federal Works Administrator; Maj. Gen. Robert M. Littlejohn (W.P. 1912) was Administrator of the War Assets Administration; Gen. Omar N. Bradley (W.P. 1915) became head of the Veterans Administration; and Joseph M. Swing (W.P. 1915) became Commissioner of Immigration and Naturalization. Other graduates "distinguished" themselves in the late 1940s: Maj. Gen. Glen E. Edgerton (W.P. 1908) became Managing Director and Chairman of the Board of the Export-Import Bank; Brig. Gen. Herbert D. Vogel (W.P. 1924) was Chairman of the Tennessee Valley Authority; and Maj. Gen. Kenneth D. Nichols (W.P. 1929) became General Manager of the Atomic Energy Commission. These few names are just examples; a complete listing would reveal approximately 150 military men in important policy posts in civilian government in 1948–50 alone.

This influx of soldiers into previously forbidden areas might seem contrary to the American experience. However, World War II had introduced a new set of rules, rules with which only the military were comfortable. At the outbreak of the war, the American people were no strangers to violence; indeed, they themselves had been the star performers in our many conflicts —the people had been the weapons. But they were not enough in World War II, for it was a war of resources, of production, of transportation and the massive application of destruction. In short, the first new rule required that the tools of violence be taken away from the people and relocated into the disciplined hands of the grand strategists, the professional soldiers. They had the training, they were given the positions, and they soon monopolized the means of war. Hiroshima and Nagasaki taught Americans the second new rule: their isolated home was technically vulnerable to attack—not just a simple invasion, but atomic devastation of a horrible magnitude. After the war these rules awaited interpretation, and the civilians and the military squared off to determine the new world reality. The struggle was over before it began. The war had given the military intensive training in coordinated economic, political, and military affairs, and no other group had had this kind of continuous experience. At the same time, the politicians abdicated their policy-making responsibilities and hid behind the technically oriented, "apolitical" soldier. Thus military men became accepted by the political and economic powers as authorities on subjects that went far beyond their historically proper domain. That the larger public placed extraordinary confidence in its military leaders was due in part to hero worship, but, more importantly, it was because of the new world circumstances—they looked to their proven saviors for counsel and guidance. The civilians never had a chance to establish a reality that was directed toward the achievement of a political and human peace. If one views politics as a struggle for power and the ultimate kind of power as violence, it follows that the military didn't have to struggle at all—they controlled the tools of violence, while the civilians were still locked in politics. The image of peace was lost and replaced by a precarious balance of armed fear and a garrison state. The professional soldier's dream of a perpetual state of high preparedness for war came true—the world was defined in terms of the "military reality." The new rules did not translate into a possible peace, they translated into a possible war. Sidney Lens in *The Military Industrial Complex* sums up the advantages of the military's new position: "The zest for expansion, for sewing up pockets of influence, has been the distinguishing feature of the armed services. All bureaucracies of course have a similar proclivity, but the Pentagon has been many times blessed. It had the adulation of the people for having won the war. It had a convenient enemy to lay before the public constantly—communism. It could conjure up images of impending horrors by mysterious weapons no one had ever seen or could question." [9]

What happened to our "apolitical" soldier? Can anyone remain apolitical in positions of such power? The professional soldier believes he does—"Duty, Honor, Country" does not mention "politics." The military have grown up with the military definition of a world reality that the nation accepted only after World War II, and they do not see it as a political mechanism. They believe in it firmly and see their actions as the ones necessary to save their country, not as partisan policies to be debated.

West Point is the key institution in fostering these military myths and subordinating rational societal goals. The harsh four years of the Academy have been most successful in breaking up the civilian values of the selected few and replacing them with a character structure that accepts without question the common military reality.

The success of West Point in warping the political sensibilities of its graduates reached its zenith with Douglas MacArthur. A few years after being removed from command by President Truman for flagrantly subverting the administration's political efforts for peace in Korea and substituting his own, MacArthur had these words for the cadets at West Point: "Yours is the profession of arms—the will to win, the sure knowledge that in war there is no substitute for victory; that if you lose, the nation will be destroyed; that the obsession of your public service must be Duty–Honor–Country. Others will debate the controversial issues, national and international, which divide men's minds; but serene, calm, aloof, you stand as the nation's war-guardian, as its lifeguard from the raging tides of international conflict, as its gladiator in the arena of battle. For a century and a half you have defended, guarded, and protected its hallowed traditions of liberty and freedom, of right and justice. Let civilian voices argue the merits or demerits of our processes of government; whether our strength is being sapped by deficit financing indulged in too long, by federal paternalism grown too mighty, by power groups grown too arrogant, by morals grown too low, by taxes grown too high, by extremists grown too violent; whether our personal liberties are as thorough and complete as they should be. These great national problems are not for your professional participation or military solution. Your guidepost stands out like a tenfold beacon in the night—Duty–Honor–Country." [10]

MacArthur saw no contradiction between these words and his actions in Korea, and he did not expect the cadets to see any either. He was speaking as a professional soldier to future professional soldiers, as one above politics to those who would soon be above politics, and as a man who had spent his life in pursuit of the military reality to those who would guard and perpetuate the reality he had finally found.

That MacArthur's fellow alumni are able to filter reality as well as he is best illustrated by the following letters from West Pointers to a small group of military-school mavericks known as Concerned Academy Graduates. The letters were responses to a 1971 CAG request for support in its efforts to end the Vietnam war. The signatures have been deleted.

In good old battlefield language—Cram it up your asses you yellow traitor bastards.

W.P. 1958 [resigned 1961 as first lieutenant]

I think that it is time that you and the dissenting politicians supported our government in its attempt to end the war. You should all return to the values of patriotism taught at our academy or disassociate yourselves from the Association of Graduates.

W.P. 1950 [resigned 1954 as captain]

I think your organization stinks. The only good thing I find about it is that, so far, you haven't found any patsey's [sic] in '50 USMA.

W.P. 1950 [resigned 1953 as first lieutenant]

Bullshit.

W.P. 1950 [resigned 1955 as first lieutenant]

Your letter is a gross insult and inexcusable disservice to the academies from which you obtained your education and also to your country. . . . Certainly, there is no need for a group of misguided and misinformed individuals who use the hallowed name of the academies to dignify and add credence to a half-baked position. . . . It would be criminal to support a group that is dissenting merely for the purpose of dissenting without a logical evaluation or real concern for the problems that confront the country, its military and its society. . . .

W.P. 1946 [retired 1967 as lieutenant colonel]

. . . Promotion of any political view through the use of an organizational name purporting to speak for Academy Graduates injures the relations of Academy Graduates with the public. It is substantially more damaging when Academy Graduates are linked with a political view generally considered radical or with a view which may not be in the best interest of our country. Use of the words "Academy Graduates" in your assumed name is, at the very least, in poor taste and a breach of the duty which you owe to other Academy Graduates. . . .

W.P. 1951 [resigned 1954 as first lieutenant]

[242]

THE APOLITICAL POLITICIANS

You ought to be ashamed of yourselves, all of you.
W.P. 1950 [resigned 1958 as captain]

You bastards are sick.
W.P. 1952 [resigned 1959 as captain]
W.P. 1943 [retired 1961 as lieutenant colonel]
W.P. 1943 [retired 1962 as lieutenant colonel]

George Psihas (W.P. 1951) didn't write a letter, but he "developed a scheme to counter the constant degradation of WP and the military that is so common today, and has even evidenced itself in some Service Acad. Grads. George suggested that we collectively sign a reaffirmation of our basic dedication to 'Duty, Honor, Country,' and perhaps have it printed in the 'New York Times' or other major newspapers; have a copy presented to the Pres. or the Congress; and possibly have a bronze presentation tablet as a gift to the Military Academy. . . ." [11]

In 1964 Robert A. Lovett, financier and former Under Secretary of State, directed the following comments to the keepers of the military reality:

I am convinced that [the widening of] proper military concern can best be built on the firm foundation of the military sciences and of the discipline and high standards of character based on the great traditions of this magnificent military academy and those of its sister services. For the virtues nourished here are your priceless inheritance from the Long Gray Line and must remain one of the few unchanging values in a radically changing world.

I submit, gentlemen, that only an expanding mind can deal with a world of expanding complexities; and that broadening your horizons will not diminish the value of your special military skills but will, on the contrary, enhance their validity and usefulness in those great Councils of Government where, as servants of the Republic, you will sit as keepers of the faith and guardians of the peace. [12]

The first line of "expanding minds," "keepers of the faith," and "guardians of the peace" can be found tucked away in the bowels of America's vast intelligence network. Leading such organizations as the Central Intelligence Agency (CIA), the Defense Intelligence Agency (DIA), the National Security Agency (NSA), Army Security Agency (ASA), and the various

Army intelligence staff sections in the Sixties were such notable West Pointers as:

Donald V. Bennett, W.P. 1940
Superintendent, USMA, 1966–68; Commanding General, Seventh Army, 1968–70; Director, DIA, 1970

William M. Breckinridge, W.P. 1928
Chief, ASA, 1960–62

Marshall Carter, W.P. 1931
Deputy Director, CIA, 1962–65; Director, NSA, 1965–69; President, George C. Marshall Research Foundation, 1970

John J. Davis, W.P. 1931
Assistant Director, NSA, 1961–65; Assistant Chief of Staff/Intelligence, Department of the Army, 1965–66; Assistant Director, Arms Control and Disarmament Agency, 1967

Charles J. Denholm, W.P. 1938
Institute for Defense Analysis, 1962–65; Commanding General, ASA, 1965

Lawrence R. Dewey, W.P. 1924
Member, CIA Board of National Estimates, 1961; Research Analysis Corp., 1963–66

Vasco J. Fenili, W.P. 1943
Office of the Assistant Chief of Staff/Intelligence, Department of the Army, 1968; Chief, NSA Europe, 1968–70

Alva R. Fitch, W.P. 1930
Deputy Director, DIA, 1964–66; Military Editor, Washington Kiplinger Letter, 1970

Robert R. Glass, W.P. 1935
Deputy Chief of Staff/Intelligence, U.S. Army Europe, 1965–67; Chief of Staff, DIA, 1967; Consultant, Planning Research Corp., 1969

Roger Hilsman, W.P. 1943
Director, Office of Intelligence and Research, State Department, 1961–63; Assistant Secretary for Far Eastern Affairs, State Department, 1963–65

Chester L. Johnson, W.P. 1937
Office of the Assistant Secretary of Defense, Internal Security Affairs, 1960–61; Deputy Assistant Chief of Staff/Intelligence, 1966–67

Samuel N. Karrick, W.P. 1943
Senior Liaison Officer, U.S. Embassy, Saigon, 1965–67; Office of the Assistant Secretary of Defense, Internal Security Affairs, 1967–69; Deputy Director, DIA, 1969

Joseph A. McChristian, W.P. 1939
Office of the Assistant Chief of Staff/Intelligence, 1962–63; Assistant Chief of Staff/Intelligence, Military Assistance Command Vietnam, 1965–67; Assistant Chief of Staff/Intelligence, Department of the Army, 1968

Jammie M. Philpott, W.P. 1943
Deputy Director, DIA, 1969

William W. Quinn, W.P. 1933
Deputy Director, DIA, 1961–64

Louis B. Umlauf, Jr., W.P. 1943
Assistant Military Attaché, Mexico City, 1963–66; Staff and Faculty member, Defense Intelligence School, DIA, 1966–68; Chief of Foreign Liaison, DIA, 1968

Lawrence K. White, W.P. 1933
Executive Director and Comptroller, CIA, 1947–70

William P. Yarborough, W.P. 1936
Commanding Officer, 66th Military Intelligence Group, 1958–61; Commanding General, Army Special Warfare Center, 1961–64; Assistant Chief of Staff/Intelligence, Department of the Army, 1966–68

The above is an incomplete listing meant only to give an idea of the depth of West Point involvement. At lower levels there are scores of additional grads.

With the establishment of these agencies in the early 1960s, the intelligence community had gained a powerful network for the collection of information. These groups constituted a tremendous potential for gathering military, political, economic, geographical, and cultural data on foreign countries. Predictably, this effort has overlapped to the point where the feedback of information has burgeoned into an unmanageable data bank. The duplication of effort in the intelligence game has become renowned, and would be humorous with the many anecdotes of spy versus spy if it were not for the reality of gross inefficiency in the management of the agencies. But the most ludicrous demonstration of how dangerous the misuse of this wealth of data is may best be seen through examination of the theories which the Pentagon has developed from this information. Armed with mountains of files describing cultural evolution in the world of the Sixties and Seventies, starting with an approach to analysis which is guided by such rigid philosophies as "Duty, Honor, Country" and directed by men who are ingrained with educations and honed by whole careers where analysis prohibits failure, this community has succeeded in reading from all its raw intelligence a definition of the world as it wants and needs to see it. Instead of learning from all this investigation, the Pentagon has sought to rearrange the facts in line with its own vital status quo.

This phenomenon flows logically from the entire process of West Point training. The assumption that one's value system is superior to all others and that that system is not to be altered but only to be reinforced and concurred with by those outside the system can be demonstrated at both ends of a West Pointer's career. On entering the Academy, he is systematically drawn into line with the established values of his predecessors in the Long Gray Line. Should he challenge the facts by offering new ones, he is singled out as someone not to be listened to or considered. He is disregarded or, at best, reminded that he is on dangerous ground because his analysis is unique. At this early stage the "cream" of the military is thoroughly drilled in the vital need for avoiding controversy. This continues to be reinforced until the graduate starts to apply these personal values to intelligence analysis. By the time he is finally called on to exercise the degree of sensitivity or flexibility vital to a successful job, he is, by definition of his own successful military career, incapable of dealing with the strange phenomena which the modern intelligence-collection machine has so generously provided him —facts. To the extent that the West Point tradition of thought has touched his inner psyche, he rejects outside values. To the extent that he views non-West Pointers as inferior, weak, and threatening to his great traditions, he sees the input of intelligence concerning foreign cultures as alien values that must be dealt with like a Beast Barracks cadet. With the same zeal with which the upperclassman beats the plebe into submission, the general sees his mission in the intelligence command as disciplining all this new data and forcing it to conform with what he is sure ought to be. The input is the enemy, and the status quo must be protected.

Given a military establishment which dealt with matters of tactics only, this zeal could be a wealth of constructive energy to be utilized in the development of a strong standing defense force. If West Point were what it purports to be—an academy which produces America's military leadership in ground warfare —such generals as Maxwell Taylor, Dwight Eisenhower, Donald V. Bennett, Marshall Carter, and William Quinn would have been confined to their honest roles as professional tacticians. But we have seen here and can observe from American history since World War II a deviation from that role which has been made increasingly possible by the steady expansion of domain by West Point's power-seeking fraternity. This expansion would be regrettable in any democracy which is supposed to shun oligarchy and nepotism, but in the intelligence community it brings a unique ramification. When the military gains appreciable control of the policy-making mechanism of government such as it has in CIA, NSA, ASA, and DIA, the result is to carry the mania for status-quo preservation into the Executive function of prescribing our foreign policy. The philosophies which are described here and which are best codified in West Point regulations and traditions have naturally been a part of the unfortunate spill-over of the military establishment beyond its prescribed limits. The danger in foreign-policy planning is that the graduates who bring to the job a high degree of success in being inflexible (as military traditions demand) inevitably read all intelligence input as calling for counter-action in order to continue the glorious status quo abroad and neutralize what they see as a threat to all they hold dear. The legacy of this influence has been the counter-insurgency stance to which the United States has become so heavily devoted in the last twenty-five years. It is the logical fulfillment of his prescribed role as the guardian of moral decency that the graduate, when interpreting intelligence data from abroad, takes a deep breath and attacks at every point where his values are not being practiced.

The Army's record of dealing effectively with "counter-insurgency" tactics, however, has not been good. Over a long period the military establishment has established by its own incompetence and lack of sensitivity a reputation for leaning always in the direction of escalated force and violence—so much so that the Executive has sought opinions beyond those of the military men. In a search for an objective analysis which would argue with scientifically researched conclusions and theories in the same way that a military man would argue with tactical and strategic theories, the Pentagon found the answer to its own lack of credibility—the think tank. If a corporation were set up exclusively to perform objective research, and were contracted by the Pentagon to make policy recommendations, the findings of these private corporations would not be seen as a general's biased view toward increased military involvement in the world. And so, during the period of increased United States military intervention abroad in the 1960s the Pentagon found itself seeking private corporations to perform such functions as "social science research," which is intelligence language for studying the internal politics of a given nation or region and determining whether or not the theme of that country's political activity is in line with United States interests or the status quo as it best serves the American national interests. In the last decade, hundreds of corporations which offer this research have sprung up from coast to coast. From the Bedford, Massachusetts, research complex through the Research Triangle in Pittsburgh to Menlo Research Park in California, numerous corporations offer this service by contract to the Pentagon either as an exclusive function or as a sideline. A half-dozen of the heaviest contractors includes the Institute for Defense Analysis, RAND Corporation, MITRE Corporation, Planning Research Corporation, Stanford Research Institute, and Research Analysis Corporation. All of these companies work closely with the intelligence agencies mentioned, and many of their policy recommendations pass directly to the President.

The Institute for Defense Analysis, at 400 Army-Navy Drive in Arlington, Virginia, is interesting not only because its president for three years in the last five was Gen. Maxwell D. Taylor (W.P. 1922) and on its trustee board and staff were such men as Gen. Alfred M. Gruenther (W.P. 1919), Gen. Sidney F.

THE APOLITICAL POLITICIANS

Giffin (W.P. 1933), and Maj. Gen. John B. Cary (W.P. 1934), but also for the way in which the corporation was developed. Founded in 1955, IDA was set up to lend respectability to the process of counter-insurgency escalation in peacetime. In its structure IDA is typical of a think-tank operation used to by-pass all the legal and constitutional restrictions controlling monopoly in defense spending. IDA combines the generals who provide the impetus for research in weaponry and "area studies" with the corporate executives of the large defense contractors who use IDA to lend credibility to the need for their products. At the same time, because IDA was a non-profit organization, there was no answerability to Congressional committees which could retard an effort at uncontrolled escalation. IDA also represented an early incorporation of the university community into research projects. University expertise was used for the Weapons Systems Evaluation Group of the Joint Chiefs of Staff and then later in such non-technical areas as counter-guerrilla modus operandi, environmental destruction, and population manipulation. This expansion was based again on the philosophies of the "forward strategists" that, due to existing threats to United States national interests, we must expand our influence and involvement wherever possible to ensure the preservation of the status quo. This argument is always vague and makes ambiguous reference to the need for the United States to assume the role of guardian general to the world's freedom. It generally follows the form of this argument put forth in IDA's first Annual Report in 1956: "Present military capabilities based on these new technologies in hostile hands present our country with a threat that is historically unfamiliar: heavy destruction by direct attack. Moreover, the era is one of war in peace, in which vast shifts in the world power framework, aggravated by implacable Communist ambitions of world domination, have brought us world responsibilities beyond the direct defense of our own territory." So, as early as the mid-1950s, the think tank was being used to argue for the necessity to expand and escalate. Although IDA took the same stance as the brinksmen in the Department of Defense, it added a note of responsible action and increased objectivity by introducing cost-effectiveness and an emphasis on management science. Other think tanks hold similar monopolies in by-passing any check-and-balance system, and all are heavily populated by graduates of West Point. The need to keep graduates on the payrolls and to have them interact between their fraternity within the Pentagon and the think tanks is vital, as can be seen in the list of graduates with five of the largest think tanks contained in Appendix B.

The scores of militarists in the intelligence community, all asserting that their values and virtues have earned them the right to interpret world conditions, have won. The acceptance of their view of reality has directed that government concentrate its power in two key areas—the advancement of science and technology and the direction of foreign affairs. The former recognizes the need for maintaining a high level of technological preparedness for war; the latter reflects the new role of the nation as a member of the world community. Together, they mean "national security," and within the new reality that becomes the responsibility of the military.

Science has become a key mechanism in perpetuating and regulating this military reality. By making possible hydrogen weapons, intercontinental missiles, and strike forces capable of multiple overkill, it has made obsolete the old method of depending on industrial mobilization to meet any threat to the national security. It has blurred the boundaries between war and peace. The advanced state of our nation's technology has become the only deterrent to war. Thus the country's energies and resources have been focused on making that technology more and more sophisticated and with it maintaining American supremacy. Agencies such as AEC, NASA, and FAA are the primary regulators and sponsors of the research and development which advance our technology, and, as such, they have become major centers of economic and political power. Along with the Department of Defense, they control 90 percent of the funds provided for the creation of new technology, military and civilian. West Pointers have been present in these agencies from the beginning, supervising, of course, the maintenance of our national security. They began with the atomic bomb.

At the end of World War II national security was defined solely in terms of nuclear capability. Because the United States possessed its secret, the atomic bomb became the fulcrum of the new U.S. role within the world community. The bomb's development had been a technological and administrative feat of monumental proportions. In four years the Manhattan Project, under the direction of Brig. Gen. Leslie R. Groves (W.P. 1918), spent $2.2 billion and mobilized 254 military officers, 1,688 enlisted men, 3,950 government workers, and 37,800 contract employees in the creation of a weapon capable of destroying the human race. West Point was involved from the start.

In October 1941 Vannevar Bush, a civilian and Director of the Office of Scientific Research and Development (OSRD), obtained White House sanction to explore the possibilities of harnessing atomic energy, but because of the gigantic task of design and construction, he felt that the project would have to be administered by the Army. Gen. George Marshall designated Brig. Gen. Wilhelm D. Styer (W.P. 1916), who was chief of staff for Gen. Brehon B. Somervell's (W.P. 1914) newly created Services of Supply, as the initial Army contact. Somervell then appointed Col. James C. Marshall (W.P. 1918), of the Corps of Engineers, as director of the preliminary work for S-1 (the code name for the Manhattan Project in OSRD). Marshall brought as his assistant Col. Kenneth D. Nichols (W.P. 1929). The first clash between the military and civilian scientists occurred almost immediately. Col. Marshall, given the responsibility for selecting the site, chose to proceed cautiously, much too cautiously for the eager scientists. Under pressure from Bush and Gen. Marshall, Somervell gave the project official status within the Corps of Engineers and made Groves the overall director. Within forty-eight hours of his assignment Groves had selected the site for the first production plants and ensured that the highest priority would be given to S-1. Guided by a top-level policy committee composed of Bush, Adm. William R. Purnell, and Gen. Styer, Brig. Gen. Groves (he received his promotion just prior to the announcement that he had taken over the Manhattan Project) would direct the program until its culmination in August 1945. Although the bulk of the work was done by civilians, Gen. Groves retained a firm grip over the project, and only a handful of men were privy to any information about its nature. The majority of the 44,000 persons under Gen. Groves' command knew only that they were part of an effort critical to the national security. Decisions were made solely by Gen. Groves and the policy committee. Even the Secretary of State was ignorant of the project until January 1945.

Initially, the scientific community was willing to abdicate any policy-making role because of the unique nature of the project, but as early as 1944 they began to realize the implications of government-controlled research. One revealing incident occurred at the Metallurgical Laboratory in Chicago, where Arthur Compton proposed a long-term basic research program designed to maintain U.S. supremacy in the field of atomic energy during the postwar period. Wielding dictatorial powers, Gen. Groves immediately shut off his attempt. At the same time, the scientists began to reflect upon the international implications of the bomb. But the international nature of science clashed directly with the military's parochial view of reality. The scientific community believed that the United States should tell the world about the bomb in order to prevent an arms race and establish effective international control for the peacetime development of atomic energy. Gen. Groves, on the contrary, felt the United States should maintain its nuclear superiority for as long as possible by surrounding the project with the utmost secrecy. In late 1944 Groves tried to prevent a French scientist who knew a great deal about the program from returning to France. When the man finally did leave, Groves attempted to have him kept under surveillance by American agents in France.

The long-range problems posed by the bomb would not be resolved until after the end of the war with Japan. In 1944, while the scientists remained troubled about the bomb's possible impact on the postwar order, the military plunged ahead planning details for its use in the immediate future. After the first successful test at Alamogordo, Secretary of War Stimson discussed these operational plans with Gen. H. H. Arnold (W.P. 1907). Arnold recommended that the actual selection of targets should be made by Gen. Carl Spaatz (W.P. 1914) and Gen. Groves. On August 6, the bomb was dropped on Hiroshima, closing the first chapter of West Point's contribution to man's new ability to destroy himself.

The successful completion of the Manhattan Project brought to an end the authorized role of the military in the development of atomic energy. To maintain U.S. supremacy in the field, it was clear that continued government support and direction were necessary, but a new mechanism was needed to administer the program. Congress had to create a new agency to take over the responsibilities of the Manhattan Engineer District (MED). The military, however, were not willing to completely relinquish control over an area that was so clearly vital to the national security, and Army lawyers drafted the first legislation presented to the House Military Affairs Committee. Reaction to the one-day hearings dealing with the future development and control of the program was severe. Scientists, in particular, disapproved of the structure of the new agency and resented the tight security restrictions included in the bill. Many said that Groves had planned it so that he could maintain complete authority in the postwar period. The fear of continued military direction of the atomic-energy program was widespread and deeply felt. In the Senate, however, a more thorough attempt was made to solicit advice from people (not necessarily military) qualified to plan for postwar organization—scientists in the Office of War Mobilization and Resources and government experts in scientific legislation. The proceedings of the Senate Special Committee on Atomic Energy reflect the controversy that raged between the civilians and the military over the nature of future developments. The committee chairman, Senator McMahon, recognizing the need to educate his committee about the operation of MED before they could intelligently consider drafting new legislation, asked for necessary information. Richard Hewlett in his history of the Atomic Energy Commission describes in detail the subsequent controversy between Gen. Groves and McMahon over the release of this classified information. Briefly, the chairman believed it essential that the committee have access to the entire history of the project; Groves felt that disclosing this information would jeopardize national security. Temporarily Groves won. He persuaded President Truman that releasing classified material might jeopardize the delicate international negotiations under way in regard to international control; but he was gradually losing any kind of public support for a continued military role in atomic energy. The probable consequences for science of continued military input were graphically illustrated by an incident in Japan in late 1945. Under the direction of Gen. Mac-Arthur, United States forces confiscated three cyclotrons from Japanese universities and dumped them in the ocean. The rationalization offered by the War Department was that the cyclotron was "of special value in atomic research which our Government believes should be prohibited to our enemies." [13] The order that directed this completely unnecessary destruction of very valuable scientific instruments had been issued under the Secretary of War's name, but he had no knowledge of it—it had come from Gen. Groves.

When the general testified before the McMahon committee he made his plans for the future development of atomic energy very clear. He indicated that it was essential to have a man with extensive military experience on the commission, someone "who is not going to forget for one minute that . . . defense must come first and other things will have to come afterward until the international situation is resolved." [14] He went on to suggest that "If any bill is adopted which does not include men with military background on the Commission, the Commission should be required by law to submit to the Joint Chiefs of Staff all matters of policy prior to adoption and before publication." [15] Most committee members felt that such a clearly militarist orientation would defeat any possibility of promoting international control and development and open an arms race that McMahon and the scientific community wanted desperately to avoid. But Groves' testimony raised the hopes of the more conservative members of the committee, and once again the question of military representation was hotly debated. Senator Vandenberg offered an amendment that would create a military-applications advisory board, appointed by the President and consisting of an equal number of military officers and civilians, which would "advise and consult with the Commission on all atomic-energy matters relating to the national defense" and would have the right of appeal to the President on all commission decisions related to national defense. McMahon felt the adoption of the amendment would "so throttle the action of the civilian commission as to amount to the abandonment of all actual control to the military." Once again he marshaled the support of the scientists to bring the issue to the public's attention. The resulting pressure forced the committee to modify the amendment and substantially reduce the power of the board. The *principle* of complete civilian control had finally been firmly established and the Atomic Energy Act was quickly approved by both House and Senate.

On the surface the battle for civilian control had been won, but underground the fight persisted. Although by law the civilian commission had authority over all aspects of atomic energy, the military maintained a substantial influence both within AEC and within the field. Gen. Groves had the most striking impact, for upon the dissolution of MED he was appointed head of the Armed Forces Special Weapons Project—the original Department of Defense division in charge of policy planning for the development and application of new nuclear weapons. He subsequently became a member of the Military Liaison Committee established by the Atomic Energy Act of 1954 to provide a channel of communication between the commission and DOD on all matters relating to the military applications of atomic energy and development of nuclear weapons. Richard Hewlett, AEC historian, characterized Groves as "a real thorn in the Commission's flesh." A strong personality conflict between him and David Lilienthal, the first chairman of the commission, nearly caused its dissolution. The general had nothing but contempt for the other commissioners and felt they were unqualified to direct the development of the atomic-energy program. At the same time, the commissioners were hypersensitive about the influence of the military and were frightened of Groves. The situation deteriorated so rapidly that, under pressure from Eisenhower, Groves decided to leave the program.

Other West Pointers, however, continued to solidify their influence within AEC, thereby ensuring that the development of atomic energy would proceed along the lines of the new military reality. Three of the general managers (chief administrators) of AEC have been military men, and of these two have been West Pointers—Gen. Kenneth D. Nichols (W.P. 1929) and Kenneth E. Fields (W.P. 1933). Gen. Nichols had a particularly detrimental effect on the commission. Partly because he had been passed over in the selection of the first general manager, Nichols came to AEC in 1953 determined to "reform" the agency. He made a definite attempt to reestablish the environment of MED, convinced that this was the optimal way of maintaining U.S. superiority in the nuclear sciences. During his term the specter of aggressive Communism dominated the American scene and created a climate in which he could command extraordinary influence. Continued progress in the field of atomic energy had once again become synonymous with national security, but the scientific community was no longer willing to tolerate a quasi-military situation which violated the fundamental international nature of science. Nichols' arrival at AEC precipitated the departure of many of its scientists.

During the same period the military succeeded in completely subverting the original intention of the founders of AEC that every aspect of atomic energy, including control of nuclear weapons, be supervised by civilians. In the original act the commission was given "custody of all assembled or unassembled atomic bombs, bomb parts, or other atomic military weapons, presently or hereafter produced except that upon the express finding of the President that such action is required in the interests of national defense, the Commission shall deliver such quantities of weapons to the armed forces as the President may specify." [16] The responsibility for overseeing the weapons program lay with the Division of Military Application, whose director has always been an active-duty officer. James McCormack (W.P. 1932) was the first to hold the position. During his term he remained responsible to a civilian authority (the commission), but subsequent West Pointers intensified the struggle to achieve complete military control of nuclear weapons and ultimately succeeded. During the Eisenhower administration AEC was forced to relinquish its monopoly over atomic weapons to the Defense Atomic Support Agency (the successor to the Armed Forces Special Weapons Project) within the Department of Defense. Exclusive civilian control was gone, and with it went the priority of using atomic energy for the betterment of mankind. In its place the manipulators of the military reality have created a new world in which the potential for total annihilation is the dominant influence. All the world knows this fear, yet the son of the man who created the bomb, Brig. Gen. Richard H. Groves (W.P. 1945), is able to say without any doubt that his father had no regrets about successfully directing both the development of the atomic bomb and the even more dangerous military takeover of its applications.[17]

The Atomic Energy Commission represented the first major federal experiment in the support of science. This coalition of government and science had been precipitated by the crisis of World War II and the fear that another nation-state, Germany, was developing a technology more advanced than ours. In 1957 a second crisis occurred—the Soviets launched the first Sputnik. Rather than applauding such a scientific feat, the American people led by their government responded with fear and paranoia. Once again another nation-state seemed to have achieved a level of technology far more advanced than our own, and we plunged once again into a technological competition which required massive federal support. The space race replaced nuclear armaments as the focus of national attention, and the National Aeronautics and Space Administration replaced the Atomic Energy Commission as the primary focus of federal funds for research and development. The military, of course, followed the attention and the money.

As in the Atomic Energy Commission, West Pointers have assumed very powerful positions within NASA. Indeed, if the United States Military Academy had not contributed two of its graduates, David Scott (W.P. 1954) and Alfred Worden (W.P. 1955), to the astronaut program, the recent Apollo 15 mission would have been without its commander on one hand and its most eligible bachelor on the other. When Scott reached the moon and exclaimed, "As I stand out here in the wonders of the unknown at Hadley, I try to understand the fundamental truth of our nature," [18] he had the answer hidden away in the lunar module *Falcon*. He and Irwin were carrying a treasure trove of 400 envelopes bearing stamps canceled at Cape Kennedy shortly after midnight on the day of lift-off and the signatures of the three astronauts. On August 7, after splashdown, additional stamps on the envelopes were canceled aboard the U.S.S. *Okinawa*, the recovery ship. Eventually 100 of the envelopes ended up in the hands of a West German stamp dealer and were sold for a total of $150,350. It seems that the honorable men from West Point were trying to set up a trust fund for their children by adding an entrepreneurial twist to the largess of the American people and their space program. NASA regulations allow astronauts to carry souvenir items, including postal covers, to the moon, but these articles must be kept by the individual or given to friends or relatives. In addition, the astronaut must obtain official permission for the items and is barred from using them for personal gain or for commercial or fund-raising purposes. NASA officials recovered 298 of the 300 envelopes retained by the capitalist spacemen and announced that Scott, Worden, and Irwin realized the impropriety of the venture and declined to accept any money from the stamp dealer. However, a NASA official acknowledged that the astronauts' change of heart came only after "all the publicity" about the envelopes.[19] For this minor quibbling with the honor code, the three Air Force colonels received official "letters of reprimand" and were barred from future flights. With the trust fund a flop, it appears that they will have to send their children to the Military Academy— the taxpayers will still foot the bill. But the Apollo program is only one part of the NASA operation, and graduates appear at all levels. At the top echelons, Jacob E. Smart (W.P. 1931) is special assistant to the NASA administrator and assistant administrator in the Office of DOD and Inter-agency Affairs; one of Smart's assistants is John C. Damon (W.P. 1938); Clare F. Farley (W.P. 1943) is executive officer; and Lawrence W. Vogel (W.P. 1942) is director of headquarters administration. In the words of Gen. Smart, "They are everywhere in the woods." [20] (The "space consultant" to Walter Cronkite and CBS News in 1969 was Charles D. Friedlander (W.P. 1950), on loan from the White House.) Within the Office of Manned Spaceflight there is an especially large contingent. The Apollo program is directed by Rocco Petrone (W.P. 1946) and he is sure to have had few problems working with such fellow alumni as Scott, Michael Collins (W.P. 1952), Edwin Aldrin (W.P. 1951), and Frank Borman (W.P. 1950).

Indeed, the high concentration of soldier-astronauts chosen for the manned flights has caused some discontent among the second generation of scientist-astronauts recruited from the civilian community. To date, only experienced military and civilian fliers have been selected for the Apollo crews. The scientist-astronauts feel that since flight and landing techniques have been perfected, scientific experimentation has come to the fore and the importance of the flier's role has declined. Yet the scientists are still being confined to such routine missions as T-38 jet-trainer flights and men such as Scott and Irwin walk around on the moon. There has been some criticism of the performance of the pilots in their new role as scientific experimenters. Said one NASA official about the performance of a recent Apollo crew: "They acted like robots, picked up rocks, put out equipment and took pictures. But they didn't really see anything." [21] It is easy to see why so many West Pointers have successfully participated in the Apollo flights. Their experience at the Academy provides the perfect foundation: they are accustomed to self-denial and hard work; they have strong technical backgrounds; and they respond well to training, although not to learning. The qualities developed at West Point can easily be reinforced within the Apollo training program to create the human automatons needed to perform the variety of tasks devised by more creative minds. Yet most of these men will never be able to take full advantage of their opportunities to expand man's knowledge of the universe, for, as the NASA official said, "they didn't really see anything."

The preponderance of military personnel within NASA's administration is seen as perfectly logical, at least by certain administrators. Gen. Smart offered this analysis: Because of the dependency of NASA on the Department of Defense for logistics and personnel support, the links between the two agencies must remain strong. Relations are improved by the active presence of military personnel within NASA. Correspondingly, he says that because DOD is both an operational and an R&D agency it must rely on outside competence for much of its work, and so it frequently turns to NASA. Such close cooperation might prompt assertions about the problem of excessive military influence within the space program, but Gen. Smart interprets it as the natural outgrowth of the initial difficulties of NASA in finding qualified personnel. At the inception of the NASA program only the military had the necessary expertise in aeronautics and it seemed logical that those who were already professional test pilots should be brought into the program. Today Gen. Smart believes that continued collaboration is advantageous for economic reasons—the mutually supportive roles of the two agencies prevents unnecessary duplication and saves the government considerable money. At the same time, it permits the extension of the Long Gray Line across the upper echelons of the technological elite in the country.

Within the federal bureaucracy, NASA and AEC are the two largest "civilian" agencies sponsoring research and development. Their combined budgets represent 37 percent of total government expenditure for R&D. Together with the Department of Defense they control 90 percent of R&D funds. There is a third federal agency whose financial support for science is minimal compared with the AEC and NASA giants, but whose influence upon the development of modern technology is substantial. The Federal Aviation Administration, along with its many predecessors, has had the responsibility of guiding and fostering the growth of the aeronautics industry throughout its modern history. And West Pointers have played an integral part in that history.

In the late Twenties the federal government first assumed a direct role in the promotion of civil aeronautics. By 1933 President Roosevelt had created the position of Director of Aeronautics (placed within the Commerce Department) and appointed Eugene L. Vidal (W.P. 1918) as first director. Vidal had to deal immediately with the controversy over the place of aviation in—where else?—military affairs. He survived that problem, only to be faced with the air-mail scandals of 1933 and 1934. Under a second reorganization Vidal became director of the Bureau of Air Commerce and remained there until 1937. In the years following, West Point control of civil aeronautics lapsed only temporarily. After the fourth reorganization of the federal aviation program in 1938, FDR appointed Col. Donald H. Connolly (W.P. 1910) first administrator of the Civil Aeronautics Administration. Connolly brought to his new job the experience gained as administrator of the Works Project Administration for Southern California between 1935 and 1939. He also brought with him as an assistant Lucius D. Clay (W.P. 1918). During Connolly's term as administrator, Congress made its first direct appropriation to a federal aviation agency for airport construction. The major criterion for allocating the $40 million in funds was that the improvements be necessary to the national defense, and the administrator, of course, had the final authority to determine whether or not an airport was vital to that purpose—the military reality had found another implementer. Following his stay at CAA, Connolly rejoined the military for World War II, during which he became director of civil aviation for the Army Air Force and, later, the commanding general of the Persian Gulf Command. At the close of the war he joined the State Department for three years. Upon retirement he went to work for the city of Baltimore as its director of aviation. The career of his former assistant, Lucius Clay, followed similar basic lines. After leaving CAA he went to the headquarters of the Army Service Forces for three years, and then became deputy military governor of the U.S. zone in Germany during 1945–46. In 1947–49 he was commander-in-chief of the European Command and military governor of the U.S.-occupied zone. Upon retirement he joined private industry and moved easily into the upper echelon of the corporate establishment, first as chairman of the Continental Can Company and later as a senior partner of Lehman Brothers in New York City. These experiences are typical of the movement of West Pointers into and out of government service during the course of their careers.

Further major organizational changes were not made in the federal aeronautics program until 1958, when the situation reached crisis proportions. CAA was unable to keep up with the growing industry and its increasing problems. Centralized agencies were needed to coordinate the civilian and military aspects of general aviation. In August 1958 the Federal Aviation Act was passed, creating two independent agencies—the Federal Aviation Administration and the Civil Aeronautics Board—to consolidate all essential management functions necessary to support the common needs of military and civilian aviation. Prior to this point the Department of Defense had maintained its own air-traffic controllers and operated within its own air space. The military did not object to the concept of a jointly staffed aviation agency so long as it was based on a "full partnership," with the post of deputy director filled by a military man. If the military were not represented in this way, they felt, the "national defense needs" would not be given proper consideration. While the generals worried about the possibility of neglecting national defense, the civilians weighed the probability of a military takeover. As in the case of the Atomic Energy Commission, however, legislative measures were taken to prevent that —in theory, at least. Thus, Title III, Section 301, of the Federal Aviation Act states that "The administrator . . . at the time of his nomination shall be a civilian." But, despite all good Congressional intent, the military have retained control. Serving on the Financial Advisory Committee of the Civil Aeronautics Board is Samuel K. Lessey (W.P. 1945)—he is also vice-president of Shearson, Hammill Co., a New York investment-banking firm, and in 1968 was assistant to the chief sergeant-at-arms at the Republican national convention. More importantly, three of the four FAA administrators have been Air Force generals, and two of the four have been graduates of West Point.

Relaxing in the plush suite of Schriever and McKee Associates on the twelfth floor of a Connecticut Avenue office building (across the hall is the AVCO Corporation; next door is the General Aviation Manufacturers Association), Gen. William McKee (W.P. 1929) explained how President Johnson called him to the White House one morning and asked him to become administrator of FAA. There was no question of his acceptance; after all, his entire career had been one of service to his country. When his President asked him to accept the position of FAA administrator, it was the Commander-in-Chief speaking and he could not refuse.[22] There were certain minor complications, however. The law required the administrator to be a civilian, and Gen. McKee was a retired Air Force officer. President Johnson turned to Congress for special legislation making an exception to the law. In a letter to Senator Warren Magnuson, chairman of the Senate Commerce Committee dated April 29, 1965, he said: "General McKee's appointment as Federal Aviation Agency Administrator does, however, present a situation requiring congressional assistance. The general's retired status and the policy developed at the time of the establishment of the agency that the administrator should be a civilian could impose upon him the burden of requiring him to make an unreasonable financial sacrifice and subject his family to the risk that they would be denied, in the event of his death, the benefits of his present retired status which they rely on for their security." [23] Johnson went on to request that special legislation be passed to avoid any hardship for Gen. McKee. Such action was not unprecedented, but it was unusual. Certainly Gen. McKee had impressive credentials. During the war he served as Deputy Assistant Chief of Air Staff for Operations, Commitments and Requirements at the headquarters of the Army Air Forces. In 1946 he became chief of staff of the Air Transport Command and then commanding general of the European Division of the Air Transport Command. Following several assignments at the headquarters of the USAFE, McKee was appointed assistant vice chief of staff of the Air Force. During 1953–61 he served as vice commander of the Air Materiel Command and then was promoted to be vice commander and subsequently commander of the Air Force Logistics Command. In 1962 he became vice commanding officer, USAF. He came to the space agency in 1964 as assistant administrator for manpower development. NASA administrator James Webb felt that since there were such close ties between his agency and the military, there should be stronger formal organizational links. He saw a specific need for greater input from the Air Force, especially at the policy level, and brought McKee to NASA for just that reason. The general undertook a comprehensive review of all the NASA programs for Mr. Webb and renewed many old friendships.

When President Johnson was looking for a new FAA administrator, both Webb and Robert McNamara recommended Gen. McKee for the position. Webb had been impressed by his work at NASA, and McKee had known McNamara for years—they had worked closely together while McKee was at the Pentagon in 1962–64. Since one of the primary responsibilities of the new FAA administrator would be the management of the new supersonic-transport program, and because McNamara was very knowledgeable about the effort that would be required, he felt that McKee should personally oversee its development. Not all felt as McNamara did, however, and some opposition to the appointment developed during the hearings before the Commerce Committee. The problem of military encroachment upon a civilian agency was highlighted in testimony by representatives of two major aviation organizations. The Aircraft Owners and

Pilots Association, represented by Joseph B. Hartranft, Jr., originally opposed McKee's appointment. They subsequently withdrew their opposition, because, as Mr. Hartranft testified, "We have also been informed that the President had compelling reasons of national interest that transcended strictly aviation affairs, in announcing his intention of appointing Gen. McKee administrator of the FAA. It is not within our power to assess those reasons. In these troubled times, when the prestige and security of our nation is threatened in many parts of the world, occasions arise when we must accept the judgment of our Chief Executive despite our strong contrary beliefs." [24] A civilian interpretation of the military reality! One wonders what kind of pressure was exerted upon AOPA to extract such a concession, for in later testimony Hartranft was adamant about the need to maintain civilian control of FAA. After noting that under an act that specifically stipulates the FAA administrator be a civilian the score was about to become two to one in favor of the military, he went on to observe:

> We must conclude that the present language is either inadequate to convey accurately and convincingly the intent of Congress with regard to statutory qualifications of candidates, or that there exists nowhere an available and capable civilian to fill the top aviation post.
>
> We cannot conceive the latter to be the case—that nowhere within the FAA itself or from outside that agency does there exist a qualified civilian. The issue of civilian leadership, we conclude, must be drawn with renewed clarity. . . .

Yet despite his renewed conviction that civilian control had to be protected, Hartranft yielded to administrative pressure. Senator Dominick, particularly concerned about what the responsibilities of FAA were besides the promotion of general aviation, asked Hartranft about the "compelling reasons" for bringing McKee to FAA. He replied that he had been informed of two: the development of supersonic transport and, as he described it, "the particular situation we find ourselves in nationally, in which he [Johnson] felt that the qualifications of Gen. McKee closely fitted the requirements with respect to that national situation. This brought into consideration, as I understand it, matters which were in addition to aviation considerations." Hartranft couched his response in the most ambiguous terms, but its intent is clear—the highest official in this country had interpreted the national situation as one of crisis, as one in which the state was threatened. The military reality had made it necessary to appoint a four-star general as head of an agency which by law should have been administered by a civilian.

While the leaders of this country were able to make policy only within the framework of the military reality, its citizens continued to fight for the establishment of a civilian reality. David Scott of the National Pilots Association posed the problem most succinctly in his testimony before the committee:

> To take action which will nullify the specific determination of Congress to suit a special situation should be warranted only on the basis that there is no acceptable alternative. We are not convinced that there is no possibility of finding a qualified civilian to serve in this important position as Administrator of the FAA or to find a place in the FAA to use the talent of Gen. McKee without changing the provisions of the law originally drafted.
>
> It has been reported that the President chose Gen. McKee for the post of Administrator because he particularly wanted a man who would accelerate the supersonic transport program. The SST is a dramatic program, but there are other activities of the agency which are most important even if not so spectacular. We feel the new Administrator of the FAA should initiate programs that would accelerate the development of practical STOL and VTOL passenger aircraft to solve the problem of mass transportation on relatively short-haul intercity travel. Although not as spectacular, this could well prove more beneficial to more people than the SST. International civil aviation problems are becoming of increasing importance, and we question whether a man with a military background is the ideal choice to deal with representatives of foreign governments in the field.

Scott's testimony had little impact upon the proceedings. Arguing within the context of a civilian reality, he was unable to relate to men who perceived the entire world order in a very different way.

McNamara's faith in McKee's ability to handle the SST was rewarded in a distinctly West Point fashion. Burdened with choosing between Boeing and Lockheed as producers of the plane, McKee agonized until one night he awoke from his sleep thinking of the Cadet Prayer—"make us to choose the harder right instead of the easier wrong." He immediately decided on Boeing. The phrase doesn't quite fit the decision, for almost all the official recommendations he had received favored Boeing rather than Lockheed as the manufacturer. Upon his resignation, McKee received a letter of commendation from President Johnson which stated, in part: "And you brought wise and prudent management to our supersonic transport program." [25]

When Nixon appointed the fourth FAA director, the score became three to one, and he encountered no difficulty in having him confirmed. He chose a military man who had resigned from the regular Air Force, one who ostensibly met the "civilian" qualifications. Nonetheless John H. Shaffer was a military man, a member of the West Point Class of January 1943, and a long-time acquaintance of Gen. McKee. He had had time, however, to establish close ties with industry before coming to FAA and there was no opposition to his appointment. But the West Point mentality operates irrespective of whether or not the carrier is in uniform. Shaffer's experience with Ford Motor Company (assistant plant manager, Metuchen, New Jersey) and with TRW, Inc. (corporate vice-president stationed in Washington) does not negate the fact that he is a West Point graduate; it only facilitates cooperation between the government and giant aeronautical corporations at the expense of the interests of the people.

FAA has total control of aviation in the United States. In a public-relations pamphlet the scope of its activities is described in this way: "FAA's responsibilities begin at the drawing boards where aircraft are conceived and end at the factories where they take shape. The federal role continues with jurisdiction over the men who dispatch the aircraft from airports, the aircrews who fly them, the aviation mechanics who maintain them and other specialists, such as parachute riggers, flight instructors, etc. FAA responsibilities include the aerospace, the navigation aids, the airway system, the airports and the research needed to continually improve the performance and enhance the safety of aircraft." The administrator, in the words of the assistant public-information officer, "has the responsibility to oversee all aspects of the FAA activities." Thus, virtual control of the entire aeronautics field lies in the hands of John Shaffer. As was the case with AEC and NASA, an agency which was established to provide clearly civilian direction for one of the most advanced fields of technology fell under military domination.

Control of AEC, NASA, and FAA by West Pointers is significant not only because it directly violates the clear intentions of Congress, but also because it places West Pointers at the very center of one of the major sources of power in the United States. Luther Hodges, former Secretary of Commerce, called research and development "the lever of rising living standards and economic growth." [26] Even such diametrically opposed personalities as Lyndon Johnson and James A. Rhodes, Governor of Ohio, recognized that investment in science was economically advantageous to their home communities. Johnson noted that bringing the new space center to Houston would "let the Southwest take the lead in the nation's economic development," and Rhodes commented that "Simply in terms of our own economic self-interest our only proper course is to increase our investment in science, technology and research as fast as we can. . . ." [27] Because of the advanced state of science, however, the federal government had had to assume the central role in sponsoring R&D. Don K. Price in *The Scientific Estate* comments that "the stakes had become too high in this gamble for more and more physical power, for anyone to ante up except the national government." [28] It has indeed assumed that responsibility. It supports the majority of R&D in industry, essentially maintains the research programs at all major universities, and sponsors its own in-house research. Since West Pointers control the major federal sponsors of R&D, they wield unlimited economic power, and since political and economic power have become virtually synonymous in modern society, the West Pointer has moved into the inner political circles, whether he chooses to acknowledge it or not. When Gen. McKee said, "West Point has had a very profound influence in this country, much more than people realize. I doubt if the average person recognized the impact," he was barely touching upon what is a fundamental reality in our society today. Samuel Huntington in *The Soldier and the State* comes a little closer to the awful truth in this extraordinary passage:

Just south of the United States Military Academy at West Point is the village of Highland Falls. Main Street of Highland Falls is familiar to everyone: the First National Bank with venetian blinds, real estate and insurance offices, yellow homes with frilly Victorian porticos, barber shops, and wooden churches—the tiresome monotony and the incredible variety and discordancy of small-town commercialism. The buildings form no part of a whole: they are simply a motley, disconnected collection of frames coincidentally adjoining each other, lacking common unity or purpose. On the military reservation the other side of South Gate, however, exists a different world. There is ordered serenity. The parts do not exist on their own, but accept their subordination to the whole. Beauty and utility are merged in gray stone. Neat lawns surround compact, trim homes, each identified by the name and rank of its occupant. The buildings stand in fixed relation to each other, part of an over-all plan, their character and station symbolizing their contributions: stone and brick for the senior officers, wood for the lower ranks. The post is suffused with the rhythm and harmony which comes when collective will supplants individual whim. West Point is a community of structured purpose, one in which the behavior of men is governed by code, the product of generations. There is little room for presumption and individualism. The unity of the community incites no man to be more than he is. In order is found peace; in discipline, fulfillment; in community, security. The spirit of Highland Falls is embodied in Main Street. The spirit of West Point is in the great, gray, Gothic Chapel, starting from the hill and dominating the Plain, calling to mind Henry Adams' remarks at Mont St. Michel on the unity of the military and the religious spirits. But the unity of the Chapel is even greater. There join together the four great pillars of society: Army, Government, College, and Church. Religion subordinates man to God for divine purposes; in its severity, regularity, discipline, the military society shares the characteristics of the religious order. Modern man may well find his monastery in the Army.

West Point embodies the military ideal at its best; Highland Falls the American spirit at its most commonplace. West Point is a gray island in a many-colored sea, a bit of Sparta in the midst of Babylon. Yet is it possible to deny that the military values—

loyalty, duty, restraint, dedication—are the ones America most needs today? That the disciplined order of West Point has more to offer than the garish individualism of Main Street? Historically, the virtues of West Point have been America's vices, and the vices of the military, America's virtues. Yet today America can learn more from West Point than West Point from America. Upon the soldiers, the defenders of order, rests a heavy responsibility. The greatest service they can render is to remain true to themselves, to serve with silence and courage in the military way. If they abjure the military spirit, they destroy themselves first and their nation ultimately. If the civilians permit the soldiers to adhere to the military standard, the nations themselves may eventually find redemption and security in making that standard their own.[29]

This is the same Huntington who emphatically maintains in his book *The Common Defense* that the military and their thinking have no significant effect on American foreign policy. He has obviously never heard of the following "defender of order" from the "monastery" at West Point.

The usurpation and abuse of power by General Anastasio "Tachito" Somoza, Jr. (W.P. 1946), dictator of Nicaragua, and of his father before him, date back to 1928. In that year Gen. Frank R. McCoy (W.P. 1897), with the help of some 6,000 U.S. Marines, ran the national elections in Nicaragua. These elections and events before and after provide some insight into the West Point foreign-policy mind in action and presage the elections supervised by the U.S. military in Vietnam some forty years later.

Nicaragua, rich in natural resources and affording the opportunity of a transoceanic canal, had long held a peculiar fascination for U.S. military men. In the 1850s Gen. William Walker, a soldier of fortune backed by some U.S. financial interests and outfitted with a motley army, managed to win control of the entire land and declare himself President of the Republic. The private services of William Walker had been requested by the liberals of León in a civil war raging within Nicaragua, but few had recognized Walker's yearning for the political. This would-be savior surrendered to a British ship in 1860 and was turned over to a Honduran army unit, which had him executed.

Nevertheless, by 1909 Nicaragua, about half the size of Kentucky, might as well have been one of the states of the American union. A U.S. lumber company owned the timber rights to some 8,000 square miles of pine forest; U.S. businessmen owned most of the mining concessions, particularly in gold; a U.S. firm owned all port facilities at Corinto on the Pacific; individual U.S. businessmen and Europeans owned coffee plantations; a U.S. navigation company enjoyed a transportation monopoly on the rivers of the Bluefield area; and a U.S. company owned banana plantations at Las Perlas on Nicaraguan government land.

Notwithstanding this near-total control, however, the dictator of Nicaragua in 1909, President José Santos Zelaya, a ruthless and dispassionate strong man, turned over business concessions to other countries—much in the spirit of free enterprise, but also much to the chagrin of the government in Washington, D.C. The death of two American soldiers of fortune in an anti-Zelaya rebellion provided the excuse for the United States to send Marines "to restore order." Secretary of State Philander C. Knox indignantly proclaimed Zelaya a "blot on the history of Nicaragua," Zelaya resigned, U.S. Marines left the Caribbean republic—and by 1910 New York banks were negotiating loans in Nicaragua.[30]

Again in 1912 U.S. Marines disembarked on Nicaraguan shores, this time at the request of President Adolfo Díaz. Their job, of course, was to put down an anti-Díaz uprising. The Marines stayed until 1925, and only two and one half months after their departure another insurrection took place. By 1928 the country was in turmoil. Augusto César Sandino, thirty-three, of peasant and working-class background, led a band of revolutionaries in the northeastern section of Nicaragua, strongly protesting the repressive Díaz regime and some 2,000 U.S. Marines who had returned to Nicaragua. Sandino, a man of charisma, was unalterably against the exploitation of Nicaraguan resources by the United States. He wrote to D. F. Sellars, U.S. Representative in Managua, "The only way to put an end to this struggle is the immediate withdrawal of the invading forces from our country. . . ."[31] In answer to Sandino, and to put an end to the civil strife threatening the vast U.S. business interests, more Marines were dispatched to Nicaragua. Col. Stimson, later U.S. Secretary of State, also negotiated with the Nicaraguan government in power for the United States to act as a mediator between all factions and to run the elections scheduled for 1928.

Gen. Frank Ross McCoy (W.P. 1897) was chosen by President Coolidge to head the U.S. electoral commission in Nicaragua. Upon graduation from West Point, McCoy had spent two years in Cuba as aide-de-camp in charge of fiscal affairs and budgetary matters under Gen. Leonard Wood, the governor-general. As a member of several committees of arbitration, investigation, and relief, McCoy had made trips to many of the Central American countries. In 1923, he had been director-general of a relief expedition to Japan following an earthquake that destroyed a large portion of that country. He had then become principal assistant in charge of civil administration in the Philippines, again serving under Gen. Wood. McCoy had fought against the Moros in the Philippines and in France during World War I, eventually serving on the staff of Gen. Pershing. He had been aide to Presidents Roosevelt and Taft and was a close personal friend of Secretary of State Stimson.

Gen. McCoy's appointment as supervisor of the Nicaraguan elections was strongly opposed by some members of Congress on the grounds that there is a basic contradiction in a military man performing a civilian function. Representative Fiorello La Guardia of New York, for example, wrote a letter to the Secretary of State:

> May I suggest that this government assign a group of experienced, sincere and impartial Americans, unspoiled of diplomatic training and bare of side arms, gatlings, and bombs. . . .
> Neither the gold braid of the Navy nor the spurred boot of the Army can assure that confidence of a fair and impartial election necessary to the successful conduct of a democratic government.[32]

Later, in April 1928, American citizens protested U.S. policy toward Nicaragua, and several Latin American newspapers protested the elections—elections in which Sandino and any other "bandits" would not be allowed to run. Editorials appeared in the newspapers of Buenos Aires, Mexico City, and other urban centers. In Balboa a Panamanian newspaper editorial criticized the suggestion that other Central American countries participate in the supervision of the Nicaraguan elections. A Mexican editorial expounded the virtues of peasants staying away from the polls on election day.[33]

To legitimize the mission to Nicaragua, the U.S. agreement with President Díaz had stated that the appointment of the U.S. commissioner was subject to the approval of the Nicaraguan Congress, a seemingly procedural stipulation. Representative Chamorro of the Nicaraguan House of Deputies, however, informed by the U.S. Department of State that he would not be diplomatically recognized should he be elected President, led a faction against passage of the "McCoy Bill." Representative Chamorro offered a substitute resolution which would have made Gen. McCoy an observer rather than a supervisor. Because of the requirement of a two-thirds majority, the bill was defeated and a less powerful compromise resolution was passed. President Díaz then issued an executive decree backed by the Nicaraguan Supreme Court declaring the compromise Congressional resolution null and void, thereby restoring to Frank McCoy his near-dictatorial powers over the Nicaraguan elections. Headlines from articles which appeared in *The New York Times* during this period are revealing: "Díaz Decree Meets Washington Approval" (March 28, 1928); "Nicaraguan Congress Adjourns Sine Die, McCoy Presses Own Plans to Supervise Elections" (March 17, 1928); and "McCoy Board Bars Rival Candidates" (July 8, 1928). Indeed, throughout the elections it was the National Election Board, of which McCoy was chairman, that decided who was allowed to run for the Presidency of the Republic.

The contradiction between a free election and the reality that McCoy was foisting upon the Nicaraguan people did not seem to bother him, perhaps because he was the epitome of a West Pointer. Writing in the *Nation,* Carleton Beals said McCoy was "one of those iron-willed, super-logical, single-track types whose stern jaw carried not an ounce of compromise." Further, wrote Beals, McCoy "had hit upon an ideal scheme for the salvation of Nicaragua—a utopian democratic perfection, which he was putting over with the faith of Loyola, and the same inquisitorial methods." During the period from August 1926 through February 1931 some 6,000 United States Marines were dispatched to Nicaragua.[34] Using his troops to ensure his utopia, McCoy is reported to have told Gen. Feland of the Marine Corps, "If you haven't gotten Sandino in a month, I will feel that you have failed and I shall so report to the State Department."[35] Sandino was not "gotten" during that month, and McCoy begins to sound more and more like the Westmoreland of days to come.

Matthew B. Ridgway (W.P. 1917), then a captain working with Gen. McCoy, also did not perceive any disparity between holding "free" elections and not allowing certain persons to run for President or not allowing persons in Sandinista-held villages to vote. Years later, after having attained the rank of general and having been stationed at other Latin American posts, Ridgway wrote of the elections: "We rewrote the election laws, translated them from English into Spanish, and distributed them throughout the country. Some ten months later, the election was held. There was no rioting, no disorder, and I am positive that no election was ever held in any land that was fairer or more impartial."[36]

In March 1928 it was announced that "Brigadier General Frank Ross McCoy, head of the Board, will return to the United States sometime before Sunday to choose the personnel who will aid him in the direct supervision. These members will be 25 or 30 Army and Navy men and civilians, all of whom must speak Spanish fluently."[37] Of the twenty-two officers McCoy chose for his Managua office, seven were Academy graduates and one was an ex-cadet. Two were retired colonels: C. C. Smith (W.P. 1894) and Ora E. Hunt (W.P. 1894). Hunt had been stationed at West Point in 1908–12 and 1914–17 as assistant professor in the Department of Modern Languages. Capt. L. V. H. Durfee (W.P. 1917), also a member of McCoy's staff, later became a professor of Spanish at West Point. Lt. Irvin Alexander (W.P. 1919) had taught law at USMA from 1924 to 1926 and was a close friend of Capt. Ridgway.

McCoy also employed thirty-two Annapolis graduates from the classes of 1926 and 1927 who ranked high in Spanish. In addition to these eminently qualified "diplomats," McCoy had help from members of the academic and political community.

Most of the Nicaraguan electoral law was written at Princeton, New Jersey, by a Professor Dodds. Professor Barrows of the University of California, a Carnegie Professor in International Relations, also wrote part of the law and advised Gen. McCoy, as did George K. Pond of the Massachusetts State Senate. Walter Wilgus, a former editor of the *Manila Times,* advised McCoy on legal and technical matters.

Being a member of the electoral commission was not all drudgery, but even the playtime was not without its minor catastrophes. Matthew Ridgway hunted crocodiles in his spare time: "The Nicaraguan lakes are full of monster crocodiles, wary creatures, but dangerous to a man alone. I hunted them by creeping up on them, crawling on my belly through the slime. I would shoot them just between those little knobs in which their eyes are set, which is all you can see sticking up when they are in the water." Ridgway bagged as many as seven crocodiles in one day, "fourteen-footers, with big wide bellies on them, weighing up to a thousand pounds each, I would guess." In this manner, clad only in shorts and shoes, Capt. Ridgway lost a treasured West Point memento: "My loosely fitting West Point ring slipped off my finger while I was stalking one big old bull and it's still there somewhere, buried in the jungle muck." [38]

In November 1928—in true U.S. fashion—the "elections" were held. Coming as no surprise to most persons, the rigging was deemed a success in the United States. Over 130, 000 votes were cast, a total 30 percent higher than the turbulent 1924 elections, which had also been run by the United States but without the same "definitiveness." President Calvin Coolidge telegraphed McCoy: "I take pleasure in congratulating you for your splendid services in supervising the elections. It is a great credit to you and I believe will be of lasting benefit to the people of Nicaragua." [39]

At the local level in Nicaragua, as the United States was later to experience in Vietnam, everything was not really so rosy. Lt. Col. Clyde H. Metcalf, a Marine who served in Nicaragua, put it this way: "By the beginning of 1929 it was becoming more and more evident that the Marines in Nicaragua had been called upon to perform an almost impossible task. They were expected to maintain order . . . without any control over the civilian population. . . . Neither the people nor their officials stood behind the Marines in their attempt to put down lawlessness." [40]

By 1929, according to Harold N. Denny, a *New York Times* reporter who had spent six months in Nicaragua, "The U.S. has ruled Nicaragua during most of the past 18 years more completely than the American Federal Government rules any state in the Union. It unquestionably has exercised a protectorate over Nicaragua, however spiritedly the State Department may disavow the word." [41] In 1929 an American citizen chosen by American bankers and the State Department was in charge of collecting Nicaragua's customs duties, one half the total revenues of the nation, and another American was manager of the National Bank of Nicaragua, and as such was comptroller of Nicaragua's currency.[42] Neither was a West Pointer; graduates, of course, are soldiers, not bankers or election brokers. After Mencada had been installed as President in early 1929, the United States decided the Marines were no longer needed in Nicaragua and all Marines left the Caribbean Republic by January 1, 1933. This opened the door for the assumption of the Somoza dynasty. Gen. Sandino, the rebel leader, had long maintained that he would lay down his arms as soon as the "invading American forces" left the country, and, true to his word, he voluntarily disarmed his army on February 22, 1933, and surrendered. A few months later Tacho Somoza, chief of the Nicaraguan army, spoke with Arthur B. Lane, the U.S. Representative, and that same evening gathered twelve officers of the Guardia Nacional together. He told them he had spoken with U.S. Minister Lane, "who has assured me that the government in Washington supports and recommends the elimination of Augusto César Sandino, because they consider him a disturber of the peace of the country." [43] The U.S. government has denied this conversation. The thirteen officers voted unanimously to kill Sandino that same night, and all signed a resolution called "The Death of Caesar" to ensure complicity of all present. Gen. Sandino and three Sandinista generals were driven to a remote airfield hours later and, under orders of Gen. Somoza, were summarily executed by machine gun.

[275]

General Somoza allowed President Mencada to continue in office until 1936, and then took over the entire country for himself. The first Nicaraguan Constitution in 1939 extended Somoza's rule to 1947, but with no provision for reelection. Somoza assured that he and the Guardia Nacional would abide by the elections of 1947, and he even supported Leonardo Argüello, who took office in that year. Twenty-five days later, after Argüello had dismissed from office several Somoza relatives, Argüello was forced to flee the country, and Somoza once again became ruler of the Republic. In 1948 and 1950 Somoza rewrote the Constitution to suit his needs and was elected for the last time on May 1, 1951. [44]

In 1963 Luis Somoza briefly stepped down as President—but only after the withdrawal and imprisonment of the principal opposition candidate. Luis Somoza's hand-picked successor, René Schick, tried to bring a breath of liberalism to the police state, but was not very successful. In the summer of 1966 Schick died of a heart attack and General Tachito Somoza, chief of the Army (W.P. 1946), lost forty pounds from his burly frame and won the "elections."

Some insight into the Somoza family can be gleaned from the elaborate means they sometimes use to protect themselves from physical harm. In March 1963, for example, John F. Kennedy met with a group of Central American presidents gathered in Costa Rica. Luis Somoza arrived, resplendent with seventy security agents and a convoy of armored cars. And although other presidents stayed at their respective embassies, Somoza's place of residence was kept secret.[45]

Rulership has been profitable for the Somoza family. Under Tacho Somoza, the country made some progress, but he made more by acquiring an estimated one tenth of the productive land of his country. During World War II and the Korean war, world cotton prices boomed and Nicaragua began showing a healthy trade surplus. Of course, much of the Nicaraguan produce sold on world markets came from the dictator's farms. A 1950–51 study of income in Nicaragua indicated that 25 percent of the national income went to one percent of the population and that that segment paid little of the tax burden. It was paid by the 99 percent whose average annual income was $100.

Somoza's sons have managed to hold on to the family fortune —an estimated 430 properties including lumber, liquor, soap, cement, utility interests, and a steamship monopoly—but not without some hardship. In 1968, Tachito had to suppress a small guerrilla movement led by Ramon Raudales, a veteran of Sandino's army, and the next year the Guardia Nacional had to dispose of a larger band of guerrillas, many of whom had been armed and trained in Fidel Castro's Cuba.[46]

The Somoza fortune has had repercussions for other Latin American countries. In the 1950s an effort was made to diversify farm production in Nicaragua and encourage light industries, but a drop of the price of coffee and cotton in the world market caused a nationwide economic decline in the late Fifties. The Central American market offered the possibilities of recovery, but under the rule of the Somozas, Nicaragua remained ripe for revolution and the nation's energies were directed toward suppressing internal dissent. Fittingly, Puerto Cabezas, Nicaragua, was a jumping-off point for Cuban-exile counter-revolutionaries in the Bay of Pigs invasion. After this abortive incursion, Tachito Somoza said he would be glad to lead an armed invasion of Cuba at the head of anti-communist volunteers. Nicaragua and the Somoza family, as a result of such displays of cooperative attitude, have long received generous grants and loans. In the early 1960s, for example, the Central American Bank, the World Bank, and a Special United Nations Fund turned $4 million over to Nicaragua. In turn, during the same period the government of Nicaragua contributed $10,000 to the campaign coffers of John F. Kennedy in 1960 and $1,500 to Representative Daniel J. Flood of Pennsylvania, a champion of a proposal that a transoceanic canal be built through Nicaragua.[47] It could be that Washington officialdom, in dealing with Tachito Somoza, relies on the wisdom laid down by President Franklin Roosevelt while speaking of the elder Somoza. "He's a sonofabitch," Roosevelt is reported to have said, "but he's ours." [48]

In 1947 the *Army and Navy Bulletin* boasted that "Today, the Army has virtual control of foreign affairs. . . . The chain of control in diplomatic hot spots, both in the execution of basic policy and in the formulation of ad hoc arrangements, lies almost totally in the hands of the military authorities." Gen.

Douglas MacArthur (W.P. 1903) ruled Japan, Lt. Gen. Geoffrey Keyes (W.P. 1913) presided over the American sector of Austria, Lt. Gen. Albert C. Wedemeyer (W.P. 1919) headed a special mission to China, Brig. Gen. Charles E. Saltzman (W.P. 1925) was Assistant Secretary of State for Occupied Areas, a former cadet named John E. Peurifoy was an Assistant Secretary of State, Lucius Clay (W.P. 1918) was Military Governor of the Occupied Zone in Europe (Professor John Galbraith recently named Clay one of the people "who have made a profession of the Cold War" [49]), Frank McCoy (W.P. 1897) was chairman of the Far Eastern Commission, and Archibald Arnold (W.P. 1912) was Military Governor of Korea. This list is incomplete; the military, dominated by West Pointers, occupied key foreign-policy positions around the globe during this period. This is not to say they were not prepared for these obligations—they often knew foreign languages, had personal contacts abroad, and, above all, were ready to follow instructions from their partners in Washington. Once established in their slots, they decided which policy issues would be raised in Washington, their class- or career-mates in the State Department and on the Joint Chiefs of Staff recommended solutions to the President, and, after they translated his decision into a course of action, instructions were relayed to their friends in the field. From top to bottom, this process was controlled by the military.

With the military reality holding sway in the postwar years, the professional civilian diplomat ceased to be an effective force in international decision-making. He had been bypassed by an extraordinarily efficient clique of high military officials. The generals arranged the Japanese peace treaty, the agreements between the armies in Germany, the disposition of the western Pacific islands captured from the Japanese, the armistice in Korea, the 1953 defense agreements with Spain, and so on. The military were very comfortable in these roles, for their view of peace as merely an interlude between wars made their negotiations immune to charges of "appeasement" or "treason." The professional diplomat with a view toward real peace did not have this advantage and very nearly vanished from sight. In sum, it seems almost inevitable that foreign policy should have been controlled by the generals: the wartime atmosphere persisted after World War II, the Soviet Union appeared aggressive and hostile, and the awesomeness of atomic weapons had the American public fearing for its safety. With these conditions as the accepted reality, it is plain to see how the military, with their emphasis on national security, enemy capabilities, and military readiness for the worst contingencies, became dominant. Civilian checks and balances on foreign policy had been irreparably eroded.

Many well-known West Pointers have been involved in the capture of foreign policy, but the whole process is best described by one not so well known, Brig. Gen. George A. "Abe" Lincoln (W.P. 1929). He was active in the initial takeover during World War II and has, over the years, remained a powerful ideologue —powerful enough to assume an important position in President Nixon's strengthening of the military reality in foreign policy.

Graduating fourth in the Class of 1929, Lincoln won a Rhodes Scholarship and attended Oxford until 1932. In 1937, after a series of Corps of Engineers assignments, he returned to West Point to teach government and economics. His students included "several hundred of the now senior leadership of the Army." [50] Following the outbreak of the war, Lincoln left West Point and soon became chief of the Strategy and Policy Group, Operations Division, War Department. As such, he was Gen. Marshall's strategic planner, serving as the War Department member of the Joint Staff and Combined Staff Planners. He attended the conferences at Quebec, Yalta, and Postdam and, near the end of the war, worked on the redeployment of American troops in the Pacific and the Japanese surrender. Asked by Eisenhower to remain a Planner in the postwar period, Lincoln wrestled "with the chores of demobilizing our giant forces, occupying and then reconstructing former enemy countries and coping with the new problems of nuclear weapons, collective security, and the obstreperous Russians." [51] He capped this period by serving as the Military Advisor to Secretary of State Byrnes at the Paris Peace Conference. Lincoln, in other words, was in the thick of applying the military reality to world affairs.

Others soon realized the value of Lincoln's expertise and decided it was time for him to train his fellows in perpetuating this new strength of the military. He was asked to return to West

Point. In the words of Col. Amos Jordan (W.P. 1946), Lincoln's protégé in the Social Science Department at USMA, the process of enticing Lincoln back to West Point went as follows: "When the Academy was authorized a second professor in the larger departments in 1946, Col. Beukema (Class of 1915) sought out Gen. Lincoln, who was interested, both because of the great admiration he had for Herman Beukema and also because he had sensed an enormous challenge in educating cadets and others for the task of adjusting to the new security environment [!]. Gen. Eisenhower first tried to dissuade him, suggesting a second star in lieu of turning his talents to a West Point professor's position. When Abe persisted, encouraged by his then boss, Lauris Norstad (Class of 1930), Ike stipulated that he stay with Norstad until passage in 1947 of the Unification Act." [52]

Another Lincoln associate in Social Sciences, Col. Roger Nye (W.P. 1946), writes: "The U.S. Military Academy has rarely been accused of raiding sister schools for its professors. It has preferred to lure them from within the far-flung fortresses and occasionally from inside the Pentagon. Never was this brand of professionalizing more successful than just after World War II, when a number of distinguished service officers were persuaded to leave the line of the Army to become officer-professors. George Arthur (Abe) Lincoln was in the 1947 draft. He was not easily shanghaied. He had grown accustomed to heavy responsibilities, had retained his Brigadier-General stars through the post-war cutbacks, and was poised for the command positions that were promised if he stayed in the line. But on September 1, 1947, he became Col. G. A. Lincoln, Professor and deputy head of the Dept. of Social Sciences, USMA." [53] Lincoln himself says, "By that time [1947], I was a brigadier general and decided that I could serve best by going back to the Military Academy as professor. . . ." [54]

These descriptions coloring Lincoln's decision to abort a bright Army future for West Point as a purely altruistic one stand in sharp contrast to the remarks of John Foster Dulles in 1957 before the Senate Foreign Relations Committee when Lincoln was being considered for appointment as Assistant Secretary of State: "You will note from that summary [of Lincoln's career] that while Col. Lincoln is a Regular Army Officer occupying a permanent professorship at the United States' Military Academy, his case is unusual in that he *was forced to accept that permanent professorship because of an unfortunate heart attack which disenabled him from continuing a more active military career.*" [55] (Emphasis added)

Whatever the real reasons for his return to West Point, Lincoln's image and academy integrity were sufficiently intact for him to join the cadre of professor-consultants who floated back and forth between "academia" and the federal national-security machine. Discussing his career before the Senate Committee on Armed Services in 1969, he said, "I have been there [USMA] for nearly 22 years, however, spending probably a third of that time on various assignments in Washington, generally for Government agencies." [56] In 1948–49 he served as Deputy to Under Secretary of the Army William H. Draper. Because Draper was heavily involved in developing the first Joint Armed Forces Budget, Lincoln assumed most of his responsibilities, including the management of the Berlin blockade. In 1950 he consulted with the Pace Committee investigating the organization and operation of the National Security Council. One year later he became the Department of Defense representative on the Interdepartmental Committee formed to design the Mutual Security Program (foreign aid to the NATO countries). Later in 1951 he became the Defense Department's advisor to the United States delegate to the Temporary Council Committee of NATO (first Averell Harriman and later Draper) and attended the NATO conferences in Rome and Lisbon. Still later Lincoln found time to consult for CIA, the Arms Control and Disarmament Agency, the Agency for International Development, the Brookings Institution, and the Council on Foreign Relations.

There are other activities which are yet to be revealed, for, as the State Department put it in 1957, "The foregoing summary of Col. Lincoln's activities is by no means exhaustive. Some of the projects relating to United States policy with which he has been connected are still highly classified and cannot be discussed in open hearing." [57]

As a consultant in propagandizing the military reality in the civilian world Lincoln appears to have been eminently successful, but his primary duty was still that of a West Point professor.

According to General Maxwell Taylor (W.P. 1922), he used both roles to maximum effectiveness:

> The Department [Social Sciences] expanded in many fields and began to attract increasing numbers of brilliant young officers into the ranks of its instructors. . . . Gradually they formed in the Officer Corps a group of officers with the Lincoln stamp and his outlook toward the basic issues of national defense. In his Department, Lincoln had taught them the necessity of blending together military and non-military components to form a national strategy of maximum effectiveness. They had acquired from him an understanding of the many facets of national power and the need for flexibility in its application. Such men have become a national asset in preparing the Armed Forces to meet the challenges of the evolving world relationships as typified by the complex situation in Vietnam.
>
> In the course of training officers of this type, Col. Lincoln has been largely responsible for projecting a new image of West Point throughout the nation. West Point is no longer viewed as a military monastery set back from the stream of national life. As Col. Lincoln himself has moved easily back and forth from academic to public life, graduates trained in his model have been conspicuously active in both military and non-military fields. If Clemenceau is correctly quoted as saying that "War is too serious a business to be left to the generals," one may say with equal cogency today that peace is too serious a business to be left entirely to civilians. Officers patterned after Lincoln are the kind needed to work closely with civilian leadership in creating and fostering conditions most favorable to the maintenance of peace.[58]

So much for the myth of the "apolitical soldier."

Thousands of individuals have had the opportunity to learn the military reality from Lincoln at West Point. In the words of Col. Amos Jordan on the occasion of Lincoln's retirement in 1969, "he leaves behind a legacy of solid achievement in the form of engraving on the minds of some 14,000 cadets and 250 officers who have passed through the Corps and the Department during his professorial years." [59] West Pointers aren't the only ones who have had their minds engraved; Dean Rusk, one of the architects of Vietnam, says, "There is a very long list of men who look to 'Abe' Lincoln as their teacher, and I am honored to be counted among them." [60] A brief list of others who have professed owing Lincoln a debt of gratitude would include the following:

Brig. Gen. Robert N. Ginsburgh (W.P. 1944): Member of the Chairman's Staff Group in the Office of the Chairman, JCS; member of the State Department's Policy Planning Council; Executive Assistant to two Air Force Chiefs of Staff; Legislative Liaison Officer in the Office of the Secretary of the Air Force; Plans Officer for the Allied Air Forces, Southern Europe; Research Fellow, Council on Foreign Relations; Commander, Aerospace Standards Institute.

Gen. Andrew J. Goodpaster (W.P. 1939): Supreme Commander, Allied Forces, Europe; Commander in Chief, United States Army, Europe; Deputy Commander, United States Military Assistance Command, Vietnam; Director of Army Studies; Director of Joint Staff; Special Assistant to the Chairman, JCS; Defense Liaison Officer and Staff Secretary to the President of the United States; Special Assistant to the Chief of Staff, SHAPE.

Gen. Charles H. Bonesteel (W.P. 1930): Commander-in-Chief, United Nations Command, Korea; Special Assistant to Ambassador Harriman in Europe; Deputy to Ambassador Spoffard with the NATO Council Deputies; Defense Department member of the National Security Council Planning Board; Special Assistant (Policy) to the Chairman, JCS; Director of Special Studies in the Office of the Chief of Staff; Senior U.S.A. Member of the Military Staff Commission of the U.N.

And a couple of young "comers":

Lt. Col. Robert G. Gard, Jr. (W.P. 1950): Military Assistant to the Secretary of Defense; Special Consultant to the Assistant Secretary of Defense, International Security Affairs (ASD-ISA); Chief of the NATO Branch of the European-Western Hemisphere Division of the Policy Planning Staff in the Office of the ASD-ISA.

Lt. Col. John W. Seigle (W.P. 1953): Chief of Army Studies; Assistant to the Director of the Office of Emergency Preparedness; Assistant Professor, USMA; Ph.D., Harvard.

With devotees of these kinds and his long record of spreading the gospel of "national security," Lincoln could not long go unnoticed by the Nixon administration. He was selected in Jan-

uary 1969 to be director of the Office of Emergency Preparedness (OEP), a position that carries with it a seat on the National
Security Council.

OEP is part of the Executive Office of the President, and, as
such, all its high-level positions are political appointments (the
three previous directors were ex-governors). It has the responsibility of assuring that the nation's civilian resources are ready to
meet any kind of national emergency, including enemy attack.
This function divides into three categories: government preparedness, disaster assistance, and resource analysis. The first
operation is designed to ensure continuity of government in case
of an attack and is, of course, untested and highly theoretical in
its workings. The second involves coordinating all federal aid
to disaster areas and, as the big publicity-getter, is the least
ambiguous of all OEP's activities. The third area, resource
analysis, deeply involves the agency in both domestic economic
policy and overall United States trade policy. In this regard,
OEP is charged with determining which material resources are
strategic and critical and sets the quality and quantities of such
materials to be stockpiled to meet national-security needs. According to Lou Neeb, one of the planners, the entire operation
is very political because either dumping excesses or stockpiling
can have a large impact on the free market.[61] In addition, OEP
is directed to safeguard our resources by protecting domestic
industries through controlling the importation of products that
may be harmful to national security, and through long-term
policy planning on industry energy demands. In the past, the
director of OEP had the added responsibility of being special
assistant to the President for state-federal relations (hence the
three ex-governors), but Nixon dropped this task and substituted a larger role for the director on the National Security
Council. More on this point later.

Why did Lincoln leave his beloved West Point and return to
the government when at one time he had supposedly been anxious to escape that very organization? Lincoln himself answers:
"First, my lifework has been to serve the United States, particularly in the broad area of national security, not only the more
narrowly military matters, but economic, political, human. And
the President asked me to undertake this responsibility. I have

been accustomed by nearly 40 years of service to react immediately to a request from the Commander in Chief as happily as the more junior officers." [62] Perhaps Lincoln had forgotten how he responded to Eisenhower's request as Army Chief of Staff for him to remain in government in 1947. Or could Dulles have been right about the heart attack? In any case, the conflicting recollections are puzzling.

Lincoln's general qualifications for the job were best summarized by a State Department official who testified, "I find that he has not specialized in any particular area. Both his responsibilities and the various consultative jobs he has done have been worldwide in scope." [63] He did, however, have some particular expertise in the defense industry, owning, jointly with his wife, stock in such companies as Litton, Textron, Westinghouse, Olin Mathieson, Air Reduction, General Motors, Reynolds Metals, Sperry-Rand, etc. Augmenting his USMA and Oxford educational background for the job, he had received an honorary Doctor of Laws from the University of Pittsburgh in 1968. It was presented by his old friend Wesley Posvar (W.P. 1946), chancellor of the university.

The major focus of Lincoln's attention since 1970 has been oil import policy. In 1969 President Nixon ordered a Cabinet Task Force to investigate oil import restrictions, which had gone unchanged since 1959. Chaired by Secretary of Labor Schultz, the group included the Secretaries of State, Treasury, Defense, Interior, and Commerce, and George Lincoln. No specific policy decisions were made by the Task Force, however, and their final report contained only recommendations and an indication of a need for a new management system to set policy for the oil import program. In response to this, Nixon created the Oil Policy Committee (OPC), an interdepartmental panel which includes the same members as the original Task Force but is chaired by Lincoln. Its function is to advise Lincoln, who was in turn delegated the responsibility of policy direction, coordination, and supervision of the oil import program. In effect, Lincoln was given the authority to define a new oil import policy as part of his overall job of "protecting domestic industry." The staff at OEP has expanded to provide Lincoln support in this role. There is now a special assistant to the director for oil and energy,

Elmer Bennett, who serves as OEP liaison with both industry and other government agencies. Also aiding Lincoln is the oil-and-energy working group, headed by Robert Shepard, a former executive assistant to Lincoln, who before coming to OEP worked with the Office of the Secretary of the Army as assistant director for research at a "research and development" center in Thailand. The executive officer for the working group is Anthony Smith (W.P. 1958). Smith came to OEP in 1970 as a replacement for John Seigle (W.P. 1953), who was Lincoln's first national-security advisor. Two more grads, John D. Simpson (W.P. 1959) and John Moellering (W.P. 1959), recently found their way into OEP and oil import policy.

The results of the oil-and-energy working group and the policy recommended by Lincoln bear little resemblance to the initial recommendations of the Task Force. For the ten years preceding the investigation, oil import restrictions were maintained by a quota system assigned in percentage terms to the various importers. The Task Force concluded: "A quota system is essentially rigid in two respects—it sets fixed limitations on the volume of oil that can be imported, and it builds up vested interests in the allocation of import benefits. Both aspects make it difficult to keep the import program responsive to current economic and national security needs in the light of energy developments at home." [64] The report went on to recommend a phased transition to a tariff system for controlling imports. Lincoln's duty under the dictates of the military reality and of the "national security" seemed clear: that is, switch to a tariff system or America will suffer. To date, however, there has been no major change in the oil policy program. There is still a finite quota system and allocations are made to each importer.

The fundamental premise behind an import restriction is that it is needed to keep the relevant industry self-sufficient in the face of threatening foreign developments. If there were no restrictions on oil: (a) foreign oil could come in at cheaper prices, causing the domestic industry to atrophy and fall behind in the development of new fields and technology; (b) the nation could be vulnerable to an interruption of imports which might be to our military, political, or economic disadvantage; (c) a cut-off might be threatened in order to affect our foreign policy;

or (d) our balance of payments might be affected, causing restrictions on other imports. All these risks were described by the
Task Force, but were later discounted in the same report as
only vague possibilities, none of which would have a serious
effect on the nation. Lincoln, however, seems to believe they
are all realistic and frightening. He says, "Our country's position in the world and its power abroad as well as at home is built
on energy and will depend greatly on how we handle our energy
problems in the future. Energy security is a vital part of national
security." [65]

From this statement it seems logical to assume that he sees the
above possibilities as real threats to national defense—or does
he? The real problem in switching to a tariff system is that it
would ultimately result in freer competition and lower the price
of domestically produced oil to a competitive level in the world
market. In 1969, the price differential between foreign and domestic oil was roughly $1.50 per barrel. By limiting imports, the
government can maintain this disparity and force the American
consumer to pay more (approximately five cents per gallon)
than he would if there were an open world market. Given the
size of the American oil industry, its influence on the economy,
and its international nature, the quota system seems politically a
very advantageous policy. With Lincoln in control, Nixon has
little to fear in the way of change, for, as one of Lincoln's West
Point aides put it, "The Director is a 'good soldier,' he is completely devoted to serving his leader and generally never advises
or criticizes." [66] Does Lincoln identify "national security" with
Nixon's political wishes? This question cannot be answered until
such men as Lincoln are publicly stripped of the protection of
the "military reality" and the myth of the "apolitical soldier."

George Lincoln also operates in another area with impunity
—the National Security Council (NSC). During the Sixties the
role of NSC was secondary in policy-making, and, consequently,
the responsibilities of the director of OEP as a member were
minimal. When Nixon reactivated NSC at the outset of his administration and made it the central machinery in the process of
policy-making for national security, it was only natural for
Lincoln to spend his first year as director working closely with
the council. In fact, Lincoln was chosen for OEP specifically

because Nixon wanted him as a member of NSC. In Lincoln's words, "the President has stated to me quite firmly that he wants me to put considerable of my personal time on the National Security Council matters." During the same hearings he added, "I recognize the great importance of the responsibilities the President has nominated me to undertake, stemming from membership in the National Security Council, which as you know is statutory and which President Nixon proposes to use a great deal, extending from there to my office in connection with national disaster assistance." [67] His appointment was the culmination of a long association with NSC beginning with the Pace Committee in 1950. In 1957 Eisenhower wanted to appoint him Assistant Secretary of State for Policy Planning and State Department representative to the NSC Planning Board (the principal policy-formulating body for NSC). His job would have been to "anticipate and identify problems affecting the security objectives, commitments, and risks of the United States, and initiate action to provide the required analyses and draft policy statements for the consideration of the Council." [68] On one of the rare occasions when civilians lashed out at the military reality, the Senate Foreign Relations Committee refused to approve Lincoln, on the grounds that he was too closely tied to the Army. The circumstances surrounding his "patriotic" departure from government in 1947 also arose in these hearings:

> SENATOR FULBRIGHT. How old is Colonel Lincoln, Mr. Secretary?
> MR. MURPHY. He is 50 years of age.
> SENATOR FULBRIGHT. And he has had a heart attack?
> MR. MURPHY. He had a heart attack several years ago.
> SENATOR FULBRIGHT. Is he on a regimen which limits his activities?
> MR. MURPHY. Well, in the sense that he has been taken out of active military service and was given this professorship assignment in which his physical condition is adequate.[69]

The defeat was only a temporary setback, however, for Lincoln had known Nixon during the Eisenhower administration and, better yet, had been a friend of Henry Kissinger for years. According to Anthony Smith, who taught at West Point with Lincoln, Kissinger had come early to Lincoln's attention as a foreign-policy strategist and was someone with whom he was in continuous contact.[70]

In 1969 "Abe's" connections paid off and he made NSC. During his first year at OEP he spent the majority of his time on NSC problems while it was doing a complete reevaluation of our foreign policy. He had two staff assistants doing background work for him—one a liaison with the Department of Defense, John Seigle (W.P. 1953), and the other a Foreign Service officer from the State Department. When Seigle returned to the Pentagon in 1970, he was replaced by another Academy man. Lincoln shows a certain fondness for old grads and they return it with fulsome praise for their boss—"a brilliant man who has no political ambitions and whose only aspiration is to serve the President faithfully"; "a scholar/government advisor type rather than a military man"; "very competent in the oil fields"; "he remembers details very well"; and "he is a good soldier." These comments are not unusual, coming from military men whose efficiency ratings are Lincoln's responsibility.

In 1971, when Lincoln was placed in charge of administering the ninety-day wage-and-price freeze, the following description appeared in a Washington newspaper: "When talking to newspapermen or congressional committees, George Lincoln puts on the air of a dumb country boy. He always begins by saying, 'Now, you know a lot more about this than I do.' But my assessment of him is that he's a sharp, shrewd country boy. He does what the White House wants him to. He's a front man and well-fitted for the job." [71]

Mr. Jones (not his real name) works in "XYZ" as an advisor and has attitudes typical of the bright young West Pointers now in government. His remarks are in quotes.

His Role in "XYZ." Jones considers himself apolitical and invisible, never signing his name to any memo, directive, etc. "The mark of a good staff man is one who remains anonymous and simply serves his boss—just like Kissinger." He perceives the power that derives from anonymity in high positions, but explains that people like himself and Kissinger are just fulfilling their functions and any accompanying political power is just too full of nuances to discuss. (This interview took place in 1971.)

Lincoln and NSC. Although Lincoln spent most of his first year as director working on NSC problems, he now comes in very late in the game, "after the spadework has been done." He doesn't have a staff doing original research; his people simply synopsize what other agencies have done and Lincoln offers policy advice to NSC on this basis. "He is a friend of Kissinger's, however, and generally will support the administration in whatever decision it decides to make."

The U.S. Domestic Situation. Jones hears talk of national crisis, of social upheaval, and of a reexamining of priorities, but states that the situation is not critical and "isn't any worse than during the Depression or the Civil War." He recognizes certain specific problems—i.e., pollution, welfare, and slums—but maintains that they are not military responsibilities. He personally would not cut military spending to divert funds into these areas. When asked about the problem of military men occupying civilian positions within a defense-oriented society, he said, "I don't see this as a problem because the men in policy-making positions are the bright ones." This reasoning is typical. Although Jones does not make value judgments and tries to examine problems in objective terms, he either simplifies or utterly ignores the moral or philosophical content of broad social issues.

West Point. "The educational system may not be the best, but in terms of its function—to train men 'in service to their country'—it is very good. If one measured the efficiency of education in terms of hours spent in class (although this admittedly may not be the best way), West Point is the most efficient school. The Academy does not go in depth into subjects, it doesn't have extensive reading courses, but the idea is to give a general education so you don't have an officer corps that is ignorant. On the other hand, you don't develop a good officer, one who follows orders, in an atmosphere of academic freedom or liberality. You need to make them disciplined." Asked about the possibility that cadets are taught to regurgitate rather than think, Jones said, "Well, five eighths of them probably don't learn, but they make good officers in a technical sense, they perform their job well. Obviously, many will be immature adolescents when they graduate. On the other hand, you have three eighths who are bright, who will question regardless of the academic situation. These are the ones who will go on to get advanced degrees and who will hopefully end up in policy-making positions." Jones graduated in the top three eighths of his class, went to graduate school, and is in a policy-making position, so, by his own standards, he must be one of the bright, thinking grads. "Admittedly," he went on, "West Point doesn't encourage people to think, but that isn't its purpose. You have to recognize that you can't compare the education at West Point with an education in a liberal-arts institution because there is just no basis for comparison." The topic of cadet isolation from outside events prompted these comments: "West Point doesn't isolate the cadets as much as you think. For example, they have to read *The New York Times*. Sometimes they are even tested on it. Besides, things aren't as bad as they used to be—when I was at West Point my first year, I only had two Saturday afternoons away from the Academy, both to go to football games."

The Honor System. "Basically, *it teaches one to respect the dignity of other men.* You do not deceive other men in any way. The first few months this is really drilled into the cadet." Asked for his interpretation of the code with regard to killing humans, he said, "In the first place, there is no occasion to kill or maim at West Point, so this is not part of the honor code." Reminded that the Army does kill people and that killing someone is not exactly showing respect for his dignity, he added, "That's different. In a military situation one is following orders, doing one's job, and the fate of the enemy is to be eliminated." Mr. Jones, then, recognizes certain limitations in West Point, but is capable of excusing them in terms of its "mission." He believes that the "bright" graduates in government can overcome their narrow West Point experience and function effectively without being tainted. He is a fundamentally neutral man, obedient to his superiors, loyal to American institutions, and utterly incapable of seeing beyond the military reality—a typical West Pointer trying very hard to prove he is also a civilian.[72]

This is a man who advises George Lincoln on the body that Nixon describes as "the principal forum for consideration of foreign policy issues." But Jones is not alone in his relationship with the National Security Council. The President's Deputy Assistant for National Security Affairs (Henry Kissinger's top aide) is Brig. Gen. Alexander Haig (W.P. 1947). John Holdridge (W.P. 1945) is the NSC staff expert on East Asia. Maj. James R. Murphy (W.P. 1957) is a member of the NSC

Program Analysis staff. Lt. Col. Bernard Loeffke (W.P. 1957) is on the NSC Planning Group.

One White House man's memories of West Point provide an interesting commentary on the mentality of graduates in government. He considers that his education at West Point was the greatest experience of his life and says that it taught him to discipline and develop his mind. Mr. Grad (not his real name) was good material for the Academy, for he characterizes himself before coming to West Point as a sloppy thinker and, "like most eighteen- and nineteen-year-olds, lazy." He believes that he needed to be trained and forced to work. Mr. Grad maintains the fiction that he learned to "think" by being examined constantly and having to do daily preparations. He admired his instructors, "who always had a specific lesson plan for each day and consistently covered the required material." He was happier with what he considered the intimate relationship with his instructors developed through constant testing and evaluation than with the professors he encountered in graduate school.

Mr. Grad does not question any of the ponderous institutional procedures of West Point. He firmly believes they all contribute to creating a highly competent and honorable officer corps. He says that the honor code builds men of strong character and believes that it serves to "flush out people who won't be truthful, who will concoct the truth. . . . The Army can't afford the risk of someone lying in the field because ultimately they will be dealing with human lives. . . . And the beauty of the system is twofold—it is run by the cadets and it teaches them that the truth can never get you in trouble." Even the rules about public displays of affection have their purpose, he says. "It is good that cadets can't hold hands in public, etc. I think we should expect our leaders to be above this. It does not look good to see an officer in uniform making public display of affection." [73]

This kind of thinking can be heard elsewhere at high levels. Mr. Ring (again, not a real name), assistant to the chief of a high-powered agency and ghost writer for many progress reports on Vietnam and the "Pentagon Papers," is another of the bright young graduates who is able to recall with a certain fondness his West Point days.

He has benefited from every opportunity provided the select

few to expand beyond the confines of West Point. His Ph.D. represents one of these opportunities. Lutian Pei, a China expert and close friend of George Lincoln, set up the Social Science Department at MIT with Ring and two other West Pointers among the first students. Strongly influenced by Lincoln's ideas, Pei wanted his department to be behavioral and quantitative, and felt that Academy men would make excellent students because of their strong mathematics background. Lincoln made sure that Pei got his boys. Even while studying there Ring found his West Point connections useful. In one course his class did a study of productivity in laboratories of four different kinds. The group gained access to two of them through the West Point Society of New England—the Gillette Laboratory (the administrative head of research is a graduate) and the MITRE Lab (the deputy director of personnel is a graduate).

After receiving his Ph.D., Ring returned to teach in the Social Science Department at USMA. He says that the department is competitive with any school in the country, at least among the sections in the top half of a class. The excuse for deficiencies in the lower sections is that one is forced to work at the Academy with a much broader spectrum of students than at most universities. This, he maintains, accounts for such "unique" procedures as the board outlines. Ring rationalized them by saying that if a cadet has to stare at the blackboard during the entire class, he might as well be looking at the three main points of the lesson. He also called it a teaching aid for the instructor. When questioned about the explicit and often hilarious teaching routines spelled out in Lincoln's manual *Teaching in the Social Sciences Department,* Ring rose to its defense by saying that it is a necessary document in terms of what Lincoln had to work with: military officers, not teachers—"consequently, they have to be disciplined." Ring could also accept the procedures used in the Math Department, which he admits is a "ham-handed anachronism," for they fit into the overall mission of West Point. The Math Department is "designed to be a reinforcement of discipline" and, despite its failures, one can say that "every West Pointer has a good quantitative background and this is very useful."

Ring can admit that "West Point may delay the period in the

cadet's life when he makes the moral decisions about what he's doing with his life" and at the same time justify it in terms of West Point's mission—"to inculcate certain functional values. Among these are apolitical loyalty to this country, a sense of duty-honor-country, and a deep respect for discipline." West Point, he says, tries to fashion a group of people who respond instinctively to these values. Therefore, "If you look at the education one gets there in that way, you evaluate it differently."

Like Mr. Jones, Ring accepts the fact that the military do play an important role in decision-making, but does not see a grave threat because the people involved are generally those who have had considerable experience and training beyond West Point. The problem is not always military advice but "the degrading of military advice, whose vitality is then sapped as an input to decision-making." "Today there is more awareness among civilians about how far the military can go. In addition, as far as decision-making and problem-solving processes are concerned, in all thinking men they are similar. When the decision is made, priorities then become relevant, and then it is a matter of who has the most influence." [74] Ring did not carry this argument to the next logical step: that the military is the group with the most influence.

Virtually every agency and office of the federal government has its quota of men anxious to talk about their days at West Point. The few concentrated upon in this discussion were selected because of the inordinate power the military have assumed in the areas of technology and foreign policy precisely at a time when these affairs are at the center of the most important national decisions. Consider, for example, Henry Kissinger's recent secret trip to China. Two of the men with him in Peking were John Holdridge (W.P. 1945) and James D. Hughes (W.P. 1946). The man who remained with the President at the Western White House and functioned as his principal foreign-policy advisor in Kissinger's absence was Brig. Gen. Alexander Haig (W.P. 1947). "Almost unnoticed, he has emerged as the one member of Kissinger's staff of 120 with any clout of his own. . . . Whatever their reasons, Mr. Nixon and Kissinger have developed a respect for Haig and, on occasion, the general fills in for his boss in private briefings for the President. Haig appears to be the sole exception to what Princeton lecturer I. M. Destler refers to as a flaw in the Kissinger apparatus: 'No one seems to be really trusted by Nixon and Kissinger but Nixon and Kissinger.' " [75] No longer are the military the apolitical tools of the policy-makers; they are the policy-makers and they are West Pointers. We have created a monster that can be found at every level of our national government from Francis G. Hall (W.P. 1963), Nixon's social aide who handles such things as the seating at Tricia's wedding and legislative liaison with the Pentagon, through the major departments like State and such agencies as FAA, to Congress with N.Y. Representative John M. Murphy (W.P. 1950) and Bill Sullivan (W.P. 1947) in Senator Dole's office, and finally into the courts with Judge H. C. Dillard (W.P. 1924) at the Palace of Justice in The Hague—"If any of our classmates gets a parking ticket in Nigeria, the Cameroons, or Bermuda—just let me know and I'll try to fix it up." [76] One chapter cannot, of course, do justice to so pervasive an influence, but it is hoped that the validity of the following quote by C. Wright Mills in *The Power Elite* can be recognized: "All over the world, the warlord is returning. All over the world, reality is defined in his terms. And in America, too, into the political vacuum the warlords have marched. Alongside the corporate executives and the politicians, the generals and admirals—those uneasy cousins within the American elite—have gained and have been given increased power to make and to influence decisions of the gravest consequences." [77]

CHAPTER 7

Defending Country and Capitalism

> . . . the Military-Industrial Complex Ghost is at
> large again, and the witch hunters in full cry; this
> is not a good time for old soldiers to be seeking
> an opportunity to remain in the main stream of
> defending our Nation.[1]
>
> —BURTON C. ANDRUS, JR. (W.P. 1941)

"THERE isn't a trick in the racketeering bag that the military
gang is blind to. It has its 'finger-men' to point out enemies, its
'muscle-men' to destroy enemies, its 'brain guys' to plan war
preparations, and a 'Big Boss'—Super-nationalistic Capitalism."

These aren't the words of a contemporary radical haranguing
the crowd at a frantic peace rally. Rather they belong to Maj.
Gen. Smedley Butler, speaking in 1933 at an Armistice Day
celebration in Philadelphia. He continues:

> It may seem odd for me, a military man, to adopt such a com-
> parison. Truthfulness compels me to do so. I spent thirty-three
> years and four months in active military service as a member of
> our country's most agile military force—the Marine Corps. I
> served in all commissioned ranks from a Second Lieutenant to
> Major General. And during that period I spent most of my time
> being a high-class muscle-man for Big Business, for Wall Street,

and for the Bankers. In short, I was a racketeer, a gangster for capitalism.

I suspected I was just a part of a racket at the time. Now I am sure of it. Like all members of the military profession, I never had an original thought until I left the service. My mental faculties remained in suspended animation while I obeyed the orders of the higher-ups. This is typical of everyone in the military service.

I helped make Mexico—and especially Tampico—safe for American oil interests in 1914. I helped make Haiti and Cuba a decent place for the National City Bank boys to collect revenues in. I helped in the raping of half a dozen Central American republics for the benefit of Wall Street. The record of racketeering is long. I helped purify Nicaragua for the international banking house of Brown Brothers in 1909–1912. I brought light to the Dominican Republic for American sugar interests in 1916. In China in 1927 I helped to see to it that Standard Oil went its way unmolested.

During these years I had, as the boys in the back room would say, a swell racket. I was rewarded with honors, medals, and promotions (two Congressional Medals of Honor and sixteen other combat decorations). Looking back on it, I feel that I might have given Al Capone a few hints. The best he could do was operate his racket in three districts. I operated on three continents.

Butler saw himself as a tool in the hands of the manipulators of capitalism, and most critics of the military-industrial complex have agreed with his implication that within the complex the role of the military is subordinate to that of the industrialists. In *The Armed Society* Tristam Coffin maintains that the military has been co-opted by the corporate rich. Julius Duscha in *Arms, Money and Politics* concludes that the military are subservient to the corporate elite because it finances their non-military activities and hires them upon retirement. Morris Janowitz in *The Professional Soldier* and William Domhoff in *Who Rules America?* agree with these interpretations. In other words, in any historical examination of the military-industrial complex it is a given that the income, wealth, and institutional leadership of the business elite give it the dominant power role in decision-making. The national corporate economy and the institutions it created and nourished gave these men their authority, and nowhere was this authority more manifest than in the manipulation of the military economy.

In defining the role of the individual military man within the complex, the above-mentioned critics concentrated on retired and active-duty officers and concluded that an insignificant number had reached or influenced the inner circles of the corporate elite and that, for the most part, they conformed to the general rule of subservience to corporate interests. This analysis does not attach enough importance to the phenomenon of militarism. On an individual level, both businessmen and military men are subservient to the militarization of society, not to each other. In this atmosphere, the corporate and military elites are equal partners, sharing the duty of preserving the status quo. While urging and directing the aggressive and warlike national policy that is the key ingredient of militarism, the businessmen have fallen prey to its evils. They have always been particularly susceptible to this because of the ordered nature of their corporate system. The objective requirements of the system—i.e., position, profit, and growth—have become the subjective aims and values of the humans involved. The system defines its members, not vice versa. When militarism became a dominant characteristic of the postwar national policy, the corporate functionaries found new meaning in their habits of blind respect for authority, their attitudes of conformity and docility, and their view of dissent as a treasonable activity. The corporate elite, on the other hand, found its moral authority and material position made even more secure by fostering these attitudes and cementing its relationships with those who exhibit them in the extreme—the military.

Military training is schooling in ceremony, unquestioning obedience, and arbitrary commands, and the more comprehensive this schooling, the more effective the habits of subordination and the less effective any habits of personal freedom and authority. What school better illustrates this type of training than West Point? The corporate elite naturally sought these people out and enlisted their aid in habituating the United States to think in terms of rank, authority, subordination, and passivity in the face of loss of freedom. West Point, with its stress on hierarchical mastery and its insistence on gradations of dignity and honor, proved to be an effective source of militaristic thought.

The corporate elite, however, has not been able to remain aloof in this process. As the military, and particularly West Pointers, applied their ideology to the pursuit of corporate goals, the elite found itself becoming habituated to their warlike, predatory way of life and easily accepted them as indispensable partners and friends in the struggle to keep America "free." The corporate and the military elites, although starting from different points, have reached a happy symbiosis of aims and values that works to perpetrate a militarized economy and people. A West Pointer, former Maj. Gen. Alvin C. Welling (W.P. 1933 and vice-president of Wyandotte Chemical Company), sums up the entire illness in these words: "Duty–Honor–Country–West Point has become Duty–Honor–Country–Wyandotte. For the long pull, the major difference between service in this company vs. service in the service will stem only from the color of the suit which one wears to work." [2]

World War II was the critical period for the welding of the Duty-Honor-Country-Capitalism concept, and the chief battle was fought over the issue of reconversion to peacetime production. The conflict arose in late 1943 because in less than two years of war the enormous productive capacity of the U.S. had managed to outstrip the demands placed on it by the war. In November 1943 the government estimated that military procurement would have to be cut back by one billion dollars a month in 1944. Cutbacks of this size meant layoffs and unemployment, particularly among the smaller firms doing defense work. All that was needed to offset this hardship was permission to reconvert to peacetime production and government allocations of materials with which to manufacture. The authority for such a move had to come from the War Production Board (WPB), which theoretically held supreme power over the nation's economy. WPB was headed by Donald Nelson, a vice-president of Sears, Roebuck—he had been recommended for the job by his boss, Gen. Robert E. Wood (W.P. 1900), then the chairman of Sears. Nelson was aided by his deputy, Charles E. Wilson, president of General Electric, and a staff of 500 other business executives. Formidable as this group appeared, the real economic power was held by Gen. Brehon B. Somervell (W.P. 1914), who was in charge of the Services of Supply, for he held the purse strings: he did the purchasing and he granted or denied the contracts. Gen. Lucius Clay (W.P. 1918) was Somervell's deputy for procurement and production. His staff included S. E. Skinner, later executive vice-president of General Motors; Frank Denton, later chairman of the Mellon National Bank; and George Woods, later in charge of the World Bank. The Services of Supply spent more money in one year than the entire federal government had expended for all operations from 1789 to 1917. In 1942, when Somervell was doling out $32 billion in contracts, *Fortune* Magazine called SOS "a holding company of no mean proportions" and added that "it makes U.S. Steel look like a fly-by-night, the A.T. and T. like a country-hotel switchboard." [3]

The big businessmen in both WPB and SOS quickly realized that reconversion would allow the smaller industries to move into civilian production first and encroach on some of their production lines, so when in November 1943 Nelson sided with the New Dealers and small business and proposed to authorize reconversion, it must have come as a great shock to his boss, Gen. Wood, and the rest of his corporate brethren. Opposition to Nelson's plan was immediate, and the military led the way, speaking of an adverse effect "on the morale of the fighting forces" [4] if the effort on the home front were relaxed. The Secretary of War announced that "the munitions production schedules for the Army had been slipping for several months" [5] and the Joint Chiefs of Staff expressed their concern lest reconversion result in "people throwing up their war jobs." [6] Undaunted, Nelson announced he was going ahead with the program, but, unfortunately, he became ill and his duties were assumed by Wilson, who, predictably, did not issue Nelson's order to proceed. Senator Harry S Truman demanded that Wilson issue the directive, saying that the program was being delayed by "some selfish business groups that want to see their competitors kept idle until they finish their war contracts . . . [and] by Army and Navy representatives who want to create a surplus of manpower." [7] The military immediately counterattacked. In July 1944 Somervell said that the loss of manpower in war plants had created a shortage of larger shells, so that "smaller shells and even rifle and machine gun fire" had to be substituted, "which inevitably meant closer fighting and greater loss of American lives." [8] The military followed with charges that workers quitting to take peacetime jobs were slowing production and shipment. In other words, soldiers were dying because of reconversion. Strangely, the WPB Progress Report for July reported that "supplies range from a low of 11 months for the non-combat vehicles to 22 months for the ammunition programs." [9] Rather than be exposed as liars by this report, the military demanded its suppression and continued their callous propaganda. By hiding facts, by using scare tactics, and by defying the civilian leaders, the corporate powers and the military succeeded in stalling reconversion until the giant businesses could return to the civilian market and protect their dominance of the economy. The conflict ended once and for all when the maverick Nelson was exiled on a special mission to China and the power of WPB was transferred to James Byrnes as the director of war mobilization and reconversion. He named Lucius Clay as his deputy director for war programs. The family remained intact.

Writing on his happy relationship with the corporate elite in World War II, Clay says, "Thus there was a constant interchange of ideas representing both the military and business aspects of our problems. Later, several of the Army officers in retirement became successful in the business and industrial world. I suspect this interchange which I saw take place in my own areas of responsibility occurred in other places, too. This did develop a mutual respect between the business and military worlds. It is possible that this also developed in World War I. However, our subsequent expenditures for defense were not a significant part of our economy and the relationships resulting from World War I did not endure. Since World War II, our expenditures for defense have been larger and thus the relationships established in World War II have endured. Today, defense is perhaps our major business. . . ." [10] Gen. Clay went on to become the head of Continental Can Company and later senior partner in Lehman Brothers. Gen. Somervell became president of Koppers Company.

Others had a different view of what had occurred during World War II. Donald Nelson in his book *Arsenal of Democracy* says that "from 1942 onward the Army people, in order to get control of our national economy, did their best to make an errand boy of the WPB." The Bureau of the Budget in a 1946 report titled "The United States at War" says that the Army tried to gain "total control of the nation, its manpower, its facilities, its economy," and when Roosevelt or Nelson got in their way, "the military leaders took another approach to secure the same result." [11] Whatever the description, the fight over reconversion had developed a smoothly functioning corporate-military team that was ready to consolidate its position in the postwar years and attempt to become the peacetime controller of America's economy.

The stakes in the game were enormous, and the new fight opened early. In January 1944 Wilson of General Electric, in a speech before the American Ordnance Association, proposed a "permanent war economy." In part, he said, "First of all such a [preparedness] program must be the responsibility of the federal government. It must be initiated and administered by the executive branch—by the President as Commander-in-Chief and by the War and Navy Departments. Of equal importance is the fact that this must be, once and for all, a continuing program and not the creature of an emergency. In fact, one of its objects will be to eliminate emergencies so far as possible. The role of Congress is limited to voting the needed funds. . . ." [12] Defining the role of big business relative to the military, he said, "Industry's role in this program is to respond and cooperate . . . in the execution of the part allotted to it; industry must not be hampered by political witch-hunts or thrown to the fanatical isolationist fringe tagged with a 'merchants of death' label." [13] The heart of this idea, the centralized control of big business by big business, was not new; it had been advocated by Wilson's predecessor at G.E., Gerard Swope, and by Gen. Hugh Johnson (W.P. 1903), head of the National Recovery Administration in 1934. Both these gentlemen were close associates of Bernard Baruch, an important advisor to Woodrow Wilson and Franklin Roosevelt. Johnson put the question of industrial "self-government" this way: "We must substitute for the old safety valve of free land and new horizons a new safety valve of economic readjustment and direction of those great forces. There is no alternative to shipwreck. We are permanently in a new era." [14] Johnson's words were prophetic, but his corporate and West Point cronies still had work to do.

If the ambitious goal of a permanent, prosperous war economy controlled by the corporate-military team was to be reached, it was obvious that a large and entrenched military machine was necessary to consume the products of the factories. And if this was to be the new reality, the American people had to be convinced of an ever present menace to their physical and material security. The military sought to achieve both through their plan for Universal Military Training (the peacetime draft), authored by J. Lawton Collins (W.P. 1917). For two years following the war, the military engaged in a colossal public-relations program to sell UMT, only to be defeated in 1947 when Congress struck down their bill. Confused but full of fight, the soldiers doubled their efforts and released their big guns. Gen. Eisenhower (W.P. 1915), Chief of Staff, told Congress that "our only real security lies in internationalism" supported by adequate military strength and that this strength could only come from UMT, "the only insurance against extinction." [15] Gen. Carl Spaatz (W.P. 1914), chief of the Air Force, warned that the U.S. faced possible devastation from the air through attacks across the North Pole. Lt. Gen. Leslie R. Groves (W.P. 1918), of Manhattan Project fame, testified that in the first five hours of an atomic attack forty million Americans would be killed. Gen. Collins, Deputy Chief of Staff under Ike, warned that World War III "would start very suddenly and come through the air" and that "the enemy would try to eliminate the United States at the outset, not making the same mistake as last time of taking on somebody else first and allowing us to prepare." [16] Speaking before mayors from all over the U.S., Lt. Gen. Harold R. Bull (W.P. 1914), chief of the Organization and Training Division of the General Staff, vividly described the horrors of an atomic attack on each of the mayors' cities. "The mayors returned to their cities carrying the message that peacetime conscription was the only way to protect the people of the big cities from destruction by the atomic bomb." [17] At the height of this campaign, *U.S. News and World Report* commented that "War scares, encouraged by high officials only a few weeks ago, so alarmed the 144 million U.S. public that top planners now are having to struggle hard to keep Congress from pouring more money into national defense than the Joint Chiefs of Staff regard as wise or necessary. It is proving more difficult to turn off than to turn on a war psychology." [18] The counselors of fear prevailed and the bill authorizing the peacetime draft was passed in June 1948. A "permanent war economy" was now possible.

The years following this artificially produced hysteria saw the corporate-military team growing more and more sophisticated as they gained experience at the reins of the economy. In the Fifties it was only logical that they should extend their influence to the educational system—the producer of manpower for their technical society. Typical of the tools used was a "Military In-dustrial Conference" held in Chicago in 1955 that sought to answer the question "How can our technical manpower be best utilized in the interests of our national welfare?" At this meeting there were two West Point speakers, one graduate on the finance and program committees, six graduates on the general committee, and six more on the arrangements committee. West Point was again in the thick of the struggle. Former Gen. Groves, vice-president of Remington Rand, set the tone for the assembled corporation presidents and West Pointers with these words: "How long can we expect to survive if our present annual pro-duction of engineers is only 20,000 and not increasing, while Russia's is 54,000 and constantly increasing? . . . The decline of the study of United States history in favor of the one-world-isms of the United Nations is analogous to the decline of the family in Communist Russia. . . . Although we hear much talk of push buttons and guided missiles, the fact remains that the women who survive any heavy bombing of our cities will be ones who can walk out of the rubble, and the men who finally win the wars of the future may well be, just as in the past, the ones who walk in and occupy the enemy territory. We must make our people more rugged physically, and the place to start that tough-ening-up process is in our junior citizens of school age." [19] The rest of the speakers emphasized this plea for a technical, moral, and physical superiority of U.S. youth over our enemies. The policy resolutions of this so-called conference are worth quoting:

1. There is at present a serious shortage of scientific and engineer-ing personnel for military, industrial, and educational needs.

This shortage would become critical in the event of an emergency.

2. The national interest requires that more emphasis and effort be directed toward increasing the supply of well-trained scientific and engineering personnel.

3. Under present circumstances, our program for selective service and the use of military reserve forces must be such as to insure that technically trained personnel be effectively used where they are most needed and of most value in the national interest.

and last, but definitely not least:

4. In view of the increasing importance of the technical aspects of warfare, it is imperative that the technical branches of the armed services maintain a high degree of professional competence and that they participate fully in the development and implementation of plans and policies.

In other words, the urgent requirement of the military and corporate machine was an adequate supply of technicians and scientists attainable by educating only the high-IQ minority while placing little emphasis upon improving the education of the masses. A rational and humanist education for all the people would work against the aims of the juggernaut, and the U.S. was once again asked to acquiesce in its judgment.

Copies of these stirring resolutions were presented to the Secretaries of Labor and Interior, the Department of Defense, the U.S. Commissioner of Education, members of the Senate and House Armed Services Committees (including former Maj. Gen. Verne D. Mudge (W.P. 1920) representing Senator Richard Russell, chairman of the Senate committee), the director of the Legislative Division of the American Legion, and several others. It should be noted that four important bills were before Congress at the time of this conference: a pay raise for the military, an extension of the "doctor draft," a National Reserve Plan, and an extension of the selective-service power to 1959.

Numerous other examples of the effectiveness and new-found sophistication of the corporate-military team can be enumerated, but again a West Pointer, Lucius Clay, provides the last words: "I think that the real factors in the improved standing which the military leader of today enjoys in comparison with the past lie first in the increased association with the business and industrial world resulting from the major role of defense spending in our national economy; and secondly, as a by-product of our emerging concern with international affairs. We have learned that foreign and military policy must go hand in hand and we have found that our military leaders, living much of their lives abroad, do have considerable knowledge of our international problems and their proper role in our international relationships." [20] Clay's observations emphasize what was pointed out in the chapter on government: technology and foreign policy have been and are now the exclusive domain of the corporate-military team.

As we have seen in the cases of AEC, NASA, and FAA, the impact on technology by West Pointers as members of the team has been extraordinary. The atomic bomb and the moon shots have been merely the most spectacular of a long series of so-called technological advancements. The Department of Defense, as the biggest spender, has contributed supersonic flight, a vast array of guided missiles, high-capacity computers, nuclear submarines, and so on in an almost endless list of destructive capabilities built in the name of national security. The direct role of the non-uniformed soldier in continuing this mad growth has been pointed out by Theodore K. Steele: "Military requirements today are so bizarre, the technology so advanced, the standards so tight that few men can bridge the gap between the vast defense market and the manufacturing capacity that must supply it. Industrial organizations that use their retired generals to bridge that gap, instead of to sell, are in the lead." [21] The question is no longer whether or not military men should be employed in the defense industry, but rather how they should be used once they are there.

In 1959 there were 768 retired colonels or higher employed by the top 100 defense contractors; in 1968 there were 2,100; and in 1969 there were 1,973. One fault of these figures is that they ignore the people who retired or resigned before reaching a high position. In the case of West Point, this is a serious omission, for a check of the firms that employed the above-mentioned 2,100 officers revealed over 600 West Pointers and by no means were all of these retired or high-ranking. The mentality that preserves the military-corporate team does not exist only among colonels and generals; the West Pointer who resigns as a captain is no less capable than a general of using his contacts and knowledge to further the interests of the juggernaut. In this regard, the Blue Ribbon Defense Panel's report on the Department of Defense in July 1970 analyzed the figure of 1,973. To determine the "extent of influence which retired officers in the [aerospace] industry could exert with the Department of Defense," [22] the panel sent questionnaires to 115 officers. Eighty-five responses were received and these were screened for answers and job descriptions that indicated some possibility of affecting the procurement process. Officers retired for more than three years were not included! Among the 45 officers remaining after the screening, there were "13 engineers, scientists and system analysts, 3 concerned with internal logistics in support of specific defense contracts, one Congressional lobbyist, and one officer in charge of testing military aircraft." The report also stated that "28 were presently working or had previously worked for their employer on specific defense contracts . . . 28 (not exactly the same persons as above) were either recruited or obtained their positions through friends . . . 28 (not exactly the same persons as above) were employed by the 11 defense contractors who receive almost half of all the business awarded to the top 100 contractors." [23] Extrapolating from their sample, the panel states that 570 of the 1,973 retired senior officers might be in some position to influence the award or administration of a contract. In the face of these interesting figures, the panel concludes that "no determination can be made as to the extent of actual influence which has been or is likely to be exerted by this class of officers" [24]—a fitting judgment for a panel whose working staff was headed by a West Pointer, J. Fred Buzhardt, Jr. (W.P. 1946). Buzhardt had to go no further than his own alumni magazine to discover the "extent of actual influence." In the Winter 1971 *Assembly* it was reported that Antonio P. Chanco (W.P. 1938), formerly commandant of cadets at the Philippine Military Academy and presently vice-president and general manager of Vinnell Corporation's Philippine Division, "was in D.C. to see how more U.S. Navy construction dollars might be put to good use with his company in the Western Pacific area." [25] Or Reynolds Keleher (W.P. 1941) writing: "If there were some way that those who are already firmly estab-

lished in the larger business enterprises could make known the
openings in those enterprises to interested classmates, it would
be a happy investment for everyone—including the Internal
Revenue Service." [26] Or Dunk Hartnell (W.P. 1948) stating that
"the labor market looks upon USMA graduates with considerable interest." [27] Or Paul Child (W.P. 1952) observing: "I think
we all might find it interesting to see to what extent the class
has infiltrated the [defense operation] and industry around the
nation's capital." [28] Buzhardt shouldn't have any trouble dis-
covering what his Washington-area classmates of 1946 are doing
—they meet once a month in the Pentagon for lunch. In fact,
West Pointers must present the Pentagon with a serious lunch-
scheduling problem because all classes in the vicinity meet sep-
arately at least once a month. One class, 1939, has forty-eight
D.C. residents, and among the forty listing jobs are found
thirteen associated with DOD, two with NASA, one with FAA,
two with the State Department, one with the Small Business
Administration, one with the Military Order of World Wars,
two with Vitro Corporation (over $30 million in military con-
tracts in 1970), and four with various computer companies
representing over $26 million in military contracts in 1970. This
happy group meets the third Monday of each month in Room
3C668 of the Pentagon for a lunch costing $2.75. Maybe some-
one could raise the question of "influence" at the next luncheon
and give his classmates something to talk about.

If Buzhardt is unfamiliar with how his fellow graduates
achieve their high "civilian" positions, the early case of Gen.
Joseph T. McNarney (W.P. 1915) may be instructive. Mc-
Narney was the top-ranking officer in the Air Force and became
general manager of the entire Defense Department under Secretary Johnson in pre-Korean war days. In 1950, when the
Navy, seeking to avoid cuts in its carrier fleet, attacked the Air
Force as the service whose arms should be cut, McNarney immediately rose to the defense. The Navy's key target, the long-
range B-36 bomber, was the general's pride and joy, but the
Navy pointed out that the plane (designed in 1941) was too
slow and vulnerable in an age of jets and missiles and therefore
should be eliminated. McNarney was outraged and insisted that,
although the plane was old, it was the best weapon in his arsenal

and production must continue. The result was millions of dollars spent on a plane that was already obsolete. McNarney retired in February 1952, and in March was employed by Consolidated Vultee, now the Convair Division of General Dynamics, the manufacturer of the B-36! McNarney, testifying before the Hébert Committee, claimed that he had received no prior offer to join Convair when he left the Air Force. Offer or not, he became the president of Convair at $75,000 a year and by 1956 had drawn $324,500 in salary and expenses plus his regular Air Force pension of $16,000 annually. When his contract as president expired, he had another waiting that would pay him $30,000 a year for ten years as a consultant to his old firm. *Business Week* commented, "McNarney knows Convair's best customer, the Pentagon, as few others do. . . . In business circles, the word has gone out: Get yourself a general. What branch of government spends the most money? The Military. Who, even more than a five-percenter, is an expert on red tape? A general or admiral. So make him chairman of the board." [29] In a more contemporary period and introducing a new wrinkle, James Ling, head of Ling-Temco-Vaught, has told how "his company studies the Pentagon promotion lists to see which officers will be likely candidates for the top positions and then picks their brains to get insight into the kinds of weaponry that might be emphasized if a particular officer became chief of staff." [30] Hundreds of other quotes and illustrations detailing "influence" can be cited for the edification of Mr. Buzhardt and his Blue Ribbon Panel and, as the remainder of this chapter will show, one does not have to stray far from the confines of West Point to find them.

In the missile and aerospace field, the most recent spectacular was the battle over the anti-ballistic missile. Gen. Maxwell Taylor (W.P. 1922) fired the opening rounds in 1957 when he said, "We can see no reason why the country cannot have an anti-missile defense for a price that is within reach." Aware of the public's lack of belief in the ABM, Taylor continued, "I am sure many of you have heard the statement that the dollar requirements for this kind of defense are astronomical and that the whole concept is beyond consideration. I can assure you that studies I have seen lead me to a different conclusion." [31] The struggle escalated through the Sixties with more generals joining. Gen. John P. McConnell (W.P. 1932), the Air Force Chief of Staff, was saying that even though the Russians could penetrate any ABM system, it should be built because it would "augment our offensive forces by introducing uncertainty into the enemy's planning, compounding their targeting problems, and causing them to divert resources from other essential tasks." McConnell must have picked up his brinkmanship from his buddy Gen. Harold K. Johnson (W.P. 1933), the Army Chief of Staff, who earlier had been saying, "The more uncertainty we can create, the greater likelihod there is of avoiding a nuclear exchange." [32] When the ABM became a major public issue in 1969, the non-uniformed military began making their contributions. The American Security Council, an organization of ancient right-wingers sired by Brig. Gen. Robert E. Wood (W.P. 1900) of Sears, Roebuck fame, financed a study by "31 leading experts" from its Subcommittee on National Strategy "to investigate the problem." One of the three leaders of the Subcommittee was Gen. Nathan F. Twining (W.P. 1919). Its findings, which were actually an update of a 1967 report for the House Armed Services Committee, were reported in *USSR vs. USA: The ABM and the Changed Strategic Military Balance*. This widely distributed report was, needless to say, highly favorable to the ABM. But it wasn't quite enough, and around the same time the Foreign Policy Research Institute of the University of Pennsylvania rushed out a volume called *Safeguard: Why the ABM Makes Sense*. Of the sixteen articles in the study, only one was against the ABM. Need it be pointed out that the book was edited by a West Pointer?—William Kintner (W.P. 1940), the deputy director of the institute.

Again, at about the same time, the Pentagon was drafting a public-relations plan designed to "sell" the reluctant American public on the ABM. Describing the plan, the *Washington Post* observed: "All of it is there—the information kits, the television films and taped radio shows, the ceaseless round of calls on Congressmen, governors, mayors, local community leaders, editors, and publishers; the articles to be written for scientific journals by Army officials and officers; the carefully prepared interviews with the press; the coordination of the whole effort with the private public relations efforts of industrial firms involved in the building of the Sentinel [ABM] System." [33] The author of this callous program was, of course, a grad, Lt. Gen. Alfred D. Starbird (W.P. 1933). After the unexpected exposure given to the propaganda scheme by the press, it was quietly "withdrawn," but somehow most of the efforts contemplated by Starbird discreetly found their way into reality. One was the blossoming of such "spontaneous" grass-roots organizations as the Citizens' Committee for Peace and Security, which placed newspaper ads all over the country extolling the virtues of the ABM. Among the signers of the ad were officials of eight companies that held more than $150 million in ABM contracts. These firms included the American Machine and Foundry Co., headed by one Rodney C. Gott (W.P. 1933). Lucius Clay (W.P. 1918), then chairman of the Republican National Finance Committee, was also among the signers. *Duty-Honor-Country-ABM* should obviously be carved in granite above the entrance to the Military Academy.

In 1963, during a lull in the furor, the Army made all the ensuing propaganda academic by awarding a contract for the short-range interceptor-missile link in the ABM system, the Sprint, to the Martin-Marietta Company. Currently involved in the missile and aerospace effort at Martin-Marietta is former Lt. Gen. William W. Quinn (W.P. 1933). He says, "We are very heavy in the ABM [1971]. We are still manufacturing the Sprint. The cutback in ABM funds occurred because the Army hadn't spent all its appropriated funds. Future sites are not being funded because we are behind in building the present ones, but the program will continue."

Quinn became vice-president of the Aerospace Group of Martin-Marietta after a thirty-three-year Army career concentrated in intelligence activities. Asked how he came to his present job, he said, "As commander of the Seventh Army in Europe, I used the Pershing missile made by Martin-Marietta. The president of the company came to see me in Germany. I was to show him the missile in combat conditions. As a result of this visit, we corresponded, visited, and at one point he indicated that he would like to hire me. It often works this way. Somewhere along the line management has observed an individual in his military environment and feels he may have something to offer the company, so he asks the person to come to the company when he retires. [Quinn retired March 1, 1966, and joined Martin-Marietta on the same day.] There is a certain paradox. People accuse individuals of having a military mind; but the military mind is very flexible. It is not frozen. Because of the nature of the military, it is trained to adapt." Quinn obviously "adapted" very rapidly.

The source of his insightful view of the military-corporate team is revealed in the following conversation about West Point.

Why did you go to West Point? "I was motivated by several things. One, a motion picture that I saw called *West Point.* William Boyd starred. I was very impressed, so I began to look into it."

What do you remember most about West Point? "Playing football and lacrosse. When you're playing a sport, it takes a tremendous amount of energy. Then you go to a training table and they stuff you like a hog. When you get back to your desk, it's hard to stay awake; it takes a great deal of face-slapping to stay awake. This was the hardest thing. And academically West Point was a very, very difficult place to be. The best thing I remember was beating Navy, and then Notre Dame. The main thing I remember, if there is anything in general, is the tremendous amount of pride at being there. It was tough; the boys didn't stay. It separated the men. When I was there, 25 percent of the boys didn't make it."

Do you still see your classmates? "Yes. We have an annual dinner dance and a golf match, and we meet for lunch once a month. There is a great deal of closeness with one's class. The academies are totally different in a sociological sense from other schools. Their students come from everywhere and then they go back everywhere. Academy people live together throughout their careers. They see each other every day of their professional lives. This develops a closeness. The military is often criticized in communities where they only socialize among themselves. This is by circumstance and not by design."

Do you find your West Point connections helpful in your business? "Yes, I have several friends who've gone to different industries. I call them up and we talk about mutual problems. I get information from them that I couldn't get otherwise." [34]

Among the friends he mentioned were John G. Zierdt (W.P. 1937), director of aerospace planning for Beech Aircraft Corporation; Orval R. Cook (W.P. 1922), former president of the Aerospace Industries Association; Duncan Hallock (W.P. 1933), an executive vice-president of ITT; and Alfred D. Starbird (W.P. 1933), now a civilian and Deputy Director of Defense Research and Engineering for DOD.

Of course, Martin-Marietta and Beech aren't the only aerospace industries to which West Pointers bring their unique talents. AVCO Corporation, which boasted almost $270 million in military contracts in 1970, employs as vice-president and group executive for its Government Products Group, James R. Dempsey (W.P. 1943). Dempsey has a long history of involvement with missiles beginning in 1945 with the Air Force's guided-missile programs. He resigned as a lieutenant colonel in 1953 and became the assistant to the vice-president for planning of the Convair Division of General Dynamics Corporation (remember Gen. McNarney?). Successively, Dempsey was director of the Atlas missile program, manager of Convair's Astronautics Division, vice-president of Convair's Astronautics Division, vice-president of the Convair Division, a vice-president of General Dynamics, president of Convair, and, finally, in 1966, a group vice-president of AVCO. Dempsey was preceded at AVCO by Gen. Albert C. Wedemeyer (W.P. 1919), who was a director and vice-president in the Fifties. Waiting for Dempsey's arrival in 1966 was Edgar D. Kenna (W.P. 1945), then a vice-president and the general manager of AVCO's Research and Development Division. Kenna is noted as the developer of the re-entry system for the ICBM. He left AVCO in 1968 to become president of Fuqua Industries, but Dempsey need not feel alone at the top, for the executive assistant to the president of AVCO is Leonard D. Henry (W.P. 1931), formerly of Aerojet General Corporation. In fact, there were no less than nineteen West Pointers in management, marketing, or engineering positions at AVCO during the Sixties. In the last five years the company has held over $581 million in contracts directly related to the Vietnam war.

TRW Inc., which held over $179 million in defense contracts

in 1970, currently has a West Pointer in charge of its aerospace efforts—Stanley C. Pace (W.P. 1943) is an executive vice-president and director of the company. He resigned in 1954 as a colonel, joined TRW, and has been in the thick of aerospace development ever since. John H. Shaffer (W.P. 1943) has had quite a similar career. He also resigned in 1954, joined TRW as a vice-president in 1957, and occupied that position until 1969, when he left to become administrator of the Federal Aviation Administration. Richard C. Snyder (W.P. 1943) was director of TRW's Legislative Affairs Office in Washington, D.C., in 1966. Three other 1943 graduates could be found in Pace's empire during the Sixties. The conversation of these six at class reunions must be rather limited. Seventeen other graduates at TRW ensure that the word about aerospace advancements is not confined to the 1943 grads.

Not to be outdone in the race for West Pointers and contracts, another aerospace giant, North American Rockwell (over $700 million in defense work in 1970), employed until very recently Arthur G. Trudeau (W.P. 1924) as assistant to the chairman of the board. Trudeau was formerly head of research and development for the Department of the Army. Among the score of other graduates working for North American Rockwell can be found the president of the Power Systems Division, a vice-president for technical growth, vice-president of the Atomics-International Division, the paymaster, and the director of the Washington office.

Needless to say, hundreds of additional West Pointers can be found by examining the other large aerospace contractors. For example, Boeing and General Electric, with a combined $1.5 billion in defense contracts in 1970, employed over 100 graduates in the Sixties, primarily in their missile and other government products areas.

Burt Andrus (W.P. 1941) sums up the brotherly situation with a report in *Assembly:* "Bill [William H. Gurnee, Class of 1941, Assistant to the President of Northrop Corp.] has been on a project for Northrop working on the same problem that Jack Christensen (W.P. 1941) has as a contract with his own consulting firm. . . . Bill went on to say that Felix Gerace (Class of 1941) had come aboard at Northrop and after scouting all over Los Angeles for a house finally found one, of all places, just a few doors from the Gurnees!" [35]

The following is a partial list of other West Point notables in aerospace companies who will not be discussed later in the chapter. The dates shown are those of their latest confirmed employment.

Mark E. Bradley	VP	Garrett Corp.	1965
Chester V. Braun	VP	McDonnell-Douglas Corp.	1969
Kenneth F. Dawalt	VP	French Aerospace Corp.	1970
Younger A. Pitts	Ass't to VP	Northrop Corp.	1966
Gabriel P. Disosway	Senior VP	LTV Aerospace Corp.	1970
Joe W. Kelly	VP	General Dynamics	1964
Don R. Ostrander	VP	Bell Aerospace Systems Co.	1966
Albert L. Bethel	VP	Westinghouse	1970

Should this wide group of "friends" ever fail to keep each other and the American public aware of the necessity of ever increasing aerospace spending, the Aerospace Industries Association (AIA) or the Air Force Association (AFA) can take over. AIA, along with its eighty-two corporate members, is designed "to foster, advance, promulgate, and promote trade and commerce, throughout the United States, its territories, possessions, and in foreign countries, in the interests of those persons, firms or corporations engaged in the business of manufacturing, buying, selling and dealing in aircraft and astronautical vehicles of every nature and description (including but not limited to pilot-less aircraft, guided missiles, rockets, and satellites, manned or un-manned), power plants for aircraft and astronautical vehicles and parts and accessories thereof of every kind and nature." This powerful lobbying group has as a member of its board of governors Stanley C. Pace (W.P. 1943). Bridging the so-called "gap" between the aerospace industry and active military personnel is the function of the Air Force Association and its 105,000 members. The more than 200 corporate members of AFA regularly receive lists containing the names, ranks, titles, and phone numbers of all key military people; notices concerning "topics of interest" within the Department of Defense sent within twenty-four hours of their discovery; and use of AFA's "research" facilities to answer questions not covered in the normal flow of information. These services are provided "to assist in obtaining and maintaining adequate aerospace power for national security and world peace." Among the national directors of this obviously public-spirited group are Nathan F. Twining (W.P. 1919) and Carl Spaatz (W.P. 1914).

West Pointers, then, are found at every turn in the machinations of the aerospace-missile industry—from the generals and special-interest groups who push the new weapons-system concepts to the corporate leaders and engineers who design, build, and sell the new tools of destruction. With their webs of communication and influence and a strength gained by general public acceptance of their military interpretation of reality, these men have become indispensable partners in the corporate pursuit of America's defense dollar.

National security, however, is not confined to exotic missiles and rockets, and neither is the West Pointer's involvement. When new defense policy requires new weapons (or is it when new weapons require a new defense policy?), the graduate is always nearby. One familiar new policy is that of "limited warfare" or "limited intervention" much like that which occurred in the Dominican Republic in 1965. The key to interventionism as a foreign policy is the capability to rapidly deploy troops and equipment anywhere in the world, and, needless to say, the military quickly moved to provide this capability and justify the policy. In 1964 the Joint Chiefs of Staff, headed by Gen. Earle G. Wheeler (W.P. 1932), released a study stating that "a demonstrated U.S. ability to move forces rapidly could cause potential enemies to have serious doubts about their chances of military success in remote areas of the world." Gen. Harold K. Johnson (W.P. 1933) chimed in with the memorable "A brigade in time may save the commitment of nine." [36] No opposition, of course, was heard from such men as Gen. John P. McConnell (W.P. 1932), Chief of Staff of the Air Force, or Gen. H. M. Estes (W.P. 1936), commander of the Military Airlift Command. The tool this far-seeing group of graduates decided upon was the now famous C-5A. Because of their deep commitment to the dubious mission of the C-5A, West Pointers naturally rose to its defense when the cost overruns plaguing the program came to public attention in November 1968. They actually, however, began their defense much earlier, and the reason the 1968 revelations did not occur sooner was the direct suppression by these men of damaging information.

In December 1966 an internal Air Force memo observed "Lockheed [the prime C-5A contractor] really busted budget No. 1 in the engineering area. Numerous overruns, several in excess of 100 percent were observed. . . ." [37] By July 1967 these overruns had reached $49 million, but in November Gen. McConnell insisted in a memo to Secretary McNamara that "We have been quite successful in controlling cost growth in the C-5A program as a result of changes." He added that when the program was complete, Lockheed's overrun would probably amount to $240 million but that "This overrun was very close to what was anticipated at the time of contract go-ahead, and is not therefore an overrun as compared to our prediction." McConnell thus dismissed an overrun of a quarter of a billion dollars by saying it was expected! West Point mathematics is, if nothing else, very versatile. Soon after, however, the comptroller of the Department of Defense disagreed with McConnell's analysis and wrote to Secretary McNamara that it:

> conveys two incorrect impressions about C-5A costs, which are worth calling to your attention.
>
> First, it mentions an anticipated overrun of $240 million for Lockheed and $54 million for G.E. Actually the Air Force's current estimate of overrun is $351 million and $69 million respectively. It is also significant that the estimated overrun has increased since May, 1967, by $165 million for Lockheed and $29 million for G.E.
>
> Second, the memorandum states that current estimated costs are below the Air Force cost estimate made in March, 1965. Actually, the estimate made in March, 1965, was $3391 million, and the current estimate is $3835 million.

So math can be used to verify a fact or so construed as to support a position. McConnell's confidence, however, remained unshaken, and four months later, in March 1968, he dispatched a fellow graduate, Lt. Gen. Duward Crow (W.P. 1941), comptroller of the Air Force, to soothe the doubts of a suddenly interested House Appropriations Committee. Crow assured them that the C-5A program was in good shape by saying: "When the program was originally drawn up some three or four years ago, it was estimated to cost about $3.2 billion total. We are still carrying that cost. . . ." Eight months later it was revealed that the total program cost had risen to over $5 billion, truly a phenomenal rise for such a short period of time—in fact, an impossible one. Why did McConnell, Crow, and the rest of the plane's supporters cover up the massive overruns? First, they probably did not feel they were covering up because, as McConnell's memo shows, the overruns were not considered serious. After all, hadn't they experienced overruns like this before? Second, the unique "I'll scratch your back if you'll scratch mine" relationship that exists between the Pentagon and the defense industries demands mutual protection when an image is about to be tarnished. The fact that over fifty West Pointers, including the senior military advisor and an executive vice-president, were employed by Lockheed during this period did not hurt communication between the two partners.

Not all interventions could be handled by air, however, and the Navy got into the picture by proposing its Fast Deployment Logistic Ship (FDL). The winner of the design competition for these ships, Litton Industries, had already begun to work on a shipyard to handle its new contract when the Senate Armed Services Committee, in a highly unusual move, denied funds for the program. Litton, however, which has had two West Point vice-presidents, one West Point member of the board of directors, and a West Point manager of the important Washington, D.C., office, did not languish, for within a few months it was awarded a $114-million contract for a Landing Helicopter Assault Ship (LHA). This contract, according to the announcement, had a potential value of over $1 billion. Much of the rationale behind the LHA can be found in a study called "Technology and Strategic Mobility," written by J. I. Coffey (W.P. 1939) for the Institute for Strategic Studies.

Not all means of troop transportation are as complex as the C-5A and the LHA, and at some point far down the scale rests the familiar Jeep. But even this lowly vehicle is not neglected by the West Pointer, for the president of Kaiser Jeep Corporation is none other than James H. Drum (W.P. 1937).

The military transportation requirements are so vast, however, that occasionally they must be met by civilian carriers. This has been particularly true in the case of Vietnam. But one graduate, Dr. John M. Christensen (W.P. 1941), president of Joint Management Consultants, understood this situation clearly and prospered by chartering aircraft for families going to Hawaii to see their servicemen on "rest and recreation" leave from Vietnam. Few opportunities manage to sneak by the alert West Pointers.[38]

The greatest windfall has come to Pan American Airways in the form of $143 million in Pentagon contracts in 1970 alone. It is the only American airline with scheduled service to Vietnam and has been the major carrier of war matériel to that country with over fifty flights per week. In view of some of the fat military contracts it was awarded, it may be of some significance that Pan Am has Alfred M. Gruenther (W.P. 1919) on its board of directors and Lawrence S. Kuter (W.P. 1927) as executive vice-president and number-three man in the company. The government also pays Pan American to support its missile test operations at Cape Kennedy. Until 1970 the superintendent of these activities for Pan American was Thomas F. Van Natta (W.P. 1954). West Pointers evidently have performed so well for Pan Am, in fact, that it recently selected William T. Seawell (W.P. 1941 and formerly senior vice-president of American Airlines) as its president and financial savior. Other airlines, of course, have placed graduates in high positions, but none has been able to emulate Pan Am's success with the Pentagon. Watching from the sidelines during the latter half of the Sixties and into the Seventies were such airline executives as James E. Colburn (W.P. 1947), vice-president, Continental Airlines; Lauris Norstad (W.P. 1930), director, United Airlines; Albert C. Wedemeyer (W.P. 1919), director, National Airlines; Frank Borman (W.P. 1950), senior vice-president, Eastern Airlines; Jack Hurst (W.P. 1950), vice-president, Eastern Airlines; Harvey P. Barnard (W.P. 1938), senior vice-president, American Flyers Airline; Howell M. Estes (W.P. 1936 and former commander, Military Airlift Command), senior vice-president, World Airways; and Milton Arnold (W.P. 1931), director, Air Express International. Aiding his fellows from the government side is Benjamin O. Davis, Jr. (W.P. 1936), the Director of Civil Aviation Security in the Department of Transportation.

WEST POINT

As in the case of the aerospace industry, an association exists among the transportation interests to ensure that they speak with a "single voice"—the National Defense Transportation Association. The "voice" of its 14,000 members echoes the interventionist thinking behind the C-5A, the LHA, etc.: "Our armed forces today rely on the transportation industry for the global mobility necessary to support national policies and objectives." NDTA is now working with the Military Airlift Command to find the "most advantageous use of new aircraft C-5A for carrying cargo tonnage and military passengers." West Point boasts two past NDTA national presidents: I. Sewell Morris (W.P. 1932), currently chairman of the Military Advisory Committee and vice-president of the Association of American Railroads, and E. C. R. Lasher (W.P. 1929), currently chairman of the nominating committee, director of the Transportation Association of America, and president of North American Car Corporation. Robert C. Tripp (W.P. 1933) is now a national vice-president of NDTA. These men truly mean that "The combined talents and efforts of the members of NDTA provide the Government with human resources, physical facilities, and equipment that can mean the difference between survival or submission in event of enemy attack." Their "combined talents and efforts" also provide very large personal bank accounts.

To bridge the gap between the sophisticated aerospace "hardware" discussed so far and the more mundane conventional weapons, and to illustrate more closely how West Pointers work together to lubricate the defense economy, the story of the Low Observation Helicopter (LOH) is appropriate.

In 1966 the Pentagon submitted a supplemental budget request to Congress for $15 billion to meet urgent needs in Vietnam. Included in the request were funds for an additional 121 LOHs. A House committee approved the monies, but noted that the cost of the LOH had increased 250 percent in the past year and decided to investigate. Attempting to stop the investigation, the Army said it didn't need the helicopters after all, but the committee proceeded nonetheless. It discovered that in the early Sixties a design competition had been held for the LOH airframe that narrowed the possible producers to three firms: Hiller Aircraft Corp., Bell Helicopter, and Hughes Tool Co.

[320]

The Navy, which was handling procurement of the LOH for the Army under an interservice agreement, decided to award the design contract to Hiller. The Army, however, felt that two contractors were needed, so Bell was added. One member of the seven-man selection board, Gen. Clifton F. Von Kann, resented the exclusion of Hughes. At the urging of a close friend, Albert W. Bayer, the vice-president for marketing at Hughes, he filed a minority report to the board and went to his immediate superior, Gen. Barksdale Hamlett (W.P. 1930), the deputy chief of staff for military operations, complaining of the injustice wrought upon Hughes. Hamlett agreed and wrote to his friend, Gen. Arthur G. Trudeau (W.P. 1924), chief of Army Research and Development, saying that he felt Hughes should be added to the list. Trudeau also agreed that an injustice had been done, so he approached his classmate Gen. Clyde D. Eddleman (W.P. 1924), the Acting Army Chief of Staff, and relayed the story. Eddleman acted by ordering the chairman of the selection board and also a classmate, Gen. Gordon B. Rogers (W.P. 1924), to reconvene his group. He complied, and within the first ten minutes of the meeting Hughes had been added to the list. John Greco (W.P. 1930), who was manager of Army programs for Hughes, and Frederick W. Coleman (W.P. 1933), a retired brigadier general who worked in Hughes' Washington office, must have been very pleased with the performance of their fellow alumni. One man wasn't happy, though; Gen. Richard D. Meyer (W.P. 1933) chose not to follow the rules and opposed, with the Navy, the decision to add Hughes. When Eddleman was told of his siding with the Navy, Meyer was transferred to another command, removed from flight status, and apprised that he would have nothing further to do with Army aviation. Meyer eventually returned to good graces, but the helicopters didn't—they were delivered late and did not meet the design standards.[39] The West Pointers involved turned out a little better: Eddleman retired in 1962, went to work for Hughes, and eventually became vice-president of UMC Corporation; Trudeau also retired in 1962 and became president of Gulf Research and Development Co.; Hamlett retired in 1964 and assumed the presidency of Norwich University; and Meyer retired in 1967 to become the assistant to the president of Firestone Tire and Rubber Co.

These men are not alone in capitalizing on their cozy relationships with defense contractors. His experience and Colt Industries provided the path to a comfortable old age for one graduate —Maj. Gen. Nelson M. Lynde (W.P. 1929). From May 1962 until February 1964 he was commanding general of the Army Weapons Command and, as such, played a key role in negotiating the initial M-16 contract with Colt. On October 4, 1963, he approved the rifle prices as negotiated and directed the preparation of approval documents for submission to higher authority. On October 31, however, he appointed his deputy, Brig. Gen. Roland B. Anderson (W.P. 1938), contracting officer for the award of the initial production contract of 104,000 M-16s and explained that he would be absent from the command at the time of the award. By August, 1964, Lynde was working for Colt as executive consultant to the company's president. He had received the job offer from Colt in mid-February and two days before his March 1, 1964, retirement he requested an advisory opinion from the Army Adjutant General on the propriety of accepting the offer. The letter he received in answer advised that no violation of federal law was apparent if he did not sell Colt products to the federal government. Three years later Lynde was asked to testify before a Congressional committee investigating suspected waste and impropriety in connection with the M-16 program. Asked what he did to justify his $20,000 a year salary from Colt, Lynde replied, "I am employed generally, you might say, as an analyst. I have visited six foreign countries. I have surveyed eleven companies, twelve heavy industrial plants, and one proving ground, all with the question of acquisition or a joint venture. These have been in Switzerland, Holland, England, France, Canada. I have made market surveys of four major countries. I have made commodity studies of at least five commodities. I also represent Colt as far as the American Ordnance Association is concerned, the Association of the U.S. Army, the National Security Industrial Association, and various other professional military associations." Questioned specifically about any post-retirement involvement with the M-16, Lynde stated, "I have refrained from association with the M-16 program. I might say that I feel that except for this decision, that I kept, I might have made a contribution, actually, had I been permitted to attend the technical meetings on that rifle, in improving communications between the Weapons Command and Colt's Firearms Co." The committee chairman then asked, ". . . have you provided any of your associates with information on present or future military requirements since your employment by industry?" Lynde responded, "Sir, I am able, by the committee hearings on military posture and the newspapers and so on, to fairly reliably predict the military program. That I have not hesitated to express. But I have not revealed anything that might be considered as confidential and which came—" and here he was cut off by the chairman.[40] The committee report from which these statements were drawn later noted, despite Lynde's protestations of non-involvement, that he had on October 26, 1964, requested from the Army a copy of a classified document dealing with the M-16 and was on Colt's distribution list for internal company memoranda on the rifle. Two fellow graduates may have been on the same list: Edward J. Roxbury (W.P. 1946), marketing manager of Colt Military Arms, and James B. Hall (W.P. 1948), Colt's head of government sales in Southeast Asia in 1967 and currently vice-president of the Pyrodynamics Division. Need it be added that during the period 1965–70 Colt held over $238 million in military contracts relating directly to the Vietnam war? Lynde, Roxbury, and Hall did their jobs well. The Congressional investigation, however, found that the government didn't come out so well—Colt was taking excessive profits and some of the rifles were being delivered defective.

There are plenty of other weapons for West Pointers to push and companies for them to lead. Rodney C. Gott (W.P. 1933), is chairman of the board of AMF, Inc., which specializes in bombs. In 1969 alone AMF received over $130 million for its 500-pounder and $50 million for its big one, the 750-pounder. The latter has been described as making "a crater about twenty-five feet across and six feet deep—quite big enough, no doubt, for the destruction of snipers and any type of native military structure." [41] Until 1965 Gott had as president of AMF's "Expansion Services" Russell L. Maxwell (W.P. 1912). In the five years following Maxwell's departure, AMF "expanded" enough to reap $339 million in Vietnam-related contracts. Bernard E.

Conor (W.P. 1946) now assists Gott as one of his division vice-presidents and group executives.

Like many corporate leaders, Gott does not confine his abilities to one company; he also serves on the board of directors of Bulova Watch Co. His chairman for this additional duty is Omar N. Bradley (W.P. 1915). Bradley's company isn't in the same ball park with Gott's when it comes to bombs; in 1971 it simply made the detonating fuses for 81-mm. high-explosive and white-phosphorus projectiles. Over the last five years, however, Bulova has made enough precision parts for use in Vietnam to rake in over $89 million in Pentagon contracts.

Another bomb-maker is Honeywell, Inc. Along with its twenty West Pointers—including two vice-presidents, C. A. Arnold (W.P. 1946) and T. C. Cronin (W.P. 1949)—this well-known "computer company" has gathered over $642 million in Vietnam-related contracts since 1965. Among its more successful products have been the XM54 white-phosphorus anti-personnel mine, the Rockeye II cluster bomb, and, at the top of the line, the BLU-26/B "guava" bomb. The use of this last weapon has been described as follows:

> The pineapples [an early version of the guava] are carried in tubes under jet aircraft, with 25 bombs to the tube. Depending on the aircraft, each plane can carry up to 20 tubes. When released, the pineapples sprout winglets which either stabilize their descent or increase dispersion patterns. The pineapple explodes on contact and spews 240 steel pellets ten meters in all directions. The steel balls are 6.3 millimeters (approximately ¼ inch) in diameter and hit with a velocity comparable to shotgun pellets fired at a distance of three to four yards. The discharge from one aircraft creates an elliptical killing zone five football fields long by two and one half football fields wide.
>
> The steel balls have no effect on military structures. They cannot pierce cement and can penetrate earthen or sandbag military revetments only to a depth of two or three inches. The one thing they can penetrate effectively is human flesh. Because of their shape and/or velocity, once they tear into the body they move in a complex path, doing great damage and complicating removal. There are cases where people have been hit by as many as 30 pellets.
>
> . . . The guava, though smaller than the pineapple, is far more

effective. Each guava holds from 340–600 steel pellets, and because it is smaller, more can be carried on each plane. . . . The guavas, or bomblets, are carried in a "mother" bomb. After release, the "mother" breaks open at an altitude of approximately 3200 feet to spew forth her "fruit." . . . When the guavas are 30 feet from the ground they explode, hurling their steel "seed" not only outwards but also downwards. . . . The guavas also have a longer killing zone—up to the length of *ten* football fields. The real advantage, however, is that because of the air bursts, people in open ditches are no longer protected.[42]

Motorola Inc., a maker of radios, televisions, stereos, and $30 million worth of bomb fuses, employs as manager of Long Range Planning for Federal Market Development, John Millikin (W.P. 1941). He and seven fellow graduates have helped Motorola to over $91 million in Vietnam-related work. Eastman Kodak has its explosives, General Motors its tanks and howitzers, FMC Corp. its anti-personnel mines, and each has a contingent of West Pointers. A list of weapons producers and graduates associated with them would contain thousands of names. These companies could surely survive without this group of employees, but why ignore such a rich and easily accessible source of weapons expertise, inside knowledge, and devotion to authority? Indeed, far from ignoring this gold mine, the corporate-military team has set up two organizations which actively foster its growth and development—the American Ordnance Association (AOA) and the National Security Industrial Association (NSIA).

According to its literature, the purpose of the fifty-two-year-old AOA is to "disseminate among scientists, engineers, industrial executives, and other patriotic citizens, knowledge of the technical progress of weapons used and required by the armed forces of the U.S.—to keep the military informed of the capabilities and limitations of industry—to provide a reservoir of technical know-how to meet any national emergency—and to advance the special working relationship between the two main partners for American defense . . ." It is not necessary to point out the identities of the "two main partners." In contrast to the previously discussed Aerospace Industries Association, Air Force Association, and National Defense Transportation Association, AOA does not confine its efforts to a particular set of industries or weapons. Instead, it directs "liaison between science, industry, and the armed forces in the research, development, and production of *superior weapons*." Its 46,000 members have assumed a broad task for themselves, and to assure success they rely heavily on the fertile West Point mind. "In Cincinnati Frank Besson (W.P. 1932) received the Charles L. Harrison award at the Annual Meeting of the American Ordnance Association with the citation read by Bill Culp (W.P. 1932), president of the Ohio College of Applied Science." [43] The executive vice-president and full-time boss of AOA is William K. Ghormley (W.P. 1929). He came to the job after retiring as commanding general of the Army Munitions Command in 1962. Aiding Ghormley full-time is John R. V. Dickson (W.P. 1936), whose title is Assistant Staff Director for the Technology and Management Advisory Service. Working parttime but holding important positions nonetheless are council member, executive-committee member, and director Arthur G. Trudeau (W.P. 1924), the former assistant to the chairman of the board of North American Rockwell Corp.; second vice-president Laurence C. Craigie (W.P. 1923), director of Air Force Requirements for Lockheed Aircraft; and advisory-board members Benjamin W. Chidlaw (W.P. 1922), formerly in charge of the Continental Air Defense Command, and John H. Hinrichs (W.P. 1928), formerly chief of Ordnance. Joining their retired friends in AOA but still on active duty are Lieut. Gen. Henry A. Miley (W.P. 1940), deputy commanding general of the Army Matériel Command and member of AOA's Army Liaison Committee, and Maj. Gen. Andrew S. Low (W.P. 1942), who works both for the Deputy Chief of Staff of the Air Force and the AOA's Air Force Liaison Committee. With this kind of organization backing him up, a West Pointer need never lack a job defending our country from inside a defense plant.

The National Security Industrial Association operates in much the same manner. Its purpose is "maintaining an effective working partnership between industry and government" (meaning military). To this end it employs Gordon H. Austin (W.P. 1936) as its staff vice-president for operations and lists S. C. Pace (W.P. 1943) of TRW, Inc., as vice-chairman of its executive

DEFENDING COUNTRY AND CAPITALISM

committee, J. H. Drum (W.P. 1937) of Kaiser Corp. as a member of the board of trustees, and seventeen retired West Point generals as "honorary members." One of their means of "maintaining an effective working partnership" is a series of "symposia" held across the country, designed to further "communication between government and industry on mutual problems, policies, plans, and procedures." One of these, held on August 11–12, 1971, and billed as the DOD (Department of Defense)–NSIA Symposium on Major Defense Systems Acquisition, is illustrative of the role of West Pointers. The morning of the first day was filled by DOD officials explaining the inner workings of "defense systems" acquisition and development. Presenting industry's response to this information in the afternoon was James R. Dempsey (W.P. 1943), vice-president of AVCO Corp. The next day brought Gen. Henry A. Miley (W.P. 1940) speaking on the "Application of DOD Policy in the Army Environment" and Gen. George S. Brown (W.P. 1941) speaking on the same subject as it applied to the Air Force "environment." In the afternoon both sat on a panel for two hours discussing their speeches and then heard an industry response given by officials from the Raytheon Co. and the Martin-Marietta Corp. This kind of "teamwork" goes far beyond the manufacture of weapons—both AOA and NSIA act as employment agencies for the military and, more importantly, as manufacturers of propaganda for the American public. Although both groups insist they are "non-profit, and non-lobbying" and dedicated only to a "strong United States as the only deterrent to aggression," their literature is rife with concern about the "missile gap," our "threatened industrial defense base," and the "neophyte legislators, unrealistic scientists, and many unthinking dupes, who would weaken the defense of the United States." This kind of material is an obvious effort to mold public opinion in the assumptions of the Cold War and continually condition it to accept an ever expanding weapons complex. Who is better qualified to orchestrate these efforts than our veteran Cold Warrior, the West Pointer? No one. And the eminently successful AOA and NSIA have discovered as much.

Not all West Pointers, however, gravitate toward the weapons-makers. Any industry that is characterized by close ties with the

[327]

government holds magnificent potential for the ambitious graduate, and the communications industry with its long-standing government-granted monopolies has been one of these. The most recent case was that of the Communications Satellite Corporation (COMSAT).

When communications satellites first became a technical possibility, priority for their use was given to the military. Lt. Gen. Arthur D. Starbird (W.P. 1933), then director of the Defense Communications Agency and manager of the National Communications System, set the tone of military discussion by stressing the importance of the communications satellite in providing the "means of establishing, on the shortest time scale, reliable communications to out-of-the-way areas where tension develops—that is to say, flexibility to extend rapidly into new areas. . . . Any system which will give a rapid, instantaneous, reliable communication to a new, troublesome out-of-the-way area will have a tremendous advantage in the future." [44] In other words, the military needed good communications for their counter-insurgency program. And they got them. In 1966, when the first global satellite communications system was in full operation, two of the eight ground stations were in Vietnam and most of the others were located in Third World countries. Starbird's wish had come true and the military had exploited their end of the new medium—but what of the non-military applications? Those were left to COMSAT.

Organized with the government's blessing as a private company in 1963, COMSAT sold half of its initial stock offering to individual investors and the remainder to 163 authorized communications carriers—AT&T, ITT, General Telephone, and RCA came up with over 90 percent of the carrier allocation and 45.5 percent of the total offering. Assured that control was in good hands, COMSAT moved to gather customers by negotiating international agreements that would give it the necessary interference-free communications channels and an adequate number of foreign message-receivers. These negotiations have been described by one observer as a "typical imperialist struggle." Writing in *Corporations and the Cold War,* Joseph D. Phillips says: "The American industry-government team, taking advantage of their lead in satellite technology, rushed 'a program for Early Bird which would supply this North Atlantic capability in 1965' in order to forestall the efforts of British and other European interests to 'get in with . . . another generation of cables' that would maintain their dominant position in international communications. The effort was successful; it 'broke the resistance of these certain European countries and resulted in . . . a highly favorable climate for cooperative participation in an early system. . . . As the Europeans have seen the determination and speed with which we have been moving, their interest in climbing aboard has intensified. And that is exactly what we wanted.' " [45]

Who were these COMSAT men who fought such a valiant battle to establish American superiority in global communications? We can be sure they were men of experience in the Cold War. The Chairman and Chief Executive Officer was James McCormack (W.P. 1932), the Director of the International Development Division was McCormack's classmate Kenneth F. Zitzman, the Special Assistant to the Vice-President for Technology was Donald P. Graul (W.P. 1929), the Assistant Chief Engineer was another McCormack classmate, Charles M. Baer, the Manager of the Western Area was Wallace M. Lauterbach (W.P. 1941), and a consultant was Gordon Blake (W.P. 1931). With Starbird pushing from one end and McCormack from the other, and with the military reality operating as their prime input, a truly international system of communications open to all countries never had a chance—it wasn't even considered.

Though important, COMSAT is dwarfed in money and influence by such giants as International Telephone and Telegraph (ITT), General Telephone and Electronics (GTE), and RCA. Excluding the weapon-makers, ITT is the government's largest support service contractor, and it has not forgotten its West Pointers; Randolph V. Araskog (W.P. 1953) is president of ITT's Defense Communications Division; Duncan Hallock (W.P. 1933) is executive vice-president of ITT Philippines Inc.; Derrick W. Samuelson (W.P. 1951) is vice-president of ITT's World Communications Inc.; John F. Johnson (W.P. 1943) is vice-president of ITT's Avionics Division; and Clerin R. Smith (W.P. 1926) was a vice-president of the parent corporation from 1957 to 1960. ITT handled $217 million in Pentagon contracts in 1970. General Telephone, with a mere $107 million in 1970, nevertheless also tries to keep graduates in top positions: Clovis E. Byers (W.P. 1920) is a vice-president; Charles Jones (W.P. 1943) is Director of Planning for GTE International; David F. Piske (W.P. 1952) is Director of Government Communications for GTE Service Corp.; and Percy G. Black (W.P. 1917) is a former vice-president of GTE Service Corp. One of GTE's subsidiaries, the well-known Sylvania Electric Products Co., employs as a vice-president Richard M. Osgood (W.P. 1941). His company was responsible for $81 million of GTE's defense contracts.

RCA, with $262 million in Pentagon contracts in 1970, employed over twenty West Pointers in the Sixties and went its competition one better by placing a graduate on the board of directors, Harry C. Ingles (W.P. 1914). He also serves on the board of NBC and RCA Communications Inc. At latest report, RCA also employed Cary J. King (W.P. 1924) as a consultant and curator of its David Sarnoff Library.

The concentration of West Pointers in the communications industry nearly parallels that found in aerospace and missiles, and their opportunities for control are just as great. But, as in all areas where large government appropriations are up for grabs, they have left nothing to chance and have formed an association—the Armed Forces Communications and Electronics Association (AFCEA). It is, of course, dominated by West Pointers.

Founded in 1946 by the RCA man, Harry C. Ingles (W.P. 1914), it has grown to over 12,000 members, who, by their membership, "indicate their readiness for their share in industry's part in national security." The executive vice-president, general manager, editor of the house organ, *Signal* Magazine, and full-time chief of this group is Willet J. Baird (W.P. 1926). Assisting him as vice-presidents are Maj. Gen. Gordon T. Gould (W.P. 1941), Maj. Gen. George E. Pickett (W.P. 1939), Lt. Gen. Richard P. Klocko (W.P. 1937), and Earle F. Cook (W.P. 1931). Listed as directors are the ever present Lt. Gen. Alfred D. Starbird (W.P. 1933) and Maj. Gen. Walter E. Lotz (W.P. 1938). The litany of these men is depressingly familiar: "We are a patriotic, educational, non-profit, non-sectarian, non-political association with no commercial interests . . . and endeavor to maintain and improve the cooperation between the Armed Forces and Industry in communications. . . ." Non-sectarian and non-political AFCEA may be, but "Individuals and industrial organizations having affiliation with the Communist Party are not eligible for membership." As part of its membership pitch, AFCEA exhorts a potential draftee to "become an active member of your country's civilian-military team through cooperation with all agencies of the government in their quest for technological advances and achievements." This kind of phraseology is perhaps the best commentary on the callousness with which West Pointers broadcast their aims through their closed and elitist associations.

Related to the field of communications in terms of the high technology involved are such firms as IBM and Control Data. Giant IBM has been particularly attractive to graduates. The 1970 Register of Graduates listed seventy-six who had successfully traded their Army attire for the IBM uniform of conservative suit, white shirt, and charcoal-gray socks. IBM's 1970 total of over $256 million in defense contracts should have made Thetus C. Odom (W.P. 1930), vice-president of the Federal Systems Division, particularly happy. Smaller Control Data has only seven West Pointers and $80 million in 1970 Pentagon contracts, but one of these gentlemen, Earle L. Lerette (W.P. 1939), functions as special assistant to the president. Another computer grad retired in 1964 after a long career in intelligence that included a tour with the United Nations: "I was in the Middle East in the late 1940s. We went to enforce the truce as U.N. observers. A—— B——, another grad, was with me and there were many others there. B—— was later an attaché to Jordan. I was involved with writing the truce with Egypt. I was in charge of the evacuation of Egyptian troops that had been guaranteed safe withdrawal from Israel. I personally surveyed, mapped out, walked, and drew many of the boundaries between Syria, Lebanon, and Jordan." Of his career he says, "If we are going to defeat the enemy in times of peace it (intelligence) was where the action was. But it is an unsung kind of work, so it is dead rot for career advancement. You have to step on the toes of your own people to get things done and this doesn't help your career. You had to lie to your own people and this isn't consistent with 'Duty, Honor, Country,' but you had to do it to get the job done." Of his new job he says, "I represent the leaders of the company on all policy matters where there is interface between the government and the company. I am neither a lobbyist or a salesman but am close to both." His views on the usefulness of his West Point friends are strangely contradictory: "I do try to keep up old ties. Our class meets once a month to have lunch. . . . If I were in sales I might find them useful, but this is not so true in the kind of work I do. I could exploit them, but I don't because I don't think you can mix policy and marketing. I have, however, contacted other grads on certain policy matters when I needed advice. For example, three years ago the Bureau of Standards was standardizing computer software equipment. We thought some elements of the standards program were injurious to the company and to the government. I had to contact officials in all the government agencies to discuss the problem. I had especially good contacts in the Pentagon. Often my contacts have developed contacts of their own. If I want to contact someone, I call and ask their help and they say, 'Sure, why don't I arrange lunch or something?' " [46] At least two West Pointers, however, are in competition with Odom, Lerette, and companies. Trying to build his own IBM is Herbert Roth (W.P. 1951), formerly president of Anelex Corp. and now president of Lab for Electronics, Inc., and chairman of the executive committee for Mohawk Data Sciences Corp. His defense contracts aren't very large yet, but who would bet against his future success as long as he is wearing his West Point ring? William F. Ward (W.P. 1950) is also in the game as a director of Scantlin Electronics, but this seems to be just a sideline. He was vice-president of Grosset & Dunlap Publishing Co. in 1967 and is now vice-president and comptroller of Dun & Bradstreet. In 1967 Ward received a citation from the VFW for his support of the troops in Vietnam: ". . . for his continuous efforts in promoting Americanism, not only on the field of battle, but by his tremendous effort to perpetuate our way of life, via the speaker's and debating rostrum. . . ." [47] In related areas are such men as Ed Harwood (W.P. 1920), a director and trustee of the American Institute for Economic Research, and J. A. Knebel (W.P. 1959), general counsel of the Small Business Administration.

Academy graduates have found big money not only in weapons and computers, but also in that old standby, oil. As in other industries, they can be found at all levels. Starting at the top, the following observation by Murray Seegar in the *Los Angeles Times* (January 11, 1971) is appropriate:

> Using levers of power that other industries do not have, the oil companies and their widespread allies have created a subgovernment in Washington that has buried pipelines deeply into the body of the real government. Those pipelines produce inside information that allows the industry to use its power most effectively.
>
> One branch of the pipeline goes directly into the White House because President Nixon insisted after taking office two years ago that oil policy was to be made by his staff. Other branches of the line go into such agencies as the Interior Department and the Federal Power Commission that are vital to the industry's well-being and into the committees of Congress that write legislation affecting the industry.
>
> As a result, the oil industry can make things happen in Washington. More importantly, the industry can prevent the government from making a decision detrimental to the companies' interest. The industry can frustrate the earnest efforts of officials with whom it disagrees . . . [and] no industry is so deeply involved in national and international politics as oil. In no other industry does the self-interest conflict so often with the public's interest.

As pointed out in the chapter on West Pointers in government, it is George A. Lincoln (W.P. 1929) and his fellow graduates who substantially comprise the oil-policy pipeline to the White House. The line to the Interior Department is the National Petroleum Council, an "advisory body" completely financed by the oil industry. The assistant director of this public-spirited group is Edmond H. Farrington (W.P. 1942). The line going to the Federal Power Commission is called the American Gas Association, a group of so-called competitors who advise the FPC on the available supply of gas and, in effect, set the price. West Point's representative with this group is Harold S. Walker (W.P. 1943), director of public affairs for Commonwealth Services, Inc. These men and several other grads represent the kind of power and control that George A. Lincoln refers to in this statement: "We are a great country largely because of our supply and use of energy. Without control of that energy supply, we could become a Samson shorn of his locks." [48]

The men inspiring these Presidential advisors and lobbyists to greater and greater efforts are well qualified to preach "Duty, Honor, Country." Sitting in the corporate boardrooms are such men as Darwin W. Ferguson (W.P. 1930), executive vice-president and a director of Sun Oil Co. (he also finds time to chair the American Petroleum Institute's Committee on Public Affairs) and Ferguson's classmate John H. Murrell, who presides over the leading oil consulting firm of De Golyer & McNaughton as chairman of the board and chief executive officer. In 1968 another member of the Class of 1930, Lauris Norstad, sat on the board of directors of Continental Oil Co. From 1962 until 1968 Arthur G. Trudeau (W.P. 1924) was president of Gulf Oil's subsidiary Gulf Research and Development, where he selected Christopher Coyne (W.P. 1939) as his director of financial services. In 1970 the superintendent of Gulf's oil-fleet operations was Robert A. Land (W.P. 1946). At latest information, Clayton E. Mullins (W.P. 1933) was managing director of Atlantic Petroleum Ltd. in London and William M. Bishop (W.P. 1957) was a vice-president of Esso. The recent Alaskan oil find also has its West Pointer, and it is only logical that he is involved in the most controversial aspect of this operation. Raymond J. Reeves (W.P. 1934) is president, chief executive officer, and director of the Alaskan Pipeline Co.

Space is too limited to do justice to the scores of other graduates involved in the tangled maze of the oil industry, but perhaps this quote from *Assembly* says enough: "Steve Avery (Class of 1954), still shoring up the financial substructure of the Capitol, was in attendance (about that Vietnamese offshore petroleum development stock, Steve . . .)." [49]

Many other West Point entrepreneurs have been slighted in this discussion, among them Lucius Clay (W.P. 1918), who can boast of service with Continental Can Co. as chairman of the board, with Lehman Bros. as a senior partner, and, finally, with the Federal National Mortgage Association, again as chairman of the board. Clay left Continental Can, but Warren J. Hayford (W.P. 1952) and Roy T. Evans (W.P. 1933) stayed on as, respectively, general manager of market and product planning and vice-president. Lauris Norstad (W.P. 1930) left the Army in 1963, became president of Owens-Corning Fiberglas Corp. in that same year, and by 1967 had been named chairman of the board. One grad, J. Lawton Collins (W.P. 1917), found his retirement niche in the drug industry as a director of Chas. Pfizer International. Another, J. K. Houssels (W.P. 1945), sought his fortune in Las Vegas and was president of that city's Tropicana Hotel in 1964. Still others have found a home in the food business: James A. Summer (W.P. 1945) is president of General Mills Inc., and H. C. Porter (W.P. 1932) is assistant to a vice-president of General Mills; Desmond O'Connell (W.P. 1928) is president of American Bakeries and his classmate Frederick L. Anderson is a director; and Thomas B. Bartel (W.P. 1939) was recently a vice-president of Quaker Oats. Mining has also attracted some eager graduates: until 1967 Robert M. Hardy (W.P. 1935) was the president of Sunshine Mining Co., the largest silver producer in the U.S., and Walter L. Frankland (W.P. 1946) was executive director of the Silver Users Association. Trade associations seem to exert a unique appeal, as the following West Pointers will attest:

Robert G. Bartlett (W.P. 1953)—President, American Road Builders Association

William McCollam (W.P. 1946)—Director, Edison Electric Institute

I. Sewell Morris (W.P. 1932)—Vice-President, Association of American Railroads

James Q. Brett (W.P. 1930)—Director and Vice-President, National Society of Industrial Realtors

James W. Coutts (W.P. 1932)—General Manager, Retail Drygoods Association

Alan H. Gould (W.P. 1947)—President, National Association of Store Fixture Manufacturers

C. Hancock Reed (W.P. 1922)—President, American Association of Textile and Garment Wholesalers

Theodore J. Altier (W.P. 1944)—President, National Shoe Retailers Association

Still other graduates are attracted by such far-right-wing corporate leaders as Patrick J. Frawley, the financier of Fred Schwarz and his Christian Anti-Communism Crusade and that diligent ferret of subversives, the American Security Council. Frawley's fortune was founded on the Paper-Mate Pen (he eventually sold the pen to the Gillette Co., which at one time had Boone Gross, W.P. 1926, as vice-president and Irving Duffy, W.P. 1926, as a director) and now includes Eversharp, Shick, and, until recently, Technicolor. These firms subsidize far-right causes to the tune of an estimated million dollars a year.[50] Helping Frawley maintain the pace of his obsession have been two appropriate men—Gary P. Thomas (W.P. 1954), vice-president of Schick, and Thomas L. Flattery (W.P. 1947), secretary and corporate counsel of Technicolor.

There are many more West Pointers and many other companies, but it is necessary only to know one thing about them —most would agree with William Quinn of Martin-Marietta when he says: "If I were ever pressed to identify the greatest thing that ever happened to me, it would be getting that diploma. There is some mystique about the place that you never get over, you never get it out of your system. You are eternally proud. You know that you belong to an unbelievable tradition of great people—Lee, Grant, Eisenhower, Patton, Bradley. It goes on so long throughout history." [51] And industry.

Today the best example of how corporate and military aims have reached a happy symbiosis is George H. Olmsted (W.P. 1922), chairman and president of the International Bank, a firm which, along with its subsidiaries and affiliates, has assets in excess of $3 billion. Olmsted heads banks, manufacturing firms, insurance companies, and credit corporations scattered all over the world. In Liberia his company is the official administrator of the Maritime Code and grants the notoriously lax registrations that have made the Liberian shipping fleet the largest in the world. It is important to Olmsted that Liberia does not permit any ship that flies its flag to enter the ports of Haiphong or Havana. He has banks in England, Luxembourg (where he preaches the tax advantages offered by that small country in setting up holding companies), Switzerland, Lebanon, the Caribbean, and so on.

Olmsted himself describes a few of the members of his industrial empire: "Our packaging company, Kliklok, on whose California-built machines are packaged over 80 percent of the American frozen foods and many other items, is now producing machines in Bristol, England, for the British and European market. . . . Foster Wheeler Corporation, our largest industrial associate, recently has built a steel mill in Turkey, a refinery and fertilizer plant in Kuwait, power plants in Spain, a distillation furnace in Normandy, and refinery installations in Trieste, Rotterdam, and Westernport, Australia. Its licensee, Ishikawajima in Japan, is building boilers for a power plant in Korea, various land installations in Japan, and marine boilers for most of the great new oil tankers that are being built in Japanese shipyards." [52] In his pursuit of the world dollar, Olmsted has relied heavily on his fellow alumni (all companies mentioned are tied to Olmsted).

William H. Baumer (W.P. 1933)
President, International General Industries;
Director of eight other companies

Henry S. Aurand (W.P. 1915)
Director, International Bank;
Director, United Services Life Insurance Co.

Orval R. Cook (W.P. 1922)
Director, International Bank

Harold K. Johnson (W.P. 1933)
Director, Financial General Bankshares, Inc.;
Director, Kliklok Corp.

Frank A. Lee (W.P. 1945)
Director, Foster Wheeler Corp.

Francis M. Greene (W.P. 1922)
Director, United Services Life Insurance Co.

Willard A. Holbrook, Jr. (W.P. 1918)
Director, United Services Life Insurance Co.

Maxwell D. Taylor (W.P. 1922)
Director, United Services Life Insurance Co.

George H. Olmsted, Jr. (W.P. 1954)
Vice-President, Arlington Trust Co.

Olmsted's office is on the twelfth floor of a brand-new office building on K Street in Washington, D.C. Huge and opulent, it offers a commanding view across the city and the Potomac River all the way to Virginia. Sitting amid this splendor is a short, almost squat man with a round face and very white hair. Gaining an interview with a man of this stature would normally be very difficult, but the words "We would like to talk to you about West Point" worked the same magic they had in every other interview and his doors were quickly opened.

Why did you leave the Army in 1923 (he was in the class of 1922)? "Right after World War I the size of the army was drastically reduced, the opportunities were limited. I had a grandfather who graduated from the Academy right after the Civil War and spent twenty years on the frontier and then retired as a major. I didn't want to stay if there was no opportunity for advancement, and I was right, for my classmates after seventeen years were still only lieutenants."

Was your education helpful to your civilian career? "Yes. It establishes and defines the importance of integrity, responsibility, devotion to duty, and the discharge of obligations. It inculcates one with the basic principles of leadership."

How did your military experience help you? "While I was director of the military assistance program, I learned things that were helpful. Almost none of the people engaged in the military assistance programs in the countries were the same people I had business contacts with later, but I learned a great deal about the countries that was useful.

"When the International Bank goes into a country, we go in as partners with the local people. We have just opened a bank in the Virgin Islands. It is 65 percent locally owned and we run the bank for them. In Liberia, 80 percent of the employees are local people.

"There are three ways that we have interests in a bank. (1) We control 80 percent of the bank. Then for tax purposes we can consolidate. (2) We own 66⅔ percent of the bank. Then we can do what we want without interference from the other stockholders. (3) Fifty percent. We don't regard this as a problem unless there is a concentration of ownership on the other side of the table. We are not even averse to having less than 50 percent so long as we don't have a concentration of interest against us. We have had certain problems, but up till now we have been able to beat them. When you have a successful bank, occasionally you have a case where raiders attempt to get control of public stock. You try to keep yourself in a position where you can keep control during an unfriendly raid. The situation can't arise in a foreign country where the people demand control of the bank, because we don't allow situations where this can happen. Only once have we had a situation where a foreign government appropriated the company—in the Dominican Republic. We had purchased from AID insurance against such expropriations. We made a claim, they resisted it, and now the case is in arbitration.

"Most large American banks abroad are there to serve Stateside customers. We are local; we have local partnerships and we serve the local people. For example, in Luxembourg we started with $200,000 capital. Now we have 25,000 customers and branches in all major cities and over $26 million in assets.

"Only in Birmingham, England, do we have a bank where we don't own the controlling interest. There we own 50 percent and the other 50 percent is owned by Sir Issac Wolfson and Lord Thomson of Fleet."

Do the countries object to the amount of money you take out of the country as profits? "Remember, we have a partnership, so we don't take out all the bank's profits. And of our profits, we usually leave at least half of them in the bank; they are put back into the business for further expansion."

Why do you have so many military men as members of the boards of directors of your companies? "A director of a corporation has a very special type of responsibility. By law he is a representative of all the stockholders, even though he may own only a small amount or else substantial shares of the company. There are rigid laws and intangible requirements as to conflict of interest, etc. There is an intense personal liability for a director, so you look primarily for good character, judgment, not technical competence. An officer of a bank must have the technical skills. So men can be very effective directors without any experience at all in banking or finance. When you get into the area of directors, of judging a man's character, there is no difference between a military man and a civilian.

"There used to be a myth in this country about the military mind. After World War I, some intense pacifists felt there were people who didn't know anything except how to be a soldier. When I was at West Point there was a feeling that all you needed to do was ride and shoot. For example, when I was there we had six hours of equitation a week. The academies have gone a long way since then, in broadening the scope of their education. Cadets are far better equipped today.

"Today you don't hear much about the military mind, and then when you do, it is from very poorly informed people. Look at Marshall, Eisenhower, Bradley, Wedemeyer. How can you accuse them of having military minds? People who make this accusation are narrow-minded bigots.

"During World War II the military found that they didn't have people trained in international politics, economics. They had to come either from the reserve or from the civilian population. Since then the Army has made great progress in giving people a broader education. The results have shown up in Korea and Vietnam.

"General Stilwell is one of the saddest representatives of the military mind. When they made him commander in the China theater, he went around calling the Generalissimo 'Peanuts,' even in front of the Generalissimo's staff. This is why he failed. I was sent out to patch up the differences between the two. I was sent because of my experience running the military assistance program. When I got to Cairo I went to bed, and when I got up the next morning I found that Stilwell had been relieved. Wedemeyer had been put in charge of the theater. I decided to go on anyway. I had known Wedemeyer at West Point. When I got there, he said, 'George, what are you doing here?' I answered, 'Al, well, the War Department just sent me out here to settle this mess.' He said, 'George, you are going to stay.' He recognized the need to have someone with experience in international supply, in international politics and economics." [53]

This is a man who has redefined old-time economic imperialism in modern Cold War terms. Combining corporate and military thought in a speech given upon receipt of the World Trade Award, George Olmsted has the last word on West Pointers and industry:

. . . . you can defend capitalism best by creating more capitalists. In order to explain our thinking let us first take a long look backward and ask a question.

Over two thousand years ago some great leaders and a great idea succeeded, in spite of the awesome limitations of travel, communication, education, lack of precedent, and the rest, in building the supreme power of Rome and in conquering and occupying the then known world.

To this day their achievements stagger the imagination and people still say with pride when they point to a road, a temple, a colosseum or an aqueduct—"That was Roman."

But the great idea of popular government was supplanted by "Bread and Circuses." The conquered became the slaves of the conquerors, rather than free men.

The great leaders were followed by successors, fewer and fewer of whom were cast in the magnificent mold of the founders—more and more of whom were there to serve themselves rather than their people and their country.

And so, in less than three hundred years from the beginning, Rome was clearly on the way to its decline and fall.

My question is "Which way America?"

We are now in the third century since our great leaders and their great idea began to emerge.

We have become the world's only super power.

A major part of the world's people today are underprivileged, uneducated, insecure, facing want and possible starvation. In the Romans' day they called the peripheral people "Barbarians" who were meant to be enslaved or destroyed.

In our day we agree these developing nations and their people should be aided. But we don't agree on the means. Should it be "Bread and Circuses," government-to-government handouts—or should it be the system under which our country has reached its present position of strength and power? I speak of the system of opportunity and reward—the system of free private enterprise—in short, capitalism.

If we believe in capitalism, it is essential that we each run our segment of the economy with success. It is also essential—it is the great challenge of the days ahead that each of us and our businesses make capitalists out of little people everywhere. Give them the chance to earn things they can hold on to and enjoy.

Herein lies the true answer to communist aggression.

The other day I was listening to a TV commentator, one of the sniveling kind. He was talking about the new communism in Rumania and glowing about the fact that they were introducing private ownership and the profit motive, lessening the control of the central bureaucracy, placing more responsibility in the hands of the plant managers, producing more consumer goods, and in general raising the standard of living of the Rumanian people. Listening to all this, I sighed, and said to myself, "Buster, we used to call that capitalism."

If there are among us those who doubt that the system of opportunity and reward will prevail, I invite you to look at the present state of the Russian economy after fifty years of communist domination and to note the direction in which it has been evolving in very recent years. Or look at Red China and Free China.

As I said before, you can defend capitalism best by creating more capitalists.[54]

CHAPTER 8

The American Insurgency

> Oh, America, and all who are proud of being her
> sons and daughters, rise up and tell your govern-
> ment at all levels, and tell the agencies of the law
> and the mass media—and tell each other—to cease
> permitting a cunning and well-organized minority
> to create chaos and anarchy.[1]
>
> —LT. GEN. (RET.) ARTHUR G. TRUDEAU
> (W.P. 1924)

WESTMORELAND (W.P. 1936) replaces Harkins (W.P.
1929)—Abrams (W.P. 1936) replaces Westmoreland—Westmoreland replaces Johnson (W.P. 1933)—Wheeler (W.P.
1932) replaces Taylor (W.P. 1922)—Taylor replaces Lem-
nitzer (W.P. 1920)—Ryan (W.P. 1938) replaces McConnell
(W.P. 1932)—so does the Long Gray Line replenish the war
against the people of Southeast Asia. Their long story of suffering and terror can be told without once leaving the rigid mental
confines of the technicians from West Point: the reduction of a
revolution to a conspiracy; the assassination of Diem; the bombing of the North; "Search and Destroy"; pacification; Vietnamization; and, finally, My Lai. There is no conspiracy here, only a
misplaced faith that small men could design and implement
large policies. West Point has bred the unifying but inter-
changeable parts in a tragic thread that begins with prisoners

[343]

who must be made free men and ends with free men who must be made prisoners.

Two key, never-to-be-questioned assumptions have been operative in West Point's prosecution of the war: first, that Communism must be stopped, preferably with destruction; and, second, that no revolution is legitimate if it threatens the established order. Dwight D. Eisenhower (W.P. 1915) provides the best illustration of how both principles go hand in hand to warp reality: "It is almost impossible to make the average Vietnamese peasant realize that the French, under whose rule his people had lived for some eighty years, were really fighting in the cause of freedom, while the Viet Minh, people of their own ethnic origins, were fighting on the side of slavery." [2]

Richard M. Nixon describes the man who reminded Eisenhower "of an Old Testament prophet," John Foster Dulles, and in so doing reveals the unsubtle roots of this recurring death wish for Communism: "Although some diplomats disapproved of his habit of discussing the struggle against communism in moral and religious terms, to Dulles that was the very crux of the problem. In the global clash between the free world and the totalitarian Communist bloc, Dulles believed that he had found as close an approximation of the struggle between good and evil as one is likely to find in this imperfect world." [3] The Military Academy has taken Nixon's "imperfect" world and made it whole by anointing a priesthood devoted to the institution of "good" and prepared to make any sacrifice to destroy the institution of "evil." The enemy is fanatical and cunning, and, in Eisenhower's words, "He is going to bluff, to threaten, and to use everything that will divide us or our nation. . . . He has no spiritual values." [4] No rules have to be formulated to deal ethically with the Communists, for, by definition of the priests, they are unethical and godless—when dealing with a diabolical heathen driven by evil itself, there is no need to stay the sword of righteousness. The only latitude this moral structure allows is whether to use a bayonet, a bullet, or a bomb.

The deceit and treachery excused by such single-minded morality is best shown, again, by Eisenhower when he had his representative to the eighth plenary session of the Geneva Agreements in 1954 declare: "[The United States] will refrain from the threat or use of force to disturb them [the Agreements] . . . and it would view any renewal of the aggression in violation of the foresaid agreements with grave concern and as seriously threatening international peace. . . . The United States reiterates its traditional position that peoples are entitled to determine their own future and that it will not join in an arrangement which would hinder this." [5] And, at the same time, the Priest-President sent teams into North Vietnam to sabotage the Agreements by attempting to destroy printing presses in Hanoi, by pouring contaminant into the engines of the Hanoi bus company, and by distributing scare leaflets falsely attributed to the Viet Minh in an effort to get people to leave the North. [6] This duplicity is logical in the West Pointers' world of black and white, of ultimate good and ultimate evil, for in their search for understanding they begin not in humble admiration but in cheapening the world to the ordinary and malleable. Their world is approached as an engineering exercise in problem-solving, and the approved solution demands finding the proper formulae and techniques. Thus, just as their Academy English classes are divided into a series of discrete though sometimes related lessons, so is their world reality, and they insist on having it in bite-sized, manageable portions—stability rather than change, control rather than consent, and order rather than participation. It is within this context that West Point has tried to understand what was happening in Vietnam.

The preoccupation of the priesthood with their own internalized moral themes led them to overlook the central aspect of the war: that it had as its basis the acute grievances of the Vietnamese people. Roger Hilsman (W.P. 1943), a key government counter-revolutionary theorist,* states the blind spot this way: "Communism and violence feed on turmoil. Peaceful construction does not. Immature political institutions, serious economic problems aggravated by population pressures, and social tensions among the new nations offer fertile ground for fomenting unrest." [7] Does he feel that oppressive conditions

---

* The Hilsman quotes are from the period 1962–68. He recently seems to have reached a new understanding (however delayed) of the nature of the war in Southeast Asia and his quoted views may not necessarily reflect his current ones.

cause no harm in themselves; that it is only when those conditions are exploited by conspirators that harm is possible? In Vietnam the conspirators are specifically identified when Hilsman says: "General Giap (Chief of the North Vietnamese Army) is actually an advance man for Chinese Communist power." [8] This conspiracy formula is the essential ingredient in a West Pointer's ability to ignore that the causes of a revolution are grounded in repression, that it represents the goals of the people, and that it is fundamentally creative in its attempts to forge new institutions. These inherently constructive aims are not only ignored, they are actively denied. Hilsman: "We sometimes forget that our positive goals of helping to build strong, viable entities among the new nations of the world are more difficult to achieve than the limited destructive aims of the Communists." [9] Or the familiar Lt. Gen. Arthur Trudeau and his unique view: "Much of the history of this world revolves around the victories of violent, ruthless minorities subjugating the peaceful, more affluent majorities in blood baths." [10]

This sadly absurd interpretation illustrates the utter inability of these men to understand a revolution flowing from the legitimate aspirations of an oppressed mass. They have no personal roots in the people; rather they are an elite, the "cream of the crop," and their historical involvement with mankind, always occurring in an authoritarian mode, reinforces this imagined exalted position. The success of the West Pointer's delusion is grounded in the appeal of his institutionalized morality to his deepest and most natural yearnings. The fact that a successful revolution can only be grounded in the same kind of appeal (without the institutionalized morality) totally escapes him—he has lost his own revolutionary heritage and denies the possibility of its existence in others. Hilsman explains: "Although different colors on maps indicate different nations, it is essential to realize that in Southeast Asia—as in much of Africa and other parts of the world—there is no pervasive national spirit as we know it." [11] Or "the stirrings of nationalism in Vietnam were still only stirrings, inchoate and formless," [12] though, at an early stage in the U.S. involvement, there was evidence that the Viet Minh should be supported if the U.S. were truly interested in a stable, unified Vietnam—

the CIA believed that the Viet Minh "had the capacity to unify Vietnam through peaceful means." [13] In a National Intelligence Report circulated in November 1956 the CIA wrote: "The Viet Minh probably now feels that it can achieve control over all Vietnam without initiating large-scale warfare. Accordingly, we believe that the Communists will exert every effort to accomplish their objectives through means short of war." [14] Even Hilsman, after denying its existence, implicitly imparts a national cohesiveness to the Vietnamese: "In the past, the villagers gradually became aroused against governments established by Western imperialists. Today, the villagers are awakening to the menace of aggression from a Communist tyranny that is a new kind of imperialism." [15] These contradictions meant little, however, and the West Pointer, by denying nationalism, succeeded in ignoring the basic reason for the success of the Viet Minh and the Viet Cong: the maintenance of a revolution depends on the sustained support of a large part of the population and such support can come only from people who have rejected their formal leaders' claims to authority—without a national spirit, there can be no such support and therefore no revolution, only an "insurgency."

The schizophrenia of West Pointers on this most crucial issue is perfectly drawn in this statement, used in reference to America and a favorite at the Academy, by G. P. Baldwin (W.P. 1916): "The Government, the press, and the people as a whole had no enthusiasm for the war, indeed failed to understand what the nation was fighting about. This showed in lack of spirit in the troops sent to the east and in failure of the people at home to support the war. *Such support is necessary in any war.* . . . Unless the people are enthusiastic about war, unless they have a strong will to win it, they will become discouraged by repeated (deferments of victory) and accept a disadvantageous peace. . . . (This) war shows that wars may be won or lost in the home country as well as on the battlefield and that no government can go to war with hope of success unless it is assured that the people as a whole know what the war is about, *that they believe in their cause, are enthusiastic for it,* and *possess a determination to win.*" [16] [Emphasis added.] If these are the conditions for prosecuting a successful war, to what do these men attribute the stubborn persistence of the Vietnamese, a people, remember, without national spirit? Their answer is a simple denial of their own thesis. Hilsman: "guerrillas can thrive even in a countryside that does not give them active support." [17] West Pointers' acclaim of the principle that public support is necessary in any war and their use of it to excuse their own failures by blaming the American people is obscene when placed alongside their contention that the feelings of the Vietnamese people bear no relation to the success of the Viet Cong. But, in the final analysis, it is these very same absurd moral and political assumptions about Communism and revolution that lead them to reject all facts that do not point to the Vietnamese conflict as a military threat to the established order, a new form of aggression to be met and destroyed.

In 1954 Eisenhower appointed Gen. J. Lawton Collins (W.P. 1917) as special Ambassador to South Vietnam, replacing a civilian, Ambassador Heath, and signaled the end to the consideration of Vietnam as a political and social problem rather than a military one by signing an agreement with the French to take over all military training duties from them. By 1961 the military view had grown so dominant that Lt. Gen. Thomas J. H. Trapnell (W.P. 1927), after a trip to Vietnam on behalf of the Joint Chiefs of Staff, could baldly suggest that the MAAG* mission should not be under the authority of the Ambassador but should be the responsibility of the senior U.S. officer so "that military directions and policy decisions will not be influenced by non-military thinking and direction in a hot war situation." [18] These developments are only too logical within the West Pointer's overall concept of the Communists' having developed a new type of aggression "in which one country sponsors internal war within another." [19] As an ardent subscriber to this theory, Eisenhower defined its ultimate extension: "The loss of Indochina would lead to the loss of Burma, Thailand, in fact, all of the great peninsula on which they are situated." [20] As recently as December 1967 he was demonstrating the strength of this aggressive-conspiracy viewpoint on the West Point mind: "You pull our armed forces from South Vietnam and it will only

---

* Military Advisory Assistance Group.

be a question of time before every country up to the border of India falls under the Communist heel. That includes Laos and Cambodia right next door as well as Thailand and Burma, and I'm not sure about India either, once they have got that far." [21]

As the war escalated through the Sixties, the graduates grew more and more firm in their denial of the real issues in Vietnam. Gen. Earle G. Wheeler (W.P. 1932), Army Chief of Staff, maintained that what the U.S. was committed to was "military action. . . . Despite the fact that the conflict is conducted as guerrilla warfare . . . it is nonetheless a military action. . . . It is fashionable in some quarters to say that the problems in Southeast Asia are primarily political and economic rather than military. I do not agree. The essence of the problem in Vietnam is military." [22] This West Point view of the war was not an isolated input to the policy-makers. During the key 1965 period Lyndon Johnson was relying on the advice of such "varied" men of wisdom as Maxwell Taylor (W.P. 1922), Harold Johnson (W.P. 1933), William Westmoreland (W.P. 1936), Earle Wheeler (W.P. 1932), John McConnell (W.P. 1932), and his personal military advisor, Robert Ginsburgh (W.P. 1944). These men possessed an extraordinary continuity of prejudices that, along with their command presence and exuberant confidence, lent their views overwhelming weight. Proof that their recommendations were followed can be found in the casualty lists of the Americans and of the Vietnamese on both sides.

True until the end to their delusions about the nature of the war, West Pointers decided it ended in 1968: "The War in Vietnam "ended" in August of 1968 when sorely battered communist troops were unable again to engage the allied war machine." [23] The same 1969 West Point textbook that contains this astute observation also gives the "accepted" reasons for the confusion and frustration surrounding the war. First, it was limited and the U.S. did not mobilize; second, the news coverage obscured the issues and "all too often reports were altered after submission to agree with the editorial policy of the home office"; third, there was disagreement over the policies and tactics for waging a limited war; and, finally, "no small cause for complexity was the oriental setting. Few Americans have achieved an understanding of the Asian, his culture, or his countries. Nuances with deep meaning often pass completely over the head of a Westerner while unimportant events can be blown up out of all proportion in the occidental mind. The so-called cultural gap can and does foment mistrust and misunderstanding." After the honesty of his last admission, the writer, Lt. Col. Dave R. Palmer (W.P. 1956), returns to form: "Comprehending, now, why the conflict was incomprehensible [!], we can turn our attention toward seeking an appreciation of the military history of the Vietnamese War." [24] So will we.

After irrevocably labeling the struggle in Vietnam an insurgency, the search for techniques to "solve the problem" began. Maj. J. W. Woodmansee (W.P. 1956) explains the research method in a West Point textbook: "America's approach to war has been the same in many respects as our approach to other problems. We have a penchant for facing the situation directly, making a rational analysis of the problem, and seeking a quick, logical solution—'once and for all.' " [25] For our Academy generals, "a quick, logical solution" was a military one, and they arrived at this conclusion in typical reverse fashion: "Our plans should not be dominated by military considerations, but at the present time in Southeast Asia, no major plans can be realistic unless they face up to the facts of violence." [26] To this end, they sought to read Mao Tse-tung in reverse and apply his guerrilla tactics against him. Mao read some of the manuals and essays that resulted from these attempts and commented that their weakness was that they ignored "the decisive political fact that . . . governments cut off from the masses could not win against wars of liberation." [27] That these efforts at understanding ignored political realities is obvious when one reads Hilsman's advice for readers of Giap's *People's War, People's Army:* "The reader must distinguish between what may be worthwhile as *observations on military tactics* and other passages that have value only as examples of beliefs Communists hold or statements Communists wish us to believe. . . . Though far less ambitious, the book can be compared with Hitler's *Mein Kampf,* which expressed a distorted view of history as seen by a fanatical personality." [28] Even if they had been directed to concentrate on the political rather than the tactical content of the literature on guerrilla warfare, it is questionable whether the

West Pointers would have gained anything, for when the 1962
chief of the Military Assistance Command in Vietnam, Gen.
Paul D. Harkins (W.P. 1929), was asked about the political
consequences of destroying villages with napalm, his sagacious
reply was that it "really puts the fear of God into the Viet Cong.
And that is what counts." [29] Nevertheless, some political considerations did creep in at the beginning. In 1961 President
Kennedy's military advisor, Gen. Maxwell Taylor (W.P. 1922),
recommended, on the basis of a visit to Vietnam, the preservation of President Ngo Dinh Diem's regime in the South by introducing U.S. troops. He felt that "nothing is more calculated to
sober the enemy and to discourage escalation . . . than the
knowledge that the United States has prepared itself soundly
to deal with aggression in Southeast Asia at any level." [30] The
problem here was how to get the troops in without ruining
America's image as peacekeeper and to enable the leaders in
Washington and Saigon to placate their respective constituencies.
The "never lie, cheat, or steal" graduate Taylor had the answer:
slip in 8,000 troops under the pretext of a flood-relief task force.
It is only ironic that the troops eventually sent have done more
damage to the country of Vietnam than any flood short of
Noah's deluge ever could.

The troops, however, did not solve the political problem posed
by Diem, who had been designated the scapegoat for American
policy failures. In private the policy-makers had decided to
eliminate him, but in public their view was similar to that of
Gen. Harkins when he donned his religious garb and said, "After
all, rightly or wrongly, we have backed Diem for eight long hard
years. To me it seems incongruous now to cut him down, kick
him around and get rid of him. The U.S. has been his mother
superior and father confessor since he's been in office and he has
leaned on us heavily." [31] But clearer heads were at work in the
back room. On August 30, 1963, Roger Hilsman (W.P. 1943),
Assistant Secretary of State for the Far East, wrote a TOP SECRET
memo to Dean Rusk on the subject of "Possible Diem-Nhu
Moves and U.S. Responses." This memo and what Hilsman
writes in his book *To Move a Nation* contradict each other on
many points. Concerning Vietnamese self-determination and the
Diem crisis, Hilsman states in his book, "Any decision [to dis-

pose of Diem] would have to be Vietnamese. . . . We could take no part in any planning or action." [32] When South Vietnamese generals, afraid of betrayal, approached the U.S. for covert help in a coup against Diem, Hilsman wrote, "The U.S. should not participate in the decision to replace the regime or in action to carry out that decision." [33] In the memo, not only does he suggest U.S. participation in making the decision for a coup but also ways in which the U.S. might help carry out that decision. Move #6 postulates a political gesture by Diem "toward the DRV (such as opening of neutralization negotiations), or rumors and indirect threats of such a move." Hilsman's recommended response was to "encourage the generals to move promptly with a coup" and "if the DRV threatens to respond to an anti-Diem coup by sending troops openly to South Vietnam, we should let it be known unequivocally that we shall hit the DRV with all that is necessary to force it to desist." Move #8 suggests that "if hostilities start between the GVN and a coup group, Diem and Nhu will seek to negotiate in order to play for time (as during the November, 1960, coup attempt) and rally loyal forces to Saigon." Hilsman's response, in part, was to "warn the coup group to press any military advantage it gains to its logical conclusion without stopping to negotiate" and "to use, or encourage the coup group to use, military measures to prevent any loyal forces outside Saigon from rallying to Diem's support. For example, we can jam radio communications between Diem and these forces and we can encourage interdiction of transportation by blowing up bridges." In Move #9 Hilsman reasons that if Diem seeks to continue "hostilities in Saigon as long as possible in the hope that the U.S. will weaken because of the bloodbath which may involve U.S. personnel," we should "make full use of any U.S. equipment available to Vietnam to assist the coup group" and "if necessary, we should bring in U.S. combat forces to assist the coup group to achieve victory." With Move #10, *"A Götterdämmerung* in the Palace," Hilsman comes into his own: ". . . destroy the palace if necessary to gain victory. . . . Unconditional surrender should be the terms for the Ngo family. . . . Diem should be treated as the generals wish." (A complete copy of the memo is contained in Appendix C.) When the news of the coup and the deaths of Diem and Nhu reached Washington, Hilsman recorded that "it shocked President Kennedy and the rest of us. . . ." [34]

The State Department is designed to be an agency that engages in the art of diplomacy with negotiation, compromise, and understanding as its tools. Hilsman is no ordinary diplomat—he is only a West Pointer in a different uniform who coldly outlined a plan for the overthrow of a government and the possible assassination of its leaders. This is the same Roger Hilsman who in 1962 wrote, "We cannot win the battle for freedom by adapting General Giap's methods, which include everything from brazen lies to cowardly assassinations." [35]

In 1964, with Diem and politics gone, Gen. Westmoreland replaced Gen. Harkins as COMUSMACV, Gen. Taylor, disguised as an ambassador, replaced Henry Cabot Lodge, and the search for "proper" means to win the war resumed in earnest. West Point never got beyond its preoccupation with technology. At one end of the technical spectrum, and in keeping with the overriding philosophy that "The average American finds it difficult to visualize nations that do not have a common tradition, or an educational system, or a communications network," [36] Hilsman suggested that the Vietnamese "need what many a pioneer American village needed a hundred years ago—a school, a hospital, a few good bridges, some all-weather roads, a sewage system." [37] This approach led to the distribution of 50,000 transistor radios to Vietnamese peasants in an attempt to further their political education! [38] At the other end of the spectrum is the "electronic battlefield" where the transistor radios are used with computers to call in artillery on "unidentified moving objects" and humans participate by pushing buttons. Somewhere in between we find the techniques most heavily used in Vietnam since 1964. A memorandum prepared by Maxwell Taylor titled "Vietnam and Southeast Asia" contains most of them: "Induce the Government of Vietnam to turn over to the United States military commander, temporarily, the actual tactical direction of the war. . . . Induce the Government of Vietnam to conduct overt ground operations in Laos of sufficient scope to impede the flow of personnel and matériel southward. . . . Arm, equip, advise, and support the Government of Vietnam in its conduct of aerial bombing of critical targets in North Vietnam and in mining the sea approaches to that country. . . . Advise and support the Government of Vietnam in its conduct of large-scale commando raids against critical targets in North Vietnam. . . . Conduct aerial bombing of key North Vietnam targets, using U.S. resources under Vietnamese cover, and with the Vietnamese openly assuming responsibility for the actions. . . . Commit additional U.S. forces, as necessary, in direct actions against North Vietnam." [39] Soon after this memo Taylor was assigned as Ambassador, and the administrative course of his first mission report from Saigon is interesting as far as the influence of West Point is concerned. It was transmitted by Col. A. R. Brownfield (W.P. 1939), acting special assistant to the JCS for counterinsurgency and special activities, to Secretary McNamara, through Col. Alfred J. F. Moody (W.P. 1941), the secretary's military assistant. Col. Brownfield's covering memo said that the report had also been supplied to the chairman of the JCS, Earle Wheeler (W.P. 1932), and Army Chief of Staff Harold K. Johnson (W.P. 1933).[40]

Taylor's recommendations evolved into the four major U.S. "techniques" of "solving the Vietnamese problem": conventional bombing and sweeping; irregular tactics such as selective terror and the Phoenix program that supposedly emulate the Viet Cong; dividing, conquering, and controlling through pacification; and "long-haul, low-cost" technological extermination through Vietnamization and the electronic battlefield. The basis for these tactics is explained in the West Point text on *Revolutionary Warfare:* "United States military doctrine is built on the spirit of the offensive, and relies on preponderant fire support and aggressive movement to seize a decisive objective. A past reluctance to give up 'an inch of ground' has led to some valiant heroics, and occasionally some unnecessary casualties. Still, it is the outgrowth of the competitive, athletic experience of American youth and is corollary to the American concepts of time and the image of success." Having established that U.S. tactics are rooted in a Little League baseball game, West Point moves on to those of the Chinese: "The Chinese military doctrine reflects another approach to space. Mao states that the prime objective of warfare is 'to preserve oneself and destroy the enemy.' Mao encouraged his army not to consider any terrain objective worthy of heavy casualties. By giving up space, Mao could prevent decisive engagements and so buy 'time' for his protracted war. . . . Another concept of space . . . is that the Chinese have no sense of spatial continuity. This is reflected by the invariable attempt of the Chinese to move on an enemy from all sides rather than to advance against him on a continuous front [those cheats!]. . . . It is a product not only of tactical doctrine but of national psychology." [41] A colorful fold-out battle map in West Point's *Readings in Current Military History* tells the story of how this "scholarly" tactical analysis translated into action on the ground. The map is of the Iron Triangle area of Vietnam and depicts the first major multi-divisional search-and-destroy operation of the war, "Cedar Falls," in January of 1967. Slender blue arrows show the movement of armored and mechanized units toward their blocking positions along the west bank of the Saigon River; a larger blue arrow of ground troops strikes boldly at the heart of the Iron Triangle and then fans out in all directions in a series of dashed lines; explanatory notes say that "B-52 strikes began on 4 Jan. . . . Six battalions helilifted into blocking positions 8 Jan."; and the reader is left with the impression that the Viet Cong were totally overwhelmed by the systematic assaults of the men in blue. But in the upper left corner of the map there is a small, inconspicuous red box that speaks volumes about the nature of this particular operation and of the nature of the war itself. The writing in the box says: "No major enemy units were in the Iron Triangle at the time of the operations." [42] If there were no "major enemy units" encountered in this massive search-and-destroy mission, who and what were these forces waging war against?

During the twenty days that American forces spent within the Iron Triangle of Binh Duong province, all signs of life within the populated Vietnamese villages of Ben Suc, Rach Bap, Bung Cong, Rach Kien, and others were destroyed; houses were burned, foodstuffs confiscated, food poisoned or urinated on, livestock killed, fruit trees and gardens destroyed, and the civilian population forceably removed and relocated into detention camps. The land areas involved were turned into free-fire zones where it was understood that American soldiers could shoot anything that moved—and they did. This operation had been planned and conducted under Westmoreland's direction by his Chief of Intelligence, Maj. Gen. Joseph A. McChristian (W.P. 1939), and the II Field Force commander, Lt. Gen. Jonathan O. Seaman (W.P. 1934). The following month, the second major search-and-destroy operation planned by these men, "Junction City," kicked off in Tay Ninh province, directed at the War Zone C area. In that operation more than twenty Vietnamese villages were eliminated from the face of the earth. Meanwhile, up north in Quang Ngai and Quang Tin provinces, Task Force Oregon, under Westmoreland's control, was ravaging the Vietnamese countryside. By August 1967, in Quang Ngai province alone, the massive terror tactics employed had generated an excess of 150,000 refugees, more than half of whom were classified as "scattered," meaning that they had not received "shelter" within the barbed-wire camps.

Such tactics are neither mindless nor random. Contrary to Hilsman's dictum that the guerrilla can "thrive" without the support of the population, the guerrilla fighter is viewed as a fish that swims in a sea of people. The guerrilla relies upon the local population for support and protection, and to get to the fish one must dry up the sea—that is to say, eliminate the people. Such a massive destruction-and-relocation formula has been openly propounded by quasi-West Pointer Samuel Huntington (America can learn more from West Point than West Point can learn from America). As he puts it:

> The principal reason for this massive influx of population into the urban areas is, of course, the intensification of the war following the commitment of American combat troops in 1965. About 1,500,000 of the total increase in urban population is accounted for by refugees, half still in refugee camps and others settled in new areas. At least an equal number of people have moved into the cities without passing through refugee camps. . . .[43]

and:

> In an absent-minded way the United States in Vietnam may well have stumbled upon the answer to "wars of national liberation." The effective response lies neither in the quest for conventional military victory nor in the esoteric doctrines and gimmicks

of counter-insurgency warfare. It is instead forced-draft urbanization and modernization which rapidly brings the country in
question out of the phase in which a rural revolutionary movement can hope to generate sufficient strength to come to power.[44]

Huntington admits that the social costs of the forced removal
of peasants by "direct application of mechanical and conventional power" have been "dramatic" and often "heart-rending"
and that conditions in refugee camps have at times been "horrendous." But he reminds us that such cultural genocide has its
happy side: "The urban slum, which seems so horrible to middle-
class Americans, often becomes for the poor peasant a gateway
to a new and better way of life." [45]

Roger Hilsman, mission-oriented to the end, sees the plight of
the peasant as something to be used, to be acted upon, not understood. In a statement to the Senate Refugee Subcommittee on
September 30, 1965, he said: "The refugees, in my judgment,
are the key to such a program [winning an honorable peace].
In the first place, they are a substantial number of the people
of Vietnam, the people whose allegiance must be won, and because their plight is so visible they will be a test case, a symbol
of whether the government does indeed care." He then con-
ceded that allies "working with the refugees start out with a strike
against them" because "it was not Viet Cong terrorism" but
"American and Vietnamese bombing and shelling" that "drove
the refugees from their ancestral homes to the cities and towns."
To Hilsman, however, this fact does not justify ending the U.S.
effort: "all this means that even greater effort must be made to
win over these people, precisely because of their initial resent-
ment." This strange moral twist is possible because he sees helping the refugees not as a goal in itself but as a useful means of
winning the war: "But beyond winning the allegiance of the refugees, it seems to me that they offer a positive opportunity for
furthering an effective counter-insurgency program." [46] So much
for the human plight of the Vietnamese peasant.

Westmoreland's policies of burning crops and villages, firing
harassment and interdiction rounds blindly into the countryside,
and establishing free-fire zones assisted the forced relocation of
peasants to areas where they could be controlled by the allies.
Current statistics give an indication of the zeal with which West-

moreland and his henchmen have gone about their task—millions of refugees, millions of bomb craters, an area the size of the state of Vermont defoliated, and so on. But such massive terror tactics are not new to the American experience. We have waged war against populations and a people before. The first Americans, the Indians, were the first unfortunate victims.

In late 1869 the Second Cavalry, commanded by Col. E. M. Baker (W.P. 1859), went after the Piegans, one of three bands of Blackfeet Indians in Montana. Baker's boss, Gen. Philip Sheridan (W.P. 1853), had decided that a winter campaign was the best way to teach the natives to behave, and his tactic worked. In January of 1870 Baker and his cavalry found and struck a Piegan camp, killing 173 and burning forty-one lodges. But almost immediately curiously conflicting stories of the attack—it was not a battle, only one soldier was killed—began to be heard, and the local peace commission sent a man to investigate. He was told by the Indian Agent for the Blackfeet that 140 of the dead were women and children, 18 were old men, and only 15 were men of fighting age. The agent, an Army lieutenant, could hardly be called a hostile witness, but Col. Baker denied his story and said that 120 of the dead had been vigorous warriors. Baker added that he deeply regretted that 53 women and children had died, and claimed that every effort had been made to spare them during the battle, but that this was not possible due to the fierceness of the fighting (one dead cavalryman!). Later one very important fact came to light. The Army refused to admit its validity, but it explained how the cavalry unit was able to take a camp of supposedly hostile Indians so completely by surprise that it lost only one man—the camp consisted of friendly reservation Indians.[47]

It was, as in Vietnam, perhaps difficult for Col. Baker to tell friend from foe, but the Indians, like the Vietnamese, should have known better. They may have been friendly, but they had no business in West Point's nineteenth-century version of the free-fire zone. It is no mere coincidence that free-fire zones in Vietnam are referred to by the GIs as "Indian Country." [48]

The few successes the Indians had against the rampaging whites served only to bring more wrath down upon them. In 1866 a Col. Fetterman and about eighty soldiers guarding a route through

Sioux hunting grounds that led to the Montana gold mines were outnumbered, outwitted, and killed by Sioux Indians under Chief Red Cloud. When told of the defeat, Lt. Gen. William T. Sherman (W.P. 1840) said, "I do not understand how the massacre of Colonel Fetterman's party could have been so complete. . . . We must act with vindictive earnestness against the Sioux, even to their extermination—men, women and children. Nothing else will reach the root of this case." [49]

If Westmoreland did not copy his population-removal tactics from the Indian fighters, he derived them from J. Franklin Bell's (W.P. 1878) innovations in the Batangas campaign of the U.S. war against the Filipinos. Brig. Gen. Bell used the method of forcing the peasant population into zoned towns to prevent them from aiding the guerrillas and authorized the starving of all hostile belligerents, whether armed or not. His orders to subordinate commanders were that they "will immediately specify and establish plainly marked limits surrounding each town bounding a zone within which it may be practical with an average size garrison to exercise efficient supervision . . . [and] will also see that orders are given at once and distributed to all of the inhabitants within the jurisdiction of towns over which they exercise supervision informing them of the danger of remaining outside of these limits and unless they move by December 25 [1901] from outlying barrios and districts with all their movable food supplies including rice, palay, chickens, livestock, etc. to within the limits of the zone established at their own or nearest town, their property found outside of one at said date will become liable to confiscation or destruction. After January 1st, 1902, any able-bodied male found by patrols or scouting detachments outside of protected zones without passes will be arrested and confined or shot if he runs away." [50]

In the Philippine war there seemed to be an honest explanation of our motives by the ruling circles. There was little talk of fighting for freedom or helping the Filipinos determine their own destiny—the American industrialists wanted the Philippines as a colony. In fact, our true motives are not denied to this day. On June 23, 1969, the late Everett M. Dirksen introduced into the *Congressional Record* a list of instances of the use of U.S. armed forces abroad during the period 1798–1945 in an effort to demonstrate that Vietnam was not unique. Number 103 on the list of 170 interventions read: "1899–1901, Philippine Islands— To protect American interests following the war with Spain and to conquer the islands by defeating the Filipinos in their war for independence." There was no illusion of fighting for a beleaguered Asian people suffering from a sinister insurgency. Brig. Gen. Bell, later to become Chief of Staff (1906–19), candidly opined, "With very few exceptions, practically the entire population has been hostile to us at heart. In order to combat such a population, it is necessary to make the state of war as insupportable as possible, and there is no more efficacious way of accomplishing this than by keeping the minds of the people in such a state of anxiety and apprehension that living under such condition will soon become intolerable." [51] To this end, Bell ordered his commanders to "avail themselves to retaliation," to select prisoners by lot and shoot one of them for every American soldier killed: "the innocent must suffer with the guilty for the sake of speedily ending the war." [52] This theory of collective responsibility worked one way for the Filipinos and a totally different way for the Americans. When a corporal in the company of Capt. Andrew S. Rowan (W.P. 1881) was killed by the boy friend of the Filipino girl he had raped, Capt. Rowan taught the natives a lesson by having the Filipino executed and his village and the raped girl's village burned to the ground. On the other hand, when the death of a Filipino due to water torture administered by one Capt. John P. Ryan (W.P. 1888) made headlines in 1903, he was acquitted by a court-martial board that made it clear that such tactics were necessary to terminate the war. J. Franklin Bell's toleration for contradiction parallels that of Westmoreland when he says that U.S. forces in the Philippines had "exercised an extraordinary forbearance and patiently adhered to a magnanimous and benevolent policy toward the inhabitants." [53]

Confused and unable to distinguish between what has worked and morality, Roger Hilsman urged a reacquaintance with the counter-revolutionary techniques used against the Filipinos: "We Americans have also forgotten that it was we who fought one of the most successful counter-guerrilla campaigns in history—in the Philippines back at the turn of the century. We learned some fundamental military lessons then, and it is time we remembered them." He goes on to relate some bloody details and then draws some "fundamental lessons" from the extermination of the "extremists" and "bands of religious fanatics" who were evil enough to fight against occupation by the U.S. His lessons include: the maximum use of native mercenaries in the style of the "famed Philippine constabulary"; a "bold and determined" American in charge of each group of native recruits; and the adoption of the "Indian fighting" tactic of surprise and night attack. Hilsman neglects to mention that the "successful" Philippine campaign was, in the words of Bernard Fall, "the bloodiest colonial war (in proportion to population) ever fought by a white power in Asia; it cost the lives of 3,000,000 Filipinos." [54] J. Franklin Bell himself estimated that one sixth (about 600,000) of the inhabitants of Luzon alone died from the direct or indirect effects of the war.[55]

Santayana's warning that "those who refuse to learn from history are doomed to repeat it" does not necessarily relate to West Pointers, since for them it is not simply a matter of refusing to learn but one of ignoring history altogether. Westmoreland is of the opinion that "he then who would command among his fellows must tell them more in energy of will than in power of intellect." [56] Brig. Gen. George A. Lincoln, advisor to Presidents and guru to Dean Rusk, offers a unique view of the "teaching" of history. When he was head of the Social Science Department at West Point and history came under his supervision, he often had to decide what to do with new instructors who lacked experience. More often than not he assigned them to the History Department. "Anyone can teach history," seemed his attitude. In fact, it was not until his departure in 1969 that the West Point academic board first offered to the cadets a course in American history. The wars against the Indians and Filipinos are irrelevant from the strictly *military*-history viewpoint as well—in the year-long course "The History of the Military Art" no time is devoted to the study of the American Indian wars and one fifty-eight-word paragraph in the two-volume *West Point Atlas of American Wars,* written by Col. Vincent J. Esposito (W.P. 1925), is devoted to the Philippine campaigns.

Those elements of the past or present that tend to mute optimism or the West Point "can do" philosophy are, understandably, ignored. This is what Westmoreland means when he talks about the "positive approach"—he does not like pessimists. Men who ignore the unpleasant and myth-contradicting aspects of American history must also be expected to totally overlook the history of the Vietnamese people. Had Westmoreland realized that in 1789 Vietnamese patriots staged a successful surprise Tet offensive against the occupation troops of the Chinese Ch'ing dynasty, he might have known better than to say of the 1968 Tet offensive, "In my opinion this is a diversionary effort to take attention away from the northern part of the country." [57] Westmoreland might also have done well to take his mind off his briefing charts for a short time and study the Vietnamese defeat of the most powerful invaders Vietnam has ever known, the horsemen of the Mongolian Emperor Kubla Khan. They outnumbered the peasant army of Vietnam at times by ten to one, but were smashed by the Vietnamese during three attempts at invasion: in 1257, in 1283–85, and in 1287–88. The architect of these Vietnamese victories in the thirteenth century was Marshal Tran Hung Dao, prince, poet, writer, and the most revered of all Vietnamese heroes. He is the author of the *Binh Thu Yeu Luoc* (*Essentials of Military Arts*), considered the first Vietnamese book on guerrilla warfare—"The enemy must fight his battles far from his home base for a long time. We must further weaken him by drawing him into a protracted campaign. Once his initial dash is broken, it will be easier to destroy him." Seven centuries later a Vietnamese professor of history, Vo Nguyen Giap, copied Dao's strategy and was at the head of the Viet Minh army when the French surrendered in 1954 at Dien Bien Phu. General Giap, in addition to being a student of the past, is a student of poetry and, like Ho Chi Minh, uses verse to inspire those serving with him. But the first great poet-warrior of Vietnam was Marshal Ly Thung Kiet (1019–1105), who was both a tactical genius and a master of psychological warfare. Once, outnumbered and in heavy fighting with the Chinese, Kiet maintained the morale of his battered soldiers by telling them of a dream in which heaven communicated to him the following poem:

The country of Viet Nam belongs to the Vietnamese Emperors.
This is a fact written in the sacred book of heaven.
Whoever dares to invade our land
Will be surely suffering defeat.[58]

The troops are still waiting to be inspired by the poetry of William Westmoreland. But Westmoreland, seemingly blind to both the present and the past of Vietnam, can only say, as he did soon after the 1968 Tet offensive, "I do not believe Hanoi can hold up under a long war." [59] If the tactical theories of counter-revolutionary warfare are not tested against Vietnamese history, they are very definitely tested against the Vietnamese people. In 1963, before a Congressional committee, Maxwell Taylor explained: "Here we have a going laboratory where we see subversive insurgency, the Ho Chi Minh doctrine, being applied in all its forms. This has been a challenge, not just for the armed services, but for several of the agencies of government, as many of them are involved in one way or another in South Vietnam. On the military side, however, we have recognized the importance of the area as a laboratory. We have teams out there looking at the equipment requirements of this kind of guerrilla warfare. We have rotated senior officers through there, spending several weeks [a long time!] just to talk to people and get the feeling of the operation, so even though not regularly assigned to Vietnam, they are carrying their experience back to their own organizations." [60]

Six years and millions of casualties later Westmoreland was saying that Vietnam had indeed been a valuable lab for testing new weapons and tactics and that these "lessons" and "devices" are "revolutionizing" the techniques of war.[61] West Point tests the validity of the new techniques in terms of operational payoffs or, put more simply, numbers. Westmoreland's *Report on the War in Vietnam* explains the key figures, the ones that "most accurately reflect significant trends in the war": "the ratio of enemy to allied casualties . . . the ratio of enemy to allied weapons losses . . . the proportion of NVA to VC combat battalions fighting in SVN . . . the relationship of U.S. and Free World fighting strength to the contribution of the Government of Vietnam . . . the overall progress of providing security to the population of SVN." [62] Numbers, not bodies, have relevance to the linear-functional mind of the graduate, and the mounting pile of Indochinese corpses finds its rationale in George A. Lincoln's favorite definition of the Army's role: "The function of the profession of arms is the ordered application of military resources to the resolution of a social problem." [63] These "military resources" include napalm, defoliants, 17,000-pound bombs, gas, mini-guns, and once again West Point is resolving, not relating to, human beings. Statistics, graphs, and sums are the impersonal tools of the technician in weighing his technique, and in his hands the mathematics of such criminal policies as forced population removal becomes a means of proving its success—in 1967 Maxwell Taylor explained the numerical logic of having millions of refugees in or around allied-controlled camps: "As an indicator of progress in pacification, there has been an encouraging increase in Government control in rural areas in recent months. Indeed, since mid-1965, there has been an increase of some three million people in rural areas clearly under government control. About 1,200,000 of this increase has occurred in the last six months. Concurrently the Vietcong-controlled population has decreased by more than a million since 1965, the remaining governmental gains having come from contested areas. In that year it was estimated that twenty-six percent of the total population (including the cities) was under Vietcong domination; now it is down to fourteen percent. If one includes the cities, the total population under secure Government of Vietnam control has increased from 6.6 million in mid-1965 to 10.8 million in mid-1967." [64] Who is free and who is a prisoner?

The optimistic daily Saigon news briefings are not essentially different from the daily mathematics recitations at West Point; the only variation is that the briefers are not required to prove an equation, they are simply required to recite enough numbers to prove that the U.S. is winning the war. In fact, Brig. Gen. William W. Bessell (W.P. 1920), academic dean at the Academy during 1959–65, felt that there was a direct relation between proficiency in math at West Point and success in the military service. His observation should not be taken lightly. Westmoreland was highly recommended by Ambassador Maxwell Taylor to McNamara and Lyndon Johnson for the job of COMUSMACV in part because he felt that his simple by-the-numbers approach would produce accurate assessments and reports on the progress of the war. Westmoreland fully lived up to their expectations and faithfully counted the number of sorties flown, bunkers destroyed, hamlets pacified, and, above all, the number of enemy killed (although in the latter he showed more proficiency in multiplication than in addition). The depth of scrutiny to which Westmoreland subjected his statistics is revealed in the following passage: "There is one more ugly souvenir of March 16, 1968. Upon being informed of the results of the operation in Song My that day, General Westmoreland reacted quickly. He could not have read the statistics saying 128 VC had been killed and only 3 weapons captured without some second thoughts. But Task Force Barker had played the game of body count well and, after all, it was Westmoreland who had put the emphasis on that grisly statistic in the first place. So he fired off a congratulatory message to the task force for its action on March 16—for the My Lai massacre." [65]

It is this very same statistical approach that has formed the basis for the unceasing flow of optimistic appraisals from Vietnam ever since the beginning—J. Lawton Collins in 1951: "There is no question that the Communist menace in French Indochina has been stopped"; [66] William Westmoreland four days before Tet in 1968: "The year ended with the enemy increasingly resorting to desperation tactics in attempting to achieve military/psychological victory, and he has experienced only failure in these attempts"; [67] and Earle Wheeler a few months after Tet: "Our forces have achieved an unbroken string of victories which, on the aggregate, is something new in our military history." [68] And so on.

The announcements of the West Point generals kept the true nature of the war hidden from the American public for a long period, and the generals felt absolutely no guilt, for, as Maxwell Taylor has said, "You don't share your secrets with the people if you're going to be successful in doing what you expect to do." [69] But when the very length of the war finally exposed their failure to understand Vietnam as a revolution and not an insurgency, the graduates began to cleave together, relying on their collective harmony to give an effortless confirmation of their innocence. They explained that their policies (which would have brought the war to swift conclusion) had not been fully acted upon; that the failures were not their fault but rather due to the lack of trained personnel, sabotage by politicians, and the failure of public will; and that they were devising new techniques which would solve these particular flaws. Their convictions became in public what they had always been in private, nothing more than rigid self-protective devices. They blamed the Vietnamese soldier —Hilsman: "The fundamental reason for pessimism about the possibility of winning inside South Vietnam with the present level of forces is not about the American effort but the Vietnamese." [70] They blamed the Viet Cong soldier—"[Capt. Donald R.] Robinson found the enemy soldiers to be dedicated, highly motivated individuals who, on occasion, and considering their general lack of formal military education [!], displayed an amazing degree of careful planning." [71] They blamed the South Vietnamese government—Hilsman: "Americans can help in giving the villagers physical protection, but they cannot win the villagers' allegiance to the South Vietnamese Government. That task can be done only by Vietnamese, and there is little evidence that enough Vietnamese are sufficiently dedicated and willing to make the necessary sacrifices." [72] They blamed the Vietnamese people— Hilsman: "Too many Vietnamese remain devoted not to the nation, but to the selfish interests of class, sect, and religion." [73] They blamed meddling U.S. politicians—Gen. Mark Clark: "The war has been fought too long with political considerations overriding sound military judgment. Halting the bombing of North Vietnam was a great mistake, which gave a big advantage to the enemy." [74] But Eisenhower finally found where the blame truly lay. He placed it squarely on those unfortunates without the disciplined, blind wisdom of the West Pointer: "A ludicrous, and dangerous, aspect of this bitter quarrel is the large number of public men who regard themselves as military experts. One large defeatist group proclaims loudly and positively that 'we can never win the Vietnam war.' Others insist, contrary to the best military judgment and to clear evidence, that our air strikes 'do no good' and we must cease all bombing of targets in the North. Instead of giving faith and backing to the men who are responsible for the conduct of the war, these armchair strategists snipe at every aspect of the conflict. . . . They are quoted endlessly and prominently in the press and on the airwaves, and of course their words give aid and comfort to the enemy and thus prolong the war." [75] This kind of moral distortion and intellectual degeneration almost naturally occurs among men who have been conditioned all their lives to believe in their supreme worthiness, their spotless devotion, and, above all, in the purity and sanctity of the institution in which their disciplined souls find salvation: "The members of this group [West Pointers] possess a modesty of behavior, an integrity of character and a selfless, fearless patriotism which is their greatest contribution to our society. . . . All West Pointers acknowledge that Father Thayer provided the inspiration which put their feet firmly on the road to their destiny and our security." [76] This humble observation was made by a general for the pleasure of his fellows, but outsiders are by no means exempted from aiding in the conditioning process. Spiro Agnew in a speech to the cadets: "This is a time when the criminal misfits of society are glamorized while our best men die in Asian rice paddies to preserve the freedoms those misfits abuse. This is a time when the charlatans of peace and freedom eulogize foreign dictators while desecrating the flag that keeps them free." [77] This very elitism finally breeds among its believers contempt for the democratic institutions they are supposed to cherish and makes it impossible for them to acknowledge the real aspirations of the people they are subduing. The emptiness of West Point's constant acclamation of democracy and moral sanctity is clearly shown in this passage from its textbook on *Revolutionary Warfare:*

Another strategic manifestation is China's reliance on the politically motivated man to overcome any technical superiority. The U.S., with its atomic weapons, is derided as a "paper tiger." As Liu Shao-ch'i retorted, "We have the spiritual atomic bomb." One official [Chinese] analyzed, in 1961, the possibilities of war in the next few years and concluded: " . . . In the last analysis, it is men upon whom we are relying. We are relying upon men and we are emphasizing the importance of political factors. We want to raise men's political awareness and to display men's power."

Well suited to this bloodless strategy of the indirect approach

[!] is the Chinese regard for the subtle, bloodless stratagem. Generalship to the western armies may involve the determination of a clear, decisive objective and the management of men, matériel, and resources to achieve this objective. But to the Chinese, generalship is directly related to destroying the enemy's will to fight without having to destroy the enemy. If western strategy is to attack the body, "Chinese strategy is the black art of attacking the enemy's mind." Ruse, stratagem, secret agent, even the call for military negotiations when the desired objective may be "time" for political development—all of these factors are more highly regarded by the Chinese than by the western military professional.[78]

This incredible statement is claiming that it is better to kill a man than try to change his mind through the "indirect approach" of politics. The smug vanity of the West Pointer's "holier-than-thou" attitude along with his criminal use of his intelligence approaches insanity. But, fittingly, the author of this denial of the fundamental premise of democracy, J. W. Woodmansee, Jr. (W.P. 1956), went on to become a White House Fellow. "Maybe all of us *are* great, but maybe it was West Point and our trying to retain that standard [a monopoly on truth] and way of life [a disciplined ignorance] that has served the nation so well." [79]

Examples of the insensitivity of the West-Point-bred intellect abound and they are always couched in the same contemptuous, managerial terms. Roger Hilsman: "Of the target systems that have not yet been bombed, the one that contributes most to the North Vietnamese war effort is the dike and irrigation system. An attack on that system would seriously affect the food supply of the North; it would also, it is said, bring large-scale flooding and loss of life. For humanitarian reasons alone, the United States is reluctant to embark on such an attack. If it did, the revulsion and political outcry around the world would be severe. *In any case, it is doubtful that bombing the dikes would have a decisive long-term effect*" [80] (emphasis added). Samuel Huntington on forced-draft urbanization: ". . . with half of the population still in the countryside, the Viet Cong will remain a powerful force which cannot be dislodged from its constituency so long as the constituency continues to exist." [81] (One of Huntington's colleagues pointed out his difficulty when he said, "Sam has simply lost the

ability to distinguish between urbanization and genocide." [82])
Hilsman again on humanity: " 'Interdiction' bombing and shelling of suspected Viet Cong huts and hamlets and of the movement of people suspected to be Viet Cong have certainly caused
many civilian deaths. The latest estimates are that the civilian
casualties for 1967 were about 24,000 killed and 76,000
wounded, while the combined total of American and South
Vietnamese *military* deaths was about 19,000. Not all the relatives of civilians killed or wounded by American and South
Vietnamese bombing and shelling turn against the Government.
Some stoically decide only that war is hell. Some may even
blame the Viet Cong for bringing on the attack. *But there can
be no doubt that many are embittered"* [83] (emphasis added).

What are numbers and "problems to be resolved" to the military chiefs are in fact living, breathing human beings. But to the
men on the trigger end of the search-and-destroy, the free-fire
zone, and the body count, the victims must not be human; they
must be dehumanized enough to be treated as the same mere
objects manipulated in the minds of the West Pointer. As a
strategic policy, racism had to be brought to the surface, for it
was far easier and less painful to kill a slope who didn't value
his life anyway than to kill a human being; "We hated these
people, we were taught to hate these people. They were gooks,
slants, dinks, they were orientals, inferior to us, they chewed
betel nuts, they were ugly, you know, they ate lice out of each
other's hair, they were not as good as us. And you could not
trust them. I did not think it was racist then, but I certainly do
now. We just hated the whole people. They were all gooks." [84]
The racism of the West Pointer's black-and-white world view is
far more subtle and disguised than that of the infantryman, but
it has been just as necessary an ingredient in all the wars that
America has waged against populations.

In 1872, when the Moduk Indians, who had been placed on
a reservation in southern Oregon, tried to return without permission to their homes on the California border, Brig. Gen.
Edward R. S. Canby (W.P. 1839) was dispatched to stop them.
After a short period of fighting, Canby attempted to negotiate,
but was killed by the Moduks in their naïve belief that if the
cavalrymen were rendered leaderless, they would lose heart and

go home. Little did the Moduks know that the Army could easily replace Canby with another West Pointer who would automatically perpetuate the policy of genocide—and, to be sure, Gen. W. T. Sherman (W.P. 1840), Commanding General of the Army, guaranteed continued slaughter in his message to the new cavalry leader, Col. Alvan C. Gillem (W.P. 1851): "You will be fully justified in their utter extermination. . . . Treachery is inherent in the Indian character." [85] The unfortunate Apaches were also on the receiving end of the Academy's concept of ultimate evil, for, as Col. William A. Ganoe (W.P. 1907) records in his book *The History of the United States Army,* they were the "most subtle savages we have ever dealt with" and "to stalk these human animals was impossible for a white man." [86] J. Franklin Bell (W.P. 1878), who fought both the Indians and the Filipinos, shows that there can be honest disagreement over the degree of evil attributed to a people: "I have seen Indian campaigns where it took one hundred soldiers to capture each Indian; but the problem here (the Philippines) is more difficult on account of the inbred treachery of the people . . . and the impossibility of recognizing the actively bad from the passively so." [87]

Col. George S. Anderson (W.P. 1871), commander of the 38th volunteers in the Philippines, testified before Congress that "it is true that the word 'nigger' was very often used as applied to the natives, probably correctly," and when asked about the indiscriminate shooting of people during the raiding of villages, he replied, "Many men were shot as they fled, but they probably all deserved it." [88] He went on to deny charges of abusing the natives. The only good Indian, a dead Indian; the only good nigger, a dead nigger; the only good gook, a dead gook. Although President Johnson once encouraged the troops at Cam Rahn Bay to "bring home the coonskin for the wall," one rarely hears generals using racial slurs—their racism is far more subtle. Or, as Maxwell Taylor put it, "We went around hat in hand . . . and that is not the way to get Asians to sit down and talk seriously with us." [89] The method Taylor used is very clear in a meeting he had with General Nguyen Chanh Thi, Air Marshal Nguyen Cao Ky, General Nguyen Van Thieu, and Adm. Cang in late December 1964. Ambassador Taylor: "Do all of you understand English? [The Vietnamese officers indicated they did, although the understanding of Gen. Thi was known to be weak.] I told you all clearly at Gen. Westmoreland's dinner we Americans were tired of coups. Apparently I wasted my words. Maybe this is because something is wrong with my French because you evidently didn't understand. I made it clear that all military plans which I know you would like to carry out are dependent on governmental stability. Now you have made a real mess. We cannot carry you forever if you do things like this. Who speaks for this group? Do you have a spokesman?" Gen. Ky: "I am not the spokesman for the group, but I do speak English. I will explain why the Armed Forces took this action last night." Throughout this meeting Taylor forced the Vietnamese to remain standing while he sat behind his desk.[90]

The racist belief in the fundamental superiority of Americans to Asians allows the generals and others to speak in condescending and idealistic terms of our efforts in Indochina. Since it is true that the Vietnamese are not quite "civilized," we can "build a nation" for them, although the Vietnamese nation and culture are ten times as old as ours and our own society is plagued with race riots, crime, deteriorating cities, pollution, and so on. The warped concept of the U.S. building a Vietnamese nation calls to mind the immortal words of Gen. George Armstrong Custer (W.P. 1861): "The Army is the Indian's best friend."

Periodically, the racism and the indifference surface at the Academy. In the Fall 1969 issue of *Assembly* Magazine there is an article entitled "The Fourth Generation Pro Comes Home." It is the story of a young marine (non-grad) in Vietnam: "A few years out of West Point his great-grandfather died in the Indian Wars . . . a grandfather was one of the army's famous polo players . . . and his father is a West Pointer and a retired Major General." His pride is West Point's pride, and parts of his letters home are reprinted in the article: "This is a picture of our scout dog. They finally got him. But he did a good job, and found two gooks while getting killed. . . . I've got a negro corporal made of iron. We captured two gooks we thought were VC, but they clammed up. He grabbed each by the neck and slammed their heads together and they started babbling all over the place. We later learned that they were prize catches." [91] West Point is proud of such "manly" behavior.

Or there is the 1968 Christmas card sent out by Col. (now Brig. Gen. George S. Patton III—W.P. 1946). At the time, he was commanding officer of the 11th Armored Cavalry Regiment. His regimental surgeon describes the event: "Col. Patton was given by the commander of the reserve cavalry troop a color photograph of a North Vietnamese bunker that had been hit by a 750-pound bomb from a B-52. What it essentially showed was a collection of dismembered bodies lying near a shell crater. Col. Patton was so impressed by this photograph that he placed it on a Christmas card over the inscription 'Peace on Earth, Col. and Mrs. George S. Patton' and sent it to a variety of people. One of the early recipients was Gen. Abrams. When Abrams saw the card he, as Patton did not, quickly appreciated the explosive political implications and ordered him to stop sending them. I think a total of perhaps ten or fifteen were finally sent out." [92] And the way Col. James L. Hayden (W.P. 1945) describes his classmate Robert Ives' return to Washington is indicative of the empathy West Point brass feels for the Vietnamese: "Bob is back from Vietnam where he terrorized the natives with his battalion. . . ." [93] If the West Point generals considered Asians at least somewhat human, we would know the name, for example, of the Vietnamese general who laid siege for so long to Khe Sanh; we would know the names of the generals responsible for the Tet offensive of 1968, and we would know the name of the general located at the illusive headquarters known as the Central Office of South Vietnam. But the West Pointers are not concerned with the personal characteristics of opposing generals who "all think alike" and need not be considered individually. Somehow the principle of knowing one's enemy is blurred if not forgotten in the jungles of Southeast Asia.

The racism and the utter contempt for Vietnamese lives and property generated by search-and-destroy, free-fire zones, and the forced removal of civilian populations contradict the official idealism ("Help the Vietnamese help themselves") publicly espoused by the war planners. On the ground, American soldiers, in what is to them an unreal, hostile environment, cannot tell friend from foe—buffalo boys, fleeting figures, young suspects, potential grenade-throwers, and other suspicious "gooks" are shot by soldiers victimized by the nature of war itself. Their contempt for the Vietnamese is the inevitable consequence of the decision to wage war against a population or "constituency." The true nature of the war took time to get through to most Americans, but a company of infantry vigorously fulfilling its mission of pacification with a photographer along helped considerably. In a free-fire zone on March 16, 1968, Lt. William Calley and his men shot anything that moved; they searched and destroyed, and got a big body count for the promotion of the majors, colonels, and generals. More than two years later Calley found himself convicted by a military court of premeditated murder. It was as if in 1890 a journalist had accompanied Col. James W. Forsyth's (W.P. 1856) 7th Cavalry to Wounded Knee Creek and had reported in excruciating detail the massacre of the helpless Indian women and children as they fled up the dry ravine. And as if, after the public disclosure, a cavalry lieutenant had been charged with murder, Col. Forsyth himself had been charged merely with "covering up," and then Forsyth's token charges had been dropped by his old friend Gen. John Schofield (W.P. 1853), the Chief of the Army. The young cavalry lieutenant would have been hard pressed to sort out the contradictions surrounding his situation. He knew that his fellow citizens, at the abstract level of manifest destiny, considered it glorious, or at least necessary, to conquer the Indians' territory and to show the "savages" that they must abide by the white man's ways. But he would have been told also that it was a heinous crime to kill hundreds of unarmed, unresisting civilians. He knew, too, that his colonel had received awards for such incidents on a smaller scale, and would have received an award for Wounded Knee had the inhumanity not been exposed by the press.[94]

The frontier analogy is imperfect but instructive, for it emphasizes the importance of social, economic, and institutional forces in conditioning one's beliefs and behavior. When Roger Hilsman can recommend the encouragement of a coup and talk matter-of-factly about high-level "proposals to end the war by attacking the North Vietnamese civilian population," [95] and when Pentagon planners admit 70 percent concern in avoiding a humiliating U.S. defeat, 20 percent concern in keeping South Vietnamese (and the then adjacent) territory from Chinese hands, and 10 percent in permitting the South Vietnamese people to enjoy a better way of life,[96] it is difficult to imagine a humane example being set for the draftees in the field. And emphasis does not flow from the bottom up, but from the top down. Westmoreland made it absolutely clear that he wanted "bodies" and that is what he got. He did not make it absolutely clear that under no circumstances would mistreatment or murder of POWs or civilian detainees be tolerated. But, as in all other areas, he made sure he was "covered" by passing out little Geneva Convention cards to incoming troops which they were required to keep in their wallets. But a commander does not ensure that his men stay awake on guard or keep their weapons clean by giving them plastic instructions for their pockets. He sets the example and, as is taught to cadets for four years at West Point, the commander assumes responsibility for the actions of his subordinates unless, of course, the issue is war crimes. Westmoreland himself said (without prompting) that he does not "feel guilty" about My Lai and that the massacre was the fault of inexperienced, poorly trained officers and NCOs. It does not occur to him that as COMUSMACV and Chief of Staff he was and is responsible for the training of the men under his command: "I have promoted Major General Koster to his present rank because of his demonstrated ability and performance. He has earned his tribute." [97]

Westmoreland identifies so strongly with West Point and the Army as institutions that an attack on either is, in his mind, an attack on himself. Thus, he must talk of war crimes as aberrant, isolated acts and not as the inevitable consequences of national war policies and the Army's (his) tactical field policies. As he himself has said: "Recently, a few individuals involved in serious incidents have been highlighted in the news. Some would have these incidents reflect on the Army as a whole. They are, however, the actions of a pitiful few. Certainly the Army cannot and will not condone improper conduct or criminal acts—and I personally assure you that I will not. We will always regard the rights of the individual and acknowledge due process of law. *But the Army as an institution should never be put on trial* as we deal with the few" [98] (emphasis added).

Westmoreland's enjoinder to ignore the institutional factors and focus on the individual helps explain behavior by other West Pointers which would otherwise seem puzzling and internally contradictory. When Gen. Koster was relieved of his post as superintendent at West Point so that he would not unnecessarily taint the image of his alma mater, the reaction of the cadets and faculty was predictable: mindless support for the "victimized" authority figure. There was a "spontaneous" parade in front of Koster's home and a standing ovation as the departing overseer of the honor code told the cadets, in mimickry of Joe Stilwell's words, "Don't let the bastards grind you down." There was no soul-searching, no attempt to examine the relationship between the "ideals" of West Point and the cover-up of a massive murder by one of its most aspiring graduates. Rather the prevailing attitude was best expressed by the comment: "I guess that's it for that poor son-of-a-bitch, wonder who the new supe's going to be." The institution cannot be attacked—cheer the superintendent, sever him from West Point, and forget about it.

Perhaps the most engaging of all the attempts to deal with the war-crimes issue is the rationalization of the man who replaced Gen. Koster, Maj. Gen. William Knowlton (W.P. 1943). In April 1971 five West Pointers—four ex-captains and one ex-major—testified publicly before an Ad Hoc Congressional Committee chaired by Congressman Ronald Dellums about war crimes they had witnessed in Vietnam. Soon after, Knowlton reacted to the "unfavorable image" projected by these men when he spoke to the West Point Board of Visitors: "The third kind of young man trafficking in the West Point name make [*sic*] up a more difficult category. There are only one or two of them. They were good cadets and started off as good officers in combat with decorations for bravery. In each case there seems to have occurred some searing experience which resulted in alienation. Such a case is Laughlin in the Class of 1965. He has recently appeared before Representative Dellum [*sic*] to denounce one or two of his commanders in Vietnam. At West Point, we just do not have the information to assess the reasons for this sort of a case. One hunch is that the cause is peer pressure in the intellectual community. In one or two other cases we have found the female of the species more deadly than the male, and have found *young men who fell under the influence of young ladies of liberal persuasion*. I am sure that the Department of the Army is analyzing these cases" [99] (emphasis added). Koster, reduced one grade in rank for "covering up" the massacre, may continue to "traffic in the name of West Point," but those who honestly attempt to report war crimes are chastised. Knowlton's distaste for those who talk about war crimes may have roots close to home—he served as the "hustling Director of the Revolutionary Development Support Directorate, Pacification Chief" in Vietnam before commanding a brigade under Gen. Julian J. Ewell (W.P. 1939), whose operations earned him a chilling reputation.

These men and Brig. Gen. Henry E. Emerson (W.P. 1947), nicknamed "Gunfighter," who used to hunt and take potshots at Vietnamese from his helicopter, would do well to read one of the few attempts at poetry by a West Pointer (he was killed in Vietnam in 1968):

> I am washed in the blood of my men;
> Their lifeless bodies I have lifted from the ground
> And carried in my arms.
> Their blood has stained my skin and
> My muscles have strained under their limp weight.
> I am detached and intermingled,
> My eyes as theirs look but do not see;
> My clothing is wet with their blood and flesh
> And my mind is numb with the sight of their death.
> I am dead with them.
> I am washed in their lives.[100]

These men are not sadists; they are merely technicians.

Gen. Mark W. Clark (W.P. 1917) once described a key element of leadership as being "a soaring optimism that rejects and *despises* the thought of failure" [101] (emphasis added), and with war crimes on the ground exposing the criminal nature of the policies above, a failure in Vietnam was imminent. Westmoreland, leader that he is, committed the Army to an "honest, 'no-holds-barred' self-examination" and shrewdly deduced that "our most perplexing problems are human." "Human" translates into "professional" for Westmoreland, and a "professional" is "characterized by fidelity and selfless devotion which presupposes self-discipline, great skill, extensive knowledge and willingness to abide by established military ethics." [102] In 1970 the Army War College did a study to determine whether or not there were any "ethics" left to "abide" by and concluded that "current Army leadership principles and the institutional concept they express are valid and appropriate for the 1970s." [103] Shortly after the insane assault on Hamburger Hill in mid-1969 a GI underground paper in Vietnam, *G.I. Says,* publicly offered a $10,000 bounty on the officer who ordered and led the attack, but despite several attempts to eliminate him, he managed to live out his tour. To ensure that this kind of popular leadership continues, Westmoreland established a study group to analyze and improve Army leadership instruction. The group is chaired by none other than the "Gunfighter," Brig. Gen. Henry E. Emerson. Another friendly board, under the direction of Maj. Gen. Frank W. Norris (W.P. 1938), is improving the Army officer education system, and still another group, under Brig. Gen. Robert G. Gard (W.P. 1950), is "supervising and coordinating Army discipline, law and order and drug abuse control measures." Typical of the recommendations of these study groups is their solution for the racial problem: "In early 1971, we added a *four-hour block* of instruction to basic combat training, emphasizing the role of the soldier in promoting racial understanding and harmony in his unit. In late 1970, 'Leadership Aspects of Race Relations' was added to our NCO courses, and to branch officer basic and advanced courses. A similar block of instruction is presented at the Command and General Staff College." [104] Here it is again, just like the Academy—a "block on race" to make the man whole.

Almost as if he realizes that his "problem-solving techniques" won't work on humans, Westmoreland is hedging his bets by trying to eliminate them from the picture: "Today machines and technology are permitting economy of manpower on the battlefield, as indeed they are in the factory. But the future offers even more possibilities for economy. I am confident the American people expect this country to take full advantage of its technology—to welcome and applaud the developments that will replace wherever possible the man with the machine." [105] To this end, the Army has been pushing forward with seven "New Initiatives":

—"Improvements for the individual soldier"—body armor, booby-trap countermeasures, etc.
—"Forward area air defense systems"—new missiles for use against low-altitude, high-performance aircraft.
—"Dynamic defense"—unattended sensors and scatterable mines, air-dropped or fired by artillery ("NATO's Central Europe frontier, which would most likely have to be given up at the outset of a Soviet attack, is a candidate for early electronic 'seeding' ").
—"Aircraft electronic warfare protection equipment"—electronic "suits" for helicopters to frustrate enemy air-defense.
—"Terminal homing"—highly accurate guidance systems of a "fire and forget" nature for artillery, missiles, helicopters, etc.
—"Integrated Battlefield Control System"—an automated command-and-control center for operations and intelligence functions.
—"Aerial Scout"—helicopters with the night-vision and targeting equipment needed to pass data to gunships.[106]

These "New Initiatives" are otherwise known as the Electronic Battlefield or, in the words of Brig. Gen. Wilson R. Reed (W.P. 1941), "an integrated battlefield control system that will tie electronically the sensors to the reaction means— the 'beep' to the 'boom,' as it were—and leave the soldiers free to do what they do best: think, coordinate, control. The potential seems limitless." [107] What Reed did not say is that what soldiers do best now is protest, write letters to Congressmen, frag their officers, become addicts, bleed, and die. Sensors, computers, and "reaction means" do none of these. In his book *1984* George Orwell describes the end sought by these West Pointers: "War is no longer the desperate annihilating struggle that it was. . . . It is a warfare of limited aims. This is not to say that the conduct of war has become less bloodthirsty or more chivalrous. On the contrary . . . but in a physical sense the war involves very small numbers of people, mostly highly trained specialists. The fighting takes place on the vague frontiers whose whereabouts the average man can only guess at."

The idea of an electronic battlefield was born in the summer of 1966 when the Institute for Defense Analysis (IDA), with Maxwell Taylor as its president, began studying the possibility of constructing an electronic fence along South Vietnam's 900-mile border to stop infiltration. By 1969 between $1.6 and $2 billion had been spent on the "New Maginot Line" and scores of West Point weapons-makers had found a new gold mine. Joseph M. Cannon (W.P. 1942), the contract administrator for FMC Corporation's Ordnance Division, was overseeing a new supersonic firebomb and incendiary-bomblet dispenser; Ralph Cooper (W.P. 1951), manager of the Government Radar Contracts Department at Texas Instruments, was busy on new forward-looking radar for computer-guided gunships and various "intrusion" detectors; Frederic W. Hartwig (W.P. 1945), vice-president and corporate chief scientist of Electro Optical Systems, was working on night-vision sights and xenon searchlights; the five West Point engineers and staff members of the Sandia Corp. were puzzling over Air-Delivered Seismic and Acoustic Intrusion Detectors; and the nine West Pointers of the MITRE Corp. were designing "strategic command and space surveillance systems." But even with all this wonderful talent and observations like "We wired the Ho Chi Minh trail like a drugstore pinball machine and we plug it in every night," infiltration between the two halves of Vietnam was never halted. Consequently, other justification for continued expenditures on the costly equipment had to be found. [108] An acoustical buoy costs $2,000; an Air-Delivered Seismic Intrusion Detector, $19,000; a Miniature Seismic Intrusion Detector, $17,000; a Starlight scope and laser rangefinder, $230,000; a stabilized night-vision gunsight, $484,000. The Army justifies these astronomically priced goodies by citing as proof of their effectiveness two battles, Khe Sanh and Firebase Crook. At Khe Sanh a secret sensor field supposedly aided in the killing of 15,000 to 20,000 NVA troops and provided "the most decisive defeat ever handed Hanoi." [109] As we shall see, if these figures were arrived at in the same way as those of Firebase Crook, they are approximately 1,000 percent too high.

The man who tells the story of Crook is Maj. Gen. Ellis W. Williamson, not a graduate but, with stars on his shoulders, a man with a lot to lose unless he acts like one (his commander for the Crook operation was Julian Ewell); his remarks are excerpted from testimony before members of the Senate Armed Services Committee. First, Williamson established his personal philosophy: "For the past 25 years I have been singing a simple tune—if you have a fight, then 'fight with bullets—not bodies.' I have conducted a constant search for ways of getting the job done with less human suffering. . . . During this first year we suffered losses of about 12 American deaths for every 100 enemy. Some people may have been satisfied with that ratio. I was not. . . ." He then explains that the ratio later changed to 3:100 and states: "The unmanned sensors . . . certainly have contributed materially to saving these American lives. I hope that I can demonstrate how these sensors have helped us to make the first step toward the automated battlefield. This is a worthwhile approach toward 'fighting with bullets instead of bodies': that is, getting the job done with minimum danger to our friendly personnel." His first war story illustrates this "minimum danger" principle: "In mid-September the division's (sensor) emplacement teams, with a platoon of mechanized infantry, set out from French Fort to place the sensors. . . . The team did not reach the emplacement area that day. They were attacked by a large NVA force about two miles from their destination. Two of the armored personnel carriers were hit and set afire by rocket-propelled grenades. *We lost two of our emplacement team members* during the initial exchange of fire. Through true gallantry that the American soldier so often displays when the chips are down, *we managed to save the sensors from the burning personnel carriers. . . .*" So much for "minimum danger" and hiding the sensor emplacement from the enemy.

"A short time later the team departed Tay Ninh with a powerful escort consisting of *two complete mechanized infantry companies and helicopter gunships covering.* The instruments were

emplaced without incident." After "trouble differentiating between rain falling on the sensors and human movement," they
"finally paid off" and two 175-mm. guns and two 81-mm. mor-
tars "opened up" on the emplacement area. Williamson reports
that it was "literally a carnage"—he found seven bodies. But,
he goes on, "I guess probably the best real war story that I have
is one called Firebase Crook. This is the story of where some
412 enemy soldiers were eliminated with the loss of one U.S.
soldier." Complete with maps, body-count diagrams, and photographs of night action, he relates how sensors provided early
warning of attacks over a two-day period that resulted in 399
enemy killed (10 were captured) by small arms, artillery, Night
Hawk helicopters, and attack planes. Of the third night he says,
"The fire base commander again held his test firing in the early
evening to check all weapons. Much to our surprise the enemy
responded with return fire. . . . This action apparently
prompted another enemy attack and cost him three more of his
soldiers. I don't know what happened to our early warning that
last night. It is possible that the enemy moved in during the day-
light while we were depending on visual observation . . ."!
Even with this final-night letdown, Williamson offers as proof of
the effectiveness of his sensors, radars, and starlight scopes 399
bodies and the observation that "I had to move two bulldozers
up to the area, just to bury the dead" [110] (emphasis added).

Williamson's knowledge of what happened at Crook was based
on a personal visit to the firebase on the morning of the third
day of the battle. Accompanying him on this trip was his aide,
Capt. Greg Hayward (W.P. 1964), a thrice-wounded, highly
decorated veteran on his second tour in Vietnam. His description
of events at Crook differs considerably from Williamson's. Hayward relates that two weeks prior to the attacks Williamson had
given Lt. Col. Carmichael, the battalion commander at Crook
and an old personal friend, some very pointed advice about his
unit's low body count and implied that Carmichael's job was in
danger unless he started to produce some dead Viet Cong. Williamson and Hayward left for Crook as soon as the reports of
the fantastic success of Carmichael's unit were received at the
headquarters of the 25th Division. On arrival, their helicopter
flew around the firebase in tight concentric circles at an altitude

of roughly twenty-five feet, covering all the area within approximately one-half mile of the base. They counted a little over thirty bodies, most of them in the barbed wire on Crook's perimeter. They then walked the area, confirmed this figure, and confronted Carmichael in his command post. Williamson asked him to explain the battle. Carmichael did so and called it very successful, with over 300 enemy dead. Williamson asked him to justify his figures in view of what he and Hayward had just counted around the perimeter. Carmichael explained that most of the dead were accounted for by ambush patrols who had observed enemy movement and called in artillery. "At this point," Hayward says, "everyone in the command post was openly snickering, it was an obvious lie. . . . But," he continues, "by the time we got there, Carmichael's body count had already been forwarded by Williamson to higher headquarters at II Field Force and he had to believe him or be made out a liar for sending in false body counts. So Williamson supported him and it became common knowledge around the Division that Carmichael had saved his job by lying." Command pressure for body count had produced "a great battle," made liars out of two senior officers, and created a false justification for the electronic battlefield. When Hayward returned to the U.S. and resigned from the Army, he sent a letter to Williamson recalling the events at Crook and asking him why he deliberately supported an outright lie. Williamson responded by turning his former aide's letter over to the Army's Criminal Investigation Division and asking them to look into Hayward's errant behavior.[111]

Another questionable aspect of the sensor program is how the differentiation between friend and foe is made from an electronic report. An exchange between Senator Cannon and Lt. Gen. John Norton (W.P. 1941) clearly illustrates the problem:

CANNON: "What is the application of sensors in a densely populated area?"

NORTON: "I believe the answer to that question, sir, goes to the question of the kinds of sensors that are available. In very densely populated areas where there are noncombatants, well, combatants [whoops!] to be considered, it would take a very precise type of sensor. For example, we find in Vietnam where we have a seismic

> intrusion device that can't distinguish between friend
> and foe, we added maybe a magnetic device and it had
> the additional capability of picking up the presence of
> enemy weapons or ammunition. So I believe in the
> populated areas we will have to make a very careful
> choice. A combination of sensors and techniques will
> give us the answer." [112]

But what about mistakes, false alarms ? "That word has been
stricken from the vocabulary. That is now a non-targetable
activation." [113] In the electronic battlefield the decision of whom
to kill will rest, as Williamson points out, with "the morality of
the man out there making an evaluation," and the identity of
this man is clear, for at the heart of the concept is the Integrated
Battlefield Control System, an automated procedure for funneling all intelligence, operations, support, and communications
data to one man. "The decision logic process will rest with the
professional soldier"—the West Pointer.

These men and their morality are changing the nature of
warfare. No longer will conscripts be necessary, only dedicated
technicians; no longer will public support be necessary, only a
free hand to push buttons; no longer will strong feelings be
necessary, only efficient performance; and no longer will prov-
ocation be necessary, only the availability of weapons will limit
the killing. Men will bomb "coordinates," not villages; "enemy
structures," not homes; "read-outs," not people; and thus be
free of the doubts and rationalizations of killing. The generals
who develop and push this technology are products of our times,
and while tyrants are sometimes overthrown, West Point technicians are merely replaced.

As the nature of war changes, so do the notions of victory,
and in Vietnam, where the U.S. sought to make men free, it
now seeks to make them prisoners. This idea is best expressed
by Professor Ithiel de Sola Pool, a budding Sam Huntington:
"In the Congo, in Vietnam, in the Dominican Republic, it is
clear that order depended on somehow compelling newly mobi-
lized [freed] strata [people] to return to a measure of passivity
and defeatism from which they have recently been aroused by
the process of modernization." [114] The development of this sophisticated denial of freedom for victory's sake took time and

many studies. Thomas L. Fisher (W.P. 1941), director of
strategic studies at Browne & Shaw Research Corporation,
contributed an "examination of potential opportunities and limitations of international peacekeeping forces in local conflicts";
Stanford Research Institute, its vice-president John M. Christensen (W.P. 1941), and its fifty-five men attached to the Thai-U.S.
Military Research and Development Center commanded by
Manob Suriya (W.P. 1937) did a series of "Remote Area Conflict" studies; the Historical Evaluation and Research Organization and its president, Trevor N. Dupuy (W.P. 1938), submitted
"Isolating the Guerrilla"; the Foreign Policy Research Institute
under William Kintner (W.P. 1940) worked up "Alternative
U.S. Strategies and America's Future"; Atlantic Research Corporation's manager of market planning, Ned Schramm (W.P.
1943), accurately foresaw the need for a series of studies on
insurgency and counter-insurgency in various South American
countries; and the RAND Corp., along with its six graduates,
came through with "Support Systems for Guerrilla and Limited
Warfare." RAND characterizes the new approach: the "main
concern of counter-insurgency efforts should be to influence the
behavior of the population rather than their loyalties and attitudes" because "people tend to be motivated, not by abstract
appeals, but rather by their perception of the course of action that
is most likely to lead to their own personal security. . . ." [115]
The obvious course, then, is to mete out massive punishment to
the populations that support the guerrillas—crop defoliation,
destruction of livestock, razing of villages. The Research Analysis Corporation and its thirty-one West Pointers recently submitted a study to the Pentagon of "Economic-Crop Destruction
as a Cold War/Counterinsurgency Weapon" and Vitro Corp.
and its four Academy analysts are developing the necessary
anti-crop agents. Bombs and reprisals might not break the social
and political links of a people, but they do, however, offer new
opportunities for imprisoning them and thereby gaining a "victory." As RAND puts it, the government must impose "restrictions that limit the availability of resources that the insurgency
can draw from the rural areas." Sir Robert Thompson, Nixon's
favorite counter-revolutionary advisor, has added a few control
techniques to the West Pointer's lists—preventive detention,

identity cards, family photographs, snap checks, inventories of belongings and visitors, and travel restrictions.[116] Maybe a survivor of the Jewish ghetto of Vilna should offer his services to the West Point analysts and teach them that the techniques they are devising are similar in design, if not in intent, to certain of those used by the Nazis to divide and conquer his people on their way to the gas chambers of Treblinka.

Is Vietnam the terminal point for America's love affair with counter-insurgency? No—not if it is up to the West Point military, whose officers have gained valuable experience in guerrilla warfare, whose new weapons have been developed and tested on the people of Asia, and whose "lessons learned" conferences have eagerly approved the new, revised techniques—totalitarian control of the population, massive dispossession of the peasantry, and ruthless technological reprisal with bombs and chemicals rather than troops against those who stray. As Robert W. Komer, the former chief of the Pacification Program in Vietnam, explained in 1969, our "gradual" escalation permitted the "guerrillas" to make "adjustments," and the "lesson" for the future is to escalate rapidly and without compassion: "snow them under," he said.[117]

The failure in Vietnam has alienated the counter-insurgency crusaders from the democratic values and institutions of their own country: the war is being lost at home rather than in the field; domestic dissent contrasts with the enviable solidarity of the enemy; and freedom allows too much choice to ever reach stability. Maxwell Taylor, the architect of so much of our Vietnam policy, is in the forefront of those West Point ideologues who seek to bring the war home. In August 1971 he wrote:

The outstanding lesson of the Vietnam war has been the vulnerability of the sources of our power at home to subversive attack—something we have never known before on a large scale. . . . The foreign crisis has coincided with a period of domestic tension and a polarization of discontented minorities divided along political, social, and racial lines. Within these groups there has been a strong quota of hard-core radicals and even revolutionaries who have been quick to *exploit the war* as a grievance symbol inviting attack. As a result, violent spokesmen from the left have arisen to attack the war, the President, and the principal political and social institutions of our country. . . . In past times such tactics—if tolerated—could have been absorbed without much damage, but not now. A new ingredient is present—the powerful support, intentional or unintentional, rendered by our publicity media to the forces of internal subversion. . . . In the course of the war, the press, radio, and TV have combined to flood the American public with truths, half-truths, and rumors, to the destruction of the critical judgment of most of those who have been subjected to the bombardment. . . . The minimal effect has been the creating of profound public confusion conducive to skepticism, suspicion, and eventually to the conviction that somehow we have been betrayed by our leaders. . . . It is this combination of forces and circumstances which accounts for the success of the campaign of defamation which has undermined respect for the Presidency, the Congress, the courts, industry, and the armed forces. In so doing, it has brought the national confidence, pride, and morale to their present low estate. . . . Surely, the defense against these subversive methods deserves a fervor equal to that which we have lavished in the past on the protection of our lives, our liberty, and our national territory. The protection of the sources of our power must be included in any adequate concept of what our national security requires today. . . . It is that the distinction between national security and domestic welfare is becoming increasingly blurred. . . . More and more, the requirements of defense and welfare tend to blend until the two are virtually indistinguishable." [118] [Emphasis added]

So, as in Vietnam, there are no legitimate grievances in the U.S., but only democratic weaknesses that are being exploited by conspirators. All the rationalizations used to deny the fact of revolution in Vietnam are being reapplied in the U.S. to classify dissent as insurgency, and the same "fervor" with which we punished the people of Southeast Asia is being demanded for punishing the people of America.

The techniques are ready. Speaking of the electronic battlefield, Gen. Deane said: "I am . . . convinced that we now have a dynamic, flexible surveillance system for future battlefield application anywhere in the world and in any type of conflict. Our ability to apply this capability to our tactical and strategic advantage will be limited only by our resourcefulness, imagination, and willingness. . . ." [119] Some of the imagination is being supplied by the vice-president of Simulmatics Corp., David Yates (W.P. 1940), who is doing research on "Urban Insurgency," and Taylor's IDA, which received a $498,000 contract to develop "new systems for the suppression of urban disorders." Unsurprisingly, IDA recommended the "application of military counter-insurgency systems to domestic police operations." The gear is already in use—the automated control of police vehicles and television monitoring of major "trouble centers" (like Times Square in New York City) have given the urban police an early form of the electronic battlefield for use against political revolts in the cities. A more refined development is the recent suggestion that the "25 million habitual criminals" in the U.S. be outfitted with irremovable transponders that would activate sensors scattered throughout the cities and thus give police a constant check of each "criminal's" whereabouts. But the electronic battlefield is not fully developed and remains only a part of the effort required.

West Pointers have been advocating the real final solution for years, and it coincides perfectly with the "lessons learned" from Vietnam: totalitarian control of the population. In April 1966 Dwight Eisenhower was saying that he believed "implicitly in freedom of speech" but that, in his opinion, "the draft card burners should be sent to jail—at least for the war's duration." [120] A few months later, in September, Eisenhower proposed another part of his solution: "Under the system that I envision, every young male American, no matter what his status in life or his plans for the future, would spend 49 weeks—one year minus three weeks vacation—in military training. . . . This year should be considered not only as their contribution to country but as part of their education. The government would, of course, provide sustenance, clothing and other necessaries, but the trainee would be paid only a small stipend—say five or ten dollars a month—in order to have a bit of pocket change for incidentals. . . . [I think] it could do much to stem the growing tide of *irresponsible behavior* and outright crime in the United States. To expose all our young men for a year to *discipline* and the *correct attitudes* of living inevitably would straighten out a lot of potential troublemakers. In this connection—although I am sure that in saying this I label myself as old-fashioned—I deplore the beatnik dress, the long, unkempt hair, the *dirty necks and fingernails* now affected by a minority of our boys. If [this training] accomplished nothing more than to produce cleanliness and decent grooming, it might be worth the price tag. . . . To me a sloppy appearance has always indicated sloppy habits of mind" [121] (emphasis added). This was in 1966. By 1969 Lt. Gen. Arthur G. Trudeau (W.P. 1924) had brought the emphasis on behavior rather than attitude to its logical totalitarian end: "the betterment of our people at home can only be accomplished in a more rational atmosphere devoid of riots, chants, burnings, murders, narcotics, crime, and godlessness. Order must be restored. . . . [We must] demand stringent action against these despoilers of America. . . . No man whose words and actions beget violence and destruction is entitled to freedom. He is a menace to any society." [122] And so, blind until the end as to whose words "beget violence and destruction," the West Pointers seek to apply the "techniques" of Vietnam to the "solution" of America's problems. Morality is their possession, order is their cry, and stability is their goal—a uniformed America marching on a West Point Plain that extends from coast to coast.

APPENDIX A

LIST OF REQUIRED COURSES AND ELECTIVE OPPORTUNITIES

ACADEMIC CURRICULUM
CORE AND ELECTIVE PROGRAMS
AY 1969–1970

THE CORE ACADEMIC PROGRAM

Fourth Class (Freshman) Year	*First Term*	*Second Term*
*Mathematics	MA 101	MA 102
*English	EN 101	EN 102
†*Foreign Language	L__ 101	L__ 102
*Environment	EV 101	EV 102
*Engineering Fundamentals	EF 101	EF 102

Third Class (Sophomore) Year		
*Mathematics	MA 205	**MA 206 (Elective)
*Physics	PH 201	PH 202
*Chemistry	CH 201	CH 202
*Foreign Language	L__ 201	L__ 202
English	EN 201	———
*Psychology	—	PL 202
History	HI 201	HI 202
(One sequence to be selected) or	HI 203	HI 204

Second Class (Junior) Year		
Electrical Engineering	EE 301	EE 304
*Mechanics	ME 301	**ME 302 (Elective)
*Mechanics	ME 303	———
*Physics	———	PH 303
Law	LW 301	LW 302
*Social Sciences	SS 301	SS 302
	Elective	Elective

* Advanced versions of these courses are offered to qualified individuals by the department concerned.

** Those cadets enrolled in the Humanities and National Security and Public Affairs areas may substitute electives for these courses.

† The Department of Foreign Languages offers programs in Chinese, French, German, Portuguese, Russian, and Spanish.

First Class (Senior) Year		First Term	Second Term
Engineering		*CE 401	*CE 402
(One sequence to	or	CE 453	CE 454
be selected)	or	*OE 401	*OE 402
	or	EE 401	EE 402
	or	GE 401	GE 402
Leadership		PL 401	
English		———	EN 402
*Social Sciences		SS 401	SS 407
History		HI 401	HI 402
		Elective	Elective
		Elective	Elective

APPENDIX B

SOME WEST POINTERS IN THE THINK TANK BUSINESS
(WHAT ARE THEY THINKING ABOUT?)

The Research Analysis Corp., Westgate Research Park, McLean, Va.

Omar Nelson Bradley (W.P. 1915)
Lawrence R. Dewey (W.P. 1924)
Charles Day Palmer (W.P. 1924)
James Edward Moore (W.P. 1924)
Armistead Davis Mead (W.P. 1924)
John Gillespie Hill (W.P. 1924)
Donald Dunford (W.P. 1925)
Willis Small Matthews (W.P. 1927)
Ralph Joseph Butchers (W.P. 1928)
Ralph Thomas Nelson (W.P. 1928)
Herbert John Vander Heide (W.P. 1929)
Robert Jefferson Wood (W.P. 1930)
Philip Campbell Wehle (W.P. 1930)
Charles Hartwell Bonesteel (W.P. 1931)
Orlando Collette Troxel, Jr. (W.P. 1931)
Daniel Parker, Jr. (W.P. 1933)
Sherburne Whipple, Jr. (W.P. 1933)
John Martin Breit (W.P. 1933)
Ernest Mikell Clarke (W.P. 1933)
Gerald Joseph Higgins (W.P. 1934)
James Martin Worthington (W.P. 1935)
Selwyn Dyson Smith, Jr. (W.P. 1936)
David Bennett Parker (W.P. 1937)
Richard Gates Williams (W.P. 1937)
Thomas Nelson Sibley (W.P. 1938)
Norman Farrell (W.P. 1939)
Raymond Leroy Shoemaker, Jr. (W.P. 1940)
Sears Yates Coker (W.P. 1941)
James Paul Forsyth (W.P. 1941)
Bradish Johnson Smith (W.P. 1941)
William Joseph Spahr (W.P. 1943)

[391]

The Stanford Research Corp. (Stanford Research International)
Menlo Park, Calif., and 1611 Kent Street, Arlington, Va.

C. Stanton Babcock (W.P. 1925)
Edwin Hugh John Carns (W.P. 1929)
Albert Joseph Mandelbaum (W.P. 1930)
Morris Oswald Edwards (W.P. 1933)
Donald Wilt Shive (W.P. 1937)
Harold McDonald Brown (W.P. 1937)
Matthew John Altenhofen (W.P. 1938)
Morrill Elwood Marston (W.P. 1940)
John Moore Christensen, Jr. (W.P. 1941)
Robert Morris Rodden (W.P. 1944)
George Arlington Daoust (W.P. 1945)
Pierce Horatio Gaver, Jr. (W.P. 1948)
Frederick Robert Westfall (W.P. 1949)
Arthur Alten McGee (W.P. 1950)
George Massie Gividen, Jr. (W.P. 1951)
Leslie Page Holcomb, Jr. (W.P. 1950)

The MITRE Corp., 5600 Columbia Pike, Bailey's Crossroads, Va,.
and Bedford, Mass.

Angelo Ralph DelCampo (W.P. 1931)
George Louis Descheneaux, Jr. (W.P. 1932)
Charles Edmund Harrison, Jr. (W.P. 1940)
John Laurence Shortall, Jr. (W.P. 1943)
Edward Burr II (W.P. 1943)
Alexander Morton Maish (W.P. 1944)
Malcolm Eldridge MacDonald (W.P. 1946)
Robert James Ellis (W.P. 1954)
Joseph Thomas Moriarty (W.P. 1959)

The RAND Corp., Santa Monica, Calif.

Ralph Edward Koon (W.P. 1928)
Lauris Norstad (W.P. 1930)
Sidney George Spring (W.P. 1935)
Lester Lewes Wheeler (W.P. 1935)
John Lindsay Bower (W.P. 1936)
Robert McChesney Smith (W.P. 1945)
William Wallace Whitson (W.P. 1948)

Planning Research Corp., 7411 Lorge Circle, Huntington Beach,
Calif.

Robert Rigby Glass (W.P. 1935)
Burton Robert Brown (W.P. 1938)
John Randle Watson (W.P. 1942)
Selmer Gustaves (W.P. 1942)
Norman Erland Pehrson (W.P. 1943)
William Edward Naylor, Jr. (W.P. 1943)
Keith Chandler Nusbaum (W.P. 1945)
Claron Atherton Robertson, Jr. (W.P. 1948)
John Francis Magnotti, Jr. (W.P. 1949)
Grady Huger Banister, Jr. (W.P. 1950)

APPENDIX C

Top Secret memo from Roger Hilsman, Assistant Secretary of State for Far Eastern Affairs, to Dean Rusk, Secretary of State, dated two months before the assassination of South Vietnamese President Ngo Dinh Diem.

TOP SECRET
DEPARTMENT OF STATE
ASSISTANT SECRETARY

August 30, 1963

TO   : The Secretary
FROM   : FE—Roger Hilsman
SUBJECT: Possible Diem-Nhu Moves and U.S. Responses

The courses of action which Diem and Nhu could take to maintain themselves in power and the United States responses thereto are as follows:

1. *Diem-Nhu Move:* Preemptive arrest and assassination of opposition military officers and/or Vice President Tho.

   U.S. Response:

   (a) We should continue to pass warnings to these officials about their danger.

   (b) CAS should explore the feasibility of prompt supply of a warning system to these officials.

   (c) If several general officers are arrested, we should invoke aid sanctions to obtain their release on the ground that they are essential to successful prosecution of the war against the Viet Cong.

   (d) Encouragement of prompt initiation of the coup is the best way of avoiding arrests and assassinations of generals.

2. *Diem-Nhu Move:* Sudden switch in assignments of opposition generals or their dispatch on special missions outside of Saigon.

   U.S. Response: We should recommend that the opposition generals delay in carrying out any such orders and move promptly to execution of the coup.

3. *Diem-Nhu Move:* Declaration of Ambassador Lodge and/or other

[393]

APPENDICES

important American officials in Viet-Nam as *personae non gratae.*
Declassified by authority of the President, 2/14/68

U.S. Response:

(a) We should stall on the removal of our officials until the efforts to mount a coup have borne fruit. This situation again shows the importance of speed on the part of both the U.S. and Vietnamese sides. We should also suspend aid.

(b) Should the GVN begin to bring physical pressure on our personnel, we should introduce U.S. forces to safeguard their security.

4. *Diem-Nhu Move:* Blackmail pressure on U.S. dependents in Viet-Nam, such as arrests, a few mysterious deaths or—more likely— disguised threats (like Nhu's recent threat to raze Saigon in case of a coup).

U.S. Response:

(a) We should maintain our sang-froid with respect to threats.

(b) We should urge American personnel to take such precautions as avoidance of unnecessary movement and concentration of families. We should also issue arms to selected American personnel.

(c) We should demand the release of any Americans arrested and should insist for the record on proper protection of Americans by the GVN. (GVN failure to furnish this protection could serve as one of the justifications for open U.S. intervention.)

(d) We should evacuate dependents and other nonofficial personnel at the earliest possible moment that Ambassador Lodge considers it consistent with the overall operation.

(e) We should intervene with U.S. forces if necessary to protect Americans during evacuation and to obtain the release of those arrested.

5. *Diem-Nhu Move:* Severance of all aid ties with the U.S., ouster of all U.S. personnel (except for a limited diplomatic staff), and demand for removal of all U.S.-controlled military equipment in Viet-Nam.

U.S. Response:

(a) We should stall in removing U.S. personnel and equipment from Viet-Nam. This move by the GVN would again, however, underscore the necessity for speed in our counteraction.

(b) If Diem-Nhu move to seize U.S.-controlled equipment, we should resist by all necessary force.

6. *Diem-Nhu Move:* Political move toward the DRV (such as opening of neutralization negotiations), or rumors and indirect threats of such a move.

U.S. Response:

(a) Ambassador Lodge should give Diem a clear warning of the dangers of such a course, and point out its continued pursuit will lead to cessation of U.S. aid.

(b) Encourage the generals to move promptly with a coup.

(c) We should publicize to the world at an appropriate moment any threats or move by Diem or Nhu toward the DRV in order to show the two-edged game they are playing and help justify publicly our counteractions.

[394]

(d) If the DRV threatens to respond to an anti-Diem coup by sending troops openly to South Viet-Nam, we should let it know unequivocally that we shall hit the DRV with all that is necessary to force it to desist.

(e) We should be prepared to take such military action.

7. *Diem-Nhu Move:* Appeal to De Gaulle for political support for neutralization of Viet-Nam.

U.S. Response:

(a) We should point out publicly that Viet-Nam cannot be effectively neutralized unless the Communists are removed from control of North Viet-Nam. If a coalition between Diem and the Communists is suggested, we should reply that this would be the avenue to a Communist take-over in view of the relative strength of the two principals in the coalition. Once an anti-Diem coup is started in South Viet-Nam, we can point to the obvious refusal of South Viet-Nam to accept a Diem-Communist coalition.

8. *Diem-Nhu Move:* If hostilities start between the GVN and a coup group, Diem and Nhu will seek to negotiate in order to play for time (as during the November, 1960, coup attempt) and rally loyal forces to Saigon.

U.S. Response:

(a) The U.S. must define its objective with crystal clearness. If we try to save Diem by encouraging negotiations between him and a coup group, while a coup is in progress, we shall greatly increase the risk of an unsuccessful outcome of the coup attempt. Our objective should therefore, clearly be to bring the whole Ngo family under the control of the coup group.

(b) We should warn the coup group to press any military advantage it gains to its logical conclusion without stopping to negotiate.

(c) We should use all possible means to influence pro-Diem generals like Cao to move to the coup side. For example, General Harkins could send a direct message to Cao pointing to the consequences of a continued stand in support of the Ngo family and the advantage of shifting over to the coup group.

(d) We should use, or encourage the coup group to use, military measures to prevent any loyal forces outside Saigon from rallying to Diem's support. For example, we can jam radio communications between Diem and these forces and we can encourage interdiction of transportation by blowing up bridges.

(e) We should encourage the coup group to capture and remove promptly from Viet-Nam any members of the Ngo family outside Saigon, including Can and Thuc who are normally in Hue. We should assist in this operation to any extent necessary.

9. *Diem-Nhu Move:* Continuation of hostilities in Saigon as long as possible in the hope that the U.S. will weaken because of the bloodbath which may involve U.S. personnel.

U.S. Response:

(a) We should maintain our sang-froid and encourage the coup forces to continue the fight to the extent necessary.

(b) We should seek to bring officers loyal to Diem over to our side by direct approaches by MACV or CAS inducements.

(c) We should encourage the coup group to take necessary action to deprive the loyal forces of access to supplies.

(d) We should make full use of any U.S. equipment available in Viet-Nam to assist the coup group.

(e) If necessary, we should bring in U.S. combat forces to assist the coup group to achieve victory.

10. *Diem-Nhu Move:* A *Götterdämmerung* in the Palace.
    U.S. Response:

    (a) We should encourage the coup group to fight the battle to the end and to destroy the Palace if necessary to gain victory.

    (b) Unconditional surrender should be the terms for the Ngo family since it will otherwise seek to outmaneuver both the coup forces and the U.S. If the family is taken alive, the Nhus should be banished to France or any other European country willing to receive them. Diem should be treated as the generals wish.

11. *Diem-Nhu Move:* Flight out of the country (this is unlikely as it would not be in keeping with the past conduct of the Ngo family).
    U.S. Response:

    We should be prepared, with the knowledge of the coup group, to furnish a plane to take the Ngo family to France or other European country which will receive it. Under no circumstances should the Nhus be permitted to remain in Southeast Asia in close proximity to Viet-Nam because of the plots they will try to mount to regain power. If the generals decide to exile Diem, he should also be sent outside Southeast Asia.

NOTES

CHAPTER 1

1. Alden Partridge, quoted by Marcus Cunliffe, *Soldiers and Civilians*, p. 106.
2. Anastasio Somoza, quoted by Samuel E. H. France, "Report from the Classes," *Assembly*, Summer 1967, p. 86.
3. *Ibid.*
4. Brig. Gen. George S. Patton III, quoted in *Washington Evening Star*, June 3, 1971.
5. Interview with Gordon Livingston.
6. Harry S Truman quoted in D. E. Halpin (ed.), "General of the Army Omar N. Bradley," *Assembly*, Spring 1970, p. 20.
7. Omar N. Bradley, quoted in *ibid.*, p. 21.
8. William H. A. Carr, *The DuPonts of Delaware*, p. 238.
9. Thomas J. Fleming, *West Point*, p. 66.
10. R. Ernest Dupuy, *Sylvanus Thayer*, p. 23.
11. U.S. Congress, House Committee on Armed Services, *Hearings Before the Special Subcommittee on the M-16 Rifle Program*, 90th Cong., 1st Sess., 1967, p. 4761.
12. U.S., *Congressional Record*, 92nd Cong., 1st Sess., May 26, 1971, Vol. 117, No. 79, p. E5091.
13. U.S., Congress, House Committee on Armed Services, *Hear-ings*, 92nd Cong., 1st Sess., March 11, 1971, pp. 2636–37.
14. Burton C. Andrus, Jr., "Report from the Classes," *Assembly*, Summer 1971, p. 88.
15. Betty Beale, "Washington Letter," *Baltimore Sun*, June 25, 1972.
16. Jack Benner, quoted in Brig. Gen. John D. Stevens, "Report from the Classes," *Assembly*, Winter 1968, p. 68.
17. Maj. Gen. William Knowlton, quoted in Col. Alexander G. Stone, "Report from the Classes," *Assembly*, Spring 1971, p. 60.
18. Col. Burton C. Andrus, Jr., "Report from the Classes," *Assembly*, Summer 1971, p. 86.
19. Maj. Charles M. Adams, "Report from the Classes," *Assembly*, Summer 1964, p. 87.
20. Paul W. Thompson, quoted in "Annual June Week Meeting of the Association of Graduates," *Assembly*, Summer 1970, p. 45.
21. Col. Burton C. Andrus, Jr., "Report from the Classes," *Assembly*, Winter 1970, p. 75.
22. Bertel E. Kuniholm, quoted in Brig. Gen. Monro MacCloskey, "Report from the Classes," *Assembly*, Summer 1970, p. 60.
23. Col. Burton C. Andrus, Jr., "Report from the Classes," *Assembly*, Fall 1969, p. 77.

24. Matthew B. Ridgway, *Soldier*, pp. 263–64.
25. Harry H. Haas, "Report from the Classes," *Assembly*, Winter 1970, p. 53.
26. Col. John N. Hauser, "Report from the Classes," *Assembly*, Spring 1966, p. 32.
27. Richard C. Hutchinson, "Report from the Classes," *Assembly*, Winter 1968, p. 62.
28. Maj. Gen. A. S. Newman, "The Forward Edge," *Army*, February 1971, p.48.
29. Correspondence from Louis P. Font, July 2, 1972.
30. Newman, p. 48.
31. Ernest B. Furgurson, *Westmoreland*, p. 289.
32. I. F. Stone, quoted in Eqbal Ahmad, "The Theory and Fallacies of Counterinsurgency," *The Nation*, August 2, 1971, p. 74.
33. Hank Royall, quoted in Col. Alexander G. Stone, "Report from the Classes," *Assembly*, Winter 1970, p. 63.
34. Col. Marvin E. Childs, "Report from the Classes," *Assembly*, Spring 1967, p. 65.
35. Col. Burton C. Andrus, Jr., "Report from the Classes," *Assembly*, Spring 1970, p. 77.
36. Col. Harrison King, "Report from the Classes," *Assembly*, Summer 1967, p. 60.
37. Arthur A. Ekirch, Jr., *The Civilian and the Military* (New York: Oxford University Press, 1956), quoted in Morris Janowitz, *The Professional Soldier*, p. 230.
38. Theodore H. White (ed.), *The Stilwell Papers* (New York: William Sloane Associates, 1948) p. 256, quoted in Janowitz, p. 230.
39. Furgurson, p. 27.
40. Roger Hilsman, "Research in Military Affairs," *World Politics*, Vol. 7 (1954), p. 502, quoted in Janowitz, p. 135.
41. R. C. Crawford, quoted in Col. John N. Hauser, "Report from the Classes," *Assembly*, Spring 1966, p. 33.
42. U.S., *Congressional Record*, 92nd Cong., 1st Sess., June 24, 1971, No. 98, Part II, p. 6627.
43. Furgurson, pp. 288–89.
44. *Ibid.*, p. 288.
45. Col. Burton C. Andrus, Jr., "Report from the Classes," *Assembly*, Winter 1970, p. 74.
46. Letter from a first-year cadet quoted in Lt. Gen. William A. Knowlton's letter to "Fellow Graduates and Friends of the Military Academy," *Assembly*, Fall 1971, inside cover.
47. Spoken to Louis P. Font, April 3, 1970. Quote provided by him.

CHAPTER 2

1. John Steinbeck, *East of Eden*, p. 25.
2. United States Military Academy, *The New Cadet*, p. 11.
3. Maxwell Taylor, "The West Point Way," *Assembly*, Summer 1967, p. 31.
4. USMA, *Room Arrangements East Barracks, U.S.C.C.*, January 26, 1966.
5. USMA, *The New Cadet*, p. 9.
6. USMA, *Bugle Notes 1970*, Vol. 62, p. 124.
7. *Ibid.*, p. 125.
8. Ramon A. Nadal, "Changes in the Fourth Class System," *Assembly*, Winter 1970, p. 15.
9. The offenses listed occurred at the U.S. Military Academy in late 1970 and early 1971. Their Special Order Numbers are, in order: S.O. 22, S.O. 5, S.O. 12, S.O. 14, S.O. 30, S.O. 195, S.O. 40, S.O. 9, S.O. 68, S.O. 75, S.O. 65, S.O. 18, S.O. 29, S.O. 60, S.O. 34, S.O. 5, S.O. 62, S.O. 34, S.O. 55.
10. Edward L. King, *The Death of the Army*, p. 120.
11. Col. Harold D. Kehm, "Re-

port from the Classes," *Assembly*, Spring 1968, p. 72.

12. Cadet Louis P. Font's Squadbook dated December 13, 1966.

13. USMA, *Regulations, United States Corps of Cadets*, January 15, 1970, p. 59.

14. Interview with a West Point athletic coach who wishes to remain anonymous, June 4, 1971.

15. USMA, *Regulations . . .* , January 18, 1971, p. 204.

16. George S. Pappas, *The Cadet Chapel, United States Military Academy*, p. 11.

17. *Ibid.*, p. 60.

18. *Annapolis Evening Capitol*, July 28, 1971.

19. J. Robert Moskin, "Who Would Ever Go to West Point Today?," *Look*, October 6, 1970, p. 36.

20. USMA, *The New Cadet*, p. 1.

21. Erich Maria Remarque, *All Quiet on the Western Front*, p. 162.

22. Steinbeck, pp. 25–26.

23. USMA, *Regulations . . .* , September 1, 1968, p. 318.

CHAPTER 3

1. Philip A. Farris, "The Academic Evolution at West Point," *Assembly*, Winter 1971, p. 12.

2. Col. C. H. Schilling, quoted in Thomas J. Fleming, "West Point Cadets Now Say 'Why Sir?,' " *The New York Times Magazine*, July 5, 1970, p. 18.

3. USMA, Office of the Dean, *Academic Program, Academic Year 1971–1972*, February 12, 1971, Section XII, p. 1.

4. George A. Lincoln, *Teaching in the Department of Social Sciences* (USMA, 1968), p. 38.

5. *Ibid.*

6. USMA, *The New Cadet*, p. 27.

7. Lincoln, p. 46.

8. *Ibid.*, pp. 37–38.

9. *Ibid.*, pp. 23–24.

10. *Ibid.*, p. 26.

11. *Ibid.*, pp. 26–27.

12. *Ibid.*, p. 28.

13. *Ibid.*, pp. 28–29.

14. *Ibid.*, p. 23.

15. *Ibid.*

16. *Ibid.*, p. 20.

17. *Ibid.*, pp. 4–5.

18. Matthew B. Ridgway, *Soldier*, p. 33.

19. Farris, p. 11.

20. Lincoln, p. 87.

21. *Ibid.*, p. 14.

22. *Ibid.*, p. 88.

23. *Ibid.*, p. 7.

24. *Ibid.*

25. *Ibid.*, p. 13.

26. *Ibid.*, p. 36.

27. *Ibid.*, p. 4.

28. Arthur E. Wise, "Selected Characteristics of the Class of 1972," *Assembly*, Fall 1968, pp. 21, 40.

29. Lincoln, p. 88.

30. *Ibid.*, p. 4.

31. *Ibid.*

32. *Ibid.*, p. 31.

33. *Ibid.*, p. 89.

34. *Ibid.*, p. 88.

35. *Ibid.*, p. 1.

36. USMA, *Cadet Notebook History of Europe and America 1500–1870*, Social Science 201, Academic Year 1968–1969, Department of Social Sciences, September 1968, p. xi.

37. Personal experience of Robert B. Johnson.

38. Lincoln, p. 88.

39. J. Arthur Heise, *The Brass Factories*, p. 144.

40. USMA, Captain E. B. Elliott, Jr., *English 102 Lesson Plan*, Academic Year 1968–1969, Lesson 29, Lesson Dates 11/14 April 1969, p. 6.

41. USMA, *Department of English Handbook*, 1969–1970, p. 5.

42. USMA, *Regulations, United States Corps of Cadets*, September 1, 1968, p. 54.

43. Fox Conner, quoted in Brig. Gen. Gerald F. Lillard, "Report

from the Classes," *Assembly,* Winter 1968, p. 59.

44. USMA, *Instructor Syllabus,* English 102, Academic Year 1968–1969.

45. Heise, p. 149.

46. Garrison H. Davidson, quoted in Brig. Gen. Gerald F. Lillard, "Report from the Classes," *Assembly,* Fall 1966, p. 46.

47. Lt. Gen. William A. Knowlton, letter to "Fellow Graduates and Friends of the Military Academy," *Assembly,* Spring 1970, inside cover.

48. Heise, p. 150.

49. D. E. Halpin, "The Dean of the USMA Academic Board: Brigadier General John R. Jannarone," *Assembly,* Winter 1971, p. 32.

50. *Ibid.*

51. "Colonel Russ Broshous: of ARMY," *Assembly,* Fall 1969, p. 46.

52. Lincoln, pp. 52–53.

53. *Ibid.,* p. 9.

54. Heise, p. 139.

55. *Ibid.,* p. 140.

56. Dave R. Palmer, *Readings in Current Military History,* USMA, Department of Military Art and Engineering, 1969, pp. 45, 110.

57. Col. Charles P. Nicholas, "Mathematics and the Making of Leaders," *Assembly,* Spring 1967, pp. 13–14.

CHAPTER 4

1. Interview with Greg Hayward, May 18, 1971.

2. Interview with Ronald Bartek, May 18, 1971.

3. U.S., *Congressional Record,* 92nd Cong., 1st Sess., May 26, 1971, Vol. 117, No. 79, p. E5091.

4. USMA, *Bugle Notes 1970,* Vol. 62, p. 98.

5. Letter to J. Arthur Heise from an ex-cadet of the Class of 1968 who wishes to remain anonymous.

6. Letter to J. Arthur Heise from Brig. Gen. Bernard W. Rogers, commandant of cadets, December 22, 1967.

7. Letter to J. Arthur Heise from Brig. Gen. Bernard W. Rogers, January 9, 1968.

8. U.S., Congress, House Committee on Armed Services, *Hearings on the Administration of the Service Academies,* 90th Cong., 1st & 2nd Sess., 1967–68, p. 10581.

9. USMA, *Regulations, United States Corps of Cadets,* July 1, 1970, p. 45.

10. *Ibid.,* p. 46.

11. *Ibid.,* p. 45.

12. *Ibid.,* p. 49a.

13. USMA, *Regulations . . . ,* September 1, 1968, p. 54.

14. USMA, *Regulations . . . ,* July 1, 1971, p. 44.

15. Col. Samuel Hays, quoted in Thomas J. Fleming, *West Point,* p. 373.

16. U.S., *Congressional Record,* May 26, 1971, p. E5091.

17. Letter to authors.

18. Interview with Stephen Phelan, July 1971.

19. Earl Blaik, *You Have to Pay the Price,* p. 290.

20. *Ibid.,* p. 281.

21. *Ibid.,* p. 282.

22. Quoted in Heise, *The Brass Factories,* p. 38.

23. Robert F. McDermott, quoted in Heise, p. 44.

24. Heise, pp. 44–45.

25. United States Air Force Academy, *Annual Report of the Superintendent for Fiscal Year 1965,* quoted in Heise, pp. 46–52.

26. Blaik, p. 291.

27. USMA, *Bugle Notes,* p. 1.

28. U.S., *Congressional Record,* May 26, 1971, p. E5091.

29. Interview with Cadet Donham.

30. Kenneth E. Hanst, Jr., "Report from the Classes," *Assembly,* Spring 1970, p. 78.

31. James Finn (ed.), *Conscience and Command,* pp. 122–31.

32. William C. Westmoreland, quoted by William A. Knowlton in the *Congressional Record,* May 26, 1971, p. E5091.

CHAPTER 5

1. Quoted in Edgar F. Puryear, Jr., *Nineteen Stars* (Washington, D.C.: Coiner Publications, 1971) p. 245.
2. Charles Winslow Elliot, *Winfield Scott,* pp. 259–67.
3. Interview with Lt. Col. Anthony B. Herbert, January 20, 1972.
4. Arthur E. Morgan, *Dams and Other Disasters,* p. 320.
5. *Ibid.,* p. 323.
6. *Ibid.,* p. 329.
7. Brig. Gen. Ellis E. Wilhoyt, Jr., *Assembly,* Spring 1965, p. 55.
8. Capt. John S. McGuire, "Founders Day, 1971," *Assembly,* Spring 1971, p. 20.
9. Abbott Boone, "To Get Ahead Requires Hard Work . . . But a Little Luck Helps," *Assembly,* Spring 1969, p. 49.
10. Matthew B. Ridgway, "Founders Day, 1971," *Assembly,* Spring 1971, p. 21.
11. Paul W. Thompson, "Founders Day, 1971," *Assembly,* Spring 1971, p. 19.
12. Lt. Col. P. S. Gage, Jr., *Assembly,* Spring 1964, p. 66.
13. Edward L. King, *The Death of the Army,* pp. 115–16.
14. *Ibid.,* p. 119.
15. Maj. Gen. Roland M. Kirks, as quoted in "Challenge Posed CGSC Graduates Wins Award," *The Army Reserve Magazine,* May 1970, pp. 8–9.
16. Chief Petty Officer Ted Casey, U.S.N., quoted in a Freedoms Foundation booklet honoring 1970 awards recipients, February 15, 1971, p. 36.
17. Capt. Thomas J. Erwin III, quoted in *ibid.,* p. 36.

18. Lt. John R. Hefferan, quoted in *ibid.,* p. 44.
19. Lt. Col. Asa E. Hunt III, quoted in *ibid.,* p. 40.
20. Lt. Col. Joseph D. Posz, quoted in *ibid.,* p. 40.
21. Capt. Samuel W. Bartholomew, quoted in *ibid.,* p. 38.
22. Elliot, p. 704.
23. Col. Vincent J. Esposito, *The West Point Atlas of American Wars,* I, 114.
24. *Ibid.*
25. Thomas J. Fleming, *West Point,* p. 178.
26. James H. Lane, quoted in Frank J. Cavaioli, *West Point and the Presidency,* p. 29.
27. *Ibid.*
28. William T. Sherman, quoted in Cavaioli, p. 28.
29. U.S. *Congressional Globe,* 37th Cong., 2nd Sess., Vol. 32, p. 162.
30. Marcus Cunliffe, *Soldiers and Civilians,* pp. 163–65.
31. *Gale's and Seaton's Register of Debates in Congress,* Feb. 25, 1830, p. 583.
32. Fleming, pp. 112–13.
33. The primary source for the information on the origins of the Academy is *The American State Papers, Vol. VII,* pp. 1–7 (Select Committee of the House of Representatives. Mr. Smith, Maine, March 1, 1837).
34. Forest G. Hill, *Roads, Rails and Waterways,* p. 13.
35. Fleming, p. 16.
36. *American State Papers,* Vol. VII, p. 7.
37. R. Ernest Dupuy, *Sylvanus Thayer,* p. 4.
38. Col. Lester A. Webb, *Captain Alden Partridge and the United States Military Academy, 1806–1833* (Northport, Ala.: American Southern, 1965), p. 108.
39. Daniel Parker to Gen. Porter, March 20, 1815, as quoted in Webb, p. 111.
40. Dupuy, p. 9.

NOTES

41. Fleming, p. 45.
42. Sylvanus Thayer, as quoted by Fleming, p. 49.
43. *American State Papers,* Vol. VII, p. 12.
44. *Ibid.,* p. 13
45. Fleming, p. 47.
46. *American State Papers,* Vol. VII, p. 14.
47. *Ibid.*
48. *Ibid.,* p. 15
49. Hill, p. 68.
50. *Ibid.,* p. 15.
51. *Ibid.,* p. 209.
52. Cunliffe, p. 20.
53. *Ibid.,* p. 21.
54. Peter Barnes, *Pawns,* p. 21.
55. William B. Hesseltine and Hazel C. Wolf, *The Blue and the Gray on the Nile* was the general guide for the material on Egypt.
56. *Ibid.,* p. 88.
57. *Ibid.,* p. 88.
58. Herbert Molloy Mason, *The Great Pursuit* (New York: Random House, 1970), p. 148.
59. *Ibid.,* p. 202.
60. Russell F. Weigley, *History of the United States Army,* p. 355.
61. Fleming, p. 305.
62. *Ibid.,* pp.305–06.
63. *Ibid.,* p. 306.
64. *Ibid.*
65. Morris Janowitz, *The Professional Soldier,* p. 28.
66. Weigley, p. 569.
67. Janowitz, p. 57.
68. Robert M. Danford, "Founders Day—USMA 1965, An Old Grad Reminisces. . . ," *Assembly,* Spring 1965, p. 10.
69. *Ibid.,* p. 11.
70. *Ibid.,* pp. 33–34.
71. *Ibid.,* p. 9.
72. Puryear, p. 57.
73. *Ibid.,* p. xi.
74. *Ibid.,* p. 72.
75. *Ibid.,* p. 73.
76. *Ibid.,* p. 160.
77. *Ibid.,* p. 161.
78. *Ibid.,* p. 70.
79. *Ibid.,* p. 71.
). *Ibid.*

81. Janowitz, p. 302, and J. Lawton Collins, *War in Peacetime,* p. 294.
82. Puryear, p. 121.
83. *Ibid.,* p. 197.
84. *Ibid.,* p. 316.
85. Martin Blumenson, *Bloody River,* p. 41.
86. *Ibid.,* p. 42.
87. *Ibid.,* p. 69.
88. *Ibid.*
89. *Ibid.,* p. 110.
90. *Ibid.,* p. 106.
91. *Ibid.,* p. 117.
92. *Ibid.,* p. 118.
93. *Ibid.*
94. *Ibid.,* p. 130.
95. *Ibid.,* pp. 131–32.
96. *Ibid.,* pp. 132–33.
97. *Ibid.,* p. 134.
98. Mark Gayn, *Japan Diary* (New York: William Sloane Associates, 1948), p. 431, quoted in D. F. Fleming, *The Cold War and Its Origins,* II, 591.
99. D. F. Fleming, II, 593.
100. *Ibid.*
101. John Gunther, *The Riddle of MacArthur* (New York: Harper & Bros., 1951), p. 169, quoted in *ibid.,* II, 595.
102. Bert Andrews, *New York Times,* June 28, 1950, quoted in *ibid.,* p. 595.
103. I. F. Stone, *The Hidden History of the Korean War,* p. 20.
104. *New York Times,* June 21, 22, 1950, quoted in D. F. Fleming, p. 596.
105. London *Times,* June 23, 1950, quoted in *ibid.*
106. Stone, p. 9.
107. Collins, p. 18.
108. Stone, p. 60.
109. Collins, p. 138.
110. *Ibid.,* p. 99.
111. Stone, p. 111.
112. *Ibid.,* p. 132.
113. Collins, p. 144.
114. Stone, p. 178.
115. *Ibid.,* p. 256.
116. *Ibid.,* p. 257.
117. Weigley, p. 562.

118. *Nashville Tennessean,* January 19, 21, 1951, quoted in D. F. Fleming, II, 630.

119. Weigley, p. 562.

120. Stone, p. 246.

121. *Ibid.,* p. 264.

122. *Ibid.,* p. 258.

123. *Ibid.,* p. 261.

124. Hearings Before the Committee on Armed Services and the Committee on Foreign Relations, U.S. Senate, 82nd Cong., 1st Sess., Pt. 1, p. 343, quoted in D. F. Fleming, p. 635.

125. Collins, p. 294.

126. Stone, p. 312.

127. *Ibid.,* pp. 308–09.

128. Collins, p. 326.

129. Stone, p. 348.

130. *The New York Times,* April 28, 1970.

131. AUSA, *The Membership and Information Guide to the Association of the U.S. Army,* second edition.

132. "Chapter Review," *The World Wars Officer Review,* March-April 1971, p. 31.

133. *Ibid.*

134. MOWW literature.

135. "New Chief of Staff for MOWW," *The World Wars Officer Review,* January-February 1971, p. 14.

136. Lester L. Wheeler, "The Law and the Order," *The World Wars Officer Review,* January-February 1971, p. 21.

137. Wheeler, "The Law and the Order," *The World Wars Officer Review,* March-April 1971, p. 11.

138. P. A. "Dick" Horton, "To Sin by Silence," *The World Wars Officer Review,* March-April 1971, p. 21.

139. Jerry W. Asher, "Danger in Disarmament," *The World Wars Officer Review,* January-February 1971, pp. 7–12.

140. TROA literature.

141. ROA literature.

142. "Carrying Out R.O.A.'s Mission in the Nation's Capital," *R.O.A. President's Manual,* p. 10.

143. *Ibid.,* p. 11.

144. *R.O.A. President's Manual.*

145. William C. Westmoreland in a Reserve Officers' Association pamphlet titled *Why R.O.A.*

146. "Table of Contents," *Army,* October 1970.

147. Bruce Palmer, Jr., "Challenges Give Unique Chance to Better Army," *Army,* October 1970, p. 30.

148. Letter to Lt. Gen. J. J. Tolson III from the unidentified lieutenant.

149. Palmer, p. 31.

150. Gen. Bruce K. Holloway, "AFA—Effective Voice of Aerospace Power," *Air Force Magazine,* January 1972, p. 72.

151. Samuel E. H. France, Report from the Classes," *Assembly,* Fall 1971, p. 82.

152. Richard Gott, *Guerrilla Movements in Latin America,* p. 116.

153. *Ibid.,* pp. 116–17.

154. *Ibid.,* p. 117.

155. Stockholm International Peace Research Institute, *SIPRI Yearbook of World Armaments and Disarmament,* Volumes for 1968/69, pp. 230–40, and 1969/70, pp. 342–54.

156. "The IPA Faculty," *The IPA Review,* January 1967.

157. David Sanford, "Agitators in a Fertilizer Factory," *The New Republic,* February 11, 1967, p. 17.

158. U.S. Government pamphlet, *The Inter-American Defense Board: An Introduction to Mutual Security Planning by the American Republics,* Washington, D.C., 1959.

159. "Inter-American Defense College Educates Officers of 22 Nations," *Army Research and Development Newsmagazine,* March 1968.

160. Matthew B. Ridgway, *Soldier,* p. 184.

161. "Bridge of the Americas," *Army Digest*, September 1968, p. 17.

162. Philippe Noure, *Le Figaro*, translated in *Atlas*, May 1968, p. 9.

163. Gott, p. 488.

164. Ridgway, *Soldier*, pp. 184–185.

165. *Ibid.*, p. 186.

166. "Bulletin Board," *Assembly*, Fall 1964, p. 26.

167. "Detail of Military Officer to Serve as Director of the Military Academy of the National Guard of Nicaragua," Agreement between the U.S.A. and Nicaragua, Executive Agreement, Series 217, May 22, 1941.

168. Executive Agreement Between the United States and Guatemala, Series 214, "Detail of Military Officer to Serve as Director of Polytechnic School of Guatemala," dated May 27, 1941. Washington, D.C.: Government Printing Office, 1941.

169. Executive Agreement, Series 214, "Detail of Military Officer to Serve as Director of the Military School and the Military Academy of El Salvador," Agreement Between the U.S.A. and El Salvador, signed March 27, 1941, effective March 27, 1941. Washington, D.C.: Government Printing Office, 1941.

170. Executive Agreement, Series 211, "Military Aviation Instructors," Agreement Between the U.S.A. and Argentina Renewing the Agreement of June 29, 1940. Washington, D.C.: Government Printing Office, 1941.

171. Executive Agreement, Series 213, "Military Mission," Agreement Between the U.S.A. and Haiti, signed May 23, 1941, effective May 23, 1941. Washington, D.C.: Government Printing Office, 1941.

172. Henry S. Aurand, "The Olmsted Foundation and West Point," *Assembly*, Summer 1964, p. 32.

173. Jose Joaquin Jimenez, "Bulletin Board," *Assembly*, Winter 1967, p. 15.

174. *Ibid.*

175. Col. William G. Davidson, Jr., "Report from the Classes," *Assembly*, Fall 1971, p. 69.

176. Ernest B. Furgurson, *Westmoreland*, pp. 73–74.

177. *The New York Times*, February 16, 1962, quoted in Gott, p. 54.

178. Alan Howard, "With the Guerrillas in Guatemala," *The New Times Magazine*, June 26, 1966, p. 18.

179. Gott, pp. 104–05.

180. David Wise and Thomas B. Ross, *The Invisible Government*, p. 177.

181. *Hispanic American Report*, Vol. XV, No. 9 (November 1962), p. 799.

182. "Bulletin Board," *Assembly*, Spring 1966, p. 24.

183. "U.S.A.F.'s Major Commands and Separate Operating Agencies," *Air Force Magazine*, May 1971, p. 109.

184. Elizabeth B. Drew, "Dam Outrage: The Story of the Army Engineers," *The Atlantic*, April 1970, p. 52.

185. *Ibid.*

186. William O. Douglas, "The Public Be Damned," *Playboy*, July 1969, p. 143.

187. Drew, p. 51.

188. Paul Brooks, "The Plot to Drown Alaska," *The Atlantic Monthly*, May 1965, quoted in Gene Marine, *America the Raped*, p. 150.

189. Drew, p. 61.

190. Barron Lyons, *Tomorrow's Birthright*, p. 151.

191. Drew, p. 61.

192. Marine, p. 37.

193. Brig. Gen. Gerald F. Lillard, "Report from the Classes," *Assembly*, Summer 1971, p. 73.

194. Maj. Gen. Charles E. John-

son, "Report from the Classes," *Assembly,* Summer 1971, p. 81.

195. Brig. Gen. Linscott A. Wall, "Report from the Classes," *Assembly,* Fall 1971, p. 74.

196. Ben Moreell, "50 Years of Engineering," *The Military Engineer,* July-August 1970, p. 230.

197. "Strategic Air Command," *Air Force Magazine,* May 1971, p. 58.

198. Alan Emory, "Official News Proposal Jolts Congress," *Washington Post,* July 12, 1971.

199. Thomas J. Fleming, p. vi.

200. Edgar Ulsamer, "Status Report on Laser Weapons," *Air Force Magazine,* January 1972, p. 63.

201. Air Force Systems Command," *Air Force Magazine,* May 1971, p. 76.

202. *Ibid.*

203. Donald Barthelme, *Unspeakable Practices, Unnatural Acts,* p. 51.

204. "Air Force Systems Command," *Air Force Magazine,* May 1971, p. 81.

205. Address by William C. Westmoreland at the Annual Luncheon of the Association of the U.S. Army, October 14, 1969, as inserted in the U.S., *Congressional Record,* 91st Cong., 2nd Sess., July 13, 1970, p. S11104.

206. *Ibid.,* p. S11105.

207. U.S., Congress, Senate Committee on Armed Forces, *Hearings Before the Electronic Battlefield Subcommittee of the Preparedness Investigating Subcommittee,* 91st Cong., 2nd Sess., 1970, p. 140.

208. William P. Schlitz, "Aerospace World," *Air Force Magazine,* April 1971, p. 13.

209. Committee on Armed Forces, *Hearings . . . Electronic Battlefield . . . ,* p. 7.

210. *Ibid.,* p. 127.

211. *Ibid.,* p. 3.

212. Gen. George S. Brown, quoted in Edgar Ulsamer, "AFSC: Foundation for the Air Force," *Air Force Magazine,* April 1971, p. 45.

213. *Ibid.*

214. Committee on Armed Forces, *Hearings . . . Electronic Battlefield . . . ,* p. 33.

215. William C. Westmoreland, quoted by Maj. Gen. William A. Knowlton in *Congressional Record,* May 26, 1971, p. E5091.

216. Barthelme, p. 52.

CHAPTER 6

1. Frank Linnell, "Report from the Classes," *Assembly,* Winter 1971, p. 71.

2. Elvin R. Heiberg, ". . . West Point . . . A.D. 2000," *Assembly,* Winter 1964, p. 13.

3. John F. Kennedy, speech to cadets, June 6, 1962, quoted in *Assembly,* Winter 1964, p. 3.

4. Edgar F. Puryear, Jr., *Nineteen Stars,* p. 321.

5. *Ibid.*

6. *Ibid.,* p. 322.

7. Adam Yarmolinsky, *The Military Establishment,* pp. 27–28.

8. Samuel P. Huntington, *The Soldier and the State,* pp. 322–23.

9. Sidney Lens, *The Military-Industrial Complex,* p. 39.

10. Douglas MacArthur, speech to cadets, May 12, 1962, USMA.

11. Lt. Col. Clinton E. Granger, Jr., "Report from the Classes," *Assembly,* Fall 1971, p. 89.

12. Robert A. Lovett, speech to cadets, May 2, 1964, USMA.

13. Richard G. Hewlett and Oscar E. Anderson, Jr., *The New World, 1939/1946,* I, 453.

14. *Ibid.,* p. 502.

15. *Ibid.,* p. 503.

16. *Ibid.,* Appendix I.

17. Interview with Brig. Gen. Richard Groves, July 8, 1971.

18. "From the Good Earth to the Sea of Rains," *Time,* August 9, 1971, p. 10.

19. Richard Egan, "Moon Mail Proves Too Hot to Handle," *National Observer*, July 22, 1972.

20. Interview with Jacob E. Smart, June 1971.

21. *Time*, June 28, 1971, p. 49.

22. Interview with William McKee, June 1971.

23. Quoted in U.S., Congress, Senate Committee on Commerce, *Hearings on S. 1900, Appointment of Wm. F. McKee to Administrator of FAA*, 89th Cong., 1st Sess., 1965, p. 2.

24. This and following testimony drawn from *ibid.*, pp. 13–25.

25. Letter from Lyndon Johnson to William McKee, quoted in "Report from the Classes," *Assembly*, Fall 1968, p. 54.

26. Don K. Price, *The Scientific Estate*, p. 22.

27. *Ibid.*, p. 23.

28. *Ibid.*, p. 31.

29. Huntington, pp. 464–66.

30. Neill MacCaulay, *The Sandino Affair*, p. 230.

31. *Ibid.*, p. 113.

32. *The New York Times*, October 10, 1927.

33. See "At Odds over Nicaragua," *The New York Times*, October 21, 1927, and "Urge Nicaraguans to Boycott Polls," *The New York Times*, April 22, 1938.

34. "Good-bye to Nicaragua," *Literary Digest*, February 28, 1931, p. 8.

35. MacCaulay, p. 127.

36. Matthew B. Ridgway, *Soldier*, p. 38.

37. *The New York Times*, March 17, 1928.

38. Ridgway, p. 38.

39. *The New York Times*, November 10, 1928.

40. Clyde H. Metcalf, *A History of the United States Marine Corps*, p. 439.

41. Harold Norman Denny, *Dollars for Bullets*, p. 9.

42. *Ibid.*

43. MacCaulay, p. 253.

44. Franklin Parker, *The Central American Republics*, p. 229.

45. *Hispanic American Report*, May 1963, p. 243, cited in Clefford A. Hauberg, *Latin American Revolutions*, p. 370.

46. MacCaulay, p. 259.

47. *Hispanic American Report*, April 1963, p. 124.

48. *Time*, November 15, 1948, p. 46.

49. G. A. Arbatov and V. A. Matreyev, "Discussions in Baltimore," *Baltimore Sunday Sun*, February 13, 1972.

50. Amos A. Jordan, Jr., "Colonel Lincoln Retires," *Assembly*, Spring 1969, p. 39.

51. *Ibid.*, p. 40.

52. *Ibid.*

53. Amos A. Jordan, Jr. (ed.), *Issues of National Security in the 1970's*, p. 3.

54. U.S., Congress, Senate Committee on Armed Services, *Hearings on Nomination of Gen. George A. Lincoln to be Director of OEP*, 91st Cong., 1st Sess., 1969, p. 14.

55. U.S., Congress, Senate Committee on Foreign Relations, *Hearings on S. 2751, Appointment of Col. George A. Lincoln*, 85th Cong., 1st Sess., August 20, 1957, pp. 2–3.

56. Committee on Armed Services, *Hearings*, p. 14.

57. Committee on Foreign Relations, *Hearings*, p. 6.

58. Jordan, *Issues . . .*, p. 15.

59. Jordan, "Colonel Lincoln Retires," p. 41.

60. Jordan, *Issues . . .*, p. 20.

61. Interview with Lou Neeb, June 1971.

62. Committee on Armed Services, *Hearings*, p. 15.

63. Committee on Foreign Relations, *Hearings*, p. 15.

64. U.S., Cabinet Task Force on Oil Import Control, *The Oil Import*

Question (Washington, D.C.: Government Printing Office, 1970).

65. George A. Lincoln, speech to National LP-Gas Association, May 5, 1971.

66. Interview, May 1971.

67. Committee on Armed Services, *Hearings*, p. 14.

68. Committee on Foreign Relations, *Hearings*, p. 4.

69. *Ibid.*, p. 18.

70. Interview with Anthony Smith, May 1971.

71. *Washington Evening Star*, August 17, 1971.

72. Interview, May 1971.

73. Interview, June 1971.

74. Interview, June 1971.

75. "Nixon Trip Planner Basks in Anonymity," *St. Louis Post-Dispatch*, January 2, 1972.

76. Brig. Gen. Monro MacCloskey, "Report from the Classes," *Assembly*, Fall 1971, p. 59.

77. C. Wright Mills, *The Power Elite*, p. 171.

CHAPTER 7

1. Burton C. Andrus, "Report from the Classes," *Assembly*, Summer 1969, p. 92.

2. Alvin C. Welling, "Report from the Classes," *Assembly*, Winter 1966, p. 57.

3. Fred J. Cook, *The Warfare State*, p. 66.

4. *Ibid.*, p. 69.

5. *Ibid.*, p. 71.

6. *Ibid.*

7. *Ibid.*

8. *Ibid.*

9. *Ibid.*, p. 72.

10. Jack Raymond, *Power at the Pentagon*, p. 82.

11. Sidney Lens, *The Military-Industrial Complex*, p. 18.

12. Cook, p. 77.

13. *Ibid.*

14. David Horowitz (ed.), *Corporations and the Cold War*, p. 111.

15. Cook, p. 119.

16. *Ibid.*, p. 120.

17. *Ibid.*, p. 121.

18. *Ibid.*

19. These quotes and the following are from the Military Industrial Conference, *Proceedings of the Papers and Discussions*, Chicago, February 10–11, 1955, pp. 8–89.

20. Raymond, p. 82.

21. Clarence H. Danhof, *Government Contracting and Technological Change*, p. 263.

22. U.S., Blue Ribbon Defense Panel, *Report to the President and the Secretary of Defense on the Department of Defense* (Washington, D.C.: Government Printing Office, July 1, 1970), p. 183.

23. *Ibid.*, p. 186.

24. *Ibid.*, p. 187.

25. Brig. Gen. William K. Skaer, "Report from the Classes," *Assembly*, Winter 1971, p. 69.

26. Reynolds R. Keleher, "Report from the Classes," *Assembly*, Summer 1964, p. 82.

27. Dunk Hartnell, "Report from the Classes," *Assembly*, Fall 1969, p. 86.

28. Paul Child, "Report from the Classes," *Assembly*, Winter 1971, p. 89.

29. Cook, p. 202.

30. Horowitz, p. 181.

31. Ralph E. Lapp, *The Weapons Culture*, p. 38.

32. Leonard S. Rodberg and Derek Shearer (eds.), *The Pentagon Watchers*, p. 302.

33. Lapp, p. 96.

34. Interview with William W. Quinn, August 1971.

35. Burton C. Andrus, Jr., quoting a letter from William Gurnee, "Report from the Classes," *Assembly*, Fall 1970, p. 80.

36. Rodberg and Shearer, p. 192.

37. The quotes and information on the C-5A were drawn from C. Merton Tyrrell, *Pentagon Partners*, pp. 15–17.

38. Burton C. Andrus, Jr., "Report from the Classes," *Assembly,* Fall 1970, p. 80.

39. Richard F. Kaufman, *The War Profiteers,* pp. 65–67.

40. U.S., Congress, House Committee on Armed Services, *Hearings Before the Special Subcommittee on the M-16 Rifle Program,* 90th Cong. 1st Sess., 1967, pp. 4760–4763.

41. James A. Donovan, *Militarism, U.S.A.,* p. 187.

42. Donald Duncan, "And Blessed Be the Fruit," *Ramparts,* May 1967, p. 30.

43. William G. Davidson, Jr., "Report from the Classes," *Assembly,* Winter 1969, p. 60.

44. Horowitz, p. 193.

45. *Ibid.,* p. 197.

46. Interview with computer company employee, August 1971.

47. Lt. Col. William B. DeGraf, "Report from the Classes," *Assembly,* Summer 1967, pp. 89–90.

48. Quoted in Joan Dew Schmitt, "Are Our Boys Dying in Vietnam for Offshore Oil?," *Coronet,* July 1971, p. 15.

49. Maj. Peter G. Jones, "Report from the Classes," *Assembly,* Fall 1967, p. 80.

50. William W. Turner, "Patrick Frawley: Right-Wing Moneybag," *Progressive,* September 1970, p. 14.

51. Interview with William W. Quinn, August 1971.

52. George H. Olmsted in a May 9, 1967, address to the Metropolitan Washington Board of Trade, "Three Roads to More World Trade—and Peace," printed by the International Bank of Washington, p. 13.

53. Interview with George H. Olmsted, August 1971.

54. Olmsted, "Three Roads . . . ," pp. 10–11.

CHAPTER 8

1. Lt. Gen. Arthur G. Trudeau, "Wake Up, America!," *Ordnance,* September-October 1968, p. 176.

2. Dwight D. Eisenhower, *Mandate for Change* (1963), quoted in William G. Effros, *Quotations Vietnam: 1945–1970,* p. 150.

3. Richard M. Nixon, "Unforgettable John Foster Dulles," *Reader's Digest,* July 1967, p. 103.

4. Dwight D. Eisenhower, speech at the Naval War College, October 3, 1961, quoted in *The New York Times,* June 20, 1971.

5. From the statement of U.S. policy delivered at the concluding session of the Geneva Conference by Under Secretary of State Walter Bedell Smith on July 21, 1954, quoted in *The Pentagon Papers* as published by *The New York Times* (New York: Bantam Books, 1971), pp. 52–53.

6. *The Pentagon Papers,* pp. 53–66.

7. Roger Hilsman, Foreword to Vo Nguyen Giap, *People's War, People's Army,* p. xv.

8. *Ibid.,* p. xviii.

9. *Ibid.,* p. xv.

10. Trudeau, p, 176.

11. Hilsman, in Giap, p. viii.

12. Roger Hilsman, *To Move a Nation,* p. 470.

13. Ralph Stavins *et al., Washington Plans an Aggressive War,* p. 9.

14. *Ibid.*

15. Hilsman, in Giap, p. xiv.

16. G. P. Baldwin, "The Strategy of the Liao-Yang Campaign," *Strategy of Russo-Japanese War* (Army War College Memorandum: Washington, D.C., March 21, 1928), pp. 30–31, quoted in Dave R. Palmer, *Readings in Current Military History,* Department of Military Art and Engineering, USMA, 1969, pp. 110–11.

17. Hilsman, in Giap, p. xvi.

18. Stavins, p. 30.

19. Hilsman, in Giap, p. ix.

20. Dwight D. Eisenhower, April 7, 1954, quoted in Effros, p. 48.

21. Dwight D. Eisenhower, December 22, 1967, quoted in Effros, p. 198.
22. Hilsman, *To Move a Nation*, p. 426.
23. Palmer, p. 110.
24. *Ibid.*, pp. 47–49.
25. J. W. Woodmansee, Jr. (ed.), *Revolutionary Warfare*, Vol. III: *China and "The People's War,"* Department of History, USMA, 1970, p. 7.
26. Hilsman, in Giap, p. xv.
27. Eqbal Ahmad, "The Theory and Fallacies of Counterinsurgency," *The Nation*, August 2, 1971, p. 81.
28. Hilsman, in Giap, p. x.
29. Hilsman, *To Move a Nation*, p. 442.
30. Maxwell Taylor's November 3, 1961, report on Vietnam to President Kennedy, quoted in *The Pentagon Papers*, p. 148.
31. Cablegram from General Harkins in Saigon to Gen. Taylor, October 30, 1963, quoted in *The Pentagon Papers*, p. 221.
32. Hilsman, *To Move a Nation*, p. 487.
33. *Ibid.*, p. 494.
34. *Ibid.*, p. 521.
35. Hilsman, in Giap, p. x.
36. *Ibid.*, p. xxiii.
37. *Ibid.*, p. ix.
38. *Ibid.*, p. xxv.
39. Memorandum from Gen. Taylor, Chairman of the Joint Chiefs of Staff, to Secretary of Defense McNamara, January 22, 1964, quoted in *The Pentagon Papers*, pp. 276–77.
40. *The Pentagon Papers*, p. 291.
41. Woodmansee, pp. 7–8.
42. Palmer, Map No. 6.
43. Samuel P. Huntington, "The Bases of Accommodation," *Foreign Affairs*, July 1968, p. 649.
44. *Ibid.*, p. 652.
45. *Ibid.*, p. 649.
46. Ahmad, pp. 80–81.

47. Ralph K. Andrist, *The Long Death*, p. 171.
48. Personal experience of authors in Vietnam.
49. Andrist, p. 124.
50. Senate Document No. 331, 57th Cong., "Hearing Before the Committee on the Philippines in Relation to Affairs in the Philippine Islands" (Washington, D.C.: Government Printing Office, 1902), pp. 1607, 1619, quoted in William J. Pomeroy, "Pacification in the Philippines, 1898–1913," *France-Asie/Asia*, Summer 1967, p. 441.
51. *Ibid.*
52. Stuart C. Miller, "Our Mylai of 1900," *Transaction*, September 1970, p. 25.
53. *Ibid.*
54. Ahmad, pp. 76–77.
55. Tran Van Dinh, "Did the U.S. Stumble into the Vietnam War?," *The Christian Century*, June 5, 1968, p. 755.
56. Ernest P. Furgurson, *Westmoreland*, p. 290.
57. William C. Westmoreland, February 1, 1968, quoted in Effros, p. 89.
58. Tran Van Dinh, "The Essence and Meaning of the Vietnamese Revolution," in *The Asian Revolution and Australia* (Australia: Times Press, 1969), p. 91.
59. William C. Westmoreland, February 25, 1968, quoted in Effros, p. 92.
60. Ahmad, pp. 74–75.
61. *Ibid.*, p. 75.
62. U. S. G. Sharp and William C. Westmoreland, *Report on the War in Vietnam* (Washington, D.C.: Government Printing Office, 1968), p. 189.
63. Thomas J. Fleming, *West Point*, p. 358.
64. Jonathan Schell, *The Military Half*, p. 71.
65. J. F. Frosch, "Anatomy of a Massacre," *Playboy*, July 1970, p. 192.

66. J. Lawton Collins, October 27, 1951, quoted in Effros, p. 64.

67. From the year-end assessment of Gen. Westmoreland delivered on January 27, 1968, and quoted in *The New York Times,* July 4, 1971.

68. Earle G. Wheeler, August 31, 1968, quoted in Effros, p. 95.

69. U.S., *Congressional Record,* 92nd Cong., 1st Sess., 1971, No. 98, Part 2, p. E 6627.

70. Roger Hilsman, "Must We Invade the North," *Foreign Affairs,* April 1968, p. 426.

71. Albert N. Garland (ed.), *Infantry in Vietnam,* p. 3.

72. Hilsman, "Must We Invade the North," p. 429.

73. *Ibid.,* p. 428.

74. Mark W. Clark, February 20, 1970, quoted in Effros, p. 216.

75. Dwight D. Eisenhower, "Let's Close Ranks on the Home Front," *Reader's Digest,* April 1968, pp. 50–51.

76. Ira Eaker, quoted in "Report from the Classes," *Assembly,* Summer 1966, p. 52.

77. Spiro Agnew, quoted in "Class of 1970," *Assembly,* Summer 1970, p. 25.

78. Woodmansee, p. 9.

79. Philip S. Cage, Jr., "Report from the Classes," *Assembly,* Spring 1968, p. 84.

80. Hilsman, "Must We Invade the North," p. 430.

81. Huntington, p. 653.

82. Ahmad, p. 81.

83. Hilsman, "Must We Invade the North," p. 428.

84. Testimony of Ken Campbell before Congressman Ronald Dellums' Ad Hoc Hearing on War Crimes Responsibility, April 29, 1971.

85. Andrist, p. 227.

86. William A. Ganoe, *The History of the United States Army,* p. 327.

87. Miller, p. 25.

88. Senate Document No. 205, Part 1, 57th Cong., 1st Sess., "Charges of Cruelty, etc., to the Natives of the Philippines" (Washington, D.C.: Government Printing Office, 1902), p. 21, quoted in Pomeroy, p. 437.

89. *Washington Evening Star,* July 5, 1971.

90. Document #89, "Account of Taylor's Meeting with Saigon Generals on Unrest," *The Pentagon Papers,* p. 379.

91. "The Fourth Generation Pro Comes Home," *Assembly,* Fall 1969, pp. 28–29, 48.

92. Interview with Gordon Livingston, November 17, 1971.

93. James L. Haydon, "Report from the Classes," *Assembly,* Winter 1968, p. 84.

94. Andrist, pp. 348–52.

95. Hilsman, "Must We Invade the North," p. 430.

96. Excerpted from memorandum written by Assistant Secretary of Defense John T. McNaughton to Secretary McNamara in 1964 and quoted in *The Pentagon Papers,* p. 255.

97. William C. Westmoreland, quoted in Kenneth F. Hanst, Jr., "Report from the Classes," *Assembly,* Winter 1968, p. 78.

98. U.S. *Congressional Record,* 91st Cong., 2nd Sess., July 13, 1970, p. S 11103.

99. U.S., *Congressional Record,* 92nd Cong., 1st Sess., May 26, 1971, p. E5093.

100. J. T. Hoskins, quoted in "Be Thou at Peace," *Assembly,* Spring 1970, p. 123.

101. Gen. Mark W. Clark, "What It Takes to Be a Leader," *Reader's Digest,* July 1967, p. 161.

102. Gen. William C. Westmoreland, "An Army Taking Stock in a Changing Society," *Army,* October 1971, p. 19.

103. *Ibid.,* p. 20.

104. Gen. Ralph E. Haines, Jr.,

"COCARC Is Pace-Setter for Army in Transition," *Army,* October 1971, p. 38.

105. William Hesseltine, "The Automated Air War," *The New Republic,* October 16, 1971, p. 17.

106. Eric C. Ludvigsen, "Army Weapons, Equipment: Looking for a Breakthrough," *Army,* October 1971, p. 123.

107. Orville Schell, *American Report,* September 27, 1971.

108. George Weiss, "Battle for Control of the Ho Chi Minh Trail," *Armed Forces Journal,* February 15, 1971, p. 18.

109. *Ibid.,* p. 19.

110. U.S. Congress, Senate Committee on Armed Forces, *Hearings Before the Electronic Battlefield Subcommittee of the Preparedness Investigating Subcommittee,* 91st Cong., 2nd Sess., 1970, pp. 39–63.

111. Interview with Greg Hayward, December 13, 1971.

112. Senate Committee on Armed Forces, *Hearings* . . . , p. 205.

113. *Ibid.,* p. 96.

114. Ahmad, p. 82.

115. *Ibid.*

116. *Ibid.,* pp. 82–83.

117. *Ibid.,* p. 84.

118. Gen. Maxwell D. Taylor, "New Concept of Security," *Ordnance,* July-August 1971, p. 31.

119. Senate Committee on Armed Forces, *Hearings* . . . , pp. 18–19.

120. Dwight D. Eisenhower, "Thoughts for Young Americans," *Reader's Digest,* April 1966, p. 90.

121. Dwight D. Eisenhower, "This Country *Needs* Universal Military Training," *Reader's Digest,* September 1966, pp. 52–55.

122. Trudeau, pp. 176–77.

BIBLIOGRAPHY

BOOKS

Alba, Victor, *The Latin Americans*. New York: Frederick A. Praeger, 1969.

Ambrose, Stephen E., *Duty, Honor, Country*. Baltimore: The Johns Hopkins Press, 1966.

Andrist, Ralph K., *The Long Death: The Last Days of the Plains Indians*. New York: The Macmillan Company, 1964.

Archer, Jules, *Battlefield President*. New York: Julian Messner, 1967.

Baldwin, Hanson W., *World War I*. New York: Harper and Row, 1962.

Barnes, Peter, *Pawns: The Plight of the Citizen Soldier*. New York: Alfred A. Knopf, 1972.

Barnet, Richard J., *The Economy of Death*. New York: Atheneum, 1969.

Barnet, Richard J., *Intervention and Revolution*. New York: The World Publishing Co., 1968.

Barthelme, Donald, *Unspeakable Practices, Unnatural Acts*. New York: Bantam Books, 1968.

Bernstein, Harry, *Venezuela and Columbia*. Englewood Cliffs, N.J.: Prentice-Hall, 1964.

Blaik, Earl, *You Have to Pay the Price*. New York: Holt, Rinehart, & Winston, 1960.

Blumenson, Martin, *Bloody River*. Boston: Houghton Mifflin Co., 1970.

Borklund, Carl W., *Men of the Pentagon*. New York: Frederick A. Praeger, 1966.

Bosch, Juan, *Pentagonism*. New York: Grove Press, 1968.

BIBLIOGRAPHY

Brown, Frederick J., *Chemical Warfare: A Study in Restraints.* Princeton, N.J.: Princeton University Press, 1968.

Burkhardt, Robert, *The Federal Aviation Administration.* New York: Frederick A. Praeger, 1967.

Buttinger, Joseph, *Vietnam: A Political History.* New York: Praeger Publishers, 1968.

Carr, William H. A., *The DuPonts of Delaware.* New York: Dodd, Mead & Co., 1964.

Catton, Bruce, *U. S. Grant and the American Military Tradition.* Boston: Little, Brown and Co., 1954.

Cavaioli, Frank J., *West Point and the Presidency.* New York: St. John's University Press, 1962.

Collins, J. Lawton, *War in Peacetime.* Boston: Houghton Mifflin Co., 1969.

Cook, Fred J., *The Warfare State.* New York: Collier Books, 1969.

Cooper, Chester L., *The Lost Crusade.* New York: Dodd, Mead & Co., 1970.

Crane, John, and James F. Kieley, *West Point: The Key to America.* New York: McGraw-Hill Book Co., 1947.

Crump, Irving, *Our Army Engineers.* New York: Dodd, Mead & Co., 1954.

Cunliffe, Marcus, *Soldiers and Civilians: The Martial Spirit in America, 1775–1865.* Boston: Little, Brown & Co., 1968.

Danhof, Clarence H., *Government Contracting and Technological Change.* Washington, D.C.: The Brookings Institution, 1968.

Denny, Harold N., *Dollars for Bullets.* New York: Lincoln Mac-Veagh, 1929.

Devillers, Philippe, and Jean Lacouture, *End of a War.* New York: Frederick A. Praeger, 1969.

Dierks, Jack Cameron, *A Leap to Arms: The Cuban Campaign of 1898.* Philadelphia and New York: J. B. Lippincott Co., 1970.

Donovan, James A., *Militarism, U.S.A.* New York: Charles Scribner's Sons, 1970.

DuBoff, Richard B., and Edward S. Herman, *America's Vietnam Policy.* Washington, D.C.: Public Affairs Press, 1966.

Dupuy, R. Ernest, *The Compact History of the United States Army.* New York: Hawthorn Books, 1961.

Dupuy, R. Ernest, *Sylvanus Thayer: The Father of Technology in the United States.* West Point, N.Y.: The Association of Graduates, USMA, 1958.

Dupuy, R. Ernest, *Where They Have Trod.* New York: Frederick A. Stokes Co., 1940.

[414]

Dwiggins, Don, *The SST: Here It Comes, Ready or Not.* Garden City, N.Y.: Doubleday & Co., 1968.

Effros, William G., *Quotations Vietnam: 1945–1970.* New York: Random House, 1970.

Eisenhower, Dwight D., *In Review.* Garden City, N.Y.: Doubleday & Co., 1969.

Elliott, Charles W., *Winfield Scott: The Soldier and the Man.* New York: The Macmillan Co., 1937.

Epstein, Benjamin R., and Arnold Forster, *The Radical Right.* New York: Random House, 1966.

Esposito, Col. Vincent J., *The West Point Atlas of American Wars.* New York: Frederick A. Praeger, 1959.

Finn, James (ed.), *Conscience and Command.* New York: Random House, 1971.

Fleming, D. F., *The Cold War and Its Origins, 1950–1960,* Vol II. Garden City, N.Y.: Doubleday & Co., 1961.

Fleming, D. F., *The Origins and Legacies of World War I.* Garden City, N.Y.: Doubleday & Co., 1968.

Fleming, Thomas J., *West Point: The Men and the Times of the United States Military Academy.* New York: William Morrow & Co., 1969.

Foner, Jack D., *The United States Between Two Wars.* New York: Humanities Press, 1970.

Forster, Arnold, and Benjamin R. Epstein, *Danger on the Right.* New York: Random House, 1964.

Furgurson, Ernest B., *Westmoreland: The Inevitable General.* Boston: Little, Brown & Co., 1968.

Galbraith, John Kenneth, *How to Control the Military.* Garden City, N.Y.: Doubleday & Co., 1969.

Galbraith, John Kenneth, *The New Industrial State.* Boston: Houghton Mifflin Co., 1969.

Gale's and Seaton's Register of Debates in Congress, 1830.

Ganoe, William A., *The History of the United States Army.* Maryland: Eric Lundberg, 1964.

Garland, Albert N. (ed.), *Infantry in Vietnam.* Georgia: Infantry Magazine, 1967.

Gavin, James, *Crisis Now.* New York: Random House, 1968.

Gettleman, Marvin and Susan, and Lawrence and Carlo Kaplan, *Conflict in Indochina.* New York: Vintage Books, 1970.

Giap, Vo Nguyen, *People's War, People's Army.* New York: Frederick A. Praeger, 1962.

Gott, Richard, *Guerrilla Movements in Latin America.* Garden City, N.Y.: Doubleday & Co., 1970.

Gurney, Gene, *A Pictorial History of the United States Army*. New York: Crown Publishers, 1966.

Hatada, Taskashi, *A History of Korea*. California: American Bibliographical Center, Clio Press, 1969.

Hauberg, Clefford A., *Latin American Revolutions*. Minneapolis: T. S. Dennison & Co., 1968.

Heise, J. Arthur, *The Brass Factories*. Washington, D.C.: Public Affairs Press, 1969.

Hensman, C. R., *From Gandhi to Guevara*. London: Allen Lane, The Penguin Press, 1969.

Hersh, Seymour M., *Chemical and Biological Warfare*. New York: The Bobbs-Merrill Co., 1968.

Hesseltine, William B., and Hazel C. Wolf, *The Blue and the Gray on the Nile*. Chicago: The University of Chicago Press, 1961.

Hewlett, Richard G., and Oscar E. Anderson, Jr., *The New World, 1939/1946*, Vol. I. University Park, Pa.: Pennsylvania State University Press, 1962.

Hill, Forest G., *Roads, Rails, and Waterways*. Norman: University of Oklahoma Press, 1957.

Hilsman, Roger, *To Move a Nation*. New York: Doubleday & Co., 1967.

Horowitz, David (ed.), *Corporations and the Cold War*. New York: Mor nly Review Press, 1969.

Howarth, David, *Panama*. New York: McGraw-Hill Book Co., 1966.

Huntington, Samuel P., *The Soldier and the State*. New York: Vintage Books, 1964.

Janowitz, Morris (ed.), *The New Military*. New York: W. W. Norton & Co., 1969.

Janowitz, Morris, *The Professional Soldier*. New York: The Free Press of Glencoe, 1960.

Jordan, Amos A., Jr. (ed.), *Issues of National Security in the 1970's*. New York: Frederick A. Praeger, 1967.

Josephson, Matthew, *The Robber Barons: The Great American Capitalists 1861–1901*. New York: Harvest Books, Harcourt, Brace & World, 1962.

Just, Ward, *Military Men*. New York: Alfred A. Knopf, 1970.

Just, Ward, *To What End*. Boston: Houghton Mifflin Co., 1968.

Kahin, George M., and John W. Lewis, *The United States in Vietnam*. New York: Dell Publishing Co., 1967.

Kaufman, Richard F., *The War Profiteers*. New York: The Bobbs-Merrill Co., 1970.

Keller, Allan, *The Spanish American War: A Compact History.* New York: Hawthorn Books, 1969.

King, Edward L., *The Death of the Army.* New York: Saturday Review Press, 1972.

Lapp, Ralph E., *Arms Beyond Doubt.* New York: Cowles Book Co., 1970.

Lapp, Ralph E., *The Weapons Culture.* New York: W. W. Norton & Co., 1968.

LeMay, Curtis E., *America Is in Danger.* New York: Funk & Wagnalls, 1968.

Lenney, John J., *Caste System in the American Army.* New York: Greenberg, 1949.

Lens, Sidney, *The Military-Industrial Complex.* Philadelphia: Pilgrim Press and the National Catholic Reporter, 1970.

Lincoln, George A., and Norman J. Padelford, *The Dynamics of International Politics.* New York: The Macmillan Co., 1962.

Lyons, Barron, *Tomorrow's Birthright.* New York: Funk & Wagnalls, 1955.

MacCaulay, Neill, *The Sandino Affair.* Chicago: Quadrangle Books, 1967.

Mailer, Norman, *The Naked and the Dead.* New York: New American Library, 1948.

Marine, Gene, *America the Raped.* New York: Simon & Schuster, 1969.

Matloff, Maurice (ed.), *American Military History.* Washington, D.C.: Army Historical Series, Office of the Chief of Military History, 1969.

May, Ernest R., *American Imperialism: A Speculative Essay.* New York: Atheneum, 1967.

McAlister, John T., Jr., *Vietnam: The Origins of Revolution.* New York: Alfred A. Knopf, 1969.

Metcalf, Clyde H., *A History of the United States Marine Corps.* New York: G. P. Putnam's Sons, 1939.

Military Industrial Conference, *Proceedings of the Papers and Discussions,* February 10–11, 1955.

Mills, C. Wright, *The Power Elite.* New York: Oxford University Press, 1959.

Morgan, Arthur E., *Dams and Other Disasters.* Boston: Porter Sargent, 1971.

Morin, Relman, *Dwight D. Eisenhower.* New York: Simon and Schuster, 1969.

New York Times, The, *The Pentagon Papers.* New York: Bantam Books, 1971.

Olsen, Jack, *Aphrodite: Desperate Mission.* New York: G. P. Putnam's Sons, 1970.

Pappas, George S., *The Cadet Chapel, United States Military Academy.* Buffalo: Holling Press, 1965.

Parker, Franklin, *The Central American Republics.* New York: Oxford University Press, 1964.

Peck, Merton J., and Frederic M. Scherer, *The Weapons Acquisition Process: An Economic Analysis.* Boston: Division of Research, Graduate School of Business Administration, Harvard University, 1962.

Petras, James, *Politics and Social Structure in Latin America.* New York: Monthly Review Press, 1970.

Price, Don K., *The Scientific Estate.* Cambridge, Mass.: Harvard University Press, 1965.

Puryear, Edgar F., Jr., *Nineteen Stars.* Washington, D.C.: Coiner Publications, 1971.

Raymond, Jack, *Power at the Pentagon.* New York: Harper & Row, 1964.

Remarque, Erich Maria, *All Quiet on the Western Front.* Boston: Little, Brown and Co., 1928.

Richardson, James D. (ed.), *The Messages and Papers of Jefferson Davis and the Confederacy,* Vols. I & II. New York: Chelsea House–Robert Hector, 1966.

Ridgway, Matthew B., *Soldier: The Memoirs of Matthew B. Ridgway.* New York: Harper & Brothers, 1956.

Robson, John M. (ed.), *John Stuart Mill: A Selection of His Works.* Toronto: Macmillan of Canada, 1966.

Rodberg, Leonard S., and Derek Shearer (eds.), *The Pentagon Watchers.* Garden City, N.Y.: Doubleday & Co., 1970.

Rodman, Selden, *The Guatemala Traveler.* New York: Meredith Press, 1967.

Rodriguez, Mario, *Central America.* Englewood Cliffs, N.J.: Prentice-Hall, 1965.

Sandoz, Mari, *Cheyenne Autumn.* New York: Avon Books, 1953.

Schell, Jonathan, *The Military Half.* New York: Alfred A. Knopf, 1968.

Schlesinger, Arthur M., Jr., *A Thousand Days.* Boston: Houghton Mifflin Co., 1965.

Speer, Albert, *Inside the Third Reich.* Toronto: The Macmillan Co., 1970.

Stavins, Ralph, *et al., Washington Plans an Aggressive War.* New York: Random House, 1971.

Steinbeck, John, *East of Eden*. New York: The Viking Press, 1952.

Stone, I. F., *The Hidden History of the Korean War*. New York: Monthly Review Press, 1952.

Swomley, John M., Jr., *The Military Establishment*. Boston: Beacon Press, 1964.

Taylor, Maxwell D., *The Uncertain Trumpet*. New York: Harper & Brothers, 1959.

Tebbel, John, *The Compact History of the Indian Wars*. New York: Tower Publications, 1966.

Tinker, C. B., and H. F. Lowry (eds.), *The Political Works of Matthew Arnold*. London: Oxford University Press, 1950.

Tucker, Glenn, *Lee and Longstreet at Gettysburg*. Indianapolis: The Bobbs-Merrill Co., 1968.

Tyrrell, C. Merton, *Pentagon Partners: The New Mobility*. New York: Grossman Publishers, 1970.

Weigley, Russell F., *History of the United States Army*. New York: The Macmillan Co., 1967.

West Point Alumni Foundation, *Register of Graduates and Former Cadets of the United States Military Academy, 1802–1970*. West Point, N.Y.: West Point Alumni Foundation, 1970.

White, Theodore H. (ed.), *The Stilwell Papers*. New York: William Sloane Associates, 1948.

Wise, David, and Thomas B. Ross, *The Invisible Government*. New York: Random House, 1964.

Yarmolinsky, Adam, *The Military Establishment*. New York: Harper & Row, 1971.

U.S. GOVERNMENT PUBLICATIONS

Hearings on the Administration of the Service Academies Before the Committee on Armed Services, U.S. House of Representatives, 90th Congress, 1st and 2nd Sessions. Washington, D.C.: Government Printing Office, 1967–68.

Hearings on S. 2751, Appointment of Col. George A. Lincoln, Before the Committee on Foreign Relations, U.S. Senate, 85th Congress, 1st Session. Washington, D.C.: Government Printing Office, 1957.

Hearings on S. 1900, Appointment of Wm. F. McKee to Administrator of FAA, Before the Committee on Commerce, U.S. Senate, 89th Congress, 1st Session. Washington, D.C.: Government Printing Office, 1965.

Hearings Before the Electronic Battlefield Subcommittee of the Preparedness Investigating Subcommittee of the Committee on Armed Services, U.S. Senate, 91st Congress, 2nd Session, Nov. 18, 19, & 24, 1970. Washington, D.C.: Government Printing Office, 1971.

Hearings on the Nomination of Gen. George A. Lincoln to Be Director of OEP, Before the Committee on Armed Services, U.S. Senate, 91st Congress, 1st Session. Washington, D.C.: Government Printing Office, 1969.

Hearings Before the Special Subcommittee on the M-16 Rifle Program of the Committee on Armed Services, U.S. House of Representatives, 90th Congress, 1st Session. Washington, D.C.: Government Printing Office, 1967.

U.S., *American State Papers, Military Affairs,* Vol. 7. Washington, D.C., 1837.

U.S., Congress, House Committee on Armed Services, *Hearings,* 92nd Congress, 1st Session, March 11, 1971.

U.S., *Congressional Globe,* 37th Congress, 2nd Session, Vol. 32, January 1863.

U.S., *Congressional Record,* 91st Congress, 2nd Session, July 13, 1970.

U.S., *Congressional Record,* 92nd Congress, 1st Session, May 26, 1971, Vol. 117, No. 79.

U.S., *Congressional Record,* 92nd Congress, 1st Session, June 24, 1971, No. 98, Part II.

U.S., *The Inter-American Defense Board: An Introduction to Mutual Security Planning by the American Republics.* Washington, D.C.: Government Printing Office, 1959.

U.S., Cabinet Task Force on Oil Import Control, *The Oil Import Question.* Washington, D.C.: Government Printing Office, 1970.

U.S., Blue Ribbon Defense Panel, *Report to the President and the Secretary of Defense on the Department of Defense.* Washington, D.C.: Government Printing Office, 1970.

U.S., G. Sharp and William C. Westmoreland, *Report on the War in Vietnam.* Washington, D.C.: Government Printing Office, 1968.

USMA DOCUMENTS

USMA, Office of the Dean, *Academic Program, Academic Year 1971–1972,* February 12, 1971.

USMA, *Bugle Notes 1970* (Vol. 62).

USMA, *Cadet Notebook History of Europe and America 1500–1870,* Social Science 201, Academic Year 1968–69, Department of Social Sciences, September 1968.

BIBLIOGRAPHY

USMA, *Department of English Handbook,* 1969–70.

USMA, Capt. E. B. Elliott, Jr., *English 102 Lesson Plan,* Academic Year 1968–69.

USMA, *Instructor Syllabus,* English 102, Academic Year 1968–69.

USMA, *The New Cadet: Information for the Parents of the Class of 1975.*

USMA, Dave R. Palmer, *Readings in Current Military History,* Department of Military Art and Engineering, 1969.

USMA, *Regulations, United States Corps of Cadets.*

USMA, J. W. Woodmansee, Jr. (ed.), *Revolutionary Warfare,* Vol. III: *China and "The People's War,"* Department of History, 1970.

USMA, *Room Arrangements East Barracks, U.S.C.C.,* January 26, 1966.

USMA, *Teaching in the Department of Social Sciences,* 1968.

MAGAZINES

Air Force Magazine, 1971–72.

Armed Forces Journal, 1971.

Army, 1970–71.

Army Digest, 1968

Army Research and Development News Magazine, 1968

Army Reserve Magazine, 1970

Assembly, 1964–71

The Atlantic, 1970

Atlas, 1968

The Christian Century, 1968

Coronet, 1971

Foreign Affairs, 1968

France-Asie/Asia, 1967

Hispanic American Report, 1962–63

The IPA Review, 1967

Literary Digest, 1931

Look, Oct. 6, 1970

The Military Engineer, 1970

The Nation, 1971

The New Republic, 1967, 1971

The New York Times Magazine, 1966, 1970

Ordnance, 1969, 1971

Playboy, 1969–70

Progressive, 1970–71

Ramparts, 1967

BIBLIOGRAPHY

Reader's Digest, 1966–68
Time, 1948, 1971
Transaction, 1970
The World Wars Officer Review, 1971

INDEX

INDEX

Beukema, Col. Herman, 24, 280
Binh Duong province (South
  Vietnam), 355–56
Biographical Data Cards, 72
Bishop, William M., 334
Bismarck, Otto von, 158
Black, Percy G., 330
Black Class (1946), 22
Black Hawk War, 126–27
Black Sparrow Hawk, 126
Blackfeet Indians, 358
Blaik, Earl, 116–17, 122
Blair, Francis P., 153
Blair, Montgomery, 138–39, 153
Blake, Gordon, 329
Blakeslee, W. S., 190
Blind-bombing technique, 231–32
Bliss, William Wallace Smith, 25,
  155
Blockbuster bomb, 229
Blue Ribbon Defense Panel, 307
Blue Steel Trophy, 226
Blurton, Craig, 7
Board of Officers, expulsion of
  cadets and, 111
Boeing Corp., 265–66, 314
Bolivia, 197, 201, 206
Bomb manufacturers, 323–25
Bomford, Col. George, 127
Bonesteel, Gen. Charles H., 163,
  283, 391
Bonus Marchers (1932), 166, 167
Boone, Abbott, 133
Borman, Frank, 258, 319
Bowen, Lt. Gen. John W. (Ret.),
  186
Bower, John Lindsay, 392
Boy Scouts, 81
Boyd, William, 312
Bradley, Mark E., 315
Bradley, General of the Army
  Omar N., 24, 136, 163, 164,
  166, 239, 324, 391
  Korean War and, 172–74
  on military-industrial
    cooperation, 25
Bradley, Mrs. Omar N., 24
Bragg, Gen. Braxton, 140
Braun, Chester V., 315
Brazil, 186, 197, 204
Breakiron, Col. Richard C., 103
Breckinridge, William M., 244

Breit, John Martin, 391
Brett, James Q., 335
Briggs, Brig. Gen. James E., 177
Brooks, Paul, 221
Broshous, Col. Russ, 93
Brown, Maj. Gen. Albert E., 171
Brown, Burton Robert, 392
Brown, Gen. George S., 31, 227–
  28, 232, 327
Brown, Harold McDonald, 392
Brown, Gen. Jacob, 127
Brown, Vance S., Jr., 209
Browne & Shaw Research Corp.,
  384
Brownfield, Brig. Gen. Albert R.
  (Ret.), 183–86, 354
Bucha, Capt. Buddy, 29–30
Buckley, William F., 30
Buckner, Gen. Simon Bolivar, 140,
  154
Buehler, Bud, 224
Buehler, Helen, 224
Bull, Lt. Gen. Harold R., 164, 303
Bull Run, first Battle of (1861),
  157
Bulova Watch Co., 24–25, 324
Bunting, Josiah, 7
Burnside, Gen. Ambrose, 140, 141,
  156, 157
Burr, Edward, II, 392
Bush, Vannevar, 251
Business
  West Pointers' influence on
    (19th century), 156
  See also Defense industry;
    Military-industrial complex
Business Week, 309
Butchers, Ralph Joseph, 391
Butler, Maj. Gen Smedley, 296–97
Buzhardt, J. Fred, Jr., 27, 307–9
Byers, Clovis E., 330
Byrnes, James, 279, 301

C-5A aircraft, 188, 316–18, 320
CAA (Civil Aeronautics
  Administration), 260–61
CAB (Civil Aeronautics Board),
  261
Cade, Kathy, 7
Cadet Prayer, quoted, 100

[426]

INDEX

Domhoff, William, 297
Dominican Republic, 196, 204,
    220, 316
Donelson, Andrew Jackson, 153
Donham, Cary, 124
Dooley, Tom, 235
Doubleday, Abner, 27
Douglas, William O., 221
Draft, peacetime, 303, 304;
    See also Selective Service
    System
Draper, William H., 281
Drug addicts, West Point's hiring
    of former, 29–30
Drum, James H., 318, 327
DSA (Defense Supply Agency),
    220
Duffy, Irving, 336
Dulles, John Foster, 172, 280–81,
    344
Dunford, Donald, 391
Du Pont, Henry, 25–26, 142, 156
Du Pont, Henry Algernon, 25, 142
Du Pont de Nemours, Pierre
    Samuel, 142
Dupuy, R. Ernest, 147, 148
Dupuy, Trevor N., 384
Durfee, Capt. L. V. H., 273
Duscha, Julius, 297
Dyer, Vice-Adm. George, 183
Dzau, Linson Edward, 212

Eagles, William, 164
Early, Gen. Jubal, 25
Eastman Kodak Co., 325
Eaton, John Henry, 153
Eckhardt, Maj. Gen. George S.,
    224
Ecological criticism of Corps of
    Engineers, 221–22
Ecuador, 204, 208, 213–15
Eddleman, Gen. Clyde D., 321
Edgerton, Maj. Gen. Glen E., 239
Educational profession, West
    Point graduates in (1802–
    67), 154
Edwards, Morris Oswald, 392
Egypt, 158–59
Egyptian Military Academy, 158–
    59

Ehrlichman, John, 32, 235
Eisenhower, General of the Army
    Dwight D., 180
    AEC and, 255, 256
    on Communist threat, 344
    on draft-card burners, 387
    on Geneva Agreements (1954),
        344–45
    Jiménez and, 209
    Brig. Gen. Lincoln and, 279,
        280, 285
    on military-industrial complex,
        25
    on military training, 303, 387–
        88
    Patton and, 167
    on Viet Minh, 344
    on Vietnam war, 348–49, 366–
        67
    in World War II, 165–67, 238
El Salvador, military academy of,
    206
Electronic (automated)
    battlefield, 229–33, 353,
        354, 377–83, 386
Eliot, Charles W., 160–61
Elitist or aristocratic attitudes of
    West Pointers, 17–18, 21,
    41–43, 64, 134–36, 141–44,
    149–50, 154, 156, 246, 367,
    368
Elliot, Charles Winslow, 401
Ellis, Robert James, 392
Ellison, Ralph, 73, 89
Elmore, Gen. Vincent, Jr., 200
Elvir, Hugo Enrique, 216
Emerson, Brig. Gen. Henry E.,
    376, 377
Emory, William H., 155
Engineering Department, 87
English Department, 81
    grading system in, 87
    typical course in, 88–90
Esposito, Col. Vincent J., 361
Estes, Gen. Howell M., 316, 319
European Command, 199
Evans, Giles L., 223
Evans, Roy T., 335
Evans, Brig. Gen. William J.,
    231
Ewell, Lt. Gen. Julian J., 100–1,
    125, 376, 380

[430]

INDEX

Lotz, Maj. Gen. Walter E., 330
Lovett, Robert A., 243
Low, Maj. Gen. Andrew S., 326
Lowry Air Force Base, 121
Lucas, Louis F., 187
Lynde, Maj. Gen. Nelson M., Jr., 26, 322

M-16 rifle, 26, 35, 322–23
MAAG (Military Assistance Advisory Groups), 219
MacArthur, General of the Army Douglas, 254, 278
  in Korean War, 172–81, 241
  on political role of West Point graduates, 241
  in World War II, 161, 166, 167, 238
MacDonald, Malcolm Eldridge, 392
MacDonald, Peter, 190
Macomb, Gen. Alexander, 127, 151, 152
Magnotti, John Francis, Jr., 392
Magnuson, Warren, 262
Mahan, Capt. Alfred Thayer, 156
Mahan, Dennis Hart, 156
Maish, Alexander Morton, 392
Malek, Frederick V., 235
Mandelbaum, Albert Joseph, 392
Manhattan Engineer District (MED), 253
Manhattan Project, 251–53
Mao Tse–tung, 69, 350, 354–55
MAP (Military Assistance Program), 218–19
March, Maj. Peyton C., 162
Marcus, Col. David, 24
Marine Corps, U.S.
  as defender of business interests in Latin America, 296–97
  in Nicaragua, 269–75
Marine Corps League, 181
Marion, Francis, 142
Marmaduke, John S., 156
Marriage, prohibition of, 108
Marshall, Gen. George C., 164–65, 174, 251, 279
Marshall, Col. James C., 251
Marston, Morrill Elwood, 392
Martelino, Pastor, 210

Martin-Marietta Co., 188, 311
Mason, James Murray, 142
MASSTER (Mobile Army Sensor System Test and Review), 230
Mathematics Department
  disciplinary role of, 293
  grading system in, 86–87
  teaching techniques in, 96–98
  training of instructors in, 96
Mather, Gen. Robinson, 201–2
Matthews, Willis Small, 391
Maxwell, Russell L., 323
McChristian, Maj. Gen. Joseph A., 245, 356
McClellan, Gen. George B., 141, 155, 156
McCollam, William, 335
McConnell, Gen. John P., 192, 225, 310, 316–18, 349
McCook, Gen. Alexander, 140
McCormack, James, 256, 329
McCormick, G. Paul, 190
McCoy, Gen. Frank Ross, 164, 196, 203, 205, 269, 271–74, 278
McCreery, Sir Richard, 168
McDermott, Robert F., 118
McDowell, Irvin, 153
McGee, Arthur Alten, 392
McGuire, Capt. John S., 132–33
McHenry, James, 145
McKee, Gen. William, 262–68
McKinly, William, 157
McLamb, Peyton F., 223
McLane, Robert M., 153
McMahon, Brien, 253, 254
McManus, James, 224
McManus, Tom, 224
McNair, Maj. Gen. Lesley J., 165
McNamara, Lt. Gen. Andrew (Ret.), T., 186
McNamara, Robert, 263, 265, 317, 354
McNarney, Gen. Joseph T., 308–9
McNeill, Albert, 151
McNeill, William G., 151, 152
McRee, Col. William, 148
Mead, Lt. Col. Dana, 32, 235
Meade, Armistead Davis, 391
Meade, Gen. George G., 139–40, 155

NASA (National Aeronautics and
Space Administration),
191, 250, 257–60, 263, 267
Nation, The (magazine), 272
National Election Board
(Nicaragua), 272
National Guard Association, 181
National Honor Society, 81
National Liberation Front
(Vietnam), *see* Viet Cong
National Merit Scholarship, 81
National Petroleum Council, 333
National Pilots Association, 265
National Security Industrial
Association, 325–27
National War College, 192
Nationalist China, Korean War
and, 177
NATO (North Atlantic Treaty
Organization), 194–95, 219
Naval Academy, U.S., 186
Navigation routes, 19th-century
development of, 151–52
Navy, U.S., aerospace industry and,
318, 320–21
Navy League of the U.S., 181
Naylor, William Edward, Jr.,
392
Nazzaro, Gen. Joseph J., 123
NDTA (National Defense
Transportation Associa-
tion), 320, 325–26
Neeb, Lou, 284
Nelson, Donald, 299–302
Nelson, Gaylord, 221
Nelson, Ralph Thomas, 391
New York Times, The, 167n, 181,
272
on Korean War, 176–78
Newgarden, Maj. Gen. Paul, 163
Newman, Maj. Gen. A. S. 38,
39
Newman, Col. George E., 128
News media, Holloway on, 226
Nhu, Ngo Dinh, 351–53, 393–95
Nicaragua
military academy of, 205–6
Sandino revolt in, 196, 270–71,
273, 275
Somoza dynasty in, 275–77
U.S. business interests in, 270–
71

Nicaragua (*cont.*)
U.S. counter-insurgency team in,
201, 204
U.S. Marines' occupation of,
269–75
U.S. supervision of 1928
elections in, 196, 203, 269,
271–74
Nicholas, Col. Charles Parsons,
96–98, 204
Nicholls, Francis R. T., 156
Nichols, Maj. Gen. Kenneth D.,
239, 251, 255–56
Nixon, Richard M., 234
Cambodia invasion and (1971),
181, 186, 193
Chapel-attendance law suit and,
62
on Communist threat, 344
on Dulles, 344
Gen. Haig and, 294–95
Gen. Lincoln and, 283, 285,
287–88
MAP and, 218
NSC and, 287–88, 291
OEP and, 284
oil policy of, 285–87, 333
paramilitary organizations and,
181–83, 186–88, 193
Somoza and, 23
Vietnam war policy of, 193
West Pointers in staff of, 31–32,
235
NORAD (North American Air
Defense Command), 219
Norris, Maj. Gen. Frank W., 377
Norstad, Lauris, 280, 319, 334,
335, 392
North American Rockwell Corp.,
314
North Atlantic Treaty Organization
(NATO), 194–95, 219
North Vietnam, bombing of, 354,
366, 368
Norton, Lt. Gen. John, 382–83
Noure, Philippe, 404
NRA (National Rifle Association),
181, 187–88
NSA (National Security Agency),
243
NSC (National Security Council),
284, 287–92

INDEX

Sverdrup & Parcel & Associates,
223
Sweet, Col. Trevor Washington,
205
Sweet, Trevor W., Jr., 134
Swift, Alexander J., 152
Swift, Brig. Gen. Joseph G., 26,
148, 152
Swift, Joseph G. (grandson), 152
Swing, Joseph M., 239
Swope, Gerard, 302
Sylvania Electronics Products Co.,
330
Systems Command (USAF), 228,
229, 232–33

TAC (company tactical officer),
function of, 57–58
Tactics Department, 72, 73, 132
Taft, William Howard, 271
Tampico (Mexico), 297
Tan Quan District Provincial
Reconnaissance Unit, 128
Tanous, Peter S., 212
Tao Hung Chang, 212
Task Force Barker, 365
Task Force Oregon, 356
Tay Ninh province (South
Vietnam), 356
Taylor, Maj. Gen. Livingston N.,
Jr., 219
Taylor, Gen. Maxwell D., 41, 248,
337, 365, 387
ABM debate and, 309
on "beating the system" at West
Point, 45
in Counter-insurgency
Committee, 197
in Korean War, 180–81
on Brig. Gen. Lincoln, 282
Vietnam war and, 349, 351, 353–
54, 363, 364, 370–71, 379,
385–86
in World War II, 180
Taylor, Zachary, 25, 154, 155
Teaching techniques, 71–77, 79–
83, 94–98
Test and Evaluation Command,
200
Tests, academic, 87–88, 108
Thailand, 194, 211

Thayer, Maj. Sylvanus, 67, 147–
51, 156, 367
Thayer Hall, description of, 66–69
Thayer Hotel, 22
Thi, Gen. Nguyen Chanh, 370–71
Thieu, Gen. Nguyen Van, 370–71
Think tanks, 248–50, 384, 391–92
Thomas, Gary P., 336
Thomas, Gen. George H., 140
Thompson, Maj. Gen. Charles,
163
Thompson, John R., 17
Thompson, Paul W., 134–35, 227
Thompson, Sir Robert, 384–85
Thomson, Lord, 339
Thornton, Charles B., 123
Throckmorton, Gen. J. L., 220
Ting Chia Chen, Maj. Gen., 211–
12
Tolson, Lt. Gen. J. J., III, 190–91,
220
Topographical Engineers, U.S.
Army, 151, 152
Torres, Onofre, 216
Totten, Col. Joseph G., 151, 155
Trade associations, 335
Transportation routes, 19th-
century development of,
151–52
Trapnell, Lt. Gen. Thomas J. H.,
348
Tredegar Iron Works, 26
Tribolet, Robert W., 205
"Trickle theory," defined, 129
Tripp, Robert C., 320
TROA (The Retired Officers
Association), 181, 186, 187
Troxel, Orlando Collette, Jr., 391
Trudeau, Gen. Arthur G., 314, 321,
326, 334, 343, 346, 388
Truman, Harry S, 253
on Bradley, 24
Korean policy of, 171, 173, 175,
241
on World War II business
interests, 300
Truman, Lt. Gen. Louis W. (Ret.),
187
TRW Inc., 313–14
TTC (Tropic Test Center), 200
Tumpane Co., 223
Turcios Lima, Luis, 217